NL ARMS

Netherlands Annual Review of Military Studies

Ministry of Defence

Series Information

The series aims to create an overview of scientific research in military sciences and it shows the extent to which researchers of the Faculty of Military Sciences (FMS) of the Netherlands Defence Academy contribute to this field of expertise.

Research at the Faculty is confined to military-relevant, multi-disciplinary areas and therefore deals with issues relating, among others, to:

- Command and control in military operations
- Leadership and ethics
- Military law and history
- Operational analysis
- Navigation
- Combat systems
- Military platforms
- Cyber warfare

The series is peer-reviewed and reflects the diversity and quality of the Faculty of Military Sciences at its best. With NL ARMS the FMS hopes to serve as a trigger for more international comparative research on military sciences.

Editorial Office

F.E.J. de Pee-Vencken MA
Faculty of Military Sciences
Netherlands Defence Academy
P.O. Box 90 002
4800 PA Breda
The Netherlands

More information about this series at http://www.springer.com/series/13908

H. Monsuur · J.M. Jansen
F.J. Marchal
Editors

NL ARMS Netherlands Annual Review of Military Studies 2018

Coastal Border Control: From Data and Tasks to Deployment and Law Enforcement

ASSER PRESS

Springer

Editors
H. Monsuur
Faculty of Military Sciences
Netherlands Defence Academy
Den Helder
The Netherlands

F.J. Marchal
Faculty of Military Sciences
Netherlands Defence Academy
Den Helder
The Netherlands

J.M. Jansen
Faculty of Military Sciences
Netherlands Defence Academy
Den Helder
The Netherlands

ISSN 1387-8050 ISSN 2452-235X (electronic)
NL ARMS
ISBN 978-94-6265-245-3 ISBN 978-94-6265-246-0 (eBook)
https://doi.org/10.1007/978-94-6265-246-0

Library of Congress Control Number: 2018942526

Published by T.M.C. ASSER PRESS, The Hague, The Netherlands www.asserpress.nl
Produced and distributed for T.M.C. ASSER PRESS by Springer-Verlag Berlin Heidelberg

Printed on acid-free paper

This T.M.C. ASSER PRESS imprint is published by the registered company Springer-Verlag GmbH, DE part of Springer Nature
The registered company address is: Heidelberger Platz 3, 14197 Berlin, Germany

Foreword

Today's world harbours a huge and fast-growing population, generating an increasing demand for food and goods. The changing climate, with progressing desertification and rising sea levels, leads to mass migration and a continuous race for natural resources. Mankind is increasingly relying on the maritime domain to alleviate its challenges and to provide cheaper alternatives for land-based variants. The question is whether the maritime environment is resilient enough to facilitate this increasing demand in a sustainable way. On a global scale, maritime professionals are working on a number of challenges, such as the increase of legal and illegal users, more offshore activities and traffic, bigger transport volumes, non-sustainable fishing and other undesirable activity like mass migration. All of these together lead to both environmental and safety concerns.

On land, State boundaries are regulated by technical means and legal agreements to an extent that they provide a feeling that governments and international institutions are 'in control'. At sea, maritime and coast guard professionals aspire to have the same level of control in the worldwide maritime domain. Unfortunately, the maritime domain, due to its nature and size, its physical characteristics and ensuing technological limitations, along with specific international laws, presents coast guard professionals with more complex challenges. These professionals are therefore continuously on the lookout for new and other means that will allow them to gain sufficient maritime domain awareness to be 'in control'. The question remains whether their efforts and progress are enough to provide 'timely and sufficient control' whilst dealing with the aforementioned challenges. New technologies, both static and mobile, provide a solution here and there, but in general they are still not enough.

In addition to scientific and technological innovations and the sufficient funding of a wide range of scientific disciplines, there is a need for an increased focus on the maritime domain. Legal experts, maritime safety- and security professionals, government policy makers and the private sector alike should expedite their efforts to face and deal with the increasing demand on the maritime domain and to contain unwanted activity.

This book provides a comprehensive study of border control. It will provide new insights and stimulate efforts that will be of help to professionals affiliated to the maritime domain and border control.

Den Helder, The Netherlands

Capt. (N) Msc. R.J. Blok
Director—Netherlands Coast Guard

Preface

NL ARMS 2018 has set out to combine a number of academic disciplines in order to provide a comprehensive view with regard to coastal border control. As a general topic of interest, border control and regulation have received more and more attention over recent years. The EU faces challenges in the form of the migrant crisis in the Mediterranean Sea, and States struggle with the approach to modern-day border security. Even though coastal border control is largely seen as a purely national issue and possibly one for coast guard or police-like entities, military assets and technology are able to play an increasing role in addressing this crisis, and there are a number of military operations activated to help States secure their borders.

The theme of **NL ARMS 2018** is **Coastal Border Control: From Data and Tasks to Deployment and Law Enforcement**, which immediately mirrors the intent behind this volume of the Netherlands Annual Review of Military Studies. The book aims to interweave articles that stem from the perspective of social sciences and the legal, with contributions that are strongly focused on the technical possibilities of new C2 frameworks, innovative technologies and the use of data. In the various chapters, the authors from the Faculty of Military Sciences of the Netherlands Defence Academy and their colleagues from other institutes provide a coherent insight into the different relevant disciplines that go hand in hand with the evolution of this topic of coastal border control.

The book consists of four parts, largely divided by their discipline and focal point, each of which gives a different but complementary vision on coastal border control. The first part contains four contributions, one of which builds on a case study on the overall developments of border control operations. The second part consists of three contributions that address command and control for difficult and dispersed border control operations. The third part then explores a number of possibilities for the use of game theory, data analysis and simulation in order to improve asset management by navies and coast guards, while the last part delves into the natural scientific aspects of border and port protection.

Through the use of different perspectives, we hope this issue of **NL ARMS 2018** provides a broad insight into the challenges arising from the evolution of coastal border control by States. The different chapters focus both on academic theory and on the practical application thereof through deployment and enforcement, adding to the value and use of this book. We hope that you will find it insightful and enjoyable.

The Editing team,

Den Helder, The Netherlands

Prof. Dr. H. Monsuur
Dr. J.M. Jansen
Lieutenant (sr grade) F.J. Marchal LLM

Contents

About the Contributors

Editors

Prof. Dr. H. Monsuur is professor Military Operations Research at the Faculty of Military Sciences of the Netherlands Defence Academy, Den Helder, The Netherlands.

Dr. J.M. Jansen is associate professor Operational ICT at the Faculty of Military Sciences of the Netherlands Defence Academy, Den Helder, The Netherlands.

Lieutenant sr grade (RNLN) F.J. Marchal, LLM is lecturer in International and Military Law at the Department of War Studies, Netherlands Defence Academy, Den Helder, The Netherlands.

Authors

Dr. A.I. Barros is principal scientist at TNO, The Hague, The Netherlands, and fellow at the Institute for Advanced Study, Amsterdam, The Netherlands

Capt(E) Dr. ir. F. Bolderheij is associate professor Sensor Systems and Integration at the Faculty of Military Sciences of the Netherlands Defence Academy, Den Helder, The Netherlands.

Prof. dr. M.T.I.B. Bollen is professor Civil-Military Interaction at the Faculty of Military Sciences of the Netherlands Defence Academy, Breda, The Netherlands.

Prof. Dr. R.J. Boucherie is professor Stochastic Operations Research, University of Twente, The Netherlands.

H.J. Fitski, MSc is senior programme and project manager at TNO Defence, Safety and Security, The Hague, The Netherlands.

J.P.H. Kalden is CIO and Security Officer at the Netherlands Coast Guard, Den Helder, The Netherlands.

J.P. Kalkman, MSc is Ph.D student Civil-Military Collaboration at the Faculty of Military Sciences of the Netherlands Defence Academy, the Department of Organization Sciences at VU University and the department of Defence, Security and Safety of TNO, Soesterberg, The Netherlands.

Dr. B.M.J.B. Klein Goldewijk is assistant professor International Security Studies at the Department of War Studies, Netherlands Defence Academy, Breda, The Netherlands.

M. Klinik, MSc is Ph.D student Operational ICT at the Faculty of Military Sciences of the Netherlands Defence Academy, The Netherlands, Radboud University Nijmegen, The Netherlands, and TNO, Soesterberg, The Netherlands.

Dr. L. Koene is assistant professor Ballistics and Ammunition at the Faculty of Military Sciences of the Netherlands Defence Academy, Den Helder, The Netherlands.

Lieutenant jr grade (RNLN) A.A. Kool serves as a Naval officer, The Netherlands.

C.M. Laan, MSc is Ph.D student Operations Research at the University of Twente, The Netherlands, Netherlands Defence Academy, The Netherlands, and TNO, The Hague, The Netherlands.

Dr. H. Nikookar is Associate Professor Sensor Systems at the Faculty of Military Sciences of the Netherlands Defence Academy, Den Helder, The Netherlands.

Dr. L. Schlicher is assistant professor Logistics and Information at the Faculty of Military Sciences of the Netherlands Defence Academy, Breda, The Netherlands.

Ir. A.J.M. Schmets is assistant professor Military Engineering at the Faculty of Military Sciences of the Netherlands Defence Academy, Den Helder, The Netherlands.

Dr. J. Stutterheim is quantitative developer at Standard Chartered Bank, Singapore, Singapore.

E.R. van Veldhoven, MSc is research scientist Military Operations at TNO Defence, Safety and Security, The Hague, The Netherlands.

Dr. ir. A.F. Vermeulen is assistant professor Electrical Engineering at the Faculty of Military Sciences of the Netherlands Defence Academy, Den Helder, The Netherlands.

Colonel (RNLAF) Dr. J.E.D. Voetelink, LLM is Associate Professor Military Law at the Department of War Studies, Netherlands Defence Academy, Breda, The Netherlands, and a senior researcher at the Amsterdam Centre of International Law (ACIL), The Netherlands.

Dr. E. de Waard is associate professor Strategic Organizing and Change at the Faculty of Military Sciences of the Netherlands Defence Academy, Breda, The Netherlands.

Part I
Law Enforcement and Border Security

Chapter 1
Flexibility in Border Security: A Case Study of the Dutch Border Security Team

E. de Waard, J.P. Kalkman and M.T.I.B. Bollen

Contents

E. de Waard (✉) · J.P. Kalkman · M.T.I.B. Bollen
Faculty of Military Sciences, Netherlands Defence Academy, Breda, The Netherlands
e-mail: ej.d.waard.01@mindef.nl

M.T.I.B. Bollen
e-mail: mtib.bollen.01@mindef.nl

J.P. Kalkman
Department of Organization Sciences, VU University, Amsterdam, The Netherlands
e-mail: j.p.kalkman@vu.nl; jp.kalkman@mindef.nl

J.P. Kalkman
TNO Defence, Safety and Security, Soesterberg, The Netherlands

H. Monsuur et al. (eds.), *NL ARMS Netherlands Annual Review of Military Studies 2018*, NL ARMS, https://doi.org/10.1007/978-94-6265-246-0_1

Abstract Flexibility in organizations is important, especially when dealing with crises that develop in an unpredictable way. Existing management theory makes clear that organizations are confronted with different environmental dynamics and, therefore, need a mix of operational, structural and strategic flexible capabilities to remain viable. The present article uses this insight to analyze the flexibility potential of the Dutch Border Security Team Concept (BST). The BST concept has been developed by the Royal Netherlands Marechaussee as a practical answer to deal with the sudden migration crisis in the Eastern Mediterranean. The findings show that the composite BST unit has the potential to be really flexible. In sum, it has proven to be a comprehensive, semi-autonomous organizational element that possesses all the necessary capabilities to cover migration-related crisis situations well. Yet, the empirical results also bring to the front that the embeddedness of the BST within the overarching Frontex constellation affects the possibility to fully reap the benefits of organizational independence. Frontex' standardized and highly formalized routines leave too little room for a customized decentralized organizational effort.

Keywords Uncertainty · Flexibility · Frontex · Crisis management · Organizational autonomy · Border Security Team

1.1 Introduction

In a globalizing world, states have come to attach renewed importance to their borders, be it in the form of border walls or stricter border control. While the European Union was probably the most prominent example of an attempt to downplay or dissolve borders between Member States, it has also reinforced its external borders in recent years due to perceived external pressures. The large inflow of migrants fleeing war and poverty in search of a better life reached its peak in late 2014 and early 2015. This European migration crisis translated in a strengthening of Frontex, the EU agency in charge of protecting the external borders. Frontex deploys individual border guards and capabilities from the Member States to border areas under pressure, such as the Greek islands near Turkey. In response to an urgent Greek request for help in its border protection during the migration crisis, the Netherlands deployed a Border Security Team (BST) in January 2015. It was the first time that a team, consisting of over 40 specialists, was deployed under the Frontex umbrella. The core of this national element was formed by the Royal Netherlands Marechaussee (KMar), the Dutch gendarme corps in charge of domestic border surveillance. The KMar leadership collaborated with civilian organizations with migration-related tasks to aid the Greek authorities in a comprehensive manner. The KMar aimed for a 'scalable, adaptive and flexible' team that could respond to local changes but would also be usable to operate in completely different contexts, such as in Libya to register and assess asylum applications before migrants cross the Mediterranean. The KMar-leadership asked the current researchers to study the flexibility of its BST-concept.[1]

As such, this chapter aims to analyze the flexibility potential of the BST concept. As a theoretical framework Volberda's flexibility mix is used.[2] This mix distinguishes between three forms of flexibility—strategic, structural, and operational flexibility. The research findings are discussed based on the subdivision of these forms of flexibility. A comprehensive discussion and conclusion finalize the chapter.

1.2 Theory

1.2.1 Organizing for Flexibility in Crisis Response

Crises are situations of intense pressure and uncertainty. Just like other crises, this migrant crisis confronted the Border Security Team with a perceived threat, considerable uncertainty, and response urgency.[3] The uncertainty was enhanced by the fact that this was the first time a full team was deployed, with which both the deploying organization (i.e. the KMar), its members (i.e. the BST), and the coordinating organization (i.e. Frontex) had no experience. The ambiguity typical for crises can take three forms: fundamental ambiguity which makes it hard to understand what is happening at all, causal ambiguity which makes it hard to understand what caused the crisis and how it will develop, and role ambiguity which makes it hard to identify the allocation of responsibilities.[4] Operational staff therefore often has to take actions without fully understanding what the consequences will be.[5] Some even argue that only by taking such actions in an ambiguous crisis situation, responders can gain an understanding of the crisis they are tackling.[6] In any case, ambiguous events demand flexibility in the response.

A flexible inter-organizational crisis response requires both formal systems to provide a basis for flexible actions, and room for creativity to respond to changing circumstances.[7] In this regard, Weick's study of the Mann Gulch disaster is interesting.[8] He recalls the story of a group of firefighters that was overwhelmed by a wildfire, which killed most of them. In his analysis, he shows that this disaster was a consequence of the disintegration of both the structural organization (i.e. their role structure) and the flexibility of mind (i.e. their sensemaking). The solutions he proposes also have both formal, structural elements (e.g. virtual role systems, norms of

[1] We are heavily indebted to the KMar for enabling this research. The KMar provided a comprehensive list of participants that could be interviewed and facilitated a field visit to Chios, the Greek island to which the Border Security Team was deployed.

[2] Volberda 1996, p. 362.

[3] Boin et al. 2005.

[4] Caroll 2015.

[5] Van Stralen and Mercer 2015.

[6] Weick 1988.

[7] Comfort and Kapucu 2006; Bigley and Roberts 2001; Faraj and Xiao 2006.

[8] Weick 1993.

interactions) and informal elements enabling room for creativity (e.g. improvisation, doubt). Similarly, Faraj and Xiao advocate, for instance, reliance on protocols and plug-and-play teams (i.e. structural elements) as well as protocol breaking and contestation (i.e. informal creativity).[9] In inter-organizational crisis response specifically, Wolbers refers to the paradox between designed coordination based on standard operating procedures, and emergent coordination through dynamic decision-making.[10]

Formal elements enabling flexibility appear to be a contradiction in terms, since the formal elements, when upheld too strictly, may become rigid and prevent the flexibility they were intended to promote. In fact, planning and preparation for crises is challenging as crises are always different than expected.[11] Thus, planning results, to a certain extent, primarily in 'fantasy documents' that are not useful nor realistic when crises strike.[12] On the other hand, it would be too pessimistic to say that it is impossible to organize for flexibility and that it somehow just needs to spontaneously develop. For example, there are High Reliability Organizations that manage to flexibly and successfully respond to unexpected, volatile situations and have a very low failure rate. Such organizations include aircraft carriers, trauma centers, and firefighting units. These organizations share some common characteristics: they are sensitive to small changes, embrace complexity, focus on the operations, are resilient, and rely on expertise.[13] To sum up, they have structural elements that facilitate flexibility under pressure.

A specifically challenging factor with regard to organizing for flexibility in the European migration response was the inter-organizational nature of the response. In fact, the migration crisis was in many ways 'transboundary' in the sense that responsibilities and jurisdiction were divided between multiple organizations.[14] For instance, different organizations were in charge of registering migrants, processing their asylum requests, and helping with voluntary repatriations. Thus, 'composition flexibility' was necessary in order to deploy a team that was optimally equipped for the tasks at hand.[15] At the same time, in a newly composed inter-organizational team, trust still needs to grow. Initially, formal control mechanisms carry the collaboration, even though this renders flexible interacting in the early stage of the response very challenging.[16] Inter-personal trust between members of different organizations may, however, quickly emerge, translating into inter-organizational trust and facilitating greater flexibility.[17] As a result, the composition flexibility resulting in a new team of unfamiliar organizations may have gone at the cost of a flexible execution of tasks in the initial stage of the deployment.[18]

9 Faraj and Xiao 2006.
10 Wolbers 2015.
11 McConnell and Drennan 2006.
12 McConnell and Drennan 2006.
13 Weick and Sutcliffe 2007.
14 Ansell et al. 2010.
15 De Waard and Kramer 2008.
16 Kalkman and De Waard 2017; Das and Teng 1998.
17 Kalkman 2016; Das and Teng 2000.
18 De Waard and Kramer 2008.

1.2.2 Types of Flexibility

From an organization and management theory perspective, organizational flexibility depends above of all on the dynamic capabilities of managers to respond at the right time in the right way to changes, opportunities or threats in the environment. It is important to realize, though, that the environment of an organization has interrelated levels of aggregation, starting at the macro-economic level cascading down to the resource pool level.[19] At the macro-economic level political, legal, economic, socio-cultural, demographic, and technological aspects influence organizations.[20] Then, at the industry level, forces such as the bargaining power of suppliers or buyers, the threat of new entrants, the threat of substitute products, and competitive rivalry have to be taken into account by organizations.[21] Others also mention the interaction with associations, interest groups, constituencies and classes of individuals and organizations that takes place at this level.[22] Next, the task environment consists of forces that have a direct impact on the goal attainment and survival of a single organization.[23] This environmental level focuses on the relationship with specific customers, suppliers, and financiers. One level further, Lawrence and Lorsch discuss in their research on differentiation and integration the importance of departmental sub environments, arguing that, for example, a research and development department can be seen as an open system, with a long-term focus and an informal way of working to stimulate innovation; a production department is more like a closed system, with a very formal, short-term focus, due to its concentration on efficiency gains.[24] Castrogiovanni describes the resource pool as the lowest environmental level.[25] The main concern at this level is the acquisition and exchange of critical organizational resources. One could for example think of a production department, receiving its raw materials from an internal logistics department.

The point is that each of these environments has its own characteristics. As such, managers from the font line to the strategic apex require a variety of dynamic capabilities to draw from. Volberda[26] distinguish four types of flexibility: steady-state, operational, structural, and strategic flexibility. These flexibility types encompass different sorts of dynamic capabilities, that depending on the variety of impulses coming from the environment and the speed of reaction that is needed can be applied.

Steady-state flexibility represents the minimally required adaptive capacity that every organization needs to have to absorb minor changes in daily work routines. Actually, it can hardly be called a form of flexibility, because it refers to "static procedures to optimize the firm's performance when the levels of throughput and the

[19] Castrogiovanni 1991, p. 545.

[20] Kottler 1988.

[21] Porter 1979.

[22] Osborn and Hunt 1974.

[23] Dill 1958; Thompson 1967; Osborn and Hunt 1974; Dess and Beard 1984.

[24] Lawrence and Lorsch 1967.

[25] Castrogiovanni 1991, p. 545.

[26] Volberda 1996.

nature of throughput remain relatively stable over time".[27] In other words, when the range of existing practices suffices to control the organization's normal workflow, an organization possesses steady-state flexibility.

Operational flexibility means exploiting routine skills within the existing organizational structure and strategy. Changing of the production volume, building up stocks and mobilizing crash teams are examples of internal operational flexibility. Using temporary staff, multi-sourcing and obtaining resources from different suppliers can be seen as forms of external operational flexibility. These kinds of skills help management to improve their capabilities to meet or influence internal or external instabilities. Operational flexibility is most of the time reactive and tightly connected to operational aspects of the organization.

Structural flexibility means adjusting the organizational structure and decision-making and communication processes in order to meet fundamental changes. Compared to operational flexibility this is a more radical form. One could think of job enlargement, job enrichment, creating multi-functional teams, changing planning and control systems and formal hierarchical responsibilities as examples of internal structural flexibility. Just-in-time (JIT) management, co-creation and co-design are examples of the external dimension.

An organization needs to have strategic flexibility when it faces unknown forces that can have dramatic consequences. It deals with substantial questions like: What is the organization's 'raison d'être'? What is its core-business? Which activities must remain and which have to be divested? The problems are always unstructured and non-routine. Abandoning the current strategy, implementing new essential technologies and fundamentally renew products are examples of internal strategic flexibility. Creating new product-market combinations, creating barriers to entry for potential entrants, and opposing trade regulations by lobbying can be seen as forms of external strategic flexibility.

According to Volberda, a flexible organization typically requires a balanced flexibility mix to be able to adapt and innovate and to simultaneously safeguard efficient and stable operational performance.[28] As such, flexibility implies continuously dealing with the inherent organizational tension of developing new capabilities and preserving existing rules, regulations, and procedures. Within the strategic management scholarly community this tension is labelled 'ambidexterity'.[29]

1.3 Methods

To study the flexibility potential of the KMar BST concept, we interviewed 49 respondents. All interviewees were involved in the BST, either as decision-makers, as a BST member, or as a key collaborative partner in the area of operations. More specifically,

[27] Volberda 1996, p. 362.

[28] Volberda 1996.

[29] Gibson and Birkinshaw 2004.

senior organizational representatives were interviewed to find out the core topics in the decision-making process in preparation of (and during the) BST deployment. Additionally, a careful selection of BST members and local collaborative partners was made to make sure that we would have a good overview of the main local developments on the island of Chios as well as of the BST's activities. BST activities included: border surveillance, document checking, screening, fingerprinting, debriefing, intelligence-gathering, and repatriation.

In terms of data analysis, we recorded and transcribed nearly all interviews. Subsequently, we analyzed the interviews and related the topics brought forward to the flexibility categories. After this first selection, we systematically defined the core flexibility questions that the KMar faced in this border security task. The empirical focus was on the concepts operational, structural, and strategic flexibility. Steady-state flexibility was not addressed in the interviews, because of its fixation on daily routines and normal working conditions. Given the fact that the deployment to Chios was an exceptional task-setting, operational flexibility (i.e. how to execute this unique task?), structural flexibility (i.e. how to compose a unit for this unique task?), and strategic flexibility (i.e. how to deal with this specific migration crisis?) formed the empirical centers of gravity. The main findings are presented below.

1.4 Findings

We focus specifically on flexibility questions (see Table 1.1 for the categorization of the findings) in relation to the KMar as the KMar provided the core of the Border Security Teams, was responsible for the planning and organization of the BST, is primarily responsible for external border protection, and is the central point of contact for Frontex. Nevertheless, KMar officials emphasize that future BSTs do not necessarily have to be managed and organized by the KMar.

Table 1.1 Categorization of the research findings [*Source* The authors]

Strategic flexibility	Structural flexibility	Operational flexibility
Expeditionary characteristics	Basic BST module	Multi-functional professionalism
Deployment approach	Rotation dynamics	Matching task and staff
	Parent organization	Integration of interpreters
		Scaling up and down
		Female representation
		Criminal investigation

1.5 Strategic Flexibility

Over the last decade, managing the arrival of large numbers of migrants and immigrants has become one of the KMar's main tasks. As a result, the organization has become interested in finding a basic organizational concept that can be used for different migration-related crises. From this perspective, the current BST deployment on Chios can be viewed as a benchmark operation, from which lessons can be drawn for possible future deployments in different contexts. Discussing strategic flexibility of the BST concept requires an exploration of its potential in alternative migration-related operations. This exploration brings up two important topics: expeditionary characteristics, and deployment approach.

1.5.1 Expeditionary Characteristics

In general, all respondents argue that the KMar possess a relatively high level of strategic flexibility. It has a military status, which means that basically every uniformed member is deployable to risky crisis situations. Moreover, the existence of different areas of expertise within the KMar organization offers the potential to create customized organizational solutions to crisis response operations. These two elements combined make the KMar a highly flexible organization that can be used for a wide variety of tasks and settings.

At the same time, focusing specifically on dealing with this migrant crisis, it is clear that the KMar does not possess all the capabilities required to cover the entire migration chain. This implies that, depending on the mission, some of these capabilities need to be attracted from other organizations. One could think of asylum and repatriation experts in particular. The question subsequently arises whether the partner organizations offering this critical expertise also have an expeditionary posture. After all, in most cases such organizations primarily have a national responsibility. To be more concrete, can a subject matter expert, such as a migration officer, be as easily deployed to a hostile or unsafe crisis area? If this is not the case, volunteers need to be selected and procedures need to be prepared and put in place. However, this takes time and, as such, may negatively influence the flexibility of the crisis response. The KMar will then have to wait to deploy until its external partner elements are ready.

In addition, it is not unthinkable that in the future another organization than the KMar may play the leading role in a migrant-related deployment. KMar units may then have to execute their tasks under the flag of another government organization. For example, if the Immigration and Naturalization Service (IND) is the largest contributor to an inter-organizational team, it may wish to also provide a team leader. Some of the respondents doubt whether the KMar possesses the flexibility to adjust to the preferences and routines of a dominant civilian organization if such a situation occurs.

1.5.2 Deployment Approach: Frontex Versus Lead-Nation Approach

All respondents make clear that using the BST deployment on Chios as a benchmark for future operations is not entirely unproblematic. The BST is part of the Frontex Poseidon Sea operation, which makes the unit subject to a strictly defined mandate and to undisputable Frontex routines, rules, and regulations. There is some consensus that deploying a unit under the umbrella of Frontex means, and will mean in the future, that being a reliable and dedicated contributor outweighs being flexible. The point is that political sensitivities and strict mandates cannot be neglected for the sake of flexibility.

Within Europe, Frontex is generally seen as a relevant EU agency that is "here to stay" and, as such, deserves proper support from the Netherlands. Considering this support for Frontex, two possible pathways come to the fore. First, Frontex operations are based on an intricate rotation scheme of individual border officials from different contributing Member States rotating in and out. It is argued that it would be best if the KMar adhered to this way of organizing, basically accepting the system as it is. Second, the KMar may prefer to deploy a large national contingent under the umbrella of Frontex. In this case, interviewees suggest the KMar to enter into an agreement with Frontex that is based on establishing a (semi-)autonomous position for the BST. Since Frontex will be hesitant to adopt this proposition, the KMar should, in advance, reconsider its initial goals and formulate more modest ambitions that better suit Frontex' regular modus operandi.

Frontex could also enhance its strategic flexibility on its own. It has recently set up a rapid reserve pool of 1500 border guards of the different Member States. When this pool is filled and operational, Frontex could in case of a Rapid Intervention also draw from this pool a certain number of people, have them flown into a regional HQ, appoint a team leader, and provide the preparatory training to this team. In this way, an internationalized BST is created in which team members have the same background knowledge and are familiar with each other upon deployment. The further development of a 'Frontex-culture' among frequently deployed border officials, through regular team meetings and co-location, may reinforce the team spirit and the affinity with Frontex in such an internationalized BST.

Lastly, for future multinational migrant crisis response missions, a few respondents advocate a lead-nation approach instead. Either outside of Frontex or even outside of Europe (e.g. Caribbean Netherlands if Venezuela disintegrates), the Netherlands could take such a leading role. They paint a picture of a crisis area in which, in the most extreme case, a BST bears complete responsibility over the entire migration chain. It is believed that under these conditions, a BST-like organization could be run effectively and could offer enough flexibility to adjust to diverse and changing local circumstances. There are of course considerable political ramifications and limitations to consider, not in the least pertaining to state sovereignty and possible accusations of imperialistic tendencies.

1.6 Structural Flexibility

Regarding the structural flexibility of the BST concept, three important topics surfaced during the interviews. Firstly, the respondents gave their view on what a basic module for a migrant-related crisis response module should look like. Secondly, rotation challenges were a recurring point of interest. Thirdly, the current practice of drawing BST staff from one brigade was a topic of discussion.

1.6.1 Designing an Organizational BST Module

The interviewees stress that the KMar consists of a wide variety of command, staff, support, and operational capabilities. This versatility facilitates the creation of temporary organizations that can be tailored for a specific job. Respondents argue that when there is a need to incorporate critical or additional external expertise or resources, it is best to follow a two-step approach. First, it has to be determined whether crucial capabilities can be supplied by other branches of the Netherlands armed forces. Second, if the required means are not available within the armed forces, to some extent, local partners can be sought. The latter condition especially applies to support services such as transport, housing, food, and IT.

Concentrating on the primary process of managing large groups of migrants, critical expertise that the KMar does not have, is possessed by civilian government organizations. If, for a deployment, the KMar wants to control the entire migration chain, all these external elements are needed. Consequently, a partnership with these organizations needs to be secured. Theoretically, when the core tasks are surveillance, registration and identification, the KMar can supply all the needed requirements itself, and may opt to follow an autonomous approach (instead of the burden-sharing option chosen for the BST). So, basically, the KMar needs to be prepared for an expeditionary continuum ranging from completely autonomous action to fully integrated action with all the relevant partners in the migration chain. Respondents are generally confident about the organization's ability to manage this.

1.6.2 Rotation Dynamics

The deployment of a mixture of units and specialists, coming from different parent organizations led in BST Chios to a mixture of rotation schedules. The KMar rotates its BST members every three months, the civilian organization in charge or migrant repatriation initially used rotation schedules of six weeks, and some police officers could stay up to a year. As a result, the BST organization as a whole was constantly changing and re-grouping.

Even though the lengthier rotations are preferred over the shorter-term individual deployments of Frontex, there is support for the plan that all participating organizations jointly establish a rotation agreement, which is acceptable to all. Having said that, the different rotation schedules also ensure that even when the KMar contingent is replaced, there are still members in the BST of other organizations which have been working in the area for a longer period of time, so that a knowledge drain is prevented. Concentrating on the KMar, one respondent suggests increasing the duration of the deployment in a creative way. Why not deploying a BST twice in two years for three months, instead of only once? The organization, then, has to create a smaller number of BSTs and the teams can benefit from the experience gained in previous rotations.

Three months seems a realistic minimum deployment time for a BST, because building and maintaining a network and developing trust are crucial aspects of the collaborative tasks involved. Some highly specific tasks, such as fingerprinting, could justify a shorter stint, but for team coherence it might be better to keep the BST together as a group. Besides, if the BST is not deployed under Frontex, job rotation between border surveillance operators, screeners, debriefers, document experts, and fingerprinters may create a fuller understanding of the entire process and foster a harmonization of activities. Under these hypothetical conditions, a deployment time of three months is preferred by staff.

Lastly, if a BST is deployed as a long-term commitment, the respondents generally support the decision to deploy the BST commander for a period of six months for two reasons. Firstly, experienced commanders can facilitate a smooth transfer of knowledge and tasks when replacements rotate in. Secondly, being six months in the mission area improves the potential to build a strong local connection with the local authorities and non-government organizations on the island, thereby establishing a relevant position. If the BST is dissolved during the commander's term (e.g. because the Rapid Intervention ends), the commander could use the knowledge and expertise in another Frontex leadership role for the remaining period.

1.6.3 Parent Organization and the BST

For the KMar, the current formation approach is to fill the BST with volunteers coming from one brigade. The underlying assumption is that a cohesive team forms the heart of the unit. Reality is somewhat more ambiguous, however. Volunteers come from different subordinate teams within the brigade. Also, BST commanders are individually selected, and as such, do not belong to the brigade where the staff originates from per se. Next, volunteers may just have finished their initial training or only recently gained a position in the brigade and are, thus, quite new organizational members. All in all, the idea that a completely cohesive team is used can be seriously debated.

While many respondents supported the brigade-based deployment, there are good reasons to compose a new team consisting of members from different brigades in any case. First, by picking staff from different brigades, the KMar can select on the basis of expertise and thus create a team with more knowledge and experience. Second, a new team reduces the risk of groupthink (i.e. the process in which people only confirm each other's views and ideas) and, instead, renders the team more innovative and creative. Third, non-KMar BST members are likely to be more easily incorporated in the team if everyone is new. In fact, a new team is generally more open and outward-oriented than a team in which many people are already familiar with each other.

There are also organizational reasons for not recruiting all KMar-staff from one brigade. A few respondents point to the fact that, by this way of organizing, the supplying brigade may be cannibalized too much. Certain tasks can no longer be executed, because a large proportion of the original workforce is missing due to an expeditionary deployment. Also, particular activities may be "frozen" until the brigade members return from their stint abroad. Thus, once returned, they straightaway face an enormous workload. Although the KMar can decide, depending on operational considerations at home, to (partly) fill the gaps by temporarily transferring personnel from other brigades, the interviewees stress that this is not always done. On the contrary, it has even happened that, because of the strategic importance of the national airport, a brigade supplying members for a BST deployment in Chios simultaneously had to send people to Schiphol to increase the capacity over there. The interviewees remark that measures like these can make people hesitant to volunteer for future crisis response deployments.

1.7 Operational Flexibility

Discussing the operational flexibility of the BST concept has delivered some findings that can be grouped in six themes. Firstly, the multifunctional professionalism of BST members facilitates quick adaptation to new circumstances. Secondly, to some extent, staff members currently deployed are overqualified, pleading for the need to reconsider the matching between tasks and staff. Thirdly, the (re)integration of interpreters in the BST may enhance operational flexibility. Fourthly, due to a lack of organizational slack and for practical reasons, scaling up or down on the basis of operational needs can be complicated. Fifthly, the underrepresentation of women in the team is discussed. Lastly, criminal investigation is mentioned as a potentially additional field of operations.

1.7.1 Multifunctional Capabilities

On the whole, the BST members displayed an extensive operational repertoire. Most respondents bring to bear the creativity and proactivity that they view as strong national selling points. They stress that it is in their national character to make the best out of any situation. Put differently, Dutch service(wo)men and other governmental workers possess a strong drive to act even when objectives are vague or hierarchical direction is perceived as limited. Potentially (and informally), they can carry out a wide variety of tasks, which makes it quite easy to anticipate and respond to local changes. Staff members were able to carry out multiple or even all of the tasks conducted in Chios. As such, when the focus of daily activities shifts due to a changing mission context, the BST operation can potentially adjust accordingly and have staff assist in the profiles that are understaffed. Noteworthy, this requires the permission of Frontex which prefers staff to only be active in one profile for efficiency purposes.

1.7.2 Matching Tasks with Staff

To enhance flexibility, some respondents suggest improving the relation between job content and personal qualifications. In Chios, mainly experienced sergeants are employed. It could be argued that for some tasks they are overqualified, especially for fingerprinting and border surveillance. The problem of scarcity mentioned earlier could, at least partially, be tackled by deploying people of a lower rank for these simpler jobs. They could even do some specified parts of a more complex task under supervision of a senior colleague. This would lower the personnel costs, enlarge the pool of potential volunteers, and improve the task commitment of individual team members.

1.7.3 Position of Interpreters

Some interviewees also point to the pivotal role that interpreters or cultural mediators play. The outcome of a registration process strongly depends on the quality and dedication of the interpreters. There is therefore support for making interpreters a fixed part of the BST (again) in order to enhance operational flexibility. During the field visit, the interpreters were freelancers hired via a civilian government organization and were not integrated within the BST. In the field, the interpreters distanced themselves from the BST, while the BST members expected more loyalty and a collaborative attitude from them.

1.7.4 Scalability

To start with, there is general satisfaction about the support operational staff receives from the higher organizational echelons in the Netherlands. Within certain financial and organizational boundaries, the BST commander has plenty freedom of action, and enough room to improvise and employ new initiatives. Still, the ability to scale up a running operation is negatively influenced by a lack of (financial and manpower) slack in the organization as a whole. This scarcity is managed by investing heavily in long-term centralized planning processes. The downside of following a strict planning approach is that planned assets become fixed, both at home as well as in a mission area. In other words, it is virtually impossible to deploy an additional unit or technological platform on short notice because these assets are already committed to other tasks. One of the respondents estimated that the actual incorporation of additional requests for external assets can at best be satisfied in the next rotation. A similar challenge occurs with down-scaling an operation, which can be complicated by the effects on the returning staff member (whose wish to contribute is cut short), while such a down-scaling may as well have adverse political repercussions (e.g. losing face). One respondent added that a quicker return may also disrupt the preparations for a longer separation made by the family and the parent organization, although this did not seem a big problem in the premature downscaling of BST-Lesbos.

1.7.5 Gender Balance

All BSTs (as well as the broader Frontex operation on the island) seem to have been strongly male-dominated. Both female members that we spoke with shared a sense of disappointment about this for a couple of reasons. While both had generally very positive perceptions of the deployment and the team spirit, they mentioned that operating in a team as the only woman is somewhat more of challenge than operating in a gender-balanced team. Additionally, they were concerned about the team's interaction with female migrants, mentioning that it is more difficult to trace woman trafficking, for instance, if you cannot meet women alone (which men, for cultural reasons, are typically unable to do). Related to that, the information retrieved by debriefing interviews can be expected to be heavily skewed to male perspectives and experiences. A vast pool of relevant information is not used without the deployment of female debriefers. A similar line of reasoning would hold for supporting a consistent membership of ethnic minorities in the BST.

1.7.6 Criminal Investigation

Lastly, BST staff consistently advocated a broader mandate and more support for criminal investigation for which the operational flexibility lacked during this deployment. As tackling human smuggling and trafficking is a duty of Frontex and an essential element in border management, the lack of room of maneuver for investigative activities surprised and discouraged BST members. In particular, border surveillance officers mention the vast amount of relevant information that can help Frontex to identify and tackle human smuggling in addition to information retrieved from debriefing interviews. The KMar may (continue to) lobby at Frontex to implement this expansion of mandate.

1.8 Discussion

Addressing the migration crisis, as described in this article, underlines the key assumption that the challenge of modern-day military deployment is to enhance organization flexibility in order to deal with unfamiliar and uncertain security risks. Organization theorist Galbraith explains that an organization confronted with a high level of uncertainty should ideally react in two ways.[30] First, it should try to increase its information-processing capacity. Second, it should try to reduce its need for information processing. Regarding this latter path, Galbraith argues that creating self-contained organizational elements is an effective way of reducing an organization's need to process and absorb an intricate web of information streams. Basically, by decreasing the number of boundary-spanning activities and communication lines organizational complexity is reduced and responsiveness enhanced.

Studying the evolutionary process of C2 from the Stone Age up to the Vietnam war, Van Creveld[31] has embraced Galbraith's theory, concluding that dealing with uncertainty has been the essence of warfare throughout the ages. In an attempt to generalize from his historical analysis, he stresses that responsive military organizations will need to make low-decision thresholds possible by creating semi-autonomous units at a fairly low organizational level. Van Creveld[32] refers to the successful blitzkrieg doctrine, which was strongly based on the operational autonomy of the German pantzer divisions and task forces *–kampfgruppen-*, to make his point. Also, he explains that the self-controlling capacity of the three division-sized military formations, each consisting of three independent brigades, was the main reason for the clear Israeli victory in 1967.

Our findings strongly support Galbraith's seminal work and Van Creveld's historical analysis. The preference of KMar personnel to operate autonomously permeates the research findings. First of all, the KMar organization and its Dutch partner organizations have most of the required expertise, people, and mindset to conduct migration-related operations independently. Second, the results point to a synergistic relationship between autonomy, strategic flexibility, and operational flexibility. Deployment under the umbrella of Frontex, where different Member States contribute with individual border officials, appears to have affected both types of flexibility.

Starting with strategic flexibility. Frontex is a EU agency that has been established to collaboratively reinforce the protection of Europe's external borders. Its mandate is, therefore, strictly defined for this purpose. For the situation on the Greek islands Frontex' narrow mandate was problematic. Of course, the migration crisis had a major

---

[30] Galbraith 1973.

[31] Van Creveld 1985.

[32] Van Creveld 1985.

impact on the security of the EU border. Yet, the broader perspective of helping the Greek authorities to set up an efficient and effective asylum process, in order to create a sustainable migration solution, was more diverse and challenging than solely the traditional border security tasks that had to be conducted to fight the partial problem of illegal border crossings. Having been a transit country for years with migrants just passing through to Germany, Norway, the UK and other 'rich' European countries, with the closing of the borders of neighboring states, Greece suddenly encountered asylum dynamics it had never experienced before. Essentially, a coherent, transparent and legally binding asylum chain had to be developed from scratch. Input based on the insights and knowledge of other European countries, was extremely valuable to avoid reinventing the wheel. Moreover, this multi-faceted developmental process had to take place conjointly with migrants arriving on the Greek islands, which caused local reception centers to fill up. As such, time pressure was enormous. Frontex' bureaucratic and formalized posture, firmly adhering to its politically-determined mandate, proved insufficient to adequately solve the complex migration puzzle on the islands. Certainly, Frontex offered an important part of that puzzle, but in crucial adjacent areas, such as supporting and advising local municipality officials and police and coast guard units, offering re-admission related knowledge and expertise, and supplying criminal investigation capabilities, Frontex did not want to get really involved. As a result, these important parts of the puzzle largely remained untouched, which affected the overall efficacy of the mission. The composite BST unit could have offered lots of these complementary capabilities, which would have made it possible for the Dutch to deliver a highly customized solution to the Greek authorities that strategically fitted the security context better than the rather standardized Frontex contribution.

Regarding operational flexibility, the findings bring to the front that organizational autonomy also makes it possible to decisively deal with changes or new stimuli within the local task-setting. Apart from the suboptimal fit between the crisis situation and Frontex' contribution restricted to border security (i.e. lack of strategic flexibility), the agency's standardized modus operandi, with its fast rotation schedule, individual-based tasking, and a centralized planning and decision-making process, made it virtually impossible to adapt to changing local circumstances. If the Dutch BST unit would have had near-complete task autonomy, it could have better anticipated upon volatile local impetuses. The Dutch identified many opportunities to do so. Just to mention a few: adjust work routines to the number of migrants landing on the islands, shifting attention to the problem of migrants illegally bordering the ferry to the main land, supporting Greek officials in setting-up a voluntary re-admission procedure, and helping the Greek police with professionalizing their criminal investigation skills.

Also, Galbraith's additional path of dealing with uncertainty—increasing the capacity to process information—has surfaced in the empirical part of the study in relation to organizational flexibility.[33] All respondents argue that it is unrealistic to believe that a situation of complete organizational autonomy will occur in future deployments. First, a BST module is a composite national organizational formation

[33] Galbraith 1973.

with essential, migration-related capabilities coming from a variety of governmental organizations. So, although from the outside a BST may look like a cohesive organizational unit, in practice it will be an ad hoc formation with unfamiliar sub elements having to work together. Going up one level of aggregation, the same applies to the international setting in which most security-related deployments take place. A Dutch organizational module will most likely fall under the umbrella of an overarching multinational task force or international organization (e.g. Frontex). Therefore, when a lead-nation approach is followed, it becomes crucial to for example invest in mechanisms to ex-ante determine common output criteria and during deployment to react in a similar fashion to changing circumstances and share experiences between the different national modules.

The present study makes clear that mutual adjustment is critical to streamline both vertical and horizontal information flows, which helps to make overall organizational performance more responsive. Thompson defines coordination by mutual adjustment as "the transmission of new information during the process of action."[34] Since it is almost impossible to process new information with already existing rules and programs or with a detailed plan, Galbraith argues that local, ad hoc choices have to be made on how to deal with new stimuli. Consequently, he suggests to bring "the level of decision making down to where the information exist rather than bringing the information up to the points of decision"[35] Creating lateral relations can help in doing so. They come in different forms such as direct contact between two employees who share a problem, formal liaison and staff positions, interdepartmental groups or task forces, integrating roles like product and brand managers, or matrix structures.[36]

Especially liaison and staff positions were used to facilitate the vertical relationship between Frontex and the Dutch BST. Focusing on the former type of relationship, a KMar liaison officer (LNO) at the Frontex headquarters in Warsaw and a KMar officer, working as a regular staff member at the operation Poseidon HQ in Piraeus, played the role of linking pin between the EU agency in general, the mission in the Eastern Mediterranean, and the local task environment of the BST in Chios. The LNO in Warsaw was a kind of corporate planner, matching the profiles asked by Frontex for all its deployments with the available military resources in the Netherlands. The officer in Piraeus was a typical operational staff member, but also responsible for translating overall mission criteria to specific demands for the Dutch BST contingent. Regarding the latter relationship, the interaction between the Frontex Support Officer (FSO) and the BST commander is worth discussing. Although the FSO hierarchically commanded the Dutch BST, as part of the Poseidon operation, he had a horizontal relationship with the commander of the BST. This commander did not have line authority, but was deployed as a national officer to internally manage the BST unit. The FSO could concentrate on the mission, while the BST commander was a clear and direct point of contact for all kinds of peripheral questions, for example concerning housing, transportation, and medical issues of the Dutch BST members.

---

34 Thompson 1967, p. 56.

35 Galbraith 1973, p. 53.

36 Mintzberg 1983.

Although both coordination mechanisms were established to foster mutual adjustment, reality was different. Regarding the role of staff and liaison officers, the study came across the well-known trap of staff elements losing connection with the operational core.[37] Where mutual adjustment was needed to overcome or deal with changing local circumstances, the relationship evolved into a centralized top down approach, with staff elements trying to enforce standardized solutions to the frontline units. Also, when Frontex' initial rapid Intervention came to an end and matters normalized, certainly after the number of arrivals dropped, the horizontal relationship between FSO and the BST commander became an issue. Because of the large size of the BST, relevant partners on Chios approached the BST commander as Frontex' key representative, overlooking the FSO who was formally in charge. This situation strained the relationship between the two and sometimes made it problematic to assertively react to changes in the task environment.

All in all, when it comes to organizational flexibility, the Dutch BST deployment under the flag of Frontex has exposed a tension between task environment and organizational configuration. With the international security environment becoming more complex and dynamic, an organizational system is needed that has the capacity to adapt. Mintzberg argues that an adhocracy fits these circumstances best.[38] The findings make clear that at the operational level it is possible to establish an organizational structure—the BST—that adheres to the basic principles of an adhocracy. However, the fact that that this BST is part of an overarching machine bureaucracy-like public organization—Frontex—puts a lot of the merits of the adhocracy at risk again. A machine bureaucracy fits a predictable environment best, and therefore, has the impulse to focus on standardization and centralization. Both characteristics are the opposite of what an adhocracy stands for. As a result, an inherent tension is built into the organization that keeps materializing when the environmental circumstances change. The organizational, then, tends to become inwardly oriented to address collaboration problems, instead of externally to get a better grip on the challenging task environment.

1.9 Conclusion

The migration crisis in the East Mediterranean has proven a difficult nut to crack. With a complex geo-political situation as the root cause, the follow-up question on how to address the crisis became ambiguous. The solution, that consisted of a European approach to overcome a European crisis, seemed logical but also further enhanced task complexity. Frontex' operational predominance in addressing the migration crisis, pushed the organizational solution in the direction of border security, whereas daily reality called for a far broader mixture of migration-related capabilities. Although the Dutch BST that was deployed to Chios possessed many

[37] Mintzberg 1983.

[38] Mintzberg 1983.

of these capabilities, its subordinate position within the larger Frontex organization made impossible to fully exploit them. Frontex was bound by its strict mandate and, as such, prohibited its operational units to start coloring outside the lines. Unintendedly, this organizational constellation avoided a potential synergistic relationship to develop between frontline autonomy, operational customization, and strategic flexibility.

References

Ansell C, Boin A, Keller A (2010) Managing Transboundary Crises: Identifying the Building Blocks of an Effective Response System. Journal of Contingencies and Crisis Management, 18(4), 195–207

Bigley GA, Roberts KH (2001) The Incident Command System: High-Reliability Organizing for Complex and Volatile Task Environments. Academy of Management Journal, 44(6), 1281–1299

Boin A, ‘t Hart P, Stern E, Sundelius B (2005) The Politics of Crisis Management. Cambridge University Press, Cambridge

Caroll, JS (2015) Making Sense of Ambiguity through Dialogue and Collaborative Action. Journal of Contingencies and Crisis Management, 23(2), 59–65

Castrogiovanni GJ (1991) Environmental Munificence: A Theoretical Assessment. The Academy of Management Review, 16(3), 542–565

Comfort LK, Kapucu N (2006) Inter-organizational coordination in extreme events: The World Trade Center attacks, September 11, 2001. Natural hazards 39(2), 309–327

Das TK, Teng BS (1998) Between Trust and Control: Developing Confidence in Partner Cooperation in Alliances. Academy of Management Review, 23 (3), 491–512

Das TK, Teng BS (2000) Instabilities of Strategic Alliances: An Internal Tensions Perspective. Organization Science 11(1), 77–101

De Waard EJ, Kramer EH (2008) Tailored task forces: Temporary organizations and modularity. International Journal of Project Management 26(5), 537–546

Dess GG, Beard DW (1984) Dimensions of Organizational Task Environments. Administrative Science Quarterly 29(1), 52–73

Dill WR (1958) Environment as an Influence on Managerial Autonomy. Administrative Science Quarterly 2(4), 409–443

Faraj S, Xiao Y (2006) Coordination in fast-response organizations. Management Science 52(8), 1155–1189

Galbraith JR (1973) Designing Complex Organizations. Addison-Wesley, Reading, MA

Gibson CB, Birkinshaw J (2004) The Antecedents, Consequences, and Mediating Role of Organizational Ambidexterity. Academy of Management Journal 47(2), 209–226

Kalkman JP (2016) Explaining the Role of the Armed Forces in the Dutch Safety Regions. In: Beeres R., Bakx G, De Waard E, Rietjens S (eds) NL ARMS: Netherlands Annual Review of Military Studies 2016: Organizing for Safety and Security in Military Organizations [185–202]. The Hague: T.M.C. Asser Press

Kalkman JP, De Waard EJ (2017) Inter-Organizational Disaster Management Projects: Finding the Middle Way between Trust and Control. International Journal of Project Management, 35(5), 889–899

Kotler P (1988) Marketing Management: Analysis, Planning, Implementation, and Control. Prentice-Hall, Englewood Cliffs, NJ

Lawrence PR, Lorsch JW (1967) Organization and Environment. Harvard Business School Press, Boston, MA

McConnell A, Drennan, L (2006) Mission Impossible? Planning and Preparing for Crisis. Journal of Contingencies and Crisis Management, 14(2), 59–69
Minzberg H (1983) Structure in Fives: Designing Effective Organizations. Prentice-Hall, Englewood Cliffs, NJ
Osborn RN, JG Hunt (1974) Environmental and Organizational Effectiveness. Administrative Science Quarterly 19(2), 231–246
Porter ME (1979) How Competitive Forces Shape Strategy. Harvard Business Review, March–April, 137–145
Thompson JD (1967) Organizations in Action. McGraw-Hill, New York
Van Stralen D, Mercer TA (2015) Ambiguity in the Operator's Sense. Journal of Contingencies and Crisis Management, 23(2), 54–58
Van Creveld M (1985) Command in War. Harvard University Press, Cambridge, MA
Volberda HW (1996) Toward the Flexible Form: How to Remain Vital in Hypercompetitive Environments. Organization Science 7(4), 359–374
Weick KE (1988) Enacted Sensemaking in Crisis Situations. Journal of Management Studies, 25(4), 305–317
Weick KE (1993) The collapse of sensemaking in organizations: the Mann Gulch disaster. Administrative Science Quarterly 38(4), 628–652
Weick KE, Sutcliffe KM (2007) Managing the Unexpected. Jossey-Bass, San Francisco
Wolbers JJ (2015) Drawing the line. Cross-boundary coordination processes in emergency management. Dissertation, VU Amsterdam

Chapter 2
Legal Challenges Surrounding Maritime Operations in the Mediterranean Sea: Focus on Migrant Flows

F.J. Marchal and J.E.D. Voetelink

Contents

Abstract Over time the nature of military and maritime operations has shifted from traditional warfare to hybrid type of operations including non-traditional forms of military action such as law enforcement activities. The changing character of operations also impacts the applicable legal framework making the conduct of these operations more challenging from an operator's point of view. This article sheds light on the legal challenges that accompany the change in operations to migrant flow operations. A case in point are recent maritime operations focused on migrant flows conducted in de Mediterranean Sea, in particular the European Union mandated Operation Sophia, in which the Royal Netherlands Navy is involved, although not on a continuous basis.

Keywords Maritime operations · Law of the Sea · European Union · EUNAVFOR MED · Operation Sophia · Refugee Law · Rules of Engagement · non-refoulement · migrants

F.J. Marchal (✉) · J.E.D. Voetelink
Faculty of Military Sciences, Netherlands Defence Academy, Breda, The Netherlands
e-mail: fj.marchal@mindef.nl

J.E.D. Voetelink
e-mail: jed.voetelink@mindef.nl

F.J. Marchal · J.E.D. Voetelink
Amsterdam Centre of International Law (ACIL), Breda, The Netherlands

H. Monsuur et al. (eds.), *NL ARMS Netherlands Annual Review of Military Studies 2018*, NL ARMS, https://doi.org/10.1007/978-94-6265-246-0_2

2.1 Introduction

Military operations in the maritime domain have long since been the best documented and regulated among the multiple types of military operations. The maritime nations that have been conducting these operations have long standing traditions and customs, dating several hundred years back, and their navies act accordingly. In the last couple of decades however, the nature of some of these operations seems to significantly change from conventional operations to more of a law enforcement type operations. The latter take place in a much more complex area of changing and overlapping legal regimes. This change therefore has implications for the operators that conduct them and the regimes that mandate and oversee such operations.

More explicitly, recent years have shown that (mass) migration from Northern Africa and the Middle East to European countries is on the rise. A large portion of the migrant[1] flows go through the Mediterranean Sea and the consequences of migrants flooding especially the coastal countries have deeply divided the nations gathered in the European Union. In reaction to these developments a number of distinct maritime operations have seen the light.[2] Out of these operations, special focus is being awarded to EU Operation Sophia, which provides ample opportunity to show the different legal challenges that are being met.

It is interesting to look at the interplay between European law and international refugee law, which in essence are relatively mild on migrants moving into Europe, the political unwillingness from (some of) the European nations to take migrants in and the actual mandate for these operations that take place in the middle of this.

European States are bound by the rule of law and the treaties they have signed several decades ago prescribe a certain legal regime when it comes to dealing with migrants and asylum seekers. On the other hand, the sheer scale of the potential consequences of letting in large numbers of migrants has led to massive domestic protests and discussion on the way forward. Conducting maritime operations in these circumstances stress the need for a clear and concise mandate, which can be challenging to find in between the different members of EU at this moment.

This article provides a brief insight into the legal challenges that surround maritime operations focused on the migrant flows in the Mediterranean Sea. The present chapter starts by analyzing the rule of law and military operations, focusing on the various categories of maritime operations. Next, the legal basis of EU led operation EUNAVFOR MED Operation Sophia is examined against the backdrop of EU and UN decisions. The chapter then continues with the law that is applicable to this operations distinguishing between the rules of engagement as part of military operational law, the law of the sea and other relevant legal regimes such as human rights law.

---

[1] In the present chapter, the term migrants refers to refugees under Article 1 of the Convention Relating to the Status of Refugees; Geneva, 28 July 1951 (Vol. 189 UNTS No. 2545), as well as economic migrants looking for a better life abroad, Coppens 2013, p. 426.

[2] E.g. EUNAVFOR MED Operation Sophia, NATO's Standing Maritime Group 2 in the Aegean operations and FRONTEX Operations Poseidon and Triton; see Vacas Fernández 2016.

2.2 The State, Rule of Law and Military Operations

The idea of the rule of law is key to modern sovereign States, not in the least to member States of the European Union (EU).[3] Rule of law is a complex concept bringing together a wide array of principles, rules and notions that cover all aspects of the exclusive powers of a State to execute its functions within its territory: to prescribe and enforce the law and administer justice. This complexity is illustrated by the United Nation Secretary-General's elaborate definition of the rule of law that addresses issues such as accountability for the law, State powers, international human rights and due process standards.[4]

At the heart of this comprehensive concept is the notion that States enact laws that apply to their citizens, as well as all State officials and organs.[5] State powers are, therefore, derived from the law and consequently governed and qualified by the law. Armed forces are without any doubt State organs and as integral part of the State bound by the concept of the rule of law. When focusing on the executing of military operations the rule of law requires the whole of military activities to be founded on a solid legal basis and executed in accordance with all applicable rules. Therefore, deployment of elements of State armed forces abroad must be justified under national and international law and military personnel participating in the operation must act in accordance with domestic and host State rules, as well as international law. Legal basis and applicable rules together constitute the legal framework of any military operation. Today, this framework is not a fixed set of rules applicable at all times, but is dependent on the nature of a specific operation. In the course of the last two decades the legal framework has become increasingly complex because of the ever-changing character of many contemporary military operations and the hybrid character of some.

Traditionally, States fielded their armed forces to wage war against other sovereign States in, what is called in legal terms, an international armed conflict. The legal framework covering such a conflict comprises the *jus ad bellum*, the right of States to use armed force and the *jus in bello*, the laws of armed conflict or in short: the law of war. The establishment of the United Nations led to a new type of operations aimed at maintaining international peace and security based on the provisions of the UN Charter.[6] Although these UN-operations can sometime be characterized as armed conflict to which the law of war applies, the majority of these operations do not reach the armed conflict threshold, thus entailing the applicability of other sets of rules. As UN mandates expanded and became more complex troops got involved in non-typical military functions such as crowd and riot control and arrest of (war) criminals as, for example, happened in UN-mandated operations on the Balkan.

---

[3] E.g. Boucher describes how rule of law is one of the core principles of EU enlargement, Boucher 2005, p. 89.

[4] UN Doc S/2004/616, Report of the Secretary-General on the Rule of Law and Transitional Justice in Conflict and Post-Conflict Society.

[5] Cf. Bingham 2011, p. 8.

[6] Charter of the United Nations; San Francisco, 26 June 1945.

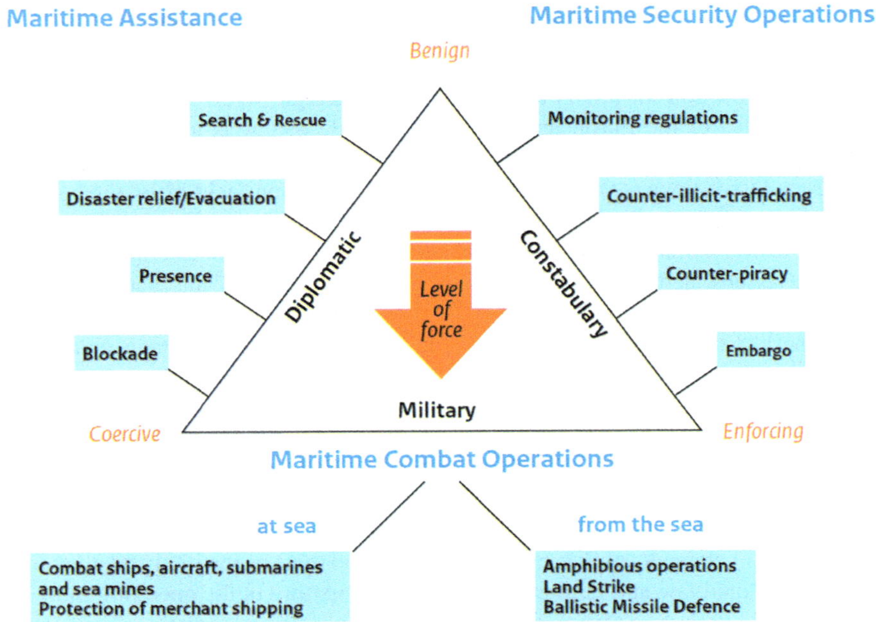

Fig. 2.1 Types of maritime operations, Netherlands Maritime Military Doctrine [*Source* Netherlands Maritime Military Doctrine, https://english.defensie.nl/downloads/publications/2015/03/03/netherlands-maritime-military-doctrine]

These functions can be best described as law enforcement type of activities that can even be the core part of a mandate. An example are the operations off the coast of Somalia to fight piracy. Although law enforcement is not a primary military task the armed forces are sometimes the best equipped to fulfill these tasks and are as first responders to a crisis situation often the only entity capable of taking effective action at that point in time. These functions also impact the legal framework as yet other rules become applicable.

The Netherlands' navy has become quite familiar with the shifting character of operations as she has been involved in counter-drugs operations in the Caribbean and anti-piracy operations off the coast of Somalia for years now, and since 2015, is conducting operations related to migrant flows in the Mediterranean Sea. Not surprisingly, this shift is reflected in the Netherlands maritime military doctrine. Part 3 of the Doctrine covers the various types of maritime operations distinguishing between Maritime Combat Operations, Maritime Assistance, and Maritime Security Operations (Fig. 2.1).[7]

Maritime Combat Operations are offensive and defensive operations taking place at sea and from sea generally within the context of armed conflict and are therefore governed by the law of war. In Maritime Assistance, on the other hand, the

[7] Netherlands Maritime Military Doctrine 2015, p. 316.

use of armed force is not the principal object as naval assets are deployed in support of diplomatic efforts or civil authorities.[8] Activities include a wide variety of actions, such as maritime capacity building, humanitarian assistance, disaster relief and evacuation, enforcement of law and order, and search and rescue actions. The exact legal framework depends on the characteristics of a specific task, which will generally take place under peacetime rules. Maritime Security Operations are defensive and offensive operations launched to protect national and international law in which naval forces may use force, e.g. by boarding and searching of ships registered abroad. Maritime Security Missions include counter-drug and anti-piracy operations and actions 'countering illegal immigration, human trafficking or slave trading'.[9] In this particular type of operations the legal framework may be more complex involving domestic and international rules, depending on the precise nature and location of the operation.

2.3 Migrant Flows and Maritime Operations in the Mediterranean; Legal Basis

The different types of maritime operations the Netherlands doctrine covers cannot be fully separated at all times adding to the complexity of the legal framework. Recent NATO and especially EU maritime operations in the Mediterranean Sea focusing on migrant flows are a case in point and clearly illustrate the broad legal challenges naval forces are facing in contemporary operations.

Before NATO and EU got involved in the control of migrant flows, the issue was largely a national issue. In 2009, facing large groups of migrants desperately trying to enter the country by sea, Italy concluded a number of bilateral agreements with Libya in an effort to stop irregular immigration. The agreements facilitated the interception of migrant vessels on the high seas and the (forced) return of the migrants to Libya.[10] Italy's push-back policy met with criticism of the European Court of Human Rights (ECtHR) as it violated the principle of *non-refoulement*,[11] the well-established rule under international law that refugees and other persons cannot be sent back to States where they run the real risk of being subjected to torture or cruel, inhuman or degrading treatment.[12] The Court decision and the drowning of more

---

[8] Military force may be used 'if civil authorities and organisations can no longer or not yet perform their tasks themselves ('safety net') or if specific military capacities are required ('structural partner')', id., p. 355.

[9] Id., p. 342.

[10] ECtRM 23 February 2012, *Case of Hirsi Jamaa and Others v Italy*, Judgement, Application No. 27765/09, p. 3.

[11] Id., p. 77.

[12] E.g., Article 33 of the Refugee Convention and Article 3 of the Convention against torture and other cruel, inhuman or degrading treatment or punishment; 10 December 1984 (Vol. 1465 UNTS No. 24841). Non-refoulement is inherent in the general terms of Article 3 of the European Convention for the Protection of Human Rights and Fundamental Freedoms; Rome, 11 August 1950

than 250 migrants near the island of Lampedusa on 3 October 2013 led to a change of policy resulting in the launch of operation *Mare Nostrum* later that month.[13]

This new maritime operation was aimed at control of Italy's borders while at the same time extending the rescue of migrants well beyond the Italian Search and Rescue (SAR) zone. People rescued at sea were no longer pushed back to Libya, but transferred to Italy. Human traffickers and migrant smugglers were arrested and handed over to the criminal justice authorities for prosecution. In the course of this operation, conducted by Italy without any assistance from other European countries, the Italian Navy rescued more than 150.000 people and transferred some 330 suspects of human trafficking to the Italian justice authorities for legal processing.[14] One year later, in October 2014, FRONTEX, the European agency for the management of operational cooperation between EU-member States at the external borders of the EU, took over the activities by launching Joint Operation Triton 2015.[15] The focus of this operation is on border control, surveillance and search and rescue in the territorial waters of Italy and parts of the search and rescue (SAR) zones of Italy and Malta.[16]

Notwithstanding these efforts, an increasing number of migrants started the perilous journey to Italy by sea leading to yet another tragedy in April 2015 when in a single accident more than 700 people drowned off the coast of Libya. As part of her comprehensive approach[17] the EU established EUNAVFOR MED, later codenamed Operation Sophia, after a girl born on a German ship participating in the operation.[18] The formal basis and mandate for this operation was the decision of the Council of the EU of 18 may 2015 approving its concept.[19] Operation Sophia is not set up as a maritime search and rescue operation as its purpose is the 'disruption of the business model of human smuggling and trafficking networks in the Southern Central Mediterranean'.[20] This military mission to fight trans-national crime qualifies as a Maritime Security Operation aimed at counter illicit trafficking in terms of the Netherlands maritime military doctrine. Although EUNAVFOR MED Operation Sophia is not

(Vol. 213 UNTS No. 2889) (ECtRM 7 July 1989, *Case of Soering v. United Kingdom*, Judgment, Application No. 14038/88, para 88).

13 18 October 2015, Italian minister of Defence: www.marina.difesa.it/EN/operations/Pagine/MareNostrum.aspx. Accessed November 2017.

14 Italian ministry of defense: www.marina.difesa.it/EN/operations/Pagine/MareNostrum.aspx. Accessed November 2017.

15 Its legal basis is discussed in Vacas Fernández 2016, p. 100.

16 UK House of Lords 2017, p. 10.

17 EU Doc COM(2011) 743 final, European Commission, 'Global Approach to Migration and Mobility, Brussel 18 November 2011 and EU Doc COM(2015) 285 final, EU Action Plan against migrant smuggling (2015–2020), Brussel, 27 May 2015.

18 House of Lords, Operation Sophia, the EU's naval mission in the Mediterranean: an impossible challenge, 13 May 2016, p. 5.

19 Council Decision (CFSP) 2015/778 of 18 May 2015 on a European Union military operation in the Southern Central Mediterranean (EUNAVFOR MED Operation SOPHIA), OJ 2015 (L 122/31). The operation was launched on 22 June 2015; Council Decision (CFSP) 2015/972 of 22 June 2015 launching the European Union military operation in the southern Central Mediterranean (EUNAVFOR MED), OJ 2015 (L157/51).

20 Council Decision (CFSP) 2015/778, Article 1(1).

set up as a search and rescue operation[21] the rescue of persons in distress at sea will have to be considered as an accompanying task,[22] making the operation even more complex.

Execution of the operation is to take place in three consecutive phases as set out in Article 2 of the Council Decision. The initial phase, which started on 22 June 2015,[23] was limited to gathering of information and patrolling the high seas in order to support the detection and monitoring of migration networks.[24] On 7 October 2015 the operation moved on to the first part of the second phase.[25] This sub-phase is also limited to the high seas authorizing the conduct of 'boarding, search, seizure and diversion on the high seas of vessels suspected of being used for human smuggling or trafficking'; all these activities are to be executed in accordance with international law.[26] The second sub-phase requires either the consent of the coastal State concerned (i.e. Libya) or a UN Security Council (UNSC) Resolution and extends the first sub-phase activities to the territorial and internal waters of the coastal States.[27] The third phase also requires the coastal State's consent or a UNSC Resolution and authorizes the operation to 'take all necessary measures against a vessel and related assets, including through disposing of them or rendering them inoperable, which are suspected of being used for human smuggling or trafficking, in the territory of that State, under the conditions set out in that Resolution or consent'.[28]

The present operation, which is still in the initial part of the second phase, is shored up by UNSC Resolution 2240 of 9 October 2015.[29] Acting under Chapter VII of the UN Charter[30] the Council authorizes UN-member States 'to use all measures commensurate to the specific circumstances in confronting migrant smugglers and human traffickers in carrying out activities' mandated in the Resolution.[31] These activities include inspection on the high seas of vessels that member States have reasonable grounds to suspect are being used for migrant smuggling or human trafficking from

---

[21] According to Butler maritime search and rescue is a competence of the EU-member States; Butler and Ratcovich 2016, p. 241.

[22] Rescue of persons in distress at sea is in international obligation that in principle does not need a formal mandate; Vacas Fernández 2016, p. 103.

[23] Council Decision (CFSP) 2015/972 of 22 June 2015 launching the European Union military operation in the southern Central Mediterranean (EUNAVFOR MED), OJ 2015 (L157/51).

[24] Council Decision (CFSP) 2015/778, Article 2(a).

[25] Political and Security Committee Decision (CFSP) 2015/1772 of 28 September 2015 concerning the transition by EUNAVFOR MED to the second phase of the operation, as laid down in point (b)(i) of Article 2(2) of Decision (CFSP) 2015/778 on a European Union military operation in the Southern Central Mediterranean (EUNAVFOR MED) (EUNAVFOR MED/2/2015), OJ 2015 (L 258/5).

[26] Id., Article 2(b)(i).

[27] Id., Article 2(b)(ii).

[28] Id., Article 2(c).

[29] UN Doc S/Res/2240 (2015); authorizations set out in the Resolution were each time for a period of one year renewed in 2016 (UN Doc S/Res/2312 (2016)) and 2017 (UN Doc S/Res/2380 (2017)).

[30] Decisions taken under Chapter VII are binding on member States (cf. Article 25 UN Charter).

[31] Paragraph 10.

Libya, provided that good faith efforts are made to obtain the consent of the vessel's flag State prior to the inspection (para 7) and, when necessary, seizure of the vessels inspected (para 8). Fink refers to these activities as Maritime Interception Operations (MIOs); an operational term for 'Naval operations that include the boarding, search and seizure of goods and the detention of persons on a foreign flagged merchant vessel, outside the territorial jurisdiction of a State'.[32]

On 20 January 2016, the EU incorporated the UN-mandate by authorizing EUNAVFOR MED Operation Sophia to conduct the activities as set out in Resolution 2240.[33] Even though the operation has not yet moved on to the next phase due to the political and security condition in Libya,[34] its mandate has been changed a number of times adding to the mission's complexity. After the Libyan Government of National Accord expressed its willingness to cooperate with the EU and the UNSC had adopted Resolution 2292[35] on the arms embargo on Libya the EU extended the mandate of EUNAVFOR MED Operation Sophia by one year adding two further supporting tasks.[36] In addition to its core tasks aimed at the disruption of the business model of human smuggling and trafficking networks and the prevention of the further loss of life at sea, the operation was to provide training to the Libyan Coast Guard and Navy[37] and to contribute to preventing arms trafficking within the Area of Operation.[38]

In December 2016 authorizations to exchange information with relevant actors, such as the International Criminal Court and the US, as well as with EU-member States, the UN Support Mission in Libya (UNSMIL), the European Police Office

---

[32] Fink 2016, 33. In the Netherlands maritime military doctrine 2015 the phrase 'Interception' is replaced by 'Interdiction'.

[33] Political and Security Committee Decision (CFSP) 2016/118 of 20 January 2016 concerning the implementation by EUNAVFOR MED operation SOPHIA of United Nations Security Council Resolution 2240 (2015) (EUNAVFOR MED operation SOPHIA/1/2016), OJ 2016 (L 258/5).

[34] Government Response UK (2017), p. 2.

[35] UN DOC S/Res/2292 (2016) of 14 June 2016.

[36] Council Decision (CFSP) 2016/993 of 20 June 2016 amending Decision (CFSP) 2015/778 on a European Union military operation in the Southern Central Mediterranean (EUNAVFOR MED operation SOPHIA), OJ 2016 (L 162/18).

[37] In 2016 the Royal Netherlands Navy contributed two ships for the training of the Libyan Coast Guard and Navy; Dutch Parliamentary Papers 2017, Evaluation Netherlands' contribution to missions and operations 2016, 15 May 2017, p. 22. https://zoek.officielebekendmakingen.nl/blg-807658. Accessed November 2017.

[38] The operation commenced capacity building and training on 30 August 2016 and started its contribution to the implementation of the UN arms embargo on 6 September 2016; Political and Security Committee Decision (CFSP) 2016/1635 of 30 August 2016 on the commencement of the capacity building and training of the Libyan Coast Guard and Navy by the European Union military operation in the Southern Central Mediterranean (EUNAVFOR MED operation SOPHIA) (EUNAVFOR MED/3/2016) OJ 2016 (L 243/11) and Political and Security Committee Decision (CFSP) 2016/1637 of 6 September 2016 on the commencement of the European Union military operation in the Southern Central Mediterranean (EUNAVFOR MED operation SOPHIA) contributing to the implementation of the UN arms embargo on the high seas off the coast of Libya (EUNAVFOR MED/4/2016), OJ 2016 (L 243/14).

(EUROPOL) and FRONTEX were enhanced.[39] In July 2017 the EU extended the mandate for another year until 31 December 2018 again adding a supporting task:[40] the conduct of surveillance activities and gathering of information on illegal trafficking, including information on crude oil and other illegal exports that are contrary to UNSC Resolutions 2146 (2014) and 2362 (2017).

Looking at the expanding combination of core and supporting tasks it is clear that EUNAVFOR MED Operation Sophia has become increasingly complex merging elements of Maritime Assistance and Maritime Security Operations. Consequently, the legal framework is broadening as well. The operation's legal basis consists of the amended 2015 Decision (CFSP) 2015/778 on a European Union military operation in the Southern Central Mediterranean and the authorizations set out in the various UNSC Resolutions and as such are the cornerstone of its legal framework.[41] The other part of the legal framework, the rules that are applicable executing the mission are addressed in the next paragraph.

2.4 EUNAVFOR MED Operation Sophia; Applicable Rules

The rule of law entails that operations are conducted in accordance with the law. As the area of operation of EUNAVFOR MED Operation Sophia has until now not been extended to coastal States or their territorial seas, the law that has to be taken in consideration is each participating State's domestic law and, more important, international law. This paragraph focuses on international law as all EU decisions and UNSC Resolutions stress that operations have to be conducted in full respect of international law, often emphasizing the particular field of international law or the specific legal instruments.

One remark on domestic law is warranted, however. Disrupting the smuggler's business model may entail detention of suspects of illegal activities (as will be further discussed below). At the moment EUNAVFOR MED Operation Sophia still hands over detainees to Italian authorities for prosecution. Consequently, intelligence collected by the participating forces must be converted in evidence admissible in Italian criminal courts.[42] In general, military personnel is not specifically trained in collecting and preserving evidence, let alone in accordance with a foreign State's rules on criminal proceedings.[43] Therefore, to ensure that the operation leads to a successful prosecution in Italy, the participating forces must be trained in more than basic board-

[39] Council Decision (CFSP) 2016/2314 of 19 December 2016 amending Decision (CFSP) 2015/778 on a European Union military operation in the Southern Central Mediterranean (EUNAVFOR MED operation SOPHIA), OJ 2016 (L 345/62).

[40] Council Decision (CFSP) 2017/1385 of 25 July 2017 amending Decision (CFSP) 2015/778 on a European Union military operation in the Southern Central Mediterranean (EUNAVFOR MED operation SOPHIA), OJ 2017 (L194/61).

[41] Cf. Butler and Ratcovich 2016, p. 248.

[42] Voetelink 2013b, p. 199.

[43] Bruggen et al. 2016, p. 2684.

ing and inspection techniques and must have some appreciation of law enforcement skills taking into account Italian law.[44] In this context, close cooperation between the participating forces and Italian criminal justice officials is crucial.[45]

The next sub-paragraphs will address the Rules of Engagement (ROE) as part of the international law of military operations,[46] the international law of the sea and refugee and migrant law. These are all regimes (of law) that have a practical impact on operators in those operations and are therefore highlighted.

2.4.1 Rules of Engagement

The 'various bodies of national and international law which are applicable to and regulate the planning and conduct of military operations' together comprise what is called military operational law.[47] This still developing field of law covers a host of subjects, including the right to use force. The military can only use (armed) force or take other coercive actions when exercising the right of self-defence or conducting operations based on a specific mandate. In the latter case the mandate will be further elaborated upon in the Operational Plan and, most important, the ROE.[48] ROE can be described as 'directives to military commanders and forces (including individuals) that define the circumstances, conditions, degree, and manner in which force, or other actions which might be construed as provocative, may, or may not, be applied. ROE are not used to assign tasks or give tactical instructions'.[49] To be clear: ROE as such are not law, but as they are closely related to a mission's legal basis and may justify otherwise possible illegal acts they will be dealt with in this chapter as part of the legal framework.

In general, ROE are classified as secret, and are therefore not published, as is the case with the ROE applicable to EUNAVFOR MED Operation Sophia.[50] Nevertheless, some general remarks can be made about the specific rules on the use of force in this particular context. As a general rule, the participating forces are entitled to use force in the exercise of their right of self-defense. Self-defense is an inherent right of an individual service member and of units participating in an operation and is as such not a part of the ROE. As the conditions and circumstances in which the EU force operates in the present phase do not reach the threshold of armed conflict the law of war is not applicable. Consequently, the use of force in this maritime context is regulated by normal peacetime rules, in particular international human rights law

---

[44] Cf. Guilfoyl 2017, pp. 318–319.

[45] Bruggen et al. 2016, p. 2685.

[46] See for a general description: Gill and Fleck 2015, 3–14.

[47] Gill and Fleck 2015, 3.

[48] Voetelink 2013a, p. 162 ff.

[49] Council of the EU, Use of Force Concept for EU-led Military Crisis Management Operations of 28 February 2006, P revision, Doc. 6877/06, as quoted in Cooper (2014), p. 192.

[50] Article 5 Decision (CFSP) 2015/778.

and the law of the sea. As the ROE build on the mission's mandate the text of the 2015 Decision (CFSP) 2015/778 (as amended) and relevant UNSC resolutions must be interpreted taking into account these fields of law.

The core task of the mission is to disrupt the business model of human smuggling and trafficking networks. The UNSC has authorized inspection, seizure and disposal of ships being used for these purposes. Detention of persons suspected of being involved in these activities is, however, not specifically mentioned in the mandate or the Resolution(s). In general, armed forces will not have the authority to arrest and detain people. Nonetheless, it would be irreconcilable with the nature of EUNAVFOR Med Operation Sophia if migrant smugglers and human traffickers were allowed to continue doing their clandestine business. Therefore, it must be accepted that the authority to detain persons is included in the UNSC authorization 'to use all measures commensurate to the specific circumstances in confronting migrant smugglers or human traffickers' and further set out in the ROE.[51] Practice supports this view as EUNAVFOR Med Operation Sophia had already arrested some 110 smugglers in July 2017.[52]

It is far from inconceivable that people involved in this profitable business will attempt to resist arrest. Therefore, military personnel authorized under the ROE to make an arrest must have the right to use some level of armed force, running the risk of killing a suspect in the process. Article 2 of the European Convention on Human Right protects the right to life, though allowing for use of force in order to effect a lawful arrest. That use of force is not unconditional, however, and must be 'absolutely necessary' and 'strictly proportionate' to make the arrest.[53] The ROE may further specify or even restrict these conditions.

Warships have the right to board and inspect vessels on the high seas under the international law of the sea. The United Nations Convention on the Law of the Sea (UNCLOS)[54] allows boarding and inspection of ships if there is reasonable ground for suspecting that a ship is engaged in slave trade, piracy,[55] is without nationality or refuses to show her flag.[56] EUNAVFOR MED Operation Sophia does not need an explicit mandate to exercise these rights, but it is probable that the authority to take the actions are part of the ROE. UNCLOS does not allow, however, taking further action, such as seizure of the vessels, or acting against ships suspected of migrant smuggling and human trafficking. That has become possible under paragraphs 7 and 8 of UNSC Resolution 2240 as described above. The authorization to take these actions will be included and possibly further specified in the ROE as well.

---

[51] A similar provision can be found in the resolutions on the arms embargo UNSC Resolution 2292, para 4.

[52] Government Response UK 2017, p. 1.

[53] ECtRM 27 September 1995, Case of McCann and others v. the United Kingdom, Judgement, Application No. 18984/91, paras 148 and 149.

[54] United Nations Convention on the Law of the Sea; Montego-Bay, 10 December 1982 (Vol. 1833 UNTS No. 31363).

[55] Article 110(1)(b) and 110(2).

[56] Article 110(1)(b) and 110(2).

2.4.2 Law Regimes Applicable to Maritime Migrant Flow Operations

2.4.2.1 Law of the Sea and the Duty to Render Assistance

It is clear from the paragraphs above that the mandate for Operation Sophia does not in the first place focus on the duty to save lives at sea. And in fact, there is no specific need to address this in an operational mandate, because the *duty to render assistance at sea* has been a longstanding maritime rule of customary law. In the last part of the previous century it has also been codified in a number of authoritative treaties, such as the SOLAS- and SAR Conventions and foremost also in UNCLOS.[57] What all these treaties have in common is the understanding that there is a positive duty, for each and every mariner including navy personnel on warships, to intervene and rescue persons in distress at sea. The starting point therefore is common ground and is it is clear what this obligation entails; save people at risk of drowning.

In practice, a number of legal challenges arise when dealing with operations in areas where mass migration occurs. Said obligation is drafted with the understanding there is a certain inherent reciprocity in the fact that every mariner would want to be rescued in case of emergency and the interdependency on each other at sea warrants such an obligation. Nevertheless, two 'problems' can occur when dealing with this traditional obligation in operations such as Sophia; when to intervene and the issue of responsibility for embarked persons. The first will be directly underneath and the second will be addressed in the following paragraph on human rights.

Firstly, when is a person really in distress? It is obvious that a sinking ship or boat is in distress and a mayday call to the SAR coordinator is a pretty good indicator that the persons on board are in need of help. But what about the multitude of dodgy and unstable vessels used by smugglers and migrants to navigate across the Mediterranean Sea? It is common to overload those vessels with people up to a point at which it is unsafe. The majority of these vessels is not equipped to traverse oceans or seas, which has been proven by the numerous accounts of migrants shipwrecking or even perishing at sea.[58] The responsibility for sailing in a seaworthy vessel lies primarily with the mariner itself. Strictly legally speaking, when a warship encounters an unstable vessel loaded with people it does not automatically follow that the warship has to render assistance. Only when it is obvious that the persons on board are in

[57] The 1974 International Convention for the Safety of Life at Sea (SOLAS), the International Convention on Maritime Search and Rescue; Hamburg, 27 April 1979 & UNCLOS Article 98.

[58] Over 2016 a rough estimate of over 5000 people lost their lives trying to cross the Med: http://www.nytimes.com/2016/12/23/world/europe/migrant-death-toll-mediterranean-europe.html. Over 2017 the UNHCR official figure shows just over 3000 death and missing: http://data2.unhcr.org/en/situations/mediterranean, accessed January 2018.

distress, i.e. are in imminent danger of losing their lives, the obligation comes into effect.[59]

So, a warship in general has two options, keep sailing or render assistance. Both are unsatisfactory to a certain degree. It could easily be understood that a warship sailing with an operational plan, scheme or transit plan does neither have the time nor inclination to disregard its plan and come to the aid of migrants, when it does not have to. In some instances, navy ships on their best behavior tried to get close to smuggling boats to provide at least some drinking water and medicine, and 'created their own SOLAS case'. Upon noticing the navy ship the suspected smugglers told the migrants to jump overboard and wave and cry for help, knowing full well that the warship would have to come in and save them, due to their duty to render assistance.[60] Suffice to say that navy commanders in general are not keen on 'the hassle' that accompanies such interventions and it is likely that they will be handed the advice to stick to their planning and thus keep sailing, even though this most likely will not be found in writing.[61] Navies would legally be perfectly in line with international law if they would indeed pass out this guidance. On the other hand, the loss of lives of migrants at sea sparks international debate and for many, such behavior would be irreconcilable with our understanding of *humanity* and human rights. Looking at it from this perspective, 'keep sailing' could then entail the disregard of a potential threat to life. Moreover, political pressure forces governments to come up with an approach to halt the loss of lives of migrants at sea, stressing the need to deploy warships in order to patrol the Mediterranean Sea and end the suffering.

In conclusion, the mere legal obligation to render assistance at sea alone presents a challenge in practice, as to the moment of intervention and where this duty actually starts and ends.

2.4.2.2 Human Rights Law and Its Effect

The second 'problem' then pertains to the situation after taking persons on board. Once embarked, all people on board of European warships are to be handled as if in jurisdiction of the Flag State of the ship, for the purpose of application of human

---

[59] Distress is defined in the SAR Convention as: "A situation wherein there is reasonable certainty that a person, a vessel or other craft is threatened by grave and imminent danger and requires immediate assistance." SAR Convention, Chapter 1, para 1.3.13.

[60] A number of those incidents occurred in recent years, is the experience of one of the authors who worked for the Netherlands Navy Maritime Headquarter from 2013 to 2015. It is however hard to produce openly accessible sources.

[61] The complexity of dealing with migrants at sea also means that there is no NATO protocol or responsibility for it and is left to national authorities of troop contributing nations. In a specific (unclassified) guidance message issued on 8 January 2015 by NATO Maritime Command in Northwood there is the notion of the possibility of an OPCON shift whenever dealing with migrants or smugglers at sea, as they would 'require follow up actions under national authority'. This guidance was issued to SNMG-1, the NATO fleet that regularly patrols the Mediterranean Sea.

rights law.[62] This means all EU regulations and more importantly the ECHR and all ensuing obligations are to be upheld. Especially the *non-refoulement* prohibition then comes into play. The principle in essence leads to a prohibition to send back migrants to the countries where they came from in Northern Africa,[63] due to the instability in that region. Then, when a number of people are residing on board, where then do warships hand them over to authorities, and also to which authorities? The *non-refoulement* principle hinders the handover to a relatively large number of countries, often the same countries that produce migrants in the first place, but provides no single guidance as to which authority then would be responsible for migrants of which the nationality appears to be unknown. Due to the SAR Convention, the Mediterranean Sea is divided into areas of responsibility (or SAR regions) in which appointed coastal states would be responsible for dealing with emergency incidents and the initial intake of survivors or persons in distress. This system however does not take into account mass migration movements on unstable vessels, states that do not want to take up migrants and the consequences of refugee law and the EU human rights system that produced the *non-refoulement* principle. In practice, states become more and more reluctant to take in migrants from the Mediterranean Sea, presenting the individual warship with even more 'hassle'.

The law of the sea is clear about the positive obligation to render assistance at sea, but the circumstances of today's mass migration movements cloud the interpretation of this obligation and increase the difficulty of applying it. Some of the ensuing obligations that stem from human rights law moreover have an effect on the longstanding naval customs and laws, in terms of practicability.

What we see is that in the maritime environment the specific body of international law of the sea interacts with human rights law. These then are mixed with an international mandate provided by the United Nations Security Council in wording that much resembles authorizations to conduct full-blown military operations. Irrespective of whether a person has been embarked in an attempt to rescue that person or because of suspicion of illicit trafficking, human rights laws prescribe certain ways of dealing with detainees. It makes operating much more complex for the commander on the ground, or in this case at sea, to be able to identify and deal with these different areas of law and apply them where necessary. To add to the confusion, another relevant body of law, summarized as *refugee law*, comes into play. It provides additional legal obligations, albeit mostly for the states receiving migrants and dealing with the

[62] The Hirsi Jamaa judgement not only dealt with the non-refoulement prohibition but also unequivocally established the extraterritorial working of the European Convention for Human Rights on EU warships outside EU territory, on the basis of effective control over all embarked persons, a.o. para 5, ECtRM 23 February 2012, *Case of Hirsi Jamaa and Others v Italy*, Judgement, Application No. 27765/09.

[63] See also above under 3. Legal basis, supra note 13&14. As an example: the Ministry of Foreign Affairs of the Netherlands regularly produces a list of 'safe countries', deemed benign enough to send migrants back to once their asylum procedure has been terminated. There are 60 countries on the list, possibly implying that roughly 133 countries all over the world would indeed not qualify as safe and therefore be prone to violation of the *non-refoulement* prohibition if migrants were sent back there. Among those are countries that are known to produce migrant flows such as Libya, Eritrea, Nigeria, Somalia, and Morocco.

asylum requests, and to a lesser extent for the warships patrolling the Mediterranean Sea. Nonetheless, they do affect their operations.

2.4.3 Refugee Law, Mass Migration and Maritime Patrols

The general laws of the sea provide for a safety net for distress cases of mariners at sea. But these were drafted with a different scope, certainly not with the aim to support mass migration by sea and the fact that a large number of fleeing refugees would take off to sea in unstable vessels. Modern day operations face a new type of challenge: the refugee. A key difference between embarking persons in distress after a maritime emergency and taking aboard migrants set out to settle in the European Union, is the fact that the latter category might also apply for asylum to their rescuers. In this case, another series of rules concerning the treatment of refugees and displaced persons appears on the field. A relatively unknown and specific body of law, especially to the likes of servicemen of armed forces serving in Operation Sophia, is the collection of rules and protocols referred to as *refugee law*. The law of the sea in general does not provide ample guidance about treatment of embarked persons (which is governed by human rights law) and says close to nothing about handling asylum seekers.[64] In fact, asylum-issues are not the responsibility of the mariner or warship that rescues persons at sea, but the responsibility of coastal states and governments. The result is that maritime operations like Sophia gain immediate attention from the government level, as well as large-scale media coverage and NGO activity.[65]

In 1951 already the Convention relating to the status of Refugees[66] (the Refugee Convention) was drafted as the main legal document with regard to the handling of asylum seekers. The *non-refoulement* principle saw the light in this convention. One could say there is relatively large consensus[67] as to whether or not a refugee should be awarded protection and asylum, if need be. But then the problem is, in an operation dealing with mass migration the majority of migrants will most likely not qualify as refugees but rather as a so-called economic migrant. The definition given

[64] The International Maritime Organization in May 2004 issued a Resolution MSC.167(78), stressing the need for States to come up with, next to the existing SAR system, systematic agreements to deal with asylum seekers picked up at sea whose responsibility is not borne by the entity performing the Rescue.

[65] Over 2016 and 2017 NGOs have started fairly large-scale rescue operations that brought some tens of thousands of migrants into the EU. They received both praise for their efforts and criticism for aggravating the situation (see https://tinyurl.com/y8qqloca). Starting mid-2017, Libyan Coastguard operators have been reported as aggressive in trying to get these NGOs to suspend their activities, which seems to be effective since a number of major NGOs have indeed done just that: (see: https://www.theguardian.com/world/2017/aug/14/three-ngos-halt-mediterranean-migrant-rescues-after-libyan-hostility) accessed January 2018.

[66] See http://www.unhcr.org/1951-refugee-convention.html for the treaty, the travaux preparatoires and commentaries, accessed January 2018.

[67] The Refugee Convention today has 145 signatories, out of 193 UN countries.

in the Refugee Convention[68] clearly states that there needs to be a 'well-founded fear of being prosecuted' before one can qualify as a refugee. How in practice would an operator be able to distinguish between the two categories, and thus determine whether or not the body of refugee law is applicable to the situation?

To add to that, hypothetically speaking, when EU Operation Sophia focuses on intercepting smugglers in the territorial waters of Libya and sending them back, one could argue that the *non-refoulement* principle will be violated.[69] Stretching this even further, if one were to reason purely from the refugee law perspective, even repressing smuggling operations on land could in fact mean obstructing a refugee's possibility to flee to a safe haven. Governments on the other hand, especially the ones dealing with a large influx of refugees, will most likely argue as a proponent for another approach, where migrant smuggling is dealt with as an illegal, or criminal, activities foremost.[70]

In fact, this approach has been on the forefront ever since the masses enjoy increased mobility and migrant movement is on the rise in the second part of the previous century. In 2000, a new multilateral treaty saw the light: the Convention Against Transnational Organized Crime, the Palermo Protocol for short. This treaty comprises of a vast majority of UN members[71] that together decided to halt the increasing practice of smuggling and trafficking persons. The latter two categories in and of itself provide another challenge, because *smuggling* and *trafficking* of people are two distinct realities, if one were to define them according to penal law. The act of trafficking requires a distinct amount of force, repression or forced labor[72] whereas

---

[68] According to the Convention a refugee is a person who [...owing to well-founded fear of being persecuted for reasons of race, religion, nationality, membership of a particular social group or political opinion, is outside the country of his nationality and is unable or, owing to such fear, is unwilling to avail himself of the protection of that country; or who, not having a nationality and being outside the country of his former habitual residence as a result of such events, is unable or, owing to such fear, is unwilling to return to it....].

[69] An insightful article uncovers a number of legal considerations with regard to this hypothesis, see P. Strauch, in his comment in the Yale Law Journal, 'When Stopping the Smuggler Means Repelling the Refugee: International Human Rights Law and the European Union's Operation to Combat Smuggling in Libya's Territorial Sea', YLJ, 126, (2017) pp. 2421–2449.

[70] Border operations and maritime operations directed at controlling migrant movement are therefore subject to danger of 'politicization': see P. Cuttita, *Repoliticization through Search and Rescue? Humanitarian NGOs and Migration Management in the Central Mediterranean*, in Geopolitics, 17 July 2017, accessible at http://dx.doi.org/10.1080/14650045.2017.1344834.

[71] 189 countries signed the treaty, according to UNODC figures: https://www.unodc.org/unodc/en/treaties/CTOC/signatures.html.

[72] The definition given by the Palermo Protocol states that Trafficking in Persons is ["the recruitment, transportation, transfer, harbouring or receipt of persons, by means of the threat or use of force or other forms of coercion, of abduction, of fraud, of deception, of the abuse of power or of a position of vulnerability or of the giving or receiving of payments or benefits to achieve the consent of a person having control over another person, for the purpose of exploitation. Exploitation shall include, at a minimum, the exploitation of the prostitution of others or other forms of sexual exploitation, forced labour or services, slavery or practices similar to slavery, servitude or the removal of organs."] which is quite a far-reaching analysis to make for an operator without any previous knowledge or intelligence of the suspected vessel and its crew.

smuggling is merely the provision of a service (be it a shady and sometimes unsafe service). International law of the sea holds provisions to tackle human trafficking, due to a likely resemblance to slave trade,[73] but not for acting against possible smugglers in the open sea. That remains within the sole custody of the coastal state to which persons are being smuggled. It is not hard to imagine that for operators patrolling the seas, distinguishing between the two is nearly impossible, but the legal implications are countless.

So, other than distinguish between distressed migrants, refugees or asylum seekers and having to save, accommodate and transfer them to safe countries, it would be helpful if maritime operations charted (and proved) the activity of the individuals in between the groups of persons responsible for smuggling or trafficking, so they are liable for prosecution.

2.5 Synthesis and Conclusion

The combination of UNCLOS obligations, ECHR jurisprudence (i.e. Hirsi), human rights and Refugee law, make for an uneasy combination and there are two opposite sides that interpret all those obligations very differently. The government approach is aimed at minimizing the influx of illegal immigrants and tackling root causes of this migration, and use a law enforcement perspective. The UN Security Council has provided a legal base for that. On the other hand, there is the humane perspective that is mostly promulgated by human rights activists and NGOs and which is represented in political systems in a multitude of EU countries in different forms. Both spheres of influence cloud interpretation of what already is a diverse and fluid assortment of types of law. In modern day maritime operations, which are largely focused on law enforcement, elements of different types of law together, such as the *non-refoulement* prohibition, the *duty to render assistance* and human rights doctrines relating to treatment of detainees make up the conditions under which operators in EU Operation Sophia have to conduct their mission.

Those maritime operations are increasingly complex, especially taking into account the huge political pressure that surround the anti-migrant operations. Three areas of law provide obligations which in practice are challenging to apply correctly. The question is what this stressed relationship with human rights will bring to the international stage. Operation Sophia is a spearhead operation that will show whether or not some human rights obligations will erode under pressure, or that we as an international society will come to bear our full responsibility under the treaties and conventions we have drafted over the years.

In the near future, navies and maritime operators will have to deal with the complexity addressed above and face the legal challenges that come their way. Consistent education, both academically and practical, and open discussion will have to lead to

[73] Article 110 UNCLOS.

understanding of the areas of law normally not within the main focus but relevant to modern day maritime operations, focused on migrant flows.

References

Bingham T (2011) The rule of law. Penguin Books, London

Butler G, Ratcovich M (2016) Operation Sophia in unchartered waters: European and international law challenges for EU naval mission in the Mediterranean Sea. Nordic J of Int'l L 85:235–259

Boucher D (2005) The Rule of Law in the modern European state. Oakeshott and the enlargement of Europe. European J of Political Theory 4(1):89–107

Coppens J (2013) Interception of seaborne migrants: The applicability of the non-refoulement principle at sea. German Y.B. of Int'l L. 56:425–455

Fundamentals of maritime operations. Netherlands maritime military doctrine (3 March 2015). https://english.defensie.nl/downloads/publications/2015/03/03/netherlands-maritime-military-doctrine. Accessed November 2017

Fink MD (2016) Maritime interception and the law of naval operations. A study of legal bases and legal regimes in maritime interception operations, in particular conducted outside the sovereign waters of a State and in the context of international peace and security. Dissertation Amsterdam University (not published)

Gill TD, Fleck D (2015) Concept and sources of the international law of military operations. In: Gill TD, Fleck D (eds) The handbook of the international law of military operations. Oxford University Press, Oxford

Government Response UK (2017): Operation Sophia: a failed mission, 13 September 2017 https://www.parliament.uk/documents/lords-committees/eu-external-affairs-subcommittee/operation-sophia-failed-mission/Government-response-operation-sophia.pdf. Accessed November 2017

Guilfoyle D (2017) Maritime Law Enforcement Operations and Intelligence in an Age of Maritime Security Int'l L Stud 93:298–321

House of Lords (2016) Operation Sophia, the EU's naval mission in the Mediterranean: An impossible challenge. 13 May 2016, p. 5

House of Lords (2017) Operation Sophia: A failed mission. 12 July 2017

Lehti J (undated) The EU military operation against human smuggling and trafficking in the Southern Central Mediterranean. Operational Maritime Law 1 (forthcoming)

Vacas Fernández F (2016) The European Operations in the Mediterranean Sea to Deal with Migration as a Symptom: From the Italian Operation Mare Nostrum to Frontex Operations Triton and Poseidon, EUNAVFOR-MED and NATO's Assistance in the Aegean Sea. SYIL 20:93–118

van Bruggen H et al (2016) Militair-justitiële samenwerking bij de aanpak van migratiestromen. Nederlands Juristenblad 36:2682–2687

Voetelink JED (2013a) Militair Operationeel Recht. Wolf Legal Publishers, Oisterwijk

Voetelink JED (2013b) EvBO: Evidence-Based Operations How to Remove the Bad Guys from the Battlefield. J of Int'l L of Peace and Armed Conflict 4:194–201

Chapter 3
Helping Migrants While Protecting Against Migration: The Border Security Team in Crisis

J.P. Kalkman, M.T.I.B. Bollen and E. de Waard

Contents

Abstract In this chapter, we study the inter-organizational response to the European migration crisis by using a collective sensemaking perspective. Collective sensemaking refers to the process by which organizations construct a shared understanding of

J.P. Kalkman (✉) · M.T.I.B. Bollen · E. de Waard
Faculty of Military Sciences, Netherlands Defence Academy, Breda, The Netherlands
e-mail: j.p.kalkman@vu.nl

M.T.I.B. Bollen
e-mail: mtib.bollen.01@mindef.nl

E. de Waard
e-mail: ej.d.waard.01@mindef.nl

J.P. Kalkman
Department of Organization Sciences, VU University, Amsterdam, The Netherlands

J.P. Kalkman
TNO Defence, Safety and Security, Soesterberg, The Netherlands

H. Monsuur et al. (eds.), *NL ARMS Netherlands Annual Review of Military Studies 2018*, NL ARMS, https://doi.org/10.1007/978-94-6265-246-0_3

an ambiguous and confusing situation, which subsequently facilitates collaboration between them. On the basis of interviews, we distill different narratives on the migration crisis for the Dutch Border Security Team (BST) and its partner organizations (i.e. Frontex, Greek authorities, and humanitarian organizations). The BST, Frontex and the Greek authorities viewed the crisis primarily in terms of a security threat, which fostered easy collaboration between them in border protection tasks. BST members, however, also deplored the suffering of migrants and found some common ground with humanitarian actors, thus becoming involved in several humanitarian actions as well. As a result, BST members ended up helping migrants while at the same time protecting Europe against migration.

Keywords border security · collective sensemaking · Frontex · Chios · migration crisis · collaboration

3.1 Introduction

The 'European migration crisis' refers to the large-scale entrance of migrants from Middle Eastern and African countries into southern Europe.[1] At the height of the crisis, in 2015–2016, over one million people crossed the sea border between Turkey and Greece arriving at one of the Greek islands, such as Lesbos and Chios.[2] The image of the drowned migrant boy Alan Kurdi confronted the European public with the perilous nature of the journey during which more than 1250 died since 2015.[3] The migrants reaching the islands initially moved on to mainland Greece on their way to Northwestern Europe, but this route became increasingly difficult as time passed. The crisis was extensively covered by media and was also one of the most politically sensitive crises that the European Union has faced in its existence, shaking its very

---

[1] The crisis has also been labelled as the 'European refugees crisis' to better reflect the fact that most people entering Europe in this way were refugees and were not leaving their countries out of free will, as the term migrant may suggest (Ruz 2015). However, we will use the word 'migrant', emphasizing that we view it as a neutral description of people crossing international borders. We recognize that the term 'migrant' includes immigrants, asylum seekers, and refugees (see Huysmans 2000, p. 752). Refugees are protected by the 1951 Refugee Convention, which defines a refugee as people who flee from persecution or armed conflict out of well-founded fears and can therefore not be returned (UNHCR 2016). Immigrant are people who leave their country for other reasons (e.g. economic reasons) and can safely return to their home country (UNHCR 2016). Asylum seekers are those people that have applied for asylum as refugee, but have not yet been acknowledged as such based on the criteria of the 1951 Refugee Convention. Asylum seekers may be defined in different ways in different countries and, in general, the decision is made in the country where the application for asylum is made (UNESCO 2017). Lastly, since most migrants on the Eastern Mediterranean Route came from Syria, Afghanistan, and Iraq (Frontex 2017a), we recognize that most of the migrants arriving at Chios were refugees.

[2] Frontex 2017a.

[3] IOM 2017.

foundation.[4] In the midst of fierce criticism, the European Union concluded a controversial deal with Turkey (henceforth: EU-Turkey deal) to incentivize the Turks to take migrants back.[5] The EU also empowered Frontex 'to ensure European integrated border management at the external borders with a view to managing the crossing of the external borders efficiently'.[6] Specifically, Frontex implemented operation Poseidon Sea 'at the external sea borders of the Eastern Mediterranean region in order to control irregular migration flows towards the territory of the Member States of the EU and to tackle cross-border crime'.[7]

The Netherlands aimed to make a noteworthy contribution to EU external border protection and provided a fully equipped Border Security Team (BST). Since Frontex usually works with individual deployments of border guards, this Dutch initiative to deploy an entire team can be regarded as a novelty. The first BST was deployed to Chios in January 2016 and a BST presence remained there for two years, while a second BST was positioned at Lesbos for three months in 2016. The Border Security Teams consisted of multiple organizations hailing from both the Ministries of Defense, and Security & Justice. The Royal Netherlands Marechaussee (KMar) provided most of the members and was responsible for the daily management as well as the coordination of the operation. Other organizations, including the police, Navy, Army, Immigration and Naturalization Service (IND), and the Repatriation and Departure Service (DT&V), provided small contributions.

Although the task of border management seemed similar to the domestic KMar-task of Mobile Security Monitoring (MTV) in advance, BST members in Chios carried out additional tasks and activities. This included out-of-mandate security tasks, such as checking documents at domestic ferries, as well as humanitarian activities, such as restoring a local graveyard. These activities seem to stem from two competing frames on migration, in which migrants are either perceived as a threat (requiring security activities) or as victims (requiring humanitarian aid). In this chapter, we will analyze why and how BST members became involved in the seemingly irreconcilable activities of border protection and humanitarian aid.

We base our analysis on sensemaking literature which describes how people or teams try to make sense of a situation or an event that does not match their expectations, such as crises. It also outlines how individuals or organizations can collaborate when they have similar or overlapping understandings of what such an uncommon situation entails and requires. After introducing sensemaking theory, we move on to a reflection on our data collection and analysis. Next, we describe how the seemingly incompatible activities of BST members can be understood and how our empirical findings contribute to the crisis sensemaking literature. A conclusion finalizes the chapter.

---

4 The Guardian 2015.

5 Kingsley and Rankin 2016; HRW 2016.

6 European Parliament and Council 2016.

7 Frontex 2017b.

3.2 Theory

3.2.1 Sensemaking

BST members were deployed in an unfamiliar and volatile environment, which bore all the characteristics of a crisis situation:[8] there was a threat to human life as migrants crossed the sea on unstable boats, there were uncertainties about the exact nature and length of the crisis, and there was an urgent need to respond. In this crisis situation, BST members were deployed as a team, a structure unique to Frontex, while for most BST members it was the first time they were deployed under Frontex. Additionally, their responsibilities were often unknown in advance or unfamiliar in general. As the understanding of the crisis was limited, the causes of the crisis complex, and the allocation of roles unclear,[9] ambiguity was the defining element upon BST members' arrival.

In situations that are ambiguous, organizational members need to make sense of the world around them. Sensemaking refers to 'the process through which individuals work to understand novel, unexpected, or confusing events'.[10] To this end, observations or experiences need to be fit into a general background frame. This background frame, based upon earlier experiences, helps to interpret observations by attributing meaning to them.[11] When an understanding of a crisis has been constructed, this will subsequently inform the appropriate actions to be taken.[12] Resulting actions, in turn, influence the crisis situation itself and provide new observations for further sensemaking.[13] For instance, fire fighters may see a wildfire and by framing it as a relatively small fire, their observations can be compared with their experiences in previous small fires so they know what actions to take.[14] Colville and his colleagues give another example: police officers, operating under a counter-terrorism frame, shot an innocent man because they interpreted their observations as if the man was a terrorist and acted accordingly.[15] If they would have seen the man as merely a suspect or a minor criminal instead, they would have interpreted his behavior very differently and used different means to stop him. These examples show that background frames are very important for how people make sense of changing and uncertain realities.

Understandings of people within one organization are usually quite similar. This is needed because coordination and collaboration within the organization could otherwise be problematic. There are various ways in which organizations steer members towards a shared understanding of the world. For instance, sensemaking of organi-

[8] Boin et al. 2005.

[9] See Caroll 2015.

[10] Maitlis and Christianson 2014, p. 58.

[11] Cornelissen et al. 2014; Weick 1995; Maitlis and Sonenshein 2010.

[12] Weick et al. 2005; Van Hulst and Yanow 2016.

[13] Weick 1988, 1995.

[14] Weick 1993.

[15] Colville et al. 2013.

zational members is influenced by organizational cultures (through socialization), that guide members' identities and provide organization-based mental maps that help members to interpret and act in a similar fashion.[16] Additionally, organizational managers can exercise considerable influence over members' sensemaking by manipulating what members observe or propagating their own understanding of reality.[17] Through organizational culture and manager interference, dominant interpretations are likely to emerge and strongly guide sensemaking of organizational members in an organization.

Sensemaking within organizations is never entirely uncontested or finished though,[18] so that minor differences in sensemaking accounts may still be distilled in any organization.[19] More specifically, different 'interpretive communities' (e.g. teams, management layers) have their own mutual relations and interactions, which can provide for a shared frame that is slightly different from the frames held by organizational members in other interpretive communities (e.g. other teams, other management layers).[20] However, these differences cannot be too significant or the organization will dissolve.

In contrast, a shared outlook helps to bring about collective action among very diverse members in an organization.[21] Dunford and Jones, for instance, reconstruct managers' top-down imposed stories, which guided towards a common understanding within three organizations after economic deregulation in New Zealand.[22] Similarly, distinct sensemaking accounts can be reconstructed for different crisis response organizations based on their organizational cultures.[23] In consequence, an organization has various mechanisms to facilitate a shared understanding among its members, but these mechanisms can usually not be used in inter-organizational collaborations.

3.2.2 Collective Sensemaking

Whereas sensemaking within one organization may sometimes be complicated by contestation and competition due to the different interpretations of different organizational members,[24] collective sensemaking over organizational boundaries (and thus inter-organizational action) is generally much more challenging. Organizations

[16] Harris 1994; Ravasi and Schultz 2006; Pratt 2000.

[17] Gioia and Chittipeddi 1991; Humphreys et al. 2011.

[18] Hope 2010; Chreim 2006; Weick 1995.

[19] Dawson and Buchanan 2005.

[20] Balogun et al. 2015.

[21] Cornelissen et al. 2014.

[22] Dunford and Jones 2000.

[23] Bergeron and Cooren 2012; Mills and Weatherbee 2006.

[24] See Hope 2010; Chreim 2006.

may have different priorities, organizational cultures, and interests,[25] which are likely to lead to divergent frames and thus differentiated sensemaking.

When different actors act on the basis of different frames, they will face coordination challenges. Such coordination challenges are reported in various crisis settings. Although disputed by some,[26] most (crisis) researchers suggest that these coordination challenges are due to the absence of a collective understanding, so that actors are likely to work in parallel at best.[27] Instead, when an understanding of a crisis is collectively construed among members of different crisis organizations (i.e. collective sensemaking), they can coordinate and implement a coherent response as they interpret observations likewise and have a similar view on which actions are necessary. More specifically, collective sensemaking may improve information exchange, since different organizational members think the same observations relevant, as well as decision-making, since the shared understanding informs the appropriate actions.[28] Thus, collective sensemaking facilitates coordination of crisis response actions through providing a sufficiently congruent crisis frame.

3.2.3 Sensemaking in the Migration Crisis

With regard to the European migration crisis, two competing frames can be distinguished: one depicting it as a security threat and the other as a humanitarian disaster. Both frames are often presented as dominant frames in migration-oriented debates and appear to be mutually exclusive.[29] This means that individuals or organizations employing either one of the frames will make different sense of observations or events than actors holding on to the other frame.

The security frame on migration resonates well within political and decision-making circles. For example, the European Union and European countries are widely perceived to actively try to securitize (Islamic) migrants (i.e. portray them as security threats).[30] This is achieved by linking migrants to criminality, terrorism, national identity threats, and welfare abuse to discursively construct an image of migrants as dangerous strangers and to foster a feeling of unease.[31] Additionally, security actors continuously treat migrants as if they are a security threat through the encampment of migrants in an isolated spot under prison-like conditions, (military) police interrogations, and screenings of migrants. Such security practices legitimate the fearful and

[25] Rosenthal et al. 1991.

[26] Donnellon et al. 1986; Kendra and Wachtendorf 2006.

[27] Balogun and Johnson 2004; Colville et al. 2013; Engwall and Westling 2004; Weick 2005.

[28] Maitlis and Sonenshein 2010; Mills and Weatherbee 2006; Weick 1993; Wolbers and Boersma 2013.

[29] See Van Gorp 2005; Figenschou and Thorbjørnsrud 2015.

[30] Bigo 2002, 2014; Huysmans 2000; Lazaridis and Skleparis 2015; Léonard 2010; Roggeband and Vliegenthart 2007.

[31] Bigo 2002; Huysmans 2000.

negative view on migration. In this regard, Frontex promotes a security perspective by carrying out its 'border protection' duties (i.e. 'securitizing practices'), which imply security threats and display elements of sovereignty and exceptionalism.[32]

The alternative to this security frame is a humanitarian frame. The humanitarian frame is embodied in international legislation for the protection of refugees (e.g. 1951 Refugee Convention) and in the work of the Office of the United Nations High Commissioner for Refugees (UNHCR) as well as in the work of non-governmental organizations (e.g. Doctors Without Borders, Save the Children). Advocates of the humanitarian frame emphasize the human face of migration by highlighting the life stories of specific migrants, portraying them as victims and telling about their struggles, concluding that we need to offer protect them to preserve human dignity.[33] By highlighting the lived realities (i.e. human interest),[34] authors challenge the Kafkaesque, dehumanizing European Union structures while pleading for more attention for vulnerable groups.[35] Freedman, for instance, argues that the European Union 'must now react to ensure that those seeking protection are able to access this and […] see how they can offer regular and safe routes to Europe for those who can no longer remain in their home countries'.[36]

Organizations responding to the European migration crisis in Chios generally operated under either one of these two frames although they had their own versions of it (i.e. their own organization-based narratives). The frame under which they operated influenced considerably how they viewed and treated arriving migrants: as potential security threat to be registered and monitored, or as refugees in need of support. After briefly elaborating on our data collection and analysis, we will summarize the narratives of the core migration-oriented organizations in Chios and subsequently describe the collective sensemaking process between the BST and its partners.

3.3 Methods

3.3.1 Case Description

We study the response to the European migration crisis on the Greek Island of Chios. Since the 'onset' of the crisis in 2015, Chios has been one of the Greek islands receiving the most migrants. The Dutch BST was therefore deployed to Chios and faced the arrival of tens of thousands of migrants until the EU-Turkey deal was closed, after which arrival numbers plummeted to several hundred per month on average

---

[32] Bigo 2014; Léonard 2010.

[33] Figenschou and Thorbjørnsrud 2015; Nickels 2007; Steimel 2010.

[34] See d'Haenens and De Lange 2001.

[35] Gerard and Pickering 2014.

[36] Freedman 2016, p. 580.

(Frontex meeting, Chios). While the situation became relatively quiet after the deal, the fact that migrants had to stay on the island led to tensions within the reception center and with the Greek population. The camps were overcrowded, hygiene and security were poor, and many migrants left the island 'illegally'.

The core responding actors during this crisis were the BST, the Greek authorities, Frontex, and humanitarian organizations. The Greek authorities that were primarily important in the crisis response are the Hellenic Coast Guard, Hellenic Police, the municipality, and the Reception and Identification Services (i.e. camp management). The BST, as deployed by the Dutch government, was formally part of Frontex, but appeared to be a separate entity in practice. In fact, the BST had a strong independent position, its own hierarchy, and partly different aims than Frontex, so we treat the BST and Frontex as distinct in this chapter and will differentiate between their narratives. Lastly, humanitarian organizations include (inter)national Non-Governmental Organizations (NGOs), UNHCR, and volunteers. As a diverse group, their narratives did not entirely overlap, but a broadly shared humanitarian account can be deduced.

By studying these narratives and the collective sensemaking consequences in the collaborate response to the crisis on Chios, we wish to explain the logic behind the different and unrelated tasks that BST members carried out. At the same time, the Chios response may function as a representative case for the relevance of narratives and collective sensemaking in other crisis situations.[37] Such case studies are very common in the literature on crisis sensemaking.[38]

3.3.2 Data Collection

The empirical part of this research was primarily based on interviews. In total, 49 people have been interviewed by means of 45 individual interviews and two double interviews. All but three of the interviews could be recorded. A deliberate selection of interviewees ensured that a variety of partner organizations were interviewed as well as BST members of different rotations.[39] This was necessary to ensure a good understanding of changes in the situation and the BST narrative. In addition, this selection guaranteed the participation of BST members of different backgrounds and showed that a dominant team narrative could indeed be distilled.[40]

The accounts of the four main players (i.e. BST, Greek authorities, Frontex, and humanitarian organizations) were constructed primarily based on their self-perceptions and complemented with others' perceptions of them. Thus, in our semi-structured interviews, we asked respondents to both describe the crisis situation and how they viewed migrants in their own words, while also asking them to reflect on their main partners.

---

[37] See Yin 2012.

[38] See Weick 1988, 1993; Cornelissen et al. 2014; Colville et al. 2013.

[39] A rotation lasted about three months.

[40] Balogun et al. 2015; Currie and Brown 2003.

3.3.3 *Data Analysis*

After data collection, all recorded interviews were transcribed. Extensive notes of the three unrecorded interviews were added to the data pool. This data was subsequently closely read to find the core elements of the various narratives. Choice of words (e.g. migrant or refugee), stories, and metaphors were insightful linguistic indicators in the analysis of interview.[41] Following the example of Dunford and Jones, we reconstruct the narratives for different actors, as can be read in the next section.[42]

3.4 Findings

In the first part of this section, we will reconstruct the dominant narratives for four of the key actors in our study: the Border Security Team, Greek authorities, Frontex, and humanitarian agencies. These narratives are based on interviews with members of these organizations, and refer to their examples and words as much as possible. In the second part of the findings, next, we present how members of different organizations made collective sense of the crisis and took collaborative actions, regardless of their divergent narratives. Specifically, we show how the BST found common ground and collaborated with security actors (i.e. Greek authorities, and Frontex) as well as with humanitarian agencies.

3.4.1 *Narratives*

3.4.1.1 Border Security Team

BST members initially primarily interpreted the crisis as a security crisis. Solid border management at the external European border was needed to reduce the number of arrivals and to mitigate multiple risks of migration. Firstly, migrants are viewed as potential terrorists. In particular, former fighters of the Islamic State of Iraq and the Levant are suspected to enter Europe via this route. One respondent mentioned that the core aim of the BST is therefore to prevent terrorist attacks by migrants that passed through Chios. Although another remarked that '*not all migrants are potential terrorists*' (Interview decision-maker), a third estimated that hundreds of terrorists entered Europe as migrants nevertheless.

Secondly, criminality and migration are often linked. Primarily young North-African men are perceived as dangerous and linked to violence, sex offences, and theft. Additionally, human smuggling is a central point of attention for border guards: border surveillance officers sought for potential smugglers in boats and debriefers

[41] See Sandberg and Tsoukas 2015; Humphreys et al. 2011.

[42] Dunford and Jones 2000.

aimed to identify smuggling routes and facilitators of human smuggling. To a large extent, the act of migration itself is criminalized: border crossings are always illegal and security checks are justified to make sure migrants do not bring weapons. Also, '*every arriving boat was guided from smuggling areas*' (Interview border surveillance officer).

Even when migrants are not seen as terrorists or criminals, they are sometimes viewed as unworthy of being welcomed in the EU. For instance, migrants are accused of reprehensible, self-centered behavior, such as getting out of the water without caring about drowning children, having no respect for women, and taking the aid of those in real need. For example, when towels and dry clothes are distributed, '*the men with wet feet are in front, while soaked women and children are standing behind*' (Interview commander). Other migrants are seen as too poorly educated, arrogant, or simply trying to take advantage of Western hospitality by taking money and a house while natives are struggling financially. The social consequences of the migrant flows are therefore deplored since '*our children will suffer from it in the future*' (Interview fingerprinter). The EU-Turkey deal is generally applauded for stopping migration flows and stronger security measures are advocated.

Counterbalancing this security perspective on migrants, BST members displayed empathy and kindness as well. One dominant reaction to the security framing was the question: what would you do? For instance, when one understands the migrants' motivations to flee, '*I can understand the refugee who comes this way*' (Interview intelligence coordinator). Similarly, migrants were accused of stealing fruits from a local farmer's land, but a BST member said that this could be understood when looking at the poor food rations. BST members thus often concluded that '*you are not against refugees as a border guard*' (Interview deputy commander).

Furthermore, human suffering undermined the security mindset. Part of this suffering took place before migrants' arrival, such as torture and exploitation, which transforms migrants into victims, feeding into the belief that '*if people really suffer somewhere else, they can come [to Europe]*' (Interview screener). But the suffering continued upon arrival, as migrants had to wait for hours outside in the winter, bus drivers charged high prices for mandatory transport to the reception center, and Greek police derided migrants or quickly resorted to violence. The reception center itself, Vial, contributes to enduring human suffering as well. The camp is overcrowded and there is bad, overused sanitation that spreads an enormous stench. Additionally, the camp is full of wasps and very warm in the summer, while being extremely cold in the summer. Overall, this creates '*horrible*' living conditions.

In response, BST staff wanted to relieve this suffering. They achieved this partly by what they called '*being humane*'. This included kindness and friendliness towards migrants as well as helping them ashore and being good hosts: '*when it was very cold, we also put people with children in the [border patrol] car when waiting for transportation with the heater on and high to protect them against hypothermia*' (Interview deputy commander). In these cases, '*being human*' and '*being humanitarian*' were spoken of as indistinguishable traits (Interview border surveillance officer).

3.4.1.2 Greek Authorities

Representatives of Greek authorities voice many concerns in accordance with the security perspectives of BST members but are somewhat more outspoken. Although they do not worry about terrorism in Greece since Western Europe is seen as a more likely target, criminality is widely perceived as a problematic consequence of migration. Firstly, migrants are believed to align with NGOs in the criminal act of human smuggling. NGOs are suspected because they are often the first to arrive at the place where migrant boats strand and thus they are suspected of having '*illegal information in some other way*' (Interview Hellenic Coast Guard). Secondly, migrants are linked to unrest and social problems, including noise nuisance, drugs use, and human trafficking. Additionally, '*they are thinking [about] how to get fake documents, how to cause trouble*' (Interview civil servant). Adding to these problems are the socio-economic challenges that the migrants are believed to cause. Since Greece is still in an economic crisis, migrants are seen as a cumbersome strain on the overburdened social services. This means that migrants are unlikely to integrate well while it appears inevitable '*to have ghetto's again in the city*' (Interview civil servant). At the same time, the social services and external assistance that migrants receive is criticized as (relatively) disadvantageous towards the local population. Moreover, the migrants are often considered lazy, because they are provided with money and food without having to work for it. One representative summarized her perspective by saying that migrants still '*have to learn how to behave*' (Interview civil servant).

As the '*biggest worry is that people will stay in Greece*' (Interview civil servant), the central Greek government and the European Union are viewed as players that need to take action. Since sea border patrol is no longer a rescue mission but is believed to have transformed into an escort mission instead, prevention of arrival is seen as a new solution. Another option mentioned is closing the facilities and speed up the process of sending migrants to the mainland or to the rest of Europe in order to reduce the stress on the island. In the meantime, the Greek authorities have to process large numbers of arrivals and even though they do feel pity sometimes, they try not to give in to it, as they are afraid migrants will take advantage of their sentiments.

3.4.1.3 Frontex

Frontex, as an EU agency, is bound by its political mandate and follows its operational plan to support the Greek authorities. Often falling back on formal guidelines, Frontex staff clarifies that this mandate means that their support takes place in two areas. Firstly, Frontex supports in surveillance activities to '*detect and intercept migrant boats*', and to detect migrants who came ashore in order to bring them to the camp (Interview Frontex staff member). Secondly, Frontex assists in the registration and identification processes in the camp.

The EU-Turkey deal is broadly viewed as an important and successful agreement by Frontex staff, as migrant numbers dropped dramatically and it operationally ended the crisis phase. Thus, '*the problems are not the new arrivals*' since '*the situation is controlled*' (Interview Frontex staff member). Nevertheless, a new problem has emerged due to the fact that people now remain on the island. The camp has grown overcrowded with migrants waiting for decisions on their asylum applications. This situation led to rising tension, which then led to fights. Additionally, migrants are free to move on the island '*and no one really controls them*' (Interview Frontex staff member). Oftentimes, migrants therefore illegally leave the island or hide. This problem is more problematic since there is concern that there are foreign terrorist fighters among the arriving migrants.

Out-of-mandate activities, whether security-related or humanitarian, are not allowed by Frontex. For instance, there is no intention or willingness to expand the operational activities to building tents in response to the problem of overcrowding: '*we don't deploy people doing this kind of tasks, we only do management of the border*' (Interview Frontex staff member). Moreover, although Frontex staff were aggravated by the fact that medical care was provided by an NGO and not by the Greek Ministry of Health, Frontex will not deploy doctors itself. In summary, Frontex staff holds on to the formal security frame restricting its activities to actions that fit in the political mandate of the (security) agency.

3.4.1.4 Humanitarian Agencies

Humanitarian organizations in this crisis aim '*to care for the needy, care for the poor, care for the hungry*' (Interview NGO). External humanitarians (e.g. large NGOs, UNHCR) came to help '*whoever needs help*' (Interview NGO), while local volunteers had more personally based motivations: '*When the children came in my home, they were crying so much and they were desperate and wet [...] I gave them clothes, they changed. Straightaway they became children [...] and I thought: okay, I can do something; small, but I can do something*' (Interview volunteer). Consequently, these actors view the crisis primarily as a humanitarian crisis and persons arriving as refugees. Looking at the countries of origin as registered by Frontex (mostly Syria, Iraq, and Afghanistan), they emphasize that these places are war-torn and mention that many refugees have lost their families and homes. They challenge the framing of arrivers as migrants, stating that many are refugees, even '*before they are recognized as refugees*', because they are '*fleeing from war*', meaning that on the islands '*we have asylum-seekers and refugees*' (Interview UN).

This means that, even though their border-crossings may be illegal, '*they are people in need*' which should set the priorities of activities straight (Interview volunteer). Even though other parties may prefer to start registration and identification quickly after an arrival to not be overloaded if new boats arrive, sometimes psychosocial support is viewed as more important. One humanitarian criticized the manner in which Frontex prioritized explaining the asylum procedure over informing the family of a deceased, saying: '*you cannot process people as if they are not people*' (Interview UN).

One of the core goals humanitarians aim for in terms of border management is what they call '*protection-sensitive border management*' (Interview UN). This means that the rights, interests, and dignity of people crossing the border are protected at all times. Additionally, victims of human trafficking and torture need to be identified and send through to relevant humanitarian agencies who can help them. Unfortunately, this protection is not yet fully incorporated in border protection practices. For instance, families have been separated during rescue operations with some family members ending up in Turkey and others in Greece. Additionally, families that are to be returned to Turkey have been detained for long periods of times in a Greek jail because carrying out the relocation was problematic.

Humanitarians lament the EU-Turkey deal as '*the worst agreement ever*' for two reasons. Firstly, '*It was the worst thing for the people, for the refugees, because I think Turkey is not a safe country for them*' (Interview volunteer). Secondly, people could no longer move on to the mainland and were stuck in Chios. Those who had their asylum requests rejected had no idea what the future would bring and were left in uncertainty. The strict border management policy was therefore heavily criticized. Some were outright opposed to the existence of borders in the first place and mentioned specifically that '*there is no need for people with guns at the borders*' (Interview volunteer). Others put the scale of the crisis in perspective to blame Europe's overly restrictive policy by pointing out that the 60,000 people, currently seeking refuge in Greece did not even match up to the total number of people in some single African refugee camps (Interview UN).

This understanding also provided the basis for criticizing camp management. Living conditions in this camp have not been improved in the two years since the beginning of the crisis and the camp is not prepared for hosting migrants when there is a sudden increase, which often happens. Families, thus, often need to sleep outside or on the floor. Furthermore, the camp '*looks like a prison*' with its barbed wire and military presence (Interview NGO). Next, because it is far removed from cities and towns, it leaves people '*marginalized*' and '*institutionalized*' (Interview NGO). In short, while functioning poorly as a transit camp, it does not function at all as a permanent camp in which it has been transformed since the EU-Turkey deal. Consequently, the local population seems to lose its compassion as well, thereby increasing the gloomy feelings of humanitarians.

3.4.2 Collective Sensemaking and Collaborate Actions

The fact that BST members could find common ground and collaborate with organizational partners as diverse as the Greek authorities and humanitarian actors is remarkable. However, BST members reported flexibility of mind and could empathize with different viewpoints: '*I could from the perspective of the refugee understand very well why it was necessary that they went [to Chios]. And on the other hand, I could see it as well from a security view and a border protection view*' (Interview deputy commander). This double-edged interpretation of reality was perceived to be elementary in the job as '*sometimes you would have to switch your perspective four times a day*' (Interview debriefer). This moving between different interpretations was also necessary to make collective sense with partners operating under very different crisis frames.

Firstly, the BST operated under the flag of Frontex in support of the Greek authorities to manage the crisis at the Greek border. These three actors were therefore primarily concerned with the security implications of migration flows and were tasked to collaborate in the same border surveillance, registration, and identification processes. This means that a strong basis for collective sensemaking was present from the moment of deployment. Their overlapping formal mandates, focusing on the provision of border security, did indeed enable quick and easy collective sensemaking. For instance, the actors found each other in the perceived link between migrant arrivals and criminality. Specifically, every border crossing was seen as illegal, rendering the migrants involved in the criminal activity of smuggling. Migrants were further suspected to violate the rules since it was commonplace that they hid themselves when their asylum requests were rejected or secretly traveled on to mainland Europe. This shared understanding fostered common support for training of the Greek police on how to deal with criminality, the decision to keep an eye on NGOs suspected of participating in human smuggling, and the purchase of stamps to emboss legal documents which migrants need in order to take the ferry to the mainland. Such actions brought about a vicious circle since migrants were likely to find ways around the new rules (e.g. falsifying embossed paper), thereby further criminalizing them and evoking new security activities.

Additionally, the Greek authorities and the BST shared a common view on the correlation between large-scale migration and social deprivation or social unrest. Both actors voiced their concern about the overburdening of social services and the societal problems that migrants pose when they '*flood*' Western societies. This shared view facilitated BST support at document checks at domestic ferries, the quest for smuggling routes on the island of Chios, and extensive trainings to Greek officials on how to recognize false documents. Many such activities are actually outside of the formal BST mandate but were carried out nevertheless as both the Greek authorities and the BST were convinced that it was important.

Secondly, BST members and humanitarians held a common empathetic interpretation of the hardships that individual migrants were facing after being confronted with their stories and living conditions. Mutual esteem varied but BST members took pains to be kind and humane, and valued the contribution that humanitarians provided to alleviate suffering. The common belief in the importance of humanitarian support facilitated information exchange and coordination of activities, including alarming each other when boats arrived and giving room for the distribution of food, water, and clothes before registration and identification began. On top of that, some BST members contributed to these humanitarian endeavors, for instance by helping a disabled child to the bathroom, distributing educational equipment, and restoring a graveyard. In response to criticism of humanitarian partners, they also showed willingness to pursue protection concerns such as supporting victims of trafficking and reconnecting separated family members. Some BST members leaned more strongly towards the humanitarian frame and managed to construct more of a shared view with humanitarians than other team members. In fact, BST members that were participating in Search and Rescue operations and providing help to new arrivals were more concerned with humanitarian ideals than those who were tasked with unveiling the nationality of migrants, taking their fingerprints, and validating the authenticity of their documents. Nevertheless, all members felt (some) empathy for migrants.

In the end, the BST's seemingly contradictory activities are logical outcomes of collective sensemaking processes with both security and humanitarian partners. Collective sensemaking with Frontex and Greek authorities expanded security-based activities intended to protect the EU against the perceived negative outfall of migration, while collective sensemaking with humanitarians facilitated empathy and the provision of support to suffering migrants.

3.5 Discussion

3.5.1 Theoretical Contributions

In the introduction, we mentioned that we aimed to show how and why BST members became involved in seemingly irreconcilable activities during their deployment. On the basis of our findings, we will now answer this question and reflect on the theoretical implications of our findings. Firstly, we found that, even though crisis frames may have a strong influence on (organizational) narratives, frames are not deterministic. Thus, multiple narratives can be derived in a crisis as well.[43] In our case, specifically, the BST, Frontex and the Greek authorities built on the frame of migration as a security issue but emphasized different themes and contexts.[44] The common frame, nevertheless, facilitated relatively easy collective sensemaking among these actors,[45] while finding common ground with humanitarian actors was more complicated. Consequently, the Greek authorities and Frontex, on the one hand, and humanitarian organizations, on the other hand, worked in parallel rather than together.[46]

The BST, however, did also manage to engage in collective sensemaking with humanitarians, since both actors lamented the poverty and despair of migrants. Thus, BST members became involved in humanitarian activities and grew concerned with protection responsibilities. BST members with Search and Rescue-tasks, in particular, managed to find common ground with humanitarians, and their collaboration

43 Dunford and Jones 2000.

44 Cf. Bergeron and Cooren 2012; Mills and Weatherbee 2006.

45 See Cornelissen et al. 2014.

46 See Balogun and Johnson 2004; Colville et al. 2013; Engwall and Westling 2004; Weick 2005.

was therefore quite extensive.[47] This reality proves that the two dominant frames (i.e. security and humanitarian) in this crisis[48] are not as mutually exclusive as often suggested. More importantly, it shows that the initial framing of this crisis as a security crisis and the development of a humanitarian counter-framing enabled BST staff to help the migrants and protect the EU against migration at the same time, even though the resulting activities appear incompatible. The apparent conflict is strongest among BST members tasked with Search and Rescue. Even though all BST members supported a dominant narrative,[49] the nature and context of the 'rescuers' left them more sensitive to humanitarian concerns. Thus, we suggest that implementation context is an important variable when studying how organizational members make sense of a crisis.

With regard to the European migration crisis specifically, this study also contributes to the literature on migration as a security threat. Specifically, it shows that the discursive framing of migration as a security issue may be widespread and broadly supported but that security practices should not be neglected in studying the association between migration and security.[50] For instance, we found that BST members contributed to the securitization of migrants by implementing out-of-mandate security tasks (e.g. introducing embosomed stamps), which evoked deviant responses of migrants (e.g. falsifications) and, when caught, contributed to their framing as criminal. Thus, border protection practices may be essential in the securitization of migrants.

3.5.2 Practical Implications

In practice, this study shows how BST members were deployed under Frontex and were tasked with the implementation of border protection responsibilities under a security frame, even though they may not have felt strongly inclined to fully commit to and enact this security frame. Many BST members commented that they were unfamiliar with Frontex before their deployment and that they primarily subscribed to the mission to offer support to those in need. The resulting tension between the securitizing mandate[51] and BST members' interpretations of reality warrants attention. In particular, several members faced strong negative emotions or described the mission as psychologically very challenging.

Additionally, when we view the Marechaussee, providing the core of the BST, as a military organization, this study shows the potential of civil-military co-action which is usually a very challenging endeavor due to cultural, organizational, opera-

---

[47] Cf. Maitlis and Sonenshein 2010; Mills and Weatherbee 2006; Weick 1993; Wolbers and Boersma 2013.

[48] Figenschou and Thorbjørnsrud 2015.

[49] Maitlis and Sonenshein 2010.

[50] Bigo 2002, 2014; Huysmans 2000; Lazaridis and Skleparis 2015; Léonard 2010.

[51] See Bigo 2014; Huysmans 2000; Léonard 2010.

tional, and normative differences.[52] In line with earlier findings on the important role that frontline members can play in bridging civil-military differences,[53] this study confirms that frontline staff are more flexible in their sensemaking and therefore have more room for collective sensemaking with unexpected partners.

3.5.3 Future Research

On the basis of our findings, we propose three areas for further research. Firstly, we show that crisis frames are not fixed but can be adapted. The security framing of the migration crisis, as adopted and employed on the strategic level of Frontex and the Dutch deploying organizations, was viewed as problematic by frontline organizational members.[54] Their observations of human suffering spoke to their emotions and destabilized their support for the enactment of a strict security frame. For instance, we described how they engaged in collective sensemaking with humanitarians. In future research, it would therefore be interesting to study the intra-organizational negotiations on the frame under which they operate.

Secondly, we encourage more research on the securitization of migration through practices. Given the fact that migration is not only discursively labeled as a threat but also practically approached as a potential threat, border protection activities may strengthen the cognitive associations between security risks and migrants (e.g. BST training of the Greek police on how to deal with criminality). While some studies already studied border protection practices in general,[55] it is particularly relevant and interesting to study real-life micro-practices of (Frontex) border officials on the ground as well as the implications of these practices.

Lastly, a noteworthy result of our study is the strong correlation between context and sensemaking, as exemplified by how BST members advocating the same narrative diverged due to their implementation of different tasks. Even though it is not a new idea that activities shape the environment and thereby the sensemaking of individuals,[56] there is little attention for the relation between diversified sensemaking and task specialization in one team.

3.6 Conclusion

The inter-organizational response to the European migration crisis was a tense and politically sensitive episode. As external border protection became a central element

[52] See Franke 2006; Salmon et al. 2011; Bollen and Rietjens 2008.

[53] Kalkman 2016; Kalkman and De Waard 2017.

[54] See Chreim 2006; Hope 2010.

[55] Bigo 2014; Léonard 2010.

[56] Weick 1988.

of the EU's response to the crisis, members of various Dutch organizations were deployed in a Border Security Team (BST) to the Greek islands of Chios in order to carry out border protection tasks under Frontex. Interestingly, these border officials became involved in the seemingly irreconcilable activities of helping the migrants while protecting Europe against migrant flows. In this chapter, we aimed to find out how this can be explained.

Using a sensemaking perspective, we describe how actors in this crisis response tried to grasp a situation that was uncommon and ambiguous to them. Collective sensemaking, then, focused on the inter-organizational process of building a common understanding of unfamiliar events. BST members initially made sense of this crisis as primarily a security crisis (i.e. security frame), rendering migration a threat to be contained. This facilitated easy interactions with the Greek authorities and Frontex which held a similar frame of the crisis. Even though the frame was shared, narratives of the situation differed among these security-focused organizations, for instance due to differences in contextual focus and mandate. Nevertheless, differences of view were relatively easily overcome as common ground could be constructed without much problems. Thus, the collaboration between Frontex, the Greek authorities and the BST was broad and pervasive. We also found that deployed BST members could not fit all their observations in the security frame as they lamented the human suffering of poor and desperate migrants, particularly those BST members tasked with Search and Rescue-tasks. BST members' humanitarian concerns opened up space for collective sensemaking with NGOs, UNHCR, and local volunteers. This fostered BST support for humane border management as well as humanitarian activities. Because of this, BST members ended up helping migrants while protecting Europe against migration.

Acknowledgements We are heavily indebted to the Royal Netherlands Marechaussee for their support throughout the data collection process. Specifically, we express our gratitude to DOPS KMar, the commander and personnel of the seventh BST-rotation at Chios, and BST members of previous rotations. Additionally, we thank the editors and an anonymous reviewer for their helpful comments.

References

Balogun J, Bartunek JM, Do B (2015) Senior Managers' Sensemaking and Responses to Strategic Change. Organization Science 26:960–979

Balogun J, Johnson G (2004) Organizational Restructuring and Middle Manager Sensemaking. Academy of Management Journal 47:523–549

Bergeron CD, Cooren F (2012) The Collective Framing of Crisis Management: A Ventriloqual Analysis of Emergency Operations Centres. Journal of Contingencies and Crisis Management 20:120–137

Bigo D (2002) Security and Immigration: Toward a Critique of the Governmentality of Unease. Alternatives 27:63–92

Bigo D (2014) The (In)Securitization Practices of the Three Universes of EU Border Control: Military/Navy—Border Guards/Police—Database Analysts. Security Dialogue 45:209–225

Boin A, 't Hart P, Stern E, Sundelius B (2005) The Politics of Crisis Management. Cambridge University Press, Cambridge

Bollen M, Rietjens B (2008) Managing civil-military cooperation. Ashgate, Hampshire

Caroll JS (2015) Making Sense of Ambiguity through Dialogue and Collaborative Action. Journal of Contingencies and Crisis Management 23:59–65

Chreim S (2006) Managerial Frames and Institutional Discourses of Change: Employee Appropriation and Resistance, Organization Studies 27:1261–1287

Colville I, Pye A, Carter M (2013) Organizing to Counter Terrorism: Sensemaking amidst dynamic complexity. Human Relations 66:1201–1223

Cornelissen JP, Mantere S, Vaara E (2014) The Contraction of Meaning: The Combined Effect of Communication Emotions and Materiality on Sensemaking in the Stockwell Shooting. Journal of Management Studies 51:699–736

Currie G, Brown AD (2003) A narratological approach to understanding processes of organizing in a UK hospital. Human Relations 56:563–586

Dawson P, Buchanan D (2005) The way it really happened: Competing narratives in the political process of technological change. Human Relations 58: 845–865

Donnellon A, Gray B, Bougon MG (1986) Communication Meaning and Organized Action. Administrative Science Quarterly, 31:43–55

d'Haenens L, De Lange M (2001) Framing of asylum seekers in Dutch regional newspapers. Media, Culture & Society 23:847–860

Dunford R, Jones D (2000) Narrative in strategic change. Human Relations 53:1207–1226

Engwall M, Westling G (2004) Peripety in an R&D Drama: Capturing a Turnaround in Project Dynamics. Organization Studies 25:1557–1578

European Parliament and Council (2016) Regulation (EU) 2016/1624 of the European Parliament and of the Council of 14 September 2016. Official Journal of the European Union L 251/1

Figenschou TU, Thorbjørnsrud K (2015) Faces of an Invisible Population: Human Interest Framing of Irregular Immigration News in the United States, France, and Norway. American Behavioral Scientist 59:783–801

Franke V (2006) The peacebuilding dilemma: Civil-military cooperation in stability operations. International Journal of Peace Studies 11:5–25

Freedman J (2016) Engendering Security at the Borders of Europe: Women Migrants and the Mediterranean 'Crisis'. Journal of Refugee Studies 29:568–582

Frontex (2017a) Risk Analysis for 2017. Frontex, Warsaw

Frontex (2017b) Poseidon Sea. http://frontex.europa.eu/operations/archive-of-operations/Lq8P8c Accessed 8 February 2018

Gerard A, Pickering S (2014) Gender Securitization and Transit: Refugee Women and the Journey to the EU. Journal of Refugee Studies 27:228–259

Gioia DA, Chittipeddi K (1991) Sensemaking and Sensegiving in Strategic Change Initiation. Strategic Management Journal 12:433–448

Harris SG (1994) Organizational Culture and Individual Sensemaking: A Schema-Based Perspective. Organization Science 5:309–321

Hope O (2010) The Politics of Middle Management Sensemaking and Sensegiving. Journal of Change Management 10:195–215

HRW (2016) Q&A: Why the EU-Turkey Migration Deal is No Blueprint. https://www.hrw.org/news/2016/11/14/qa-why-eu-turkey-migration-deal-no-blueprint Accessed 8 February 2018

Humphreys M, Ucbasaran D, Locket A (2011) Sensemaking and sensegiving stories of jazz leadership. Human Relations 65:41–62

Huysmans J (2000) The European Union and the Securitization of Migration. Journal of Common Market Studies 38:751–777

IOM (2017) Missing Migrants: Tracking deaths along migratory routes. https://missingmigrants.iom.int/ Accessed 8 February 2018

Kalkman JP (2016) Explaining the Role of the Armed Forces in the Dutch Safety Regions. In: Beeres R et al (eds) NL ARMS: Netherlands Annual Review of Military Studies 2016: Organizing for Safety and Security in Military Organizations. T.M.C Asser Press, The Hague, pp 185–202
Kalkman JP, De Waard EJ (2017) Inter-Organizational Disaster Management Projects: Finding the Middle Way between Trust and Control. International Journal of Project Management 35:889–899
Kendra J, Wachtendorf T (2006) The waterborne evacuation of Lower Manhattan on September 11: A case of distributed sensemaking. Preliminary Paper #355, University of Delaware Disaster Research Center
Kingsley P, Rankin J (2016) EU-Turkey refugee deal – Q&A. https://www.theguardian.com/world/2016/mar/08/eu-turkey-refugee-deal-qa Accessed 8 February 2018
Lazaridis G, Skleparis D (2015) Securitization of migration and the far right: the case of Greek security professionals. International Migration 54:176–192
Léonard S (2010) FRONTEX and the Securitization of Migrants through Practices. European Security 19:231–254
Maitlis S, Christianson M (2014) Sensemaking in Organizations: Taking Stock and Moving Forward. The Academy of Management Annals 8:57–125
Maitlis S, Sonenshein S (2010) Sensemaking in Crisis and Change: Inspiration and Insights From Weick (1988). Journal of Management Studies 47:551–580
Mills JH, Weatherbee TG (2006) Hurricanes Hardly Happen: Sensemaking as a Framework for Understanding Organizational Disasters. Culture and Organization 12:265–279
Nickels HC (2007) Framing Asylum Discourse in Luxembourg. Journal of Refugee Studies 20:37–59
Pratt MG (2000) The Good the Bad and the Ambivalent: Managing Identification among Amway Distributors. Administrative Science Quarterly 45:456–493
Ravasi D, Schultz M (2006) Responding to organizational identity threats: exploring the role of organizational culture. Academy of Management Journal 49:433–456
Roggeband C, Vliegenthart R (2007) Divergent Framing: The Evolution of the Public Debate on Migration and Integration in the Dutch Parliament and Media 1995–2004. West European Politics 30:524-548
Rosenthal U, 't Hart P, Kouzmin A (1991) The Bureau-Politics of Crisis Management. Public Administration 69:211–233
Ruz C (2015) The battle over the words used to describe migrants. http://www.bbc.com/news/magazine-34061097 Accessed 8 February 2018
Salmon P, Stanton N, Jenkins D, Walker G (2011) Coordination during multi-agency emergency response: issues and solutions. Disaster Prevention and Management 20:140–158
Sandberg J, Tsoukas H (2015) Making sense of the sensemaking perspective: Its constituents, limitations, and opportunities for further development. Journal of Organizational Behavior 36:6–32
Steimel SJ (2010) Refugees as People: The Portrayal of Refugees in American Human Interest Stories. Journal of Refugee Studies 23:219–237
The Guardian (2015) We will hurt EU if migrant crisis is not fixed, says Italian PM Matteo Renzi. https://www.theguardian.com/world/2015/jun/15/we-will-hurt-eu-if-migrant-crisis-is-not-fixed-says-italian-pm-matteo-renzi Accessed 8 February 2018
UNESCO (2017) Asylum Seeker. http://www.unesco.org/new/en/social-and-human-sciences/themes/international-migration/glossary/asylum-seeker/ Accessed 8 February 2018
UNHCR (2016) UNHCR viewpoint: 'Refugee' or 'migrant' – Which is right? http://www.unhcr.org/news/latest/2016/7/55df0e556/unhcr-viewpoint-refugee-migrant-right.html Accessed 8 February 2018
Van Gorp B (2005) Where is the frame? Victims and intruders in the Belgian press coverage of the asylum issue. European Journal of Communication 20:484–507
Van Hulst M, Yanow D (2016) From Policy "Frames" to "Framing": Theorizing a More Dynamic Political Approach. American Review of Public Administration 46:92–112
Weick KE (1988) Enacted Sensemaking in Crisis Situations. Journal of Management Studies 25:305–317

Weick KE (1993) The collapse of sensemaking in organizations: the Mann Gulch disaster. Administrative Science Quarterly 38:628–652
Weick KE (1995) Sensemaking in Organizations. Sage Publications Inc., Thousand Oaks
Weick KE (2005) Managing the Unexpected: Complexity as Distributed Sensemaking. In: McDaniel RR, Driebe DJ (eds), Uncertainty and Surprise in Complex Systems. Springer, Berlin, pp 51–65
Weick KE, Sutcliffe KM, Obstfeld D (2005) Organizing and the Process of Sensemaking. Organization Science 16:409–421
Wolbers J, Boersma K (2013) The common operational picture as collective sensemaking. Journal of Contingencies and Crisis Management 21:186–199
Yin RK (2012) Applications of Case Study Research. Sage Publications, Thousand Oaks

Chapter 4
Border Security, Boat Migration and Mediterranean Operations in the Frames of Securitisation and Law Enforcement: Causal Explanation and Process Tracing

B.M.J.B. Klein Goldewijk

Contents

Abstract The Central Mediterranean route is currently the main one for migrants crossing the European Union's (EU) external borders. Boat migration and border security will be approached here within two main frameworks for analysis: a securitisation frame and a law enforcement frame. First, the pathways of securitisation will be traced in the context of the discourse and military-naval operations conducted by Frontex and its partaking EU Member States, with an emphasis on EU Operation *Sophia*. Second, a seemingly opposing process of desecuritisation of migration will be analysed, where the implications of the legal *Hirsi* Judgement are at the core. Categorisation and contentious data analysis will be explored in connection to both frames. The central research question is why and how the *outcome* of the (de)securitisation of Mediterranean borders and boat migration has been reached.

B.M.J.B. Klein Goldewijk (✉)
Faculty of Military Sciences, Netherlands Defence Academy, Ministry of Defence, Breda, The Netherlands
e-mail: bmjb.kleingoldewijk@mindef.nl

H. Monsuur et al. (eds.), *NL ARMS Netherlands Annual Review of Military Studies 2018*, NL ARMS, https://doi.org/10.1007/978-94-6265-246-0_4

This is a 'how is this possible' or effects-oriented question, by taking the outcome of securitisation processes as its point of departure. The major objective is primarily theoretical: to contribute to strengthening securitisation theory by focussing on its disputed capacity of a *causal* explanation of social mechanisms and facilitating conditions. This will be realised by engaging in interpretivist process tracing: by so doing the relevance of this research strategy within international security studies will be confirmed. It is concluded that (de)securitisation processes can be explained by their paradoxical effects: they enable the protection of the rights of migrants but also create new divisions through current external border operations, and so establish ambiguities within both frameworks.

Keywords Securitisation · Law Enforcement · Boat Migration · Border Security · Mediterranean Operations · Causal Explanation · Process Tracing

4.1 Introduction

Boat migration has become a key symbol of the Mediterranean with images of migrants crammed on boats and risking their lives while crossing to Europe. For the wider public and the international media, migration by boat is associated with the most visible side of border security and control: intercepted migrant boats, coast guards patrolling territorial waters, and permanent surveillance by search and rescue (SAR) vessels.[1] The stories of massive deaths at sea, predominantly on the Central Mediterranean route between Libya and Italy, have become a cause of great international concern with wide-ranging impacts on countries of destination, transit and origin.

Migration dynamics are quickly and continuously changing. Since 2011, and particularly after 2014, an unprecedented number of people have been crossing the Mediterranean to reach Europe, with 2015 marking the sharpest increase. By then, 90% of those arriving on the shores of the Greek islands originated mainly from Syria, Afghanistan and Iraq, whereas this number dropped to 41% in 2016. By the end of 2016, the International Organization for Migration (IOM) recorded the total number of arrivals as 387,739, which is in considerable contrast to the 1,046,599 arrivals recorded in 2015. In the year 2015, 3,770 were reported dead/missing, with 2,892 on the Central Mediterranean route. In 2016, 5,082 were held dead/missing, with 4,579 on the Central Mediterranean.[2] Overall, between 2011 and 2016, some 630,000 irregular migrants disembarked in Italy via the Central Mediterranean, either via successful human smuggling across the sea, or by rescue at sea. In this period, more than 13,000 lost their lives in crossing, in addition to the many more who died

[1] Moreno-Lax 2018; Ghezelbash et al. 2018; Little and Vaughan-Williams 2017; Fargues and Bonfanti 2014.

[2] IOM 2016, 2017.

travelling through the Sahara.[3] Mainly after the EU-Turkey political agreement of March 2016, the migration flows through the Eastern Mediterranean and the Western Balkan route were halted. By consequence, arrivals to Italy increased, shifting to mainly nationals from Africa (Nigeria, Eritrea and the Gambia), whereas the share of arrivals from Syria, Iraq and Afghanistan decreased. Since 2017 the Central Mediterranean route, with Libya as main gateway, has continued to revive, which is the focus of this chapter.

Existing categories fail to adequately capture the complex and messy realities involved. Terms such as migrant and refugee are not neutral or objective: they are politicised in Europe's migration crisis and also reflect various assumptions that make any straightforward differentiation impossible.[4] Whereas refugees are defined and protected by international law,[5] there is no common legal definition of migrants. In addition, individuals may change status or simultaneously fit into different categories. Moreover, political arrangements may change the protection status under international refugee law. This was demonstrated when the EU signed the 2016 agreement with the Afghan Government, allowing EU member states to deport those who seek asylum, while obliging the Afghan Government to receive them.[6] The above not only represents a growing gap between the international legal protection regime and current forms of migration and national measures, but also requires care when using these categories.

Two main complementary frames for analysing border security and boat migration will be discussed in this chapter: a securitisation frame (in Sect. 4.3) and a law enforcement frame (in Sect. 4.4). Securitisation as an analytic frame will encompass an exploration of recent Frontex' discourse and military-navy strategies of border control, involving search and rescue (SAR) operations, and practices of coastal patrolling and interception of migrant boats across the Mediterranean Sea. Second, the law enforcement frame will reveal some reforms that have contributed to a desecuritisation process of boat migration and border control. This is surrounded by quite a few disagreements and ambiguities in the interpretation of international and EU law that will be analysed. This frame further helps to distinguish and clarify the scope of binding legal obligations of the Member States, involving the law of the sea, human rights, and refugee law. Third, the domain of contentious data analysis and categorisation will be explored (Sect. 4.5). This is not a third analytic frame but rather a realm that can be seen as somehow distinct from but also permeating the two mentioned frames. This realm involves the role of data collection and data analysis, mainly by Frontex, the European Border and Coast Guard Agency. This is the area of interlinked databases with smart technologies and surveillance that inform, among others, Frontex' risk-conception. Sub-conclusions from each of these sections build up towards the final Conclusion (Sect. 4.6).

---

[3] European Commission (EPSC) 2017, p. 1.

[4] Crawley and Skleparis 2018, pp. 49–50.

[5] 1951 Convention Relating to the Status of Refugees, 189 UNTS 150 (Refugee Convention), entered into force 22 April 1954, and its 1967 Protocol.

[6] European Commission 2016b.

Both the securitisation and the law enforcement frames, as well as the realm of data analysis, share some connections to what Didier Bigo has framed as the three main different universes of EU border control.[7] Each universe represents a distinct understanding of borders and border security, as will be explained below. The next part sets the stage and sheds light on the drivers of the research agendas to be unfolded (Sect. 4.2).

4.2 Causal Analysis and the Explanatory Capacity of Securitisation

Border security and boat migration in the Mediterranean will be approached here in terms of securitisation, which is a key component of security studies. Securitisation can be understood as a process in which an emerging issue is treated as a threat. It is a social construction that brings "threats into being".[8] The function of securitisation has been defined as "to enable imperative and exceptional measures to deal with it [threat]."[9] This is a strategic process: securitisation affects common knowledge by rereading the 'real' situation and reinserting the resultant perceptions into public discourse. This also raises the question of how this is possible and effected.

Securitisation comprises at least three layers: it is a *concept* that advances an understanding of what security is; it provides a *framework* for analysis; and it is an empirical and political *theory*.[10] There is much debate about these different components and how they are to be distinguished or connected. What stands out from such discussions as relevant for this chapter is the "explanatory status"[11] of securitisation *theory*, as Stefano Guzzini phrases it. Securitisation, in its capacity of a *theory*,[12] will be of specific relevance here in order to see how far it can guide an explanation of the *causes* of changing processes of security. In this way, securitisation theory runs as a main thread through this chapter.

The major *objective* here is primarily theoretical: to contribute to strengthening securitisation theory by focussing on its disputed capacity of providing a *causal* explanation of social mechanisms. This objective integrates into an emergent debate on the explanatory relevance of securitisation theory. The central *research question* is why and how the *outcome* of the securitisation of Mediterranean borders and boat migration has been reached. This is a 'how is it possible' or effects-oriented question, by taking the outcome of securitisation processes as its point of departure, and asking why and how (in how far), and under which mechanisms and conditions, such an outcome has been achieved. This requires a research effort to explain causal patterns that generate effects.

---

[7] Bigo 2014.

[8] Balzacq 2011b, p. XIII (Preface).

[9] Buzan and Waever 2003, p. 491.

[10] Guzzini 2011, p. 330; see also Waever 2011.

[11] Guzzini 2011, p. 329.

[12] Balzacq 2011b, 2016; Balzacq and Guzzini 2015.

4.2.1 Social Mechanisms and Facilitating Conditions

Causal patterns can be seen as social mechanisms (or constellations) and facilitating conditions involved in an analysis of different securitisation processes. By focussing on *causal analysis* in securitisation theory, an effort is undertaken here to explore and reinforce the explanatory capacity of this theory by which it can *explain* securitisation practices and process dynamics that implicate different audiences. Thus far, the securitisation literature has barely begun to identify causal mechanisms with the main exception of Stefano Guzzini:[13] his work has offered a major spur for this chapter.

As a research strategy, this study offers a process tracing approach, which has come into the realm of international security studies only recently.[14] This is mainly due to Nina Tannenwald in her studies to explain the nuclear taboo.[15] The debate on how process tracing can be used in the area of *critical* security studies got a particular boost in studies by Thierry Balzacq[16] and is flourishing since. The earlier largely absent role of process tracing in security studies may be understood by reason of its inherent link to causal explanation: this was mostly delegated to (neo)positivism and had no place in interpretivist approaches.[17] Only a few scholars, including Guzzini, have taken up this method in connection to securitisation processes and securitisation theory,[18] thereby raising the above issues on causal explanations of social mechanisms. This is a noteworthy and innovative development, since the research output of security studies for a large part depends on the methods and methodologies involved. This chapter joins and contributes to such debates.

The research method of process tracing is more than a simple option for a method to detect the paths of securitisation and trace how process dynamics work towards involving wider publics. When, basically, this method reveals and explains social mechanisms, a certain concept of causality is involved. Actually, causal explanations have received considerable attention in the social sciences and in the philosophy of science. Recurrently, (neo)positivist concepts of causality have dominated, where causality is seen as correlational analysis or discovering regularities in an empirical process. Yet, revealing a correlation of factors does not explain a process.[19] Reducing process tracing to an idea of social mechanisms seen as a sequence of intervening variables may end up in a chain of descriptive notions, a tendency that has been noted in earlier work by Alexander George and Andrew Bennett.[20] Developing an interpretivist approach to process tracing requires to take a distance from such view.

---

[13] Guzzini 2011, 2017a, b.

[14] Tannenwald 2015; Mahoney 2015; Bennett 2015.

[15] Tannenwald 2005, 2007.

[16] Balzacq 2011b, in particular Balzacq 2011a.

[17] Robinson 2017, p. 506; Balzacq 2011a.

[18] Balzacq 2011a; Guzzini 2011, 2017a, b; Robinson 2017; Oliveira 2017.

[19] Hedström and Ylikoski 2010; Hedström and Swedberg 1998; Guzzini 2011, pp. 332–333.

[20] George and Bennett 2005; Guzzini 2011, p. 332. For George and Bennett's revision, see Guzzini 2017b, p. 435; Guzzini 2017a, p. 749.

Departing from (neo)positivist concepts of causality calls for efforts to develop other approaches of causal explanation.[21] In this regard, causal mechanisms will be seen here in their triggering capacity: whether a social mechanism is triggered in a securitisation process, or not, however, is contingent, and not a necessary or automatic and regular course of a process.[22] This is also why analysing securitisation as a process adds facilitating conditions to social mechanisms. The triggering capacity of causal mechanisms will be activated only under certain conditions that depend on their interaction with how the specific process unfolds.[23]

4.2.2 *No Fixed, Linear or Regular Course of Securitisation*

In this research, I will explore only one main causal mechanism of securitisation theory. This emerged from process tracing in previous research on securitisation and was first, to my knowledge, identified by Stefano Guzzini and further elaborated by Corey Robinson.[24] The central causal mechanism is what I would call *reification*, which means converting an idea, a concept into a concrete thing or regarding it as real (Guzzini and Robinson name it a 'self-fulfilling prophecy').[25] A famous example of the working of this mechanism can be found when the dynamics of the worldwide financial crisis after 2008 created their own momentum: it became common in the public discourse to believe that some banks would become insolvent and, as an effect, depositors panicked and withdrew their funds, thereby causing bank runs and bankruptcy.[26] Reification brings a reality into being by aligning it with beliefs that get causal effects. It is a social dynamic in which public definitions of a situation become an integral part of the situation and affect the ensuing developments.[27] In other words, a particular definition of a situation evokes a new behaviour that makes the conception become reality. In brief, reification is a social mechanism of misapprehension and delusion of a reality in which manifold social actors are involved. Reification as a causal social mechanism is taken here at the analytically general level.

This social mechanism will be identified by briefly exploring two paradigmatic cases that can be seen as *counterexamples* within the two main frames: the first case, the EU naval military operation *Sophia* in the Mediterranean, actually triggers securitisation, whereas the second case, apparently in opposition, has activated desecuritisation. The latter is the case of the *Hirsi* Judgment by the European Court of Human Rights (ECtHR), the first and only case in the context of search and rescue

[21] Guzzini 2017b, p. 433.

[22] Guzzini 2011, p. 336.

[23] Guzzini 2012, p. 264; Robinson 2017, p. 510.

[24] Guzzini 2012, 2017b; Robinson 2017.

[25] See, among others, Guzzini 2017b, pp. 435–436; Robinson 2017, pp. 516–517.

[26] Robinson refers to a similar parable by Robert Merton (1948), who originally elaborated the term self-fulfilling prophecy.

[27] This quotation is from Robinson who quotes Merton, see Robinson 2017, p. 516.

(SAR) operations. The two cases are relevant together, since they rebut any idea of a fixed, linear or regular course of securitisation processes.

Taking up and further exploring an *a priori* identified key causal mechanism means that it will not inductively be derived from the cases but rather examined in its working through the cases. Even so, when exploring how reification as a causal mechanism "travels"[28] in the cases, this study is neither entirely deductive in the sense of hypothesis testing. Rather, meeting points of inductive and deductive analysis will be exposed as significant to further explanations.

In terms of its relevance, this study engages in several research agendas. First, it contributes to the call for developing methods and methodological frameworks in critical security studies, as launched by Claudia Aradau (et al.).[29] This is realised by elaborating interpretivist process tracing as an integral part of international security studies. Second, the analysis of securitisation as a process will be broken down in causal social mechanisms and facilitating conditions that link to the outcome of securitisation.[30] This undertaking can be understood as an effort to further advance securitisation theory. This theory not only assumes that securitisation is part of a dynamic process that responds to threats and risks via exceptional measures, but also regards securitisation as a whole of routinized practices, where large databases and technologies assume a key role.

4.3 Securitisation Frame: Boat Migrants and Border Control

This section of the chapter focuses on border security and boat migration in connection to Mediterranean maritime operations. These operations are realised under bilateral agreements between Mediterranean countries, such as Greece, Italy or Malta, or under coordination by Frontex, the European Union (EU) agency for external border management. Briefly, a process of military-navy strategic operations of border control will be traced. This sketch will reveal a configuration of facilitating conditions for such operations, in order to build up an explanation of the causes of securitisation under this frame.

The difference between three universes of border control, as mentioned before, is based on Bigo's extensive interviews with personnel at the Warsaw headquarters of Frontex and at manifold training sessions of border guards all over Europe, from Brussels to Lampedusa.[31] The perception of border that prevails among the military and the policy makers involved in this first realm of naval operations is not so much a traditional military vision of defending state-related borders, solid walls or EU boundaries. Rather, the central vision of the employees involved in border control and

[28] Guzzini 2011, p. 338.

[29] Aradau et al. 2015, p. 15.

[30] Robinson 2017, p. 508.

[31] Bigo 2014, p. 210, see also note 2 at p. 221 on Bigo's research protocol and techniques used.

practices of interception at sea, as Bigo notes, is one of containment and deterrence that would benefit migrants by regulating unsafe migration flows and preventing tragedies of travelling by insecure boats at sea.[32]

4.3.1 Irregular Migration and Shifting Migrant Routes

The Mediterranean border region of Europe affects all those who seek to transgress it as irregular migrants. It involves migrants' opportunities to be rescued, and get access to safety and protection. It also includes a myriad of local and (inter)national actors intervening in the border region. Though there is no universal standard definition of the term migration, as indicated above, irregular migration can be seen as a movement of crossing (inter)national boundaries: (a) outside the regulatory norms of the countries of origin, transit, or destination, and (b) without the needed authorisation or personal documents required under immigration regulations. Irregular migration has to be distinguished from illegal migration, which is a notion mostly used for human smuggling and trafficking in persons.[33]

Migration routes, trends and patterns are quickly changing, by which the Central Mediterranean route has revived. The most significant recent development at the EU's external borders with North Africa and the Middle East is this reversing trend, with various implications. In 2017, the Eastern Mediterranean and Western Balkan routes successively had the greatest decline in absolute figures of irregular migrants, as Frontex' *Risk Analysis for 2018* notes, whereas the earlier sudden fall on the Central Mediterranean route was reversed in the second half of 2017. In conformity with such changes on the migratory routes, Africans (by early 2018) account for nearly two-thirds of the irregular migrants arriving at the external borders of the EU. The share of Africans increased, when compared with 2016, due to a quickly raising number of voyages through and from Maghreb countries in North Africa. Frontex links this trend to the implementation of the EU-Turkey Statement issued by the European Council (2016) and its consequences with regard to regaining control of the Western Balkan transit corridor.[34] The implementation of this agreement required Turkey to impede irregular exit and to readmit that all new irregular migrants crossing into Greek islands "will be returned to Turkey;" that for every Syrian being returned "another Syrian will be resettled from Turkey to the EU;"; and that "Turkey will take any necessary measures to prevent new sea or land routes for illegal migration opening from Turkey to the EU."[35] With the EU-Turkey deal and the closure of the Western Balkan route, the Central Mediterranean has revitalised as the main entry for arriving in the EU by sea, where the Italian peninsula holds a significant place.

---

32 Bigo 2014, pp. 212–213.

33 International Organisation for Migration (IOM), at https://www.iom.int/key-migration-terms, Accessed on 28-01-2018.

34 Frontex 2018, pp. 6, 8, 16, 19, 34.

35 European Council 2016, p. 1; see also European Commission 2016a.

Another development after the EU-Turkey-closures is the increase in what Frontex calls an "ever-changing *modus operandi* of the smugglers," involving their "networks and the general increase in their level of sophistication," where "ever more dangerous methods are used by criminals to smuggle migrants across borders."[36] In this view, which is shared more commonly in the EU, practices of smugglers are adapting to changing circumstances, making "illegal crossings" cheaper, more frequent and riskier.[37] This means that migration, after the EU-Turkey agreement, became more closely associated with illegally crossing, as is clearly visible in Frontex' Risk Analysis for 2018.[38] Frontex concludes this report by arguing: "[i]rregular migration by sea, and more specifically via the Mediterranean routes, will remain the main *modus operandi* for illegally crossing the EU's external borders and also one of the most dangerous forms of migrant smuggling and one which often requires humanitarian assistance efforts."[39] This justifies, according to Frontex, more *detections*: not only of cross-border crimes, drugs transports, or document fraud, which would be evident, but detections of 'illegal crossings.' Throughout its full Risk Analysis for 2018, Frontex now speaks in terms such as "irregular migrants detected on the Central Mediterranean" and "migrants who go undetected."[40]

It may have become clear by now that the border security *discourse* on migrants by Frontex has substantially shifted in response to EU Council policies, involving the EU-Turkey Statement, and the changing migration routes involved. First, Frontex' discourse portrays human smugglers as perpetrators of abuse and fatalities at sea. The basic thought that comes to light is that migrants have to be rescued to spare them the dangers of the voyages, to save lives and combat smugglers. Migrants are seen *as a risk* to border security (a threat), are considered to be *at risk* because of human smugglers,[41] and are additionally identified as illegal crossers who *bring risk*. The effect is a *triple reification*. The discourse unveils that migrants fulfil three roles: they are a danger for the borders, they are exposed to danger, and they disclose danger. In sum, boat migrants are considered as a threefold threat to border security.

Second, the developing perception of migrants in this discourse also seems to justify a manifest strategic instrument to realise the goal of the reduction of unauthorised arrivals in the Mediterranean: *detection*. This instrument appears not only to be aimed at cross-border criminality, such as trafficking in persons and smuggling of goods, but detection presently also involves irregular migration as illegal border crossing. Detection now seems to fulfil the threefold role of reducing unauthorised arrivals, saving the lives of migrants, and combating illegal trafficking. The effect of this changing perception on boat migrants in association with detection was a quick *diversion* of migration routes, as explained above.

---

36 Frontex 2018, pp. 6 and 17.

37 European Commission (EPSC) 2017, p. 1.

38 The shift is most visible at Frontex 2018, pp. 8–9, 19, 28, 29.

39 Frontex 2018, p. 41.

40 Frontex 2018, p. 8, see also 9.

41 Moreno-Lax 2018, p. 120.

4.3.2 Operation Sophia

The borders of states are perhaps the most striking institutions in international relations, particularly when it concerns international security.[42] Borders and border security (walls, fences and barriers) are integral part of the international system of states, including the EU's external borders (between EU Member States and third countries). Yet border control activities move beyond territorial borders, and extend to the high seas and to third countries via search and rescue (SAR) operations within an international framework of SAR zones and jurisdictions. These search and rescue areas are still undefined in many ocean regions.[43] State-related issues of who is responsible for rescuing and saving lives have not been settled since the International Maritime Organisation (IMO) distinguished SAR areas on the oceans after the SAR Convention was adopted.[44]

In its *FRAN Q2 Report*, Frontex signals a share of 78% of the overall number of irregular migrants entering the EU on the Central Mediterranean during the second quarter of 2017.[45] In response to the revival in 2017 of the Central Mediterranean route, in regard of the major fatalities that had occurred in 2015 and 2016, and in support of Italy, Frontex launched in the early months of 2018 a new Joint Operation *Themis* that spans the Central Mediterranean Sea and substitutes the earlier Operation *Triton* launched in 2014. In operation *Themis*, SAR-activities will continue, in addition to an explicitly enhanced law enforcement focus of the mission: tracking down criminal activities and cross border crime as well as foreign fighters and other terrorist threats at the external borders.[46] The contours of this development can be traced back to Operation *Mare Nostrum* and Operation *Sophia*.

In the aftermath of the ship wreckage off the coast of Lampedusa (on 16 October 2013), Italy launched Operation *Mare Nostrum*, a humanitarian/military operation of border control, deployed in the Italian, Maltese and Libyan SAR zones.[47] *Mare Nostrum* had an active SAR-focus but was politically controversial: in Italy due to the uneven burden on this country, and elsewhere in the EU for its feared pull-factor or magnet-effect by which it would attract new or continuous flows of boat arrivals. The operation was quickly discontinued.

In acknowledgement of the height of the following migration crisis in 2015, with major shipwrecks in the Central Mediterranean, the European Council's Ten-Point Action Plan projected the establishment of an EU-led Naval Force Operation in the Mediterranean (EUNAVFOR MED), launched with Operation *Sophia*.[48] This EU

---

[42] Figueiredo 2011, pp. 155, 158, 164.

[43] European Commission (EPSC) 2017, p. 10.

[44] International Convention on Maritime Search and Rescue (adopted 27 April 1979, entered into force 22 June 1985) 1405 UNTS 119 (SAR Convention).

[45] Frontex 2017 (FRAN Q2), p. 8.

[46] Frontex (2018) 'Frontex Launching New Operation in Central Med,' Press Release, 31 Jan.

[47] European Commission (EPSC) 2017, p. 3; see also Moreno-Lax 2018, p. 126; Borelli and Stanford 2014.

[48] European Council Decision 2015/972 (n 129); see also European Commission 2015.

military operation would function *next* to Frontex operations and aimed "to better contain the growing flows of illegal migration" and disrupt "migrant smuggling".[49] Because of lacking EU jurisdiction on the extraterritorial use of military force, an authorisation of the UN Security Council was obtained (UN Resolution 2240), which permits Member States "to use all measures commensurate to the specific circumstances"[50] to disrupt organised criminal enterprises engaged in migrant smuggling and human trafficking, by which they can inspect, seize, and possibly dispose of vessels on the high seas off the coast of Libya.

Operation *Sophia*, with an anti-smuggling mandate, was designed to operate within the Libyan SAR zone and would contribute to fighting instability in the region. Documents made available by WikiLeaks revealed the position of EU Defence Commanders who exposed the flaws in the design of the mission and foresaw that EUNAVFOR Med would fail, as it would endorse diversion of migration to alternative routes in the Mediterranean, further destabilise the region and rather strengthen human trafficking.[51] Presumably, one of the flaws of *Sophia* was the fact that its design was based on Operation *Atlanta* in a similar model. *Atlanta* was an EU anti-piracy mission in Somalia that included the permission to destroy vessels ashore.[52] However, with the more robust surveillance operations involved in *Sophia*, also the business plans of human smugglers adapted: instead of such plans and their execution being disrupted or destroyed, new opportunities were created for cheaper ways to reach EU territories.[53]

4.3.3 Sub-conclusions

Interpretivist process tracing does not aim at identifying variables and then correlate them: it is not correlational analysis that would (only) discover regularities in securitisation processes.[54] Different from an understanding of causality in conjunction theory or in probabilistic theories of causation,[55] an interpretivist approach does not perceive causality in terms of process regularities and then call it a mechanism. As mentioned before, an interpretivist redefinition of causality requires to take some distance from models of explanation based on correlation.[56]

---

[49] EU Council Conclusions (EUCO 22/15) of 26 June 2015, p. 1. See also EU Council Decision (CFSP) 2015/778 of 18 May 2015; see also Ghezelbash et al. 2018, p. 19.

[50] UNSC Resolution 2240 (9 Oct. 2015).

[51] Ghezelbash et al. 2018, p. 20; Bevilacqua 2017, p. 165.

[52] Roberts 2018, p. 222.

[53] European Commission (EPSC) 2017, p. 1; Roberts 2018.

[54] Guzzini 2017a, b, p. 433.

[55] Hedström and Ylikoski 2010.

[56] Guzzini 2011, p. 333.

The securitisation frame contributes some clear insights. First, it was exposed that search and rescue (SAR) operations of boat migrants have become securitised.[57] The discourse on EU external borders operates according to a borderless logic of 'saving lives', yet the 'irregular' of migrants in need of rescue is invoked as exceptional. By consequence, border-related interventions of Member States under coordination by Frontex now predominantly aim at stopping the illegal transport of people and stem migratory flows. Second, securitisation is clearly part of an ongoing social construction of reality. The regional security crisis in the Mediterranean arose because the discourses of different actors (the EU, Frontex, Member States) *simultaneously* became involved in securitising migrants, which so constituted a process in various episodes. This evidently raises the question of causality.

As traced above, rescues in the high seas at the EU external borders have become more robust surveillance operations, paradoxically intertwined with humanitarian approaches. In fact, it has more widely been remarked that there is an increasing entanglement of securitisation and humanitarianism in the context of border control and migration management.[58] The question then is whether the humanitarian purpose of save and rescue operations has become compromised in view of more robust border security. The established SAR provisions seem to have been either relegated or merged into law-enforcement operations in response to human smuggling and trafficking, as a result of which the fatality rates in the Mediterranean area are recently quickly raising again.[59]

This requires a supplementary explanation of the *causes* of the Mediterranean securitisation processes. The starting point, from an interpretivist approach, is how such recurring events have been understood in policy discourses, as outlined above.[60] However, the securitisation frame may be misleading in this regard, since it has a restricted ability, when taken on its own, to explain in-depth the dynamics of border security and boat migration. This is the reason why securitisation, as a *theory* became relevant in the foregoing as well, reconnecting to the social mechanism of reification and the conditions that have facilitated the securitising outcome under this frame.

The narrative of connecting boat migrants to security, risk and detection already existed when Frontex became operational in 2004 and was certainly not generated by this European agency and the partaking Member States. But, as seen above, the evolution of Frontex' discourse converges for a great deal with that of the EU Commission and EU Council, which also involves Frontex' central role in providing successive risk analyses (as will further be shown below). The fact that such discourses converge may have contributed to producing the effect of a triple reification of irregular migrants as a risk to border security, as victims of human trafficking, and as illegal crossers associated with trans-border crimes. Such discourse thereby breeds the dynamics of reification.

---

57 See also Bigo 2014; Ghezelbash et al. 2018.

58 Little and Vaughan-Williams 2017; Moreno-Lax 2018.

59 Ghezelbash et al. 2018, p. 35 and 20.

60 Guzzini 2017a, b, p. 436.

Critical realists have deepened and broadened the concept of cause by articulating causal mechanisms in terms of a *causal complex*, a move elaborated by Gilberto Carvalho de Oliveira.[61] Something of such a causal complex can be identified in the above-mentioned facilitating conditions that produced the discourse and the mechanism of reification in this situation. In addition, securitising definitions of the situation emerged in risk analyses (linking irregular migration to detection) that became available to the wider public but without evidence, proper verification, or proof of the threats.[62] In any case, such beliefs stabilised, affected subsequent international developments and influenced the ensuing course of events. This evidently links to what has been clarified earlier about reification, since the consequences of such discourse brought an operational reality into being that was in alignment with the initial and consequent beliefs. Such beliefs about a threatening situation become true by a reality that apparently adapts to such beliefs. Security actors are reifying a vision of reality and do not always recognise that such beliefs are (and become) constitutive of reality itself.

4.4 Law Enforcement Frame: Entitlements and Desecuritisation

This section undertakes an effort to explain how securitisation works when analysed in a law enforcement frame and traces a few reforms in the securitisation process that will be interpreted in terms of desecuritisation effects. Some clarifications will also be given of the main obligations in international and European law binding upon the EU Member States when they operate at sea. This illuminates in particular how boat migration and border security connect to a complex setting, involving (at least) the law of the sea, human rights and refugee law.

The law enforcement frame provides an approach that makes it possible to lay out, distinguish and clarify the scope of binding legal obligations of the Member States when they operate at sea. The question is how the procedural mechanisms of international and EU law can be effective in protecting persons in distress, in this case Mediterranean boat migrants, and what remedies have been provided through the law. If (regional) security crises emerge because discourses from different actors at certain moments converge in securitising migrants, would this also be the case for desecuritisation processes under a law framework? Why did desecuritisation happen in connection to the strong *Hirsi* Judgement by the European Court of Human Rights? In a broader view, how was it possible that certain processes in international and EU law have contributed to a desecuritisation of the Mediterranean situation?

Law enforcement comprises the management of open and secure borders, filtering individual cases, sorting out legal from illegal arrivals, genuine from false claims, and policing who is allowed to enter and who should be detained or repatriated. This is the

[61] Oliveira 2017.

[62] See also Robinson 2017, p. 516.

area where the large majority of EU border guards and police is employed in terms of risk assessment and intelligence gathering, tasked with the "external dimension of [Europe's] internal security."[63] The employees working in this realm primarily justify their work, as Bigo saw from his interviews, as "immanent justice," or being the "eyes and arms of justice.[64] The *perception* of border security by EU officials and Frontex border guards in this universe, Bigo notes, is not one of patrolling and interception (as in the first universe) but rather of following the migration flows and managing flexible EU borders, based on a view of European cooperation and obligations of the Member States. They decidedly regard themselves as distinguished from non-EU contexts with military practices of harsh interdiction, as in Australia or the US. They rather frame their work as a Europeanised form of border control with the protection of borders that need to remain open while being kept secure. The justifications provided by employees are grounded on two main ideas about legitimate protection: the protection of migrants against criminals who exploit them and the protection of a European democratic legal order.[65]

4.4.1 International Law, EU Law, and Non-Refoulement

Both international law and EU law impose considerable obligations on the EU Member States with regard to persons in distress at sea. The situation of boat migrants in the Mediterranean, who may seek asylum after rescue, has provoked among the EU Member States various disagreements and non-compliance. The effective implementation of such obligations is often analysed as being hampered by the inconsistent way in which the obligations falling on Member States are interpreted.[66]

Although the right to life of migrants is protected under a number of international human rights treaties,[67] it remains uncertain in the law of the sea as to whether migrants rescued (or to be rescued) fall under the jurisdiction of the rescuing state, being the coastal state and/or flag state of a rescuing unit. In addition, it is disputed in regard of the law of the sea whether a search and rescue (SAR) operation entails the exercise of jurisdiction: in principle, the coastal state is responsible for rescuing persons in distress. When such a state is not capable, another country can render assistance and hand over the rescued persons to a coastal state connected to a specific SAR region. Moreover, the law of the sea neither establishes exactly where rescues should be disembarked, nor does it precisely allocate responsibility in their

---

[63] Bigo 2014, p. 213.

[64] Bigo 2014, p. 214.

[65] Bigo 2014, pp. 213–216.

[66] Moreno-Lax 2011, p. 176.

[67] Among others: International Covenant on Civil and Political Rights (adopted 16 Dec. 1966, entered into force 23 March 1976) 999 UNTS 171; European Convention for the Protection of Human Rights and Fundamental Freedoms (adopted 4 Nov. 1950, entered into force 3 Sept. 1953) 213 UNTS 221.

regard.[68] This becomes an issue when governments appear to be unwilling to permit the disembarkation of rescued migrants into their territory and attempt to turn responsibility over to other jurisdictions.[69] A famous example of 2009 is that of a Turkish cargo vessel (MV Pinar), rescuing 154 African migrants between the Italian island of Lampedusa and Malta, resulting in a four-day standoff as both Italy and Malta claimed that the other State was responsible for accepting the migrants based on the location of the incident and the different SAR zones involved.

The European Commission has clearly admitted a persistent "disunity within the EU over which obligations arise from EU fundamental rights and international human rights and refugee law, and how these obligations relate to the law of the sea."[70] Some solutions have been developed: in conformity with the Maritime Conventions, it is for the shipmaster and the states involved in the rescue operation to determine the appropriate place of safety. But evidently, this latter provision creates new disputes again. The effect is that the rights and obligations in SAR-operations at sea are interpreted inconsistently at least.

Integral part of the dynamics of securitisation is the substantial transformation of the role played by human rights in the Mediterranean.[71] The narrative of rescue and saving lives is without migrants' access to protection: the procedures required to implement this have not been clarified in view of the extraterritorial applicability of (migrants') human rights. By consequence, migrants are rescued in current Mediterranean state-based maritime operations, often coordinated by Frontex, but they are *not protected*: they cannot activate their rights since extraterritorial human rights duties tend to be disclaimed. This is a flagrant violation of migrants' needs that must be explained from the core content of international human rights law: fundamental freedoms and basic entitlements. This is what we have elsewhere called an 'entitlement failure:'[72] needs are not met as a result of entitlement failures by states (and state-related agencies) that are duty-holders and bound by obligations in regard to basic entitlements.

Frontex claims to have "become an essential actor in law enforcement on the European level."[73] To explain this, the agency argues it has advanced much in the area of *returns*, which increased in 2017 to about a third more than the previous year. Member States, coordinated by Frontex, returned in 2017 more than 14,000 people whose asylum applications were rejected, who did not receive subsidiary status, or who were no longer eligible to remain. By consequence, due to malfunctioning entitlement systems, human rights serve to justify detection (so as to rescue and save lives) and returns, often without access to protection in Europe. Paradoxically, the

---

[68] Trevisanut 2014, pp. 3–4 and Moreno-Lax 2011, p. 175.

[69] Ghezelbash et al. 2018, p. 24. For the MV Pinar incident, see also p. 2.

[70] Reinforcing the Management of the European Union's Southern Maritime Borders, COM(2006) 733, 11 Nov. 2006, para 35.

[71] Moreno-Lax 2018.

[72] Klein Goldewijk and de Gaay Fortman 1999, pp. VII–XIV; also Klein Goldewijk et al. 2002; Klein Goldewijk 2008.

[73] Frontex 2018, p. 7.

invocation of human rights in Frontex' cooperation with Member States thus tends to restrain (migrants') human rights and obstructs the implementation of international and EU human rights obligations.[74] This alters the position of human rights in Europe: rather than functioning as an international law-based check on SAR, human rights end up as a tool of securitisation, implemented by detections and returns.

However, different maritime positions have also been developed that sought to provide remedies through the law. The adoption of the 2010 Maritime Guidelines Decision (MGD)[75] in 2014 substituted by the Maritime Surveillance Regulation (MSR), marked an adaptation that "purported to remedy the most appalling concerns".[76] A more humanitarian language was used, which may have echoed the overall climate of the humanitarian crisis at the time in North Africa and the emergent stages of the civil war in Syria, in the wake of the Arab Spring. The 2010 Maritime Guidelines, in strong terms, articulated clear obligations of SAR and *non-refoulement*, which is a principle of international law that prohibits forced returns to any country in which one is liable to be subjected to persecution and threats to life or freedom. The MGD required maritime operations coordinated by Frontex "in a way that does not put at risk the safety of the persons intercepted or rescued", and mandated that "no person shall be disembarked or otherwise handed over to the authorities of a country in contravention with the principle of non-refoulement", with the special needs of persons for international protection "considered throughout all the operation".[77] Apparently, this forceful statement resonated somehow in the 2011 Frontex Recast Regulation (FRR). The MGD prohibition of disembarkation in breach of non-refoulement was integrated in terms of the "special needs", not just to be taken into account, but to be "addressed" as part of the binding obligation to "protect human rights".[78] However, no legal safeguards, no specific procedural steps, and no facilities were mentioned in the 2011 Frontex Recast Regulation to realise practice to such effect.

4.4.2 Hirsi *Judgement*

In the context of SAR operations, only one case has been heard before an international judicial body concerned with human rights violations. This was the 2012 *Hirsi Jamaa and others v Italy* case[79] of the European Court of Human Rights. In this case, the Court dealt with an application by eleven Somali nationals and thirteen Eritrean nationals, who were intercepted by Italian ships on the high seas and forced to return to Libya. Italy's 2009 so-called push-back campaign of Libyan migrants provoked

[74] Follis 2017; Moreno-Lax 2018.

[75] Maritime Guidelines Decision 2010/252/EU, [2010] OJ L111/20 (MGD); Maritime Surveillance Regulation 656/2014, [2014] OJ L189/93 (MSR).

[76] Moreno-Lax 2018, p. 123, see also 125–126.

[77] Paragraphs 1.1–3, Annex, Part I, MGD.

[78] Article 1a, Frontex Recast Regulation 1168/2011, [2011] OJ L304/1 (FRR).

[79] ECtHR, Grand Chamber, Hirsi Jamaa v. Italy, Appl. 27765/09, 23 Febr. 2012.

the *Hirsi* Judgment, which condemned these push-backs and promoted revision and remedy strategies in the then prevailing legal scenario.

The European Court of Human Rights affirmed that Italy was exercising its jurisdiction over the rescued migrants because they were taken on board of a naval unit at location. The ECtHR held that "whenever the State through its agents operating outside its territory exercises control and authority over an individual, and thus jurisdiction, the State is under an obligation under Article 1 to secure to that individual the rights and freedoms' under the Convention."[80] In other words, the Mediterranean maritime context cannot justify that there would be areas outside the law[81] where individuals would not be covered by a legal system that protects their rights under the European Convention on Human Rights. The rescued persons were therefore consequently under the *de facto* and *de jure* control of the flag state. This conforms with Article 92 of the United Nations Convention on the Law of the Sea (UNCLOS),[82] which affirms the exclusive jurisdiction of the flag state on the high seas.[83] This also connects to the 1979 SAR Convention,[84] which comprises an international system for coordinating rescue operations that guarantees safety. The SAR Convention relates to Article 98(2) of the UNCLOS, which states that neighbouring states shall cooperate through regional agreements to promote and maintain adequate and effective SAR services.[85]

In such legal documents, the duty to render assistance at sea is extended to the disembarkation and delivery of rescued persons to a *place of safety*,[86] as regulated in the amended Article 3(1)(9) of the SAR Convention, which was in these terms modified via Resolutions of the Maritime Safety Committee (MSC) of the International Maritime Organization (IMO).[87] This has much relevance for the persistent risks of violation of the principle of non-refoulement.[88] The 1951 Refugee Convention provides that: "No Contracting State shall expel or return ('refouler') a refugee in any manner whatsoever to the frontiers of territories where his life or freedom would be threatened on account of his race, religion, nationality, membership of a particular social group or political opinion."[89] What follows from the Hirsi Judgement is that non-refoulement not only applies to expulsions or removals from the territory of Member States, but also to how persons should be treated who are intercepted by

---

[80] Ibid., para 178.

[81] Santos Vara and Sánchez-Tabernero 2016, p. 80. See also Giuffré 2012.

[82] United Nations Convention on the Law of the Sea (adopted 10 Dec. 1982, entered into force 16 Nov. 1994) 1833 UNTS 397 (UNCLOS).

[83] Trevisanut 2014, p. 2.

[84] Convention on Maritime Search and Rescue (adopted 27 April 1979, entered into force 22 June 1985) 1405 UNTS 97 (SAR Convention).

[85] Trevisanut 2014, p. 6; Ghezelbash et al. 2018, p. 4.

[86] Article 3(1)(9) SAR Convention; see also Trevisanut 2014, pp. 5–6.

[87] IMO, MSC.155 (78), 20 May 2004.

[88] See for example Trevisanut and Ippolito 2016.

[89] Article 33(1) Refugee Convention.

vessels on the high seas and in the territorial waters of the States of departure.[90] The effect of this Judgement and the non-refoulement prohibition is that intercepted boat migrants should not be released back into any place which is not safe.

4.4.3 Sub-conclusions

It can be concluded from the above that securitisation processes of borders and migration are pervading the area of law enforcement and interact with it. The question to be dealt with now is how the causes of the above traced dynamics can be properly explained from within a law enforcement frame.

The law enforcement frame provides various explanations but seems to represent an objectivist approach through which it appears to be unable to find decisive solutions for what triggers the insecurity of EU borders. One reason for this, as seen above, is that the Member States involved *persistently* disagree on their interpretation of the canvas of overlapping international and EU law, involving the law of the sea, human rights regimes, and refugee law. Since this is the case, and because of such disagreements, a significant part of the problem may also lie elsewhere—namely in the objective laws themselves, their contents, what they mean and the way they have been interpreted. This offers an explanation that somewhat differs from those that mainly focus on how international and EU law function in disputes, or rather, what these laws do, their performance.

The desecuritisation process that was triggered by the *Hirsi* Judgement, and somehow by the preceding Maritime Guidelines, was not a single act under the authority of the obligations of the law. It was not this Judgement in itself that constitutes a 'cause' for desecuritisation in the narrow sense. It was embedded in a wider prevailing public discourse of humanitarianism in civil society, politics and the judiciary, in connection to the Arab Spring, and armed conflict-related turbulence in North Africa and the Middle East: this environment produced a gradual change that affected the procedural logic of discourses in international law as well.

In this case, in fact, the outcome is influenced by the same type of reifying mechanism. But now it has an opposite effect and triggers desecuritising moves:[91] under different facilitating conditions and in a different context (of the law), the mechanism also gets a different content: in this configuration, the discourse is *dereifying* and de-essentialising the identity of migrants. As Guzzini notes: "Both securitizing and desecuritizing moves can be part of self-fulfilling prophecies by becoming shared beliefs – and then affecting pre-existing routine action-complexes related to them."[92] This implies that desecuritisation is a routine response as well as securitisation is. A desecuritising movement, indeed, in a certain episode, may seek to prevent the

[90] Giuffré 2012; Santos Vara and Sánchez-Tabernero 2016, p. 80.

[91] Robinson 2017, p. 517.

[92] Guzzini 2011, p. 336.

emergence or further advancement of reification. Yet its effect on the overall process remains indeterminate.

For the further analysis of securitisation as a process, both the social mechanism and the facilitating conditions are relevant—as well as how they are precisely connected. In this case, first, the working of the reification mechanism, in its prompting (or triggering) capacity of desecuritisation, was dependent on the facilitating conditions, being contextual and contingent. Second, the mechanism seems to be indeterminate in its effect on the larger process of securitisation. This reaffirms Guzzini's view that the exact character and the content of the mechanism cannot be understood outside of how it works in concrete contexts, including the discursive situations in which it operates.[93]

By now, two aspects have been explained: first, that the working of the mechanism in its triggering capacity is contingent; second, that the mechanism is indeterminate in its effect on the larger process of securitisation. This still leaves the question open where to locate the causal mechanism in concrete historical process-terms: would the mechanism *only trigger* processes of securitisation and desecuritisation, and invoke a constellation of discourses, actions and events (as a routine)? Would it also impact on which *type* of constellation is activated, or would it comprise the historical process taken as a *whole*?[94]

4.5 Contentious Data, Categorisation and Frontex' Risk Analysis

The securitisation frame as well as the law enforcement frame need to be complemented by an analysis of the role of the data that produce the risk analyses for border security. The way in which the EU border control agency Frontex organises information, collects and analyses data, has generated considerable research on the role of Frontex' risk analysis in EU-level border control.[95] Of interest is the way Frontex generates its data, how data are processed, how such data-based information impacts on its risk analysis, and what the implications would be for border security and securitisation processes. This section mainly focuses on the sources of the risk-conception by Frontex.

This has a wider relevance: the general policy debate on border enforcement seems to be largely data-based. The debate appears to be divided between two conflicting sides: those who argue that porous borders have most effectively and successfully been closed for illegal entry by means of law enforcement, and critics who claim that such efforts are futile—pointing at the continuation of bypassing, trafficking and illegal entry despite enforcement measures.[96] Both sides present evidence based on

---

93 Guzzini 2011, p. 338.

94 See for this also Guzzini 2011, p. 337.

95 See mainly Horii 2016; Paul 2017.

96 Alden 2017.

data and both make their points by referring to either targeted successes at enforced border closings or the sustained illegal entry notwithstanding such enforcement.

This involves the third universe that Didier Bigo distinguishes in his interviews with officials and border guards (as explained above), one of interoperable databases, data-specialists and technicians, mostly grouped in the EU agency for large-scale IT-systems (EU-LISA) or Frontex.[97] This area is somewhat disconnected from the frames of securitisation and law enforcement, since it represents a network of large-scale computer systems, permanent surveillance (dataveillance), massive data collection, biometrics and predictive software, collecting timelines and traces of individuals, or identifying groups through profiling and algorithms. Specialists here do not work from a traditional approach of guarding borders and border checks to stop migrants, as Bigo notes, but hold a perception of physical borders as being irrelevant or digitised, since borders are seen as dots of entry and exit. They justify their work as being preventive, in support of migrants by means of pre-control before departure or risk avoidance at dangerous routes in the "dynamics of passage and traces that are left".[98] They do not have to rely on the narratives of individual migrants but collect identifications and build profiles by focussing on high speed between distant bureaucracies of consulates and intelligence services, undertaking smart surveillance.

Frontex' risk analysis is not simply a recollection of data for operational border checks and surveillance activities but, as Satoko Horii notes, should be considered as "a particular form of knowledge with an important political effect."[99] Though Frontex itself is not involved in policy making and does not decide on EU policies, the agency's databased knowledge and technologies impact on governance policies made by the EU and Frontex Member States "to track and target migrants for interception in the 'pre-frontier'."[100] As such, Frontex' data and risk analyses have effects on policy making as well as presumed political effects, in addition to the allocation of financial resources and investments.

In fact, Frontex designs its risks analyses, as its 2018 Report confirms, "to provide an overview which will help make informed decisions on both common European investments and concerted actions to improve the management of external borders and uphold the internal security of the Union."[101] Risk analysis is key for all areas of Frontex' Joint Operations at any of the three border types (sea, land and air). Independently of the specifics of the operations, all Joint Operations are following the same process of being based on Frontex risk analysis documents. Under the supervision of the European Commission and Member States, Frontex has developed two main strands of risk analysis: one based on a categorisation of irregular migration and asylum, the other providing assessments of EU external borders, the latter with

[97] Bigo 2014, pp. 216–220.

[98] Bigo 2014, p. 217.

[99] Horii 2016, p. 242.

[100] Follis 2017, p. 1003.

[101] Frontex 2018, p. 11.

the aim to determine whether an EU Member State is legitimately able to reinstate the border checks at its internal border.[102]

Frontex provides comprehensive and systematic risk analyses. The data, such as those conveyed for the 2017 FRAN Quarterly Report (Q2) by the Frontex Risk Analysis Network (FRAN), are wide-ranging. Such data collection through FRAN involves Member State border-control authorities (for the Q2 Report a total of 31 states),[103] in cooperation with the EU Document-Fraud Risk Analysis Network (EDF-RAN). Qualitative analysis is added as well, on the basis of a wide array of primary data sources (interviews by intelligence officers with migrants), in addition to secondary sources such as narrative reports (by intelligence analysts, daily accounts by coast guard personnel, open source data), also involving information from Frontex Joint Operations. All data provided for such reports is analysed by the Warsaw Frontex Risk Analysis Unit (RAU) to offer an "overview of irregular migration at the EU's external borders, based on the irregular migration data exchanged."[104] Frontex explicitly recognises that data collection and reporting practices may be at some points be hampering (not only in third countries), due to the quality and speed of identification.[105]

Since 2009, such data are statistically analysed by the use of eight irregular migration indicators and one asylum indicator, aggregated at the level of event-data and disaggregated by border type.[106] As from 2014, the Member States monthly collect and upload quantitative information on these indicators so as to harmonise data exchange at EU level. Nevertheless, some issues require attention in regard of the more specific indicators involved under this overall framework. In regard of the law-enforcement indicators, for example, the Frontex' 2018 Risk Analysis points to the fact that the number of detections of illegal border-crossing and refusals of entry connect both to detecting migrants and to the actual movements of irregular migrants to the EU. In this way, Frontex clarifies, figures of more detections of illegal border-crossings might be due to an absolute increase in the movements of irregular migrants, or may be the result of more available resources to detect them. Improved capacities thus may in some cases produce an upsurge in reported detections, but then cover a decrease in the irregular migratory movements.[107]

A few observations need to be made about the way in which Frontex generates and processes data in its variegated risk analysis reports. First, at the start of each published Frontex risk analysis, for example Frontex 2017 FRANQ2, the agency refers to "the pursuit of factual exactness, truth and exhaustive analysis".[108] In view of the latter, it must be admitted that the large variety of sources, constant updates, as well as catching data on actors, dates, locations, and event-specific details is

[102] Horii 2016.

[103] Frontex 2017 (FRAN Q2), p. 4.

[104] Frontex 2017 (FRAN Q2), p. 3.

[105] Frontex 2017 (FRAN Q2), pp. 5 and 33.

[106] Frontex 2017 (FRAN Q2), p. 33.

[107] Frontex 2018, p. 13.

[108] Frontex 2017 (FRAN, Q2), p. 2.

certainly notable. Nonetheless, the accurateness of the collection of data requires some remarks. On a closer look at the specific event-based data, some Joint Reports of the Africa-Frontex Intelligence Community (Frontex-AFIC) include ACLED-data, of which the 2017 Frontex-AFIC report offers a representative example (in addition to its 2013 report). Such reports contain assessments of conflict (re)location and instability in the Sahel and the Horn of Africa, involving possible surges in migration and the spread of jihadi groups as Boko Haram in Nigeria and al-Qaeda in the Islamic Maghreb. However, in regard of disaggregated ACLED event-data, Christine Eck already warned that those interested in subnational analyses of conflict should be wary "because of uneven quality-control issues which can result in biased findings if left unchecked."[109]

Second, multiple transnational databases, developed and used by Frontex and other institutions, have become integral part of innovative technologies, predominantly *surveillance technologies*. These are used to control the external borders of the EU, involve equipment and systems for border control (radars and sensors), border checks (inspection devices) and numerous other means for border security. It has been argued that current technological innovations, such as technologies of vision, remote tracking, biometrics, or the use of drones for monitoring frontier zones, not only transcend the physical limits of territories but fundamentally alter the conception and nature of national borders, as remarked above.[110] Raffaella Del Sarto and Chiara Steindler phrase this as the "growing disaggregation of the classical functions of borders"[111] that defined territory, state authority, and nationality in the Westphalian state model. Third, against the above backgrounds, it may certainly be said that intelligence and gathering data is an ongoing process and in Frontex subject to constant reassessment. Yet Frontex and its partners basically appear to formulate their assessment of the situations on the basis of an inherited or embedded set of collective notions (in fact, the nexus migrants-security already existed before Frontex became operational), presumably by routine or by what has been called "institutional habitus".[112]

All in all, some caveats have been raised in relation to the generation and use by Frontex of data and risk analysis. Yet, data collection and information processing could become a means for further enhancing cooperation: shared data and analyses are useful for all actors involved, including for operational staff and coast guards working on irregular migration.

[109] Eck 2012, p. 126.

[110] Follis 2017; also Bigo 2014, pp. 216–220.

[111] Del Sarto and Steindler 2015, p. 369.

[112] Robinson 2017, p. 516.

4.6 Conclusions

Securitisation processes articulate and project conceptions of security that are routinized through discourses. Securitisation, when perceived as an analytical framework, has attracted much policy interest as well as a vast scholarship that has much been advanced by the strand of critical security studies. The basic concepts, assumptions, practices and implications involved in analyses of securitisation are rooted, as explained, in a broader empirical and political theory of security.

Process tracing provided a research strategy, a route for detecting the pathways of securitisation processes, by which this chapter focused on process-mechanisms and facilitating conditions, and how they work out to enable explanations when studying border security and boat migration. By taking the outcome of securitisation processes as its point of departure, the research was driven by a 'how is this possible' or effects-oriented central question, in order to explain which specific constellations were causally appropriate to converge in producing the *outcome* of the securitisation of Mediterranean borders and boat migration. It may be concluded that (de)securitisation processes have paradoxical effects: they enable the protection of the rights of migrants but also create new divisions through current robust external border operations, thus establishing ambiguities within both frameworks. This explanation may be relevant for recognising some upcoming tendencies in Frontex' coordination of the Member States to subsume SAR under border control operations, whereby the powers are increased to intercept irregular migrants attempting to reach the EU external borders.

The debate on the explanatory capacity of securitisation theory recently started, to which this article has contributed by focussing on causal explanations. It was demonstrated and validated under two frames that for the analysis of securitisation as a process, both social mechanisms and facilitating conditions are relevant as well as how they are connected. It was thereby reaffirmed and reiterated that securitisation theory needs to be strengthened in its overall capacity of *causal explanation* of social mechanisms, by which it can increase its interpretative relevance for the study of securitisation practices and processes. The aim of introducing *causal analysis* into the securitisation of boat migration and border control was precisely to reinforce the explanatory assets and 'status' of this theory by which it can lay out and interpret the dynamics of securitisation practices and processes. Such efforts are part of the further development of non-positivist and interpretative frameworks for causal explanation to which Stefano Guzzini has provided the major impetus.

The links between the cases studied under the two main frames and how they connect to the central causal mechanism of reification—and thereby to security theory as such, was not found in any inductive generalization of the cases. Rather, it was revealed how both cases, operation *Sophia* within the securitisation frame and the *Hirsi* Judgement within the law enforcement frame, *specify* the central mechanism of reification. This was realised by opening the black box of historical processes, and then analysing how empirical situations interact with key concepts and collective notions with which security actors operate. Of course, the same holds for scholars who do research on these processes: attentiveness is required of how existing categories, theories and collective repositories inform actual understandings. In brief, beyond any inductive-deductive schedules this study specified the working of the mechanism.

The effects of adopting the two frames demand a final remark on the research agendas advanced here. The frames of securitisation and law enforcement embody distinctions, oppositions, as well as overlaps. It may be confirmed by now that the strengths of both frames are not mutually exclusive but rather reinforcing each other. Each framework contributes to understanding and both have their specific limits.

What can be concluded at this point is that there is not a single process line of (de)securitisation that unfolds through different cases. It was rather demonstrated, first, that each constellation of facilitating conditions for securitisation is contextual, historically specific to the cases in certain episodes, and dependent on how the concrete actors involved interpret such conditions. Second, the rather different and autonomous (de)securitisation processes, studied under the two frames, interact and intersect within a concrete period of time and harvest a longer-term outcomes. Different pathways, as was demonstrated, produce converging outcomes, but the specific historical processes also prompt different securitising discourses and therefore require contextualised explanations. Meanwhile, the social mechanism of reification trips through the cases, in each case linked through process tracing to an improvement of the explanatory capacity of securitisation theory.

The social mechanism of reification triggers a (de)securitising constellation. By analysing these paths, this chapter has contributed to tracing what kind of analysis securitisation theory may produce and how this theory may have systematic impacts on explaining real-life issues and concerns. In the end, this is the politics of securitisation, in the sense of politics as practised through theory design.

References

Alden E (2017) Is Border Enforcement Effective? What We Know and What It Means. Journal on Migration and Human Security 5 (2): 481–490

Aradau C, Huysmans J, Neal A, Voelkner N (eds) (2015) Critical Security Methods: New Frameworks for Analysis. Routledge, London/New York

Balzacq T (2011a) Enquiries into Methods: A New Framework for Securitization Analysis, 31–53. In: Balzacq T (ed) Securitization Theory: How Security Problems Emerge and Dissolve. Routledge, London/New York

Balzacq T (ed) (2011b) Securitization Theory: How Security Problems Emerge and Dissolve. Routledge, London/New York

Balzacq T, Guzzini S (2015) What Kind of Theory – If Any – Is Securitization? International Relations 29 (1): 97–102

Balzacq T, Léonard S, Ruzicka J (2016) "Securitization" Revisited: Theory and Cases. International Relations 30 (4): 494–531

Bennett A (2015) Using Process Tracing to Improve Policy Making: The (Negative) Case of the 2003 Intervention in Iraq. Security Studies 24 (2): 228–238

Bevilacqua G (2017) Exploring the Ambiguity of Operation Sophia Between Military and Search and Rescue Activities, 165–189. In: Andreone G (ed) The Future of the Law of the Sea: Bridging Gaps Between National, Individual and Common Interests. Springer, Cham

Bigo D (2014) The (In)Securitization Practices of the Three Universes of EU Border Control: Military/Navy - Border Guards/Police - Database Analysts. Security Dialogue 45 (3): 209–225

Borelli S, Stanford B (2014) Troubled Waters in the *Mare Nostrum*: Interception and Push-backs of Migrants in the Mediterranean and the European Convention on Human Rights. Review of International Law and Politics 37(10): 29–69

Buzan B, Wæver O (2003) Regions and Powers. Cambridge University Press, Cambridge

Crawley H, Skleparis D (2018) Refugees, Migrants, Neither, Both: Categorical Fetishism and the Politics of Bounding in Europe's "Migration Crisis". Journal of Ethnic and Migration Studies 44 (1): 48–64

Del Sarto R, Steindler C (2015) Uncertainties at the European Union's Southern Borders: Actors, Policies, and Legal Frameworks. European Security 24 (3): 369–380

Eck K (2012) In Data we Trust? A Comparison of UCDP, GED and ACLED Conflict Events Datasets. Cooperation and Conflict 47 (1): 124–141

European Commission (2015) A European Agenda on Migration, COM(2015) 240, 13 May

European Commission (2016a) Progress Report: Fourth Report on the Progress Made in the Implementation of the EU-Turkey Statement, COM(2016) 792, 8 December

European Commission (2016b) Joint Way Forward on Migration Issues between Afghanistan and the EU, Brussels, Afghanistan Donor Conference, 4 October

European Commission (EPSC) (2017) Irregular Migration via the Central Mediterranean: From Emergency Responses to Systemic Solutions. European Political Strategy Centre, EPSC Strategic Notes 22, 2 February

European Council (2016) EU-Turkey Statement, Press Release 144/16, 18 March

Fargues P, Bonfanti S (2014) When the Best Option is a Leaky Boat: Why Migrants Risk Their Lives Crossing the Mediterranean and What Europe is Doing About It. Policy Brief (5). Migration Policy Centre, European University Institute, Florence

Figueiredo P (2011) Muros do Mediterrâneo: Notas Sobre a Construção de Barreiras nas Fronteiras de Ceuta e Melilla. Cadernos De Estudos Africanos (22): 153–175

Follis K (2017) Vision and Transterritory: The Borders of Europe. Science, Technology, & Human Values 42 (6): 1003–1030

Frontex (2017) (FRAN Q2) FRAN Quarterly, Quarter 2 (April-June 2017), Warsaw, Poland: Frontex Risk Analysis Unit (December 2017)

Frontex (2018) Risk Analysis for 2018, Warsaw, Poland: Frontex Risk Analysis Unit (February 2018)

Frontex-AFIC (2017) Africa-Frontex Intelligence Community Joint Report 2016, Warsaw, Poland: Frontex Risk Analysis Unit (April 2017)

Ghezelbash D, Moreno-Lax V, Klein N, Opeskin B (2018) Securitization of Search and Rescue at Sea: The Response to Boat Migration in the Mediterranean and Offshore Australia. International and Comparative Law Quarterly: 1–37 (first access, online ahead of print, 16 January 2018, https://doi.org/10.1017/s0020589317000562)

Giuffré M (2012) Watered-Down Rights on the High Seas: Hirsi Jamaa and Others v. Italy. International and Comparative Law Quarterly 61 (3): 728–750

George A, Bennett A (2005) Case Studies and Theory Development in the Social Sciences. MIT Press, Cambridge, MA/London

Guzzini S (2011) Securitization as a Causal Mechanism. Security Dialogue 42 (4–5): 329–341

Guzzini S (2012) The Return of Geopolitics in Europe? Social Mechanisms and Foreign Policy Identity Crises. Cambridge University Press, Cambridge

Guzzini S (2017a) Power and Cause. Journal of International Relations and Development 20 (4): 737–759

Guzzini S (2017b) Militarizing Politics, Essentializing Identities: Interpretivist Process Tracing and the Power of Geopolitics. Cooperation and Conflict 52 (3): 423–445

Hedström P, Swedberg R (1998) Social Mechanisms: An Introductory Essay, 1–31. In: Hedström P, Swedberg R (eds) Social Mechanisms: An Analytical Approach to Social Theory. Cambridge University Press, Cambridge

Hedström P, Ylikoski P (2010) Causal Mechanisms in the Social Sciences. Annual Review of Sociology 36 (1): 49–67
Horii S (2016) The Effect of Frontex's Risk Analysis on the European Border Controls. European Politics and Society 17 (2): 242–258
IOM (2016) Mixed Migration: Flows in the Mediterranean and Beyond: Compilation of Available Data and Information 2015. International Organization for Migration (IOM), Geneva
IOM (2017) Mixed Migration Flows in the Mediterranean and Beyond: Compilation of Available Data and Information 2016. International Organization for Migration (IOM), Geneva
Klein Goldewijk, B (2008) Why Human? The Interlinkages of Security, Rights and Development. Security and Human Rights 19 (1): 24–36
Klein Goldewijk B, de Gaay Fortman B (1999) Where Needs Meet Rights: Economic, Social and Cultural Rights in a New Perspective. WCC Publications, Geneva
Klein Goldewijk B, Contreras Baspineiro A, Carbonari P (eds) (2002) Dignity and Human Rights: The Implementation of Economic, Social and Cultural Rights. Intersentia/Transnational Publishers/TMC Asser Press, Antwerp/Oxford/New York/Zurich/The Hague
Little A, Vaughan-Williams N (2017) Stopping Boats, Saving Lives, Securing Subjects: Humanitarian Borders in Europe and Australia. European Journal of International Relations 23 (3): 533–556
Mahoney J (2015) Process Tracing and Historical Explanation. Security Studies 24 (2): 200–218
Moreno-Lax V (2011) Seeking Asylum in the Mediterranean: Against a Fragmentary Reading of EU Member States' Obligations Accruing at Sea. International Journal of Refugee Law 23 (2): 174–220
Moreno-Lax V (2018) The EU Humanitarian Border and the Securitization of Human Rights: The 'Rescue-through-Interdiction/Rescue-without-Protection' Paradigm. Journal of Common Market Studies 56 (1): 119–140
Oliveira Carvalho G (2017) The Causal Power of Securitisation: An Inquiry into the Explanatory Status of Securitisation Theory Illustrated by the Case of Somali Piracy. Review of International Studies: 1–22 (first access, online ahead of print, 29 November 2017, https://doi.org/10.1017/s0260210517000559)
Paul R (2017) Harmonisation by Risk Analysis? Frontex and the Risk-Based Governance of European Border Control. Journal of European Integration 39 (6): 689–706
Roberts P (2018) The Militarisation of Migration: From Triton to Sofia: Assessing the Credibility of the EU's Naval Interventions Against Migrant Smuggling in the Mediterranean, 217–233. In: Reitano T, Bird Ruiz-Benitez de Lugo L, Jesperson S (eds) Militarised Responses to Transnational Organised Crime: The War on Crime. Palgrave Macmillan, Cham
Robinson C (2017) Tracing and Explaining Securitization: Social Mechanisms, Process Tracing and the Securitization of Irregular Migration. Security Dialogue 48 (6): 505–523
Santos Vara J, Sánchez-Tabernero S (2016) In Deep Water: Towards a Greater Commitment for Human Rights in Sea Operations Coordinated by Frontex? European Journal of Migration & Law 18 (1): 65–87
Tannenwald N (2005) Stigmatizing the Bomb: Origins of the Nuclear Taboo. International Security 29 (4): 5–49
Tannenwald N (2007) The Nuclear Taboo: The United States and the Non-Use of Nuclear Weapons since 1945. Cambridge University Press, Cambridge
Tannenwald N (2015) Process Tracing and Security Studies. Security Studies 24 (2): 219–227
Trevisanut S (2014) Is There a Right to be Rescued at Sea? A Constructive View. Questions of International Law 2: 3–15
Trevisanut S, Ippolito F (2016) Migration in the Mediterranean: Mechanisms of International Cooperation. Cambridge University Press, Cambridge
Waever O (2011) Politics, Security, Theory. Security Dialogue 42 (4–5): 465–480

Part II
Command and Control for Border Security Applications

Chapter 5
Dynamic Resource and Task Management

M. Klinik, J.M. Jansen and F. Bolderheij

Contents

Abstract Carrying out maritime missions comprises many phases from preparation to execution. In the long term, we would like to have an integrated toolchain that supports the crew at every phase. In this chapter, we study concepts for resource and task management in the execution phase. When the tasks to be executed have been identified, the question arises who should be assigned to them. This is both a

M. Klinik
Radboud University, Nijmegen, The Netherlands
e-mail: m.klinik@cs.ru.nl

J.M. Jansen (✉) · F. Bolderheij
Netherlands Defence Academy, Den Helder, The Netherlands
e-mail: jm.jansen.04@mindef.nl

F. Bolderheij
e-mail: f.bolderheij@mindef.nl

H. Monsuur et al. (eds.), *NL ARMS Netherlands Annual Review of Military Studies 2018*, NL ARMS, https://doi.org/10.1007/978-94-6265-246-0_5

scheduling and an assignment problem. We narrow down what kind of problem we have at hand to get an understanding what a first step towards an integrated command and control system could look like. This also enables us to classify our problem with the existing literature on planning and scheduling. We develop a domain model for tasks and resources, their connection via capabilities, together with assessment functions to compare assignments. We study what kind of information would be needed to give useful scheduling advice.

Keywords command and control · mission management · online task scheduling · online resource assignment · workflow modelling

5.1 Introduction

In previous work[1] we developed prototype Command and Control applications for reasoning about mission goals and tasks to achieve the goals. These applications dealt with assignments of resources to tasks. We studied examples from the maritime domain, that is navy ships with their tasks and resources. The concepts of tasks and resources were defined with the maritime domain in mind, which led to definitions that were too domain specific. In this chapter we want to generalize some of these concepts, and then specialize them back to the maritime domain. Our concepts should be general enough to be specialized to a variety of different scenarios, and to different levels of granularity inside one scenario.

The core goal of this chapter is the concept of a system that provides interactive decision support for on-line scheduling for command and control on board of navy ships. With this in mind, we define the concepts of tasks and resources, together with a way for tasks to specify their resource requirements. We describe how resources specify which tasks they can execute. We define a quality metric to determine which resources are most suitable for executing a task. Resources can be subject to degradation, which allows modelling broken machines and tired people.

These definitions serve as basis for a literature study to identify techniques that are useful to us. We demonstrate how the system would handle an example scenario.

The long term vision of this work is a tool for command and control that takes workflows from a planning phase as input, and finds suitable assignments of resources to tasks so that they can be performed efficiently. A supervisor monitors execution of tasks and stays in contact with the crew to solve problems when they occur. The supervisor has overview over the current state of affairs, running tasks, busy resources, and remaining capacities. Crew members carry some kind of smart device with an app that displays all tasks they are currently assigned to, in the form of a checklist. They can communicate with the supervisor by marking tasks as *in progress*, *paused*, *done*, or maybe *impossible to progress*. Tasks that require more complex

[1] Chapter 6 of this volume, Kool 2017.

interactions can have an extended user interface that allows, for example, entering data. The app can notify crew members when they are assigned to high priority tasks.

5.2 A Model for Tasks and Resources

The main goal of this work is the development of a model for tasks and resources that is abstract enough to be applicable to a variety of situations and granularities.

In this chapter we talk about three kinds of roles, the modeller, the planner, and the supervisor. The modeller identifies tasks, resources, and capabilities in the domain of discourse and formalizes them in our system. Such a formalization is called a *model*. The planner uses the model to solve the problems of a particular scenario. Planning involves picking the right tasks to achieve a goal and assigning the right resources to do so efficiently. Once planning is done and execution of a plan starts, the supervisor monitors progress of the plan and makes adjustments to it as necessary.

These three roles are not necessarily performed by different people, nor do they happen at distinct phases. Modelling and planning can go hand in hand, as can planning and supervision.

5.2.1 *Running Example: Making Pizza*

We illustrate the design decisions of this chapter using a recurring example. The example is simple, but shows many of the issues we want to be able to handle. The example serves to check that our system is expressive enough to model a common scenario, to discuss granularities where it makes sense to stop modelling, and to get an idea about what conclusions can be drawn from some given information. The example will be developed further in subsequent sections, and discussed in more detail in Sect. 5.5.

Imagine a family planning their dinner. The family consists of four people, Mom, Dad, Alice and Bob. They decide that they want to make pizza. For the sake of our discussion, making pizza consists of two tasks, preparing the dough and finishing the pizza. Our family has enough ingredients at home to prepare the dough, but for the toppings someone needs to shop groceries. The family owns a car and a bike, but only Mom and Dad have a driver's license.

5.2.2 *Tasks and Resources*

At the heart of our system lies the assignment of resources to tasks. A *task* is a unit of work that we want to be able to plan and manage. A *resource* is a scarce, uniquely identifiable or quantifiable object that a task must exclusively claim in order to be executed.

The important aspect here is that resources must be able to be claimed exclusively. One goal of our system is reasoning about resource conflicts, and conflicts can not occur when something can be infinitely shared. For example people, hammers, matchsticks, fuel, and storage space can be resources in our model, but time can not.

Georgievski and Aiello[2] argue that time is a consumable resource. We argue that time cannot be regarded as a resource at all, because time lacks the exclusivity that is essential for something to be considered a resource. Consider time and fuel. If we have five liters of fuel and two tasks that require four liters each, then these two tasks can neither be executed in sequence nor in parallel. If we have a deadline five minutes from now then we can execute as many four-minute tasks as we want in parallel, provided that all other resource requirements are met. Furthermore, time cannot be saved up. If we do not use some fuel now, we still have it later. Time is gone once it has passed, no matter whether we execute a task in it.

We do not differentiate between *performers*, which are the resources that actually perform tasks, and passive resources like tools and materials.

5.2.3 Capabilities and Assignments

When a modeller wants to specify that a task needs some resource, he usually does not specify a particular individual, but rather describes it in abstract terms. For example, the modeller might specify that making pizza requires a cook, but he would not immediately specify that it specifically requires Bob. Furthermore, Bob might have many more skills besides making pizza. To express this indirect coupling between tasks and resources, we introduce the concept of *capabilities*. Capabilities are descriptions of the roles of the resources that a task requires. In turn, resources specify all the roles they are capable of fulfilling. In case modellers want to specify a particular resource, they can do so by using a capability that only one resource has.

Capabilities also always specify a capacity. This way modellers can specify that a task needs a certain quantity of some resource, for example five liters of fuel. There is a difference between one two-capacity capability and two one-capacity capabilities. For example, if a task needs two mechanics, the modeller has to specify two one-capacity capabilities. If the modeller specifies one mechanic with capacity two, then this requirement can never be met, because people have a capacity of one for their capabilities.

During planning, once the desired tasks have been chosen, a scheduler can consider capabilities and some optimization criterion to find an optimal assignment of particular resources to the tasks. Resources that are assigned to a task are said to be *claimed* by the task.

[2] Georgievski and Aiello 2015.

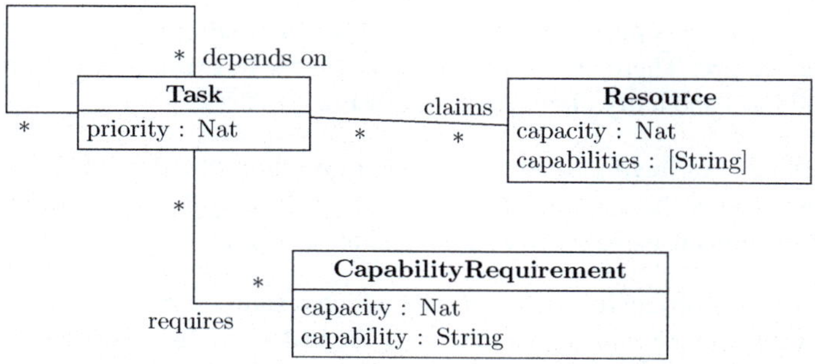

Fig. 5.1 UML class diagram for Tasks, Resources, and Capabilities [*Source* M. Klinik, J.M. Jansen, F. Bolderheij]

Figure 5.1 shows a UML class diagram for tasks, resources, and capabilities, and the relations between them. A task can require many capabilities, a resource can have many capabilities, and a task can claim many resources. A resource can be claimed by many tasks if its capacity permits it.

Another aspect we want to be able to capture is partial dependencies between tasks. Sometimes tasks depend on other tasks, which constrains the order in which they can be executed. Dependencies express that a prerequisite task has to be completed before another one can be started. The possibility to model such dependencies is represented in Fig. 5.1 by the relation from Task to Task. One task can depend on many other tasks, and one task can be prerequisite for many other tasks.

5.3 Capability Functions

If there are multiple candidate resources that can be assigned to a task, a decision must be made which resource to pick. In order to do this, we would like to have a quality measure that estimates how good a resource will perform a task.

We express quality as a percentage.

Quality does not only encode the skill level of a resource, but can be used to encode all kinds of preferences. Our system uses *capability functions* to determine the quality with which a resource can execute a given task. Whether degradation should be factored directly into quality or requires independent handling requires further investigation.

The result of a capability function is a percentage. To understand what the input should be, consider the following examples.

Example 5.3.1 On board of a marine ship are two radars. The task is to track a helicopter that has already been detected. Tracking means having high-frequency, high-accuracy updates of the helicopter's position.

Example 5.3.2 A gas pipe is on fire in room A1 on board of a ship. The task is to extinguish the fire. There are two methods available to extinguish the fire: a water mist installation and a dry chemical extinguisher.

Example 5.3.3 For having dinner, someone must shop groceries. On the shopping list is, among other things, some fresh fish. The fishmonger on the weekend market is five kilometers away. There are a bike and a car available.

In order to determine, for each scenario, which resources are best suited to execute the task, we must take into account not only the tasks and the resources, but also the helicopter, the fire, and the shopping list.

The quality of a radar track depends on the type of the target to be tracked, it's distance to the ship, and the weather. The quality of extinguishing a fire depends on the type of the fire and who is closest to the location of the fire. The quality of a person and a vehicle to do shopping depends on the items on the shopping list.

In each case, the signature of the capability function must be different, in both the number of arguments and their type. This makes it hard to construct a generic scheduler that, without domain knowledge, can assess the quality of assignments in different scenarios.

In order to have uniform capability functions, we introduce two new concepts, targets and systems. A *target* is the reason why a task must be executed. The targets in our examples are the contact of type helicopter, with it's position and speed, the fire with its location and type, and the shopping list with its contents. Other examples for targets are customer complaints, software bugs, or expected threats.

A *system* is a combination of resources which jointly provide a capability. Systems are needed when the quality of a resource can not be determined in isolation. Systems have two attributes: the capability they provide and a list of capabilities they require to do so. An assignment of concrete resources to the required capabilities of a system is called a *system assignment*. Single resources can act as systems, in cases where the quality of a single resource can be judged in isolation.

In Example 5.3.3, it is the combination of driver and vehicle whose suitability for shopping must be judged, not driver and vehicle in isolation. Mom with the car is well suited, while both Bob or Mom with the bike are less suited, and Bob with the car is not suited at all, because Bob doesn't have a driver's license.

In Example 5.3.2 we have two ways of achieving the same goal. The fire can be extinguished by the water mist installation, or by a person with a fire extinguisher. This can be modelled as a task that requires a single capability *fire brigade*, and two systems that provide this capability. The first system requires a capability *water mist*, while the second system requires two capabilities *fire fighter* and *fire extinguisher*.

Many capability functions also require access to the *environment*, a database with the current operational picture. The environment contains things like the weather conditions and the topology of the surrounding area.

All these considerations suggest the following signature for capability functions.

Definition 5.3.4 (*Capability function*) The quality of a system for a task depends on the system assignment, the task, the capability the system provides for the task, the task's target, and the environment. The expected quality is given as a percentage.

capability **:** (SystemAssignment, Task, Capability, Target, Environment) −> Percentage

5.3.1 Extensibility of the Scheduler

As modellers model scenarios by creating tasks, resources, targets, and systems, they also have to create capability functions. To provide the algorithmic expressiveness some capability functions need, they are best specified in a programming language. This requires modellers to be at least somewhat skilled in programming.

There are three common ways to let users specify input with algorithmic content. First we could provide a small domain specific language, specifically tailored for specifying capability functions. Second, we could make the system extensible by providing an interface to a scripting language like Python or Lua. Third, we could let modellers use the same language the system itself is implemented in.

The first option requires substantial implementation effort to provide features of a general purpose programming language, and even more if modellers want access to external libraries. The second option still requires some implementation effort to make the interface of the scheduler available to the scripting language. For a first prototype implementation, the third option is the best way, as it makes a general purpose programming language available to modellers at very low implementation overhead, as all interfaces and data structures can readily be accessed.

5.4 Human in the Loop

When a resource becomes degraded during execution of a plan and some tasks can no longer be finished, a change in plan is required. Dealing with unexpected situations often requires flexibility, creativity and improvisation, all abilities where humans perform better than computers. On the other hand, in order to make informed decisions, humans need insight into the current state of affairs. Information needs to be distributed quickly and stored accurately, and big numbers of possibilities must be assessed in a short time, all jobs where computers outperform humans.

We fall into line with Johnson[3] and Bradshaw et al.[4] who argue that for effective human-robot collaboration, full autonomy of the team members is not desirable: "Resilience in human-machine systems benefits from a teamwork infrastructure designed to exploit interdependence". He defines interdependence as the complementary relations that participants in a joint activity rely on in order to remedy their lacking capabilities.

---

[3] Johnson 2014.

[4] Bradshaw et al. 2013.

At the core of Johnson's model for human-machine collaboration lies the concept of OPD, which stands for observability, predictability, and directability. Observability means making relevant aspects of one's own status, knowledge and environment available to others. Predictability means that others can rely on their prediction about one's own behavior when planning their actions. Directability means the ability to influence the behavior of others, and being influenced by others.

For our application, observability means that the ship needs an up-to-date picture of the degradation of systems and people on board. The other way around, the ship's internal picture should be accessible to the supervisor. Predictability means that in similar situations, the system should come up with similar plans, and small changes in the environment should lead to small changes in a plan. Directability means that the supervisor can influence planning and always override any decision the system makes. For example the supervisor should be able to make plans that are nonsensical to the system, or start tasks whose resource requirements are not fully met.

We propose two categories of actions which allow supervisors to intervene in the execution of a plan. The first category is called *plan B* and includes decisions that can be made before a plan is executed. The second category is called *dynamic planning* and includes actions to modify a plan while it is being executed.

5.4.1 Plan B

A plan B is an alternative plan to achieve the same goal, using different tasks and resources. In the extreme case, plan B uses completely different tasks and resources. Realistically, there is some overlap between plans A and B.

If plans A and B overlap at some resource, and this resource becomes degraded, then B also can no longer be executed. Consequently, for an alternative plan to be useful, an estimation of *expected degradation* is required. Plans should not overlap in resources that are likely to degrade. Our system should give insight into resource overlap.

The advantage of alternative plans is that they can be activated quickly. Coming up with them however requires additional planning beforehand.

5.4.2 Dynamic Planning

Dynamic planning allows supervisors to change plans while they are being executed. The system should give supervisors the freedom they need to improvise.

There are two reasons why a dynamic change in plan becomes necessary. First, a resource required for execution of a running task becomes degraded. Second, a new goal is identified, and new tasks must be executed to achieve it.

When a running task becomes disabled because one of its assigned resources degrades, the supervisor has the following options.

- Keep the task running, but change its resource assignment. This is useful for tasks that allow the new resources to pick up the work where the degraded resources left it.
- Cancel the current task, start new tasks and assign different resources to them. Cancelling is useful for tasks that can not be handed over to other resources.
- Pause parts of plan A, start new tasks with new resources to repair the degradation, then continue with plan A.

Both pausing and cancelling a task frees all its assigned resources.

When additional tasks must be started because new goals have been identified, supervisors need similar actions. Goals have priorities, and tasks have priorities derived from them. A *resource conflict* exists if a set of new tasks cannot be executed because there are not enough resources available. Supervisors must find ways to resolve such conflicts, and our system must give them the tools to do so. This includes querying the current status to find solutions, and modifying the current status to implement them. For example, given a new task, the system displays all tasks with lower priority such that when they are paused, their freed resources allow the new task to be executed. The supervisor can then pick some running tasks and either cancel or pause them to free their resources.

5.5 Making Pizza

In this section we look at a situation in the daily life of a four-person family. They are sitting at the breakfast table on a Saturday morning, planning their dinner. We walk through the planning process while identifying relevant tasks and resources. The goal of this study is to make sure that our system is expressive enough to describe the scenario. Furthermore, we discuss the granularities where it makes sense to stop modelling.

The family consists of four people, Mom, Dad, Alice and Bob. The family decides that they want to have pizza for dinner today. This suggests that there is a task *make pizza*.

5.5.1 Making Pizza

Whenever we identify a new task, we must consider two questions. First, does it make sense to split the task into subtasks? Second, which resources are required to execute the task?

Making pizza consists of many subtasks, as is evident by reading any pizza recipe, and we could go even further and specify subtasks down to the level of individual hand movements. This is of course too fine grained, and even the individual steps in the recipe are too detailed for the purpose of planning dinner. The goal of planning is to provide actors with the necessary instructions to perform their tasks independently.

Being too specific is not useful, and so is being too general. Instead of having a task *make pizza*, it is conceivable to have a generic task *cook meal* that is parameterized by a recipe. The recipe would then determine which subtasks there are and which ingredients and appliances are required to execute the task. At this point, we might as well take the recipe itself as the task, which would make the *cook meal* task useless.

For our scenario we assume that the family members are sufficiently skilled in cooking so that the instruction *make pizza* is enough for them to know what to do. There is however one subtask we do want to make explicit. Preparing the dough is a subtask that can reasonably be performed independently and even by a different person.

For the sake of discussion, let's say that there are enough ingredients for the dough, but not for the topping. The family decides that one person can start making the dough, while another person shops for the remaining ingredients. After both these tasks are completed, the pizza can be finished. This suggests three tasks in total: *make dough*, *shop groceries*, and *finish pizza*. The task *finish pizza* depends on both *make dough* and *shop groceries*.

These three tasks have the right granularity that allows performers to execute them without further instructions.

5.5.2 Required Resources

The next step in the modelling phase is to identify for each task what resources it needs. The goal is to be reasonably realistic and specify only those resources that are relevant for identifying conflicts.

All three tasks need a person to execute them, and we have to specify the required capabilities. There are many possibilities of how precise we want this specification to be. For example, we could be very precise and model that for making dough, we need someone with the capability *make dough*. We could also model that we need a *cook*, or even that we just need a *person*. In this example, we go with the capability *cook* for both tasks *make dough* and *finish pizza*. For the task *shop groceries* we say that we need a *shopper*.

When considering the required materials and tools for the task *make dough*, we again have to think about the right precision. Do we explicitly model every required kitchen appliance, including the oven and individual spoons, or do we just specify that a functional kitchen is needed? Do we specify all the ingredients in the recipe? The answer is again guided by the conflicts we want the system to be able to detect. On the one hand, more information means the system can draw more conclusions. On the other hand, the more precisely we specify the resource requirements of a task, the more work it is to model the resources themselves, and to be useful this information must be kept in sync with the real world.

Table 5.1 Tasks [*Source* M. Klinik, J.M. Jansen, F. Bolderheij]

Name	Required capabilities
Make dough	Cook, kitchen
Shop groceries	Shopper, vehicle
Finish pizza	Cook, kitchen

Table 5.2 Resources [*Source* M. Klinik, J.M. Jansen, F. Bolderheij]

Name	Capabilities
Mom	Cook, shopper
Dad	Cook
Alice	Cook, shopper
Bob	Shopper
Bike	Vehicle
Car	Vehicle
Kitchen	Kitchen

For our scenario, we do not specify the ingredients, but we specify that a functional kitchen is required. We do the same for the task *finish pizza*, and specify that it needs a cook and a kitchen.

At this point, the modeller has to be careful. We just specified that two tasks need the same resource, a kitchen, and if we assume that only one kitchen exists, our system does not allow these tasks to be executed in parallel. In this particular case that is not a problem, because the second task depends on the first one anyway, but there might be situations where we want two tasks in parallel in the same kitchen. Sometimes two people can work in one kitchen on different tasks, so the kitchen is not exclusively claimed by either. In this sense, the kitchen does not qualify as a resource according to our definition. To capture the situation in our system, the modeller could split the kitchen into a number of shares, and specify that the cooking subtasks require one share each.

The task *shop groceries*, in addition to a shopper, also requires a vehicle. We assume that the family has two vehicles, a bike and a car. When assigning resources to this task, not all combinations of shoppers and vehicles make sense, because only Mom and Dad have a driver's license. Modellers can exclude impossible combinations of resources with capability functions, which are discussed in Sect. 5.3.

With the information gathered so far, the model is precise enough for the purpose of this example. Tables 5.1 and 5.2 summarize the identified tasks and resources. We could have been more precise, and also modelled that *shop groceries* requires money, or that *finish pizza* requires ingredients for the topping. Again, this comes down to the detail of the instructions the system should give to the people involved.

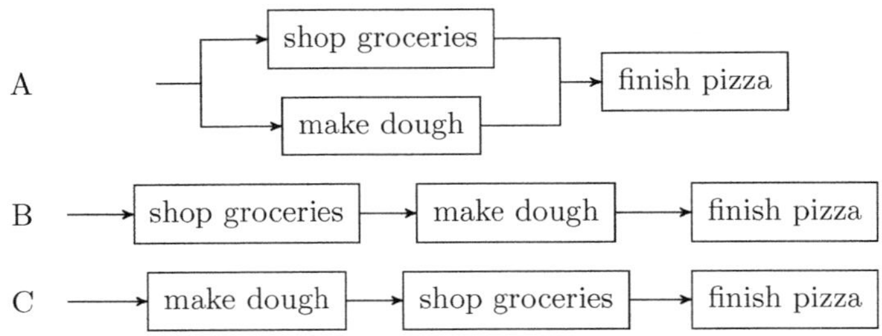

Fig. 5.2 Three ways of making pizza [*Source* M. Klinik, J.M. Jansen, F. Bolderheij]

5.5.3 Scheduling

With the information gathered about the scenario so far, it is possible to construct schedules. A *schedule* consists of two parts. First, a *workflow*, which is a complete specification of the order in which to execute tasks. Second, an *assignment* of resources to the tasks in the workflow.

The three tasks of our example and their dependencies permit three possible workflows. They are shown in Fig. 5.2. Workflow A specifies that *shop groceries* and *make dough* must be executed in parallel. Parallel execution for us means that they are to be started at the same time and that they cannot share any resources. Workflows B and C specify that all three tasks have to be executed in sequence. In both cases, the same person can be assigned to all of them. With our resources and the requirements for the tasks, there are 42 possible assignments for workflow A, and 54 for each of B and C, which makes a total of 150 ways of making pizza.

Without additional information for assessing schedules, a scheduler can do little more than list all possibilities. A scheduler could optimize for least total resource usage, which means it tries to reuse resources as much as possible, for example by assigning the same person to all three tasks in B and C. We, however, would like to have an objective function that tells which schedules are the best, according to some optimization criteria.

When estimations of the durations of tasks are available, these criteria can be ones that have been studied extensively in scheduling literature, like maximum completion time or sum of completion times.

For now, we want to focus on the quality with which a resource can execute a task, rather than durations. In this example we choose workflow A, with Mom and the car as best suited for shopping, while Dad prepares the dough and finishes the pizza, because he has the most experience with these tasks.

5.5.4 *Execution*

With responsibilities settled, the family begins execution of the tasks. Mom drives with the car to the supermarket, while Dad starts making the dough.

On the way to the supermarket, the car breaks down. In our system, this is modelled by marking both Mom and the car as degraded. Now that the goal of having pizza for dinner can no longer be reached, alternative solutions must be found.

The task *shop groceries* must be stopped, as it does not make sense to see it as a task that can be taken over by other resources. This frees the resources Mom and car, but as they are degraded, they will not be considered when looking for alternatives. When starting a new instance of *shop groceries*, the system offers two possible assignments: Alice with the bike, or Bob with the bike. However, we still have Mom waiting in the broken car, and getting her home has higher priority than making pizza. Dad knows how to get the car running again, because he has repaired the same problem before. The solution to the problem looks like this: Dad grabs his tools and takes the bus to repair the car. Alice takes his place in the kitchen and continues preparing the dough where Dad left off. Bob takes his bike and shops groceries.

In order to implement this solution in our system, the system must grant a supervisor the following possibilities.

1. The resources Mom and car must be marked as degraded.
2. The task *shop groceries* must be cancelled.
3. A new task *repair car* must be created. This task has not been conceived in the planning phase, so the supervisor must have the ability to create new tasks on the fly.
4. The task *make dough* must be paused, so that Dad becomes free for the repair task.
5. Alice is assigned to *make dough*, and the task can be resumed.
6. A new instance of *shop groceries* is started, with Bob and the bike as resources.

The supervisor must perform steps 1 to 3 by hand, while the system offers advice for steps 4 to 6. In particular, the system should figure out that when the high-priority task *repair car* pops up, there still is a solution to make pizza.

5.6 Related Work

Kuhn[5] showed that the assignment problem can be solved in polynomial time with the Hungarian method. The assignment problem asks to distribute n people to n jobs, where each person is differently qualified for each job, such that the total quality is maximized. Our assignment problem is a bit different however, because in general

[5] Kuhn 1955.

we require multiple resources per task, and when tasks run in sequence the same resources can be assigned to different tasks.

The literature on machine scheduling has results about machines that can process different kinds of jobs, which are called *multi-purpose machines*. It appears that our concept of resources can be seen as multi-purpose machines. Scheduling with multi-purpose machines and arbitrary processing times is NP-hard.[6]

Task that require multiple resources seem similar to what is known as *multiprocessor tasks* in the scheduling literature. Scheduling tasks that require two dedicated processors is already strongly NP-complete.[7]

Seeing that we have a combination of the assignment problem with multi-purpose machines and multiprocessor tasks, it appears that we have to resort to heuristic methods to find solutions. A promising method has been described by Mencía et al.,[8] using genetic algorithms to find schedules for tasks with precedence and skilled operators.

5.7 Future Work

The two most important next steps are further literature study and a minimal viable prototype implementation. We already know that finding exact solutions to our scheduling problem is infeasible, so we have to see what kind of techniques exist for heuristically finding okay solutions. After hopefully finding such a technique, and most probably adapting it, we have to make an implementation which allows us to run example scenarios. This lets us verify that we are on the right track, that the data model covers the relevant aspects of our domain, and that the answers we get are interesting and have the potential to become useful.

A user-friendly interface is not a goal for the prototype. In subsequent work it would be interesting to study how the differences between qualitatively similar solutions can be highlighted to the user. This is especially interesting when the choice of resources doesn't matter, for example when permutations of a set of resources all lead to solutions with identical quality. Furthermore we would like to find out how to present the consequences of choosing a particular solution for the remaining tasks.

5.8 Conclusion

In this chapter we study the problem of resource allocation in command and control scenarios. We narrow down the kind of problem we want to solve to get an understanding of how a first step towards an integrated command and control system

[6] Brucker et al. 1997.

[7] Kubale 1987.

[8] Mencía et al. 2015.

could look like. We identify what kind of information such a system needs in order to provide useful answers.

The central components in our system are *tasks* and *resources*, and their connection via *capabilities*. Tasks require capabilities while resources provide capabilities. An abstraction we call *systems* can be used to express that a capability can only be provided jointly by several resources. Every system has a *capability function* that indicates the level of quality with which a given set of resources provides the system's capability.

Given a scenario with tasks, resources and systems, we want to solve a combination of an assignment and a scheduling problem. We want to find an ordering of the tasks together with an assignment of resources to the tasks such that the overall quality is as high as possible.

One goal of identifying the problem we want to solve is comparison with the scheduling literature. It turns out that the complexity of our problem makes exact optimization impossible. The best we can hope for is to find some form of heuristic that gives us a feasible solution if one exists and points out conflicts if no solution exists. This is acceptable, because in a realistic scenario, quickly finding some okay solution that gets the job done is more important than eventually finding the optimal solution.

Acknowledgements We would like to thank the Manning and Automation Team at TNO, Rinus Plasmeijer, Bas van der Eng, and Terry Stroup for many hours of fruitful discussion. This research is funded by the Royal Netherlands Navy and TNO.

References

Bradshaw JM, Hoffman R, Woods DD, Johnson M (2013) The seven deadly myths of "autonomous systems". IEEE Intelligent Systems, 28(3): 54–61

Brucker P, Jurisch B, Krämer A (1997) Complexity of scheduling problems with multi-purpose machines. Annals of Operations Research, 70(0): 57–73, 1997. ISSN 1572-9338

Georgievski I, Aiello M (2015) HTN planning: Overview, comparison, and beyond. Artif. Intell, 222: 124–156

Johnson M (2014) Coactive Design: Designing Support for Interdependence in Human-Robot Teamwork. PhD thesis, Technische Universiteit Delft

Kool AA (2017) Integrated mission management voor C2-ondersteuning. Bachelor's thesis, Netherlands Defence Academy

Kubale M (1987) The complexity of scheduling independent two-processor tasks on dedicated processors. Information Processing Letters, 24(3): 141–147

Kuhn HW (1955) The Hungarian method for the assignment problem. Naval Res. Logist. Quart., 2: 83–97

Mencía R, Sierra MR, Mencía C, Varela R (2015) Schedule generation schemes and genetic algorithm for the scheduling, problem with skilled operators and arbitrary precedence relations. ICAPS, pages 165–173, AAAI Press

Chapter 6
A Mission-Driven C2 Framework for Enabling Heterogeneous Collaboration

F. Bolderheij, J.M. Jansen, A.A. Kool and J. Stutterheim

Contents

F. Bolderheij (✉) · J.M. Jansen
Netherlands Defence Academy, Den Helder, The Netherlands
e-mail: f.bolderheij@mindef.nl

J.M. Jansen
e-mail: jm.jansen.04@mindef.nl

A.A. Kool
Royal Netherlands Navy, Den Helder, The Netherlands
e-mail: aa.kool.02@mindef.nl

J. Stutterheim
Standard Chartered Bank, Singapore, Singapore
e-mail: jurrien.stutterheim@sc.com

H. Monsuur et al. (eds.), *NL ARMS Netherlands Annual Review of Military Studies 2018*, NL ARMS, https://doi.org/10.1007/978-94-6265-246-0_6

Abstract The deployment of naval vessels requires much specialised knowledge. Firstly, about the mission: what goals have to be reached (the command-aim), and what has to be done to achieve this aim? Secondly, about the situation: how can sufficient information about the situation be gathered to determine whether the planned tasks can still be executed successfully? Thirdly, about the available systems and operators: what are their capabilities and capacities, and how can these be utilised to their full extent? This knowledge is also required to determine the consequences of system failure or the non-availability of human resources. This chapter models these categories, constructs relationships between them and uses them to answer the aforementioned questions. This is done in two phases. First, a formal model is described that translates the command aim into operational tasks, determines which resources are the most suitable to execute these tasks, and determines which alternative resources are available. The model can also be used to reason about the viability of the command-aim, should certain resources become unavailable. Second, the viability of this model is investigated by implementing an executable prototype using highly portable declarative programming techniques. The model and the implementation can be used to experiment with how ship design decisions can have operational consequences on the systems and the command aim, both at design time and during operational use. To determine whether they are generally applicable, it was tested in a realistic scenario involving a potential terrorist threat on a drilling rig in the North Sea and in a damage control operation.

Keywords Command and Control · Task Oriented Programming · Resource Management · Declarative Programming

6.1 Introduction

The use of Armed Forces is the last resort of governments and organisations like the UN and NATO to enforce their will when other options like diplomacy or negotiations have failed. Because armed forces can be deployed anywhere in the world under widely varying geographical, climatological and meteorological conditions, and in different sociological circumstances, these forces depend on personnel that is highly trained to deploy sophisticated systems in order to be superior in combat situations and well educated to deal with different and often unforeseen situations. This makes them also very suitable to be deployed in other dangerous operations like counter-drugs, counter-insurgency and disaster-relief operations. To maintain combat readiness, both the military personnel and the systems that are at their disposal have to be kept at a sufficient qualitative and quantitative level. Because this is expensive, and the sacrifice of human lives is less and less acceptable, governments are striving to execute military missions with as little personnel as possible by investigating reduced manning concepts and acquire more and more unmanned and even autonomous systems. In order to be able to function (partly) autonomous, these systems have to have some notion of the mission that is assigned to the platform and how they may contribute to a successful completion of this mission and more important, how they assess the situation the platform is in and recognise those elements that endanger a successful completion of the mission so they can be neutralised effectively.

The deployment of these platforms requires a lot of specialised knowledge. This knowledge can be roughly divided into three categories. Firstly, knowledge about the mission: what goals have to be reached, or in other words: what is the command-aim, and consequently, what tasks have to be executed to achieve this aim? Secondly, knowledge about the situation: how can sufficient information about the situation be gathered to determine whether the planned tasks can still be executed successfully? Thirdly, knowledge about the available systems and operators: what are their capabilities and capacities, and how can these capabilities and capacities be utilised to their full extent to accomplish the aforementioned tasks? This knowledge is also required to determine the consequences of system failure or the non-availability of human resources.

Section 6.3 of this chapter describes the construction of a framework that models a military mission and the related mission elements. This framework uses the formulated mission goals to describe the activities that have to be executed to achieve these goals. The framework then proposes a method that analyses the capabilities of available resources (personnel, systems and consumables) to determine the most suitable resource, or combination of resources to execute each activity and consequently composes tasks that are assigned to the selected resources. The framework also contains methods that observe developments in the environment and determine if the mission goals can still be met or that either the assigned tasks or the formulated goals need to be adapted.

From this framework a system is developed that is tested within two scenario's. In the first scenario the system is used to handle the start-up phase of a mission: given a possible threat, an Oceangoing Patrol Vessel (OPV) of the Netherlands Navy must prepare itself for dealing with this threat. A plan must be made, and the platform, weapon and sensor systems must be brought in the right operational setting. In the second scenario the system is confronted with internal calamities in a fire fighting and damage control scenario. For this scenario a crude model of a ship including its systems is created by means of a newly developed graphical editor. This editor enabled the experimentation with different system configurations. Furthermore, a simple simulator was also included in the system, thus allowing for reasoning about the operational consequences of ship design decisions.

With this simulator, calamities can be initiated in the ship model. The system then shows how these calamities affect the different systems on board. Additionally, the system can be used to reason about how calamities can influence the command-aim and whether the command-aim can still be achieved. In short, the system allows reasoning about ship configurations and calamities both at design time and during operational deployment. The rest of this chapter is structured as follows. Section 6.2 starts with presenting the context for this work. Section 6.3 describes the already mentioned framework. Sections 6.4 and 6.5 describe the Task Oriented Programming Framework that is used to implement the scenario's that are described in more detail in Sects. 6.6 and 6.7. Finally, Sect. 6.8 concludes and takes a look into the future.

6.2 Motivation

In the introduction was mentioned that because of cost reduction reasons and the unacceptability of casualties, armed forces strive to reduce the number of personnel required to execute missions. The RNLN is therefore involved in a number of research projects in order to determine the level of automation that can be reached without jeopardising the mission objectives. The "Manning and Automation" project is aiming at a significant crew-size reduction by far-reaching integration of the resources. Traditionally the resources on board of the ships of the RNLN are roughly divided into three categories:

1. the platform systems that take care of the propulsion, power generation and the accommodation of the crew,
2. the combat systems consisting of the sensor systems, the weapon systems and the command and control (C2) systems that are deployed for warfare related tasks,
3. the bridge systems that are used for the navigation of the ship.

Within the "Manning and Automation" project, these systems are integrated by means of a common infrastructure called GAUDI (Gemeenschappelijke ArchitectUur Defensie en Industrie: Common Architecture Defence and Industry) that was developed by the close cooperation of the Netherlands Defence Material Organisation, the Netherlands Research Organization for Applied Physics (TNO) and Industry. As Fig. 6.1 shows, the original separate systems are left intact in order to still allow the manufacturer to separately market their systems.

The common infrastructure however allows the separate systems to utilise the information that is available in the other systems; e.g. roll and pitch data from an inertial navigation system can now be used by a weapon system for stabilisation purposes. What is more important, new applications can be developed that integrate the information of the separate system and provide services that could previously only be provided by operators, like the impact of fire or flooding on the (future) deployment of combat systems. This innovative integration concept will be part of the design of the platforms that are going to replace the current generation of frigates, submarines and mine counter measure vessels of the RNLN.

6.3 Mission Framework

When the moment has come that a government or an organisation decides to deploy armed forces to enforce its will, high-level orders are drafted that state the goals of the deployment and the permissions and limitations with respect to the use of force. These high-level orders are then broken down in to operation and mission specific orders that assigned to specialised elements of these armed forces, from now on referred to as entities. The proposed framework uses these orders to support the construction

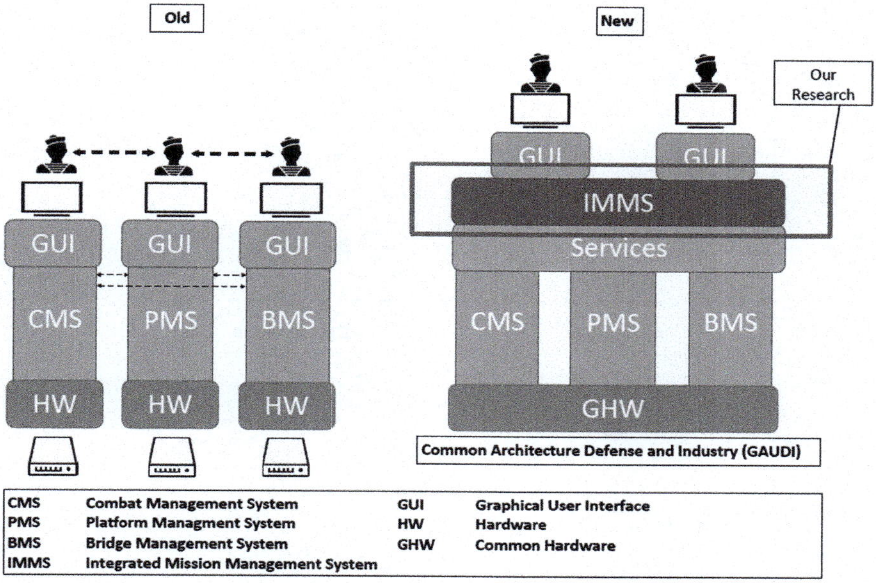

Fig. 6.1 Proposed Architecture for Future Combat Vessels [*Source* F. Bolderheij, J.M. Jansen, A.A. Kool, J. Stutterheim]

of mission goals and consequently the activities that have to be executed to achieve these goals. These activities are then related to the available resources (systems) of the entity and the most appropriate resource is *tasked* to execute a specific activity.

This framework therefore has to contain methods that:

- supports the construction mission goals in relation to the capabilities of the entity,
- derive activity sets from these goals,
- construct resource tasks from these activity sets,
- monitor the condition of the resources,
- select the most appropriate resource to execute an activity,
- monitor the execution of these tasks
- observe the environment with respect to threats that endanger the execution of these tasks and the consequent failure of the mission,
- adapt the tasks if the mission goals cannot be met,
- reformulate the mission goals if they cannot be achieved.

In order to be able to construct these methods, first the concepts *entity* and *mission* have to be analysed and modelled.

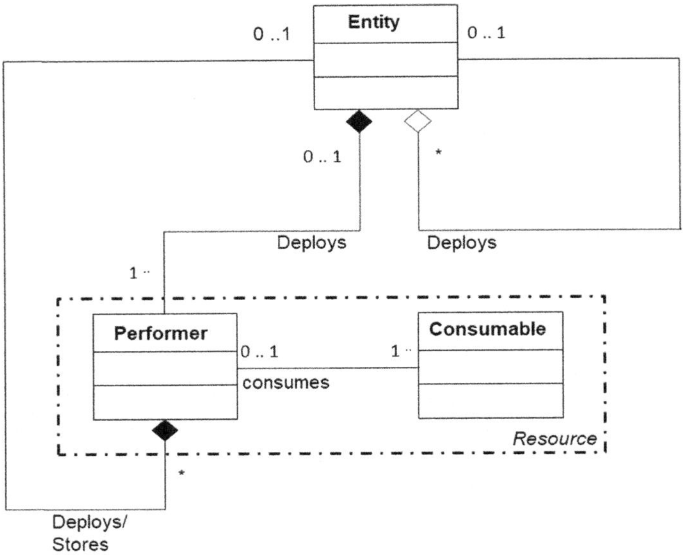

Fig. 6.2 Entities in C2 [*Source* F. Bolderheij, J.M. Jansen, A.A. Kool, J. Stutterheim]

6.3.1 The Concept Entity

As defined earlier, an entity is a specialised element of the armed forces capable of executing a specific mission. From this definition can be seen that an entity can range from a single member of the armed forces to a platoon or a brigade, complex platforms like aircraft carriers and to groups (networks) of platforms. The entity concept is modelled as an UML class-model in Fig. 6.2.

Note that the model contains recursion: an entity can be a resource of another entity or a resource can deploy an entity. If an aircraft that has taken off from a carrier is commanded by the staff of that aircraft carrier it is considered to a resource, but if the pilot operates on his own, it becomes a separate entity. This recursive concept allows the modelling of the idea of Command and Control: in the first case, the staff of the carrier command the aircraft while the pilot is in *control*. In the second case, the pilot has both the *command* and the *control* of the aircraft.

It is now necessary to take a closer look at the definition of the concept *resource*: a resource is defined in this chapter as a *performer* like a hardware system, a software system, a human expert or a mixture thereof in combination with *consumables* like fuel, ammunition, food or information that are required by the performer to function properly.

6.3.2 The Concept Mission

The Oxford Learners dictionary[1] defines a mission as: *a special task, assigned to an individual or unit of the armed forces*. Using the definition of an entity as given earlier, it can now be seen that a mission is executed by an entity. This special task has specific stages and elements. The Fundamentals of Maritime Operations[2] (GMO, Fig. 6.3) of the Royal Netherlands Navy (RNLN) describes the four stages of a Maritime Operation (mission) as:

1. Analyse stage: in this stage the operation, the goals of an operation are clarified, the area where the operation takes place is analysed and the opponent is assessed. This stage can be summarised as: what has to be done.
2. Planning stage: this stage describes how the available means have to be deployed in order to maximise the probability of success, i.e. the achievement of the mission goals that were formulated within the assess stage.
3. Execution stage: in this stage the plans that were constructed are executed and revised if required in order to obtain the goals.
4. Assess stage: in this stage the execution of the previous three stages are analysed and *lessons learned* are constructed that describe why the formulated goals were, were not ore were partially achieved and if the mission was efficiently and/or effectively analysed, planned and executed. These *Lessons Learned* can be utilised to support the execution of future missions.

These stages now have to be described in more detail to identify the processes that are executed within each stage.

The Analysis Stage

Within this stage, the mission order is reviewed to identify specific aspects of the mission. The Combat Estimate seven questions booklet[3] provides a guideline that enable commanding officers to determine the important mission elements:

- The goals that have to be achieved (objectives, effects),
- The opponent,
- The operation area, including environment, meteorology, climate, etc.,
- The timeline along which the mission has to be executed,
- The means (resources) that are available to execute the mission,
- Control Measures like Rules of Engagement ROEs) and Emission Control (EMCON) plans that impose constraints and restraints with respect to the deployment of these resources.

This means that for each of these mission elements a process can be constructed that identifies and describes these elements. The identified elements can now be used to construct plans.

---

[1] Hornby and Wehmeier 2000.

[2] Ministry of Defence 2014.

[3] Horton 2016.

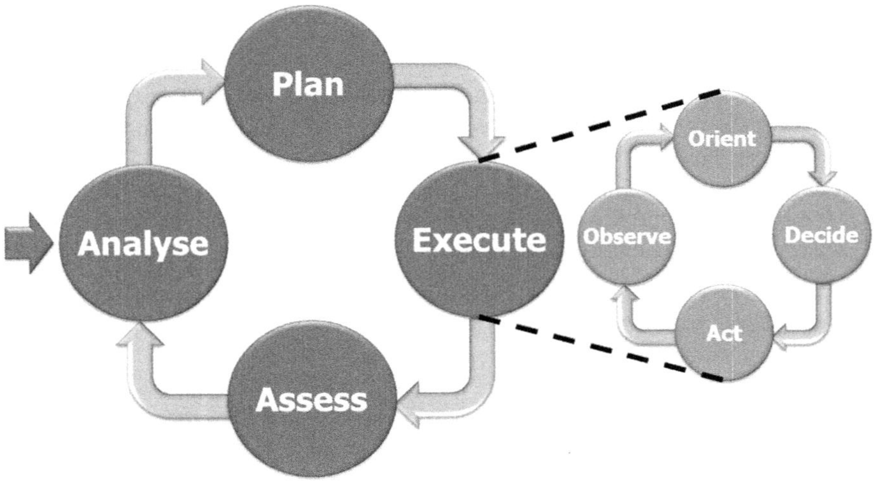

Fig. 6.3 C2-processes breakdown [*Source* F. Bolderheij, J.M. Jansen, A.A. Kool, J. Stutterheim]

The Planning Stage

Taking the mission goals that were formulated within the analysis stage as a starting point, at this point in the planning stage has to be described what has to be done to achieve these goals. A set of actions has to be constructed that lead to the achievement of these goals. These actions can take the shape of escorting a High Value Unit, intercepting drugs runners, protecting cities or groups of people, disabling communication systems etc. This chapter proposes the breaking down of these actions into *elementary elements*. An action is designated as elementary if this action can be assigned to a single resource. Thus the goals can be achieved by executing all required elementary actions. These elementary actions can then be assigned to the available resources: at this stage is determined how these actions are executed.

To be able to select the most suitable resource for an elementary action, the capabilities of these resources have to be known. Our method proposes the use of capability functions that use the requirements of an elementary action as the input parameters and yield the Quality of Service (QoS) with which the action is executed as the output. Examples of capability functions are detecting objects in the vicinity of the entity, neutralising an object and intercepting a object ; the corresponding QoSs are probability of detection, hitting accuracy and intercept speed. If a platform has more than one resource at its disposal to execute an action, the action can be assigned to the resource with the highest QoS: e.g. a radar system can detect an incoming aircraft at a much larger distance than a human look-out. The assignment of actions to specific resources may also differ from entity to entity: on the older platforms (entities like ships or aircraft) many tasks are executed by human operators, while on more modern platforms some of them are automated. These capability functions are embedded in the entity class model as the methods that are incorporated in the

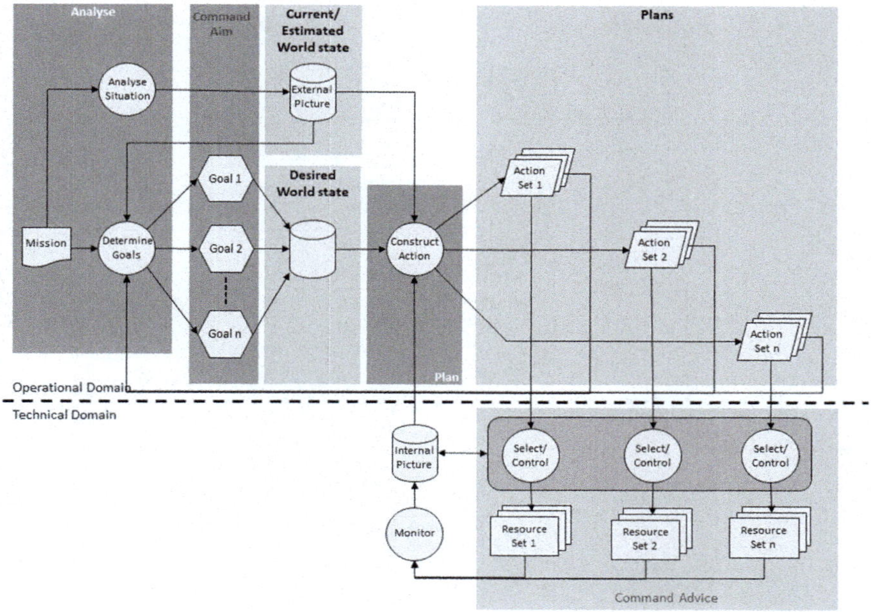

Fig. 6.4 The C2 workflow [*Source* F. Bolderheij, J.M. Jansen, A.A. Kool, J. Stutterheim]

resource class (Fig. 6.2). The assignment of an action to a resource is called a task within this framework. The execution of the analysis stage and the planning stage is outlined in Fig. 6.4.

Besides the *primary actions* that have to be executed to achieve the mission goals, also supporting or *secondary actions* need to be performed. Examples of these supporting actions are: e.g. fusing of data, loading a gun, generation of electric power and refuelling. After the primary actions are assigned to specific resources, the secondary actions have to be determined that are required to be able to execute the primary actions. By consequently detailing these secondary actions, it is possible to derive the logistic supplies necessary to execute the mission like required ammunition, food and fuel.

The constructed set of primary and secondary tasks, can be seen as the initial planning of the mission. This planning can be refined by simulating the actions, the estimated actions of the opponent and the influence of the environment in which the mission takes place.

This planning can also be analysed with respect to multiple deployment of performers or conflicting workflows: if a performer is capable of executing multiple tasks, like e.g. a multi-function radar and its usage is planned within different workflows, it is possible that it is required to execute these tasks simultaneously. If this is the case the most important task will be executed and the less important task may

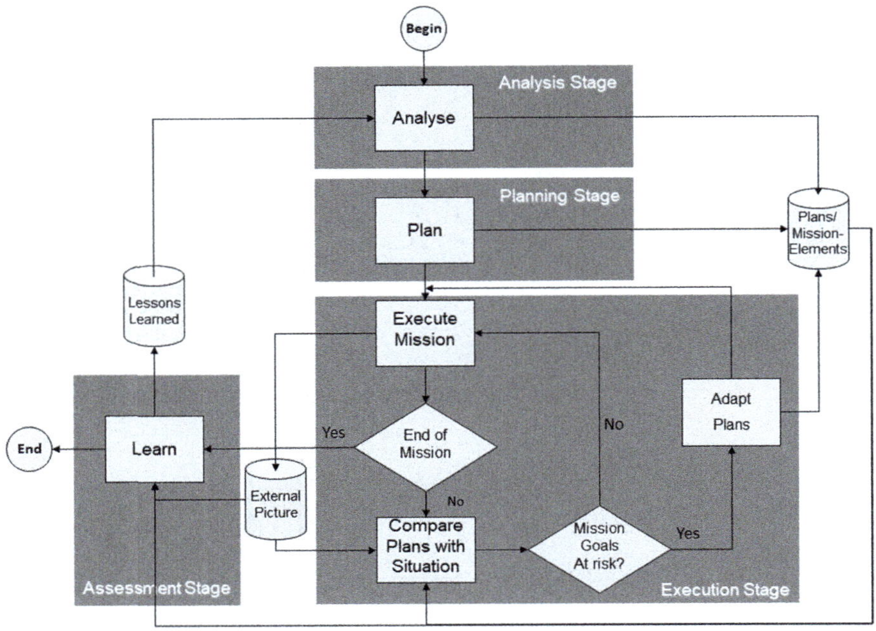

Fig. 6.5 Flow of mission processes [*Source* F. Bolderheij, J.M. Jansen, A.A. Kool, J. Stutterheim]

be assigned by the next best resource based on de QoS. The means that a prioritising mechanism like described in Bolderheij[4] needs to be implemented.

The planning in combination with the designated mission elements are now stored in the mission data store.

The Execution Stage

Because the third stage of the mission is the actual execution of this mission, this stage can be described in more detail by Boys Observe-Orient-Decide-Act (OODA) loop[5] (Fig. 6.3). It is widely accepted that if one party within a conflict is able to go through this loop faster and more accurate than its opponent, this party is likely to be the winner of the conflict. In this stage, the constructed planning is compared with the actual situation: if the current situation is as predicted during the planning stage, the mission execution can continue, otherwise the plans have to be modified. This flow is depicted in Fig. 6.5.

It is also possible that the developing situation calls for the adaptation of the goals. Bolderheij and van Genderen[6] have broken down the OODA loop further for sensor management purposes. Their sensor management framework can easily be expanded for resource management purposes. In this framework, Situational Awareness (SA)

---

[4] Bolderheij et al. 2005.

[5] Boyd 1987–1992.

[6] Bolderheij and van Genderen 2004.

is used to determine how the available sensors have to be (re) deployed in order to maintain the required level of SA. SA is described by Endsleigh et al.[7] as: the perception of environmental elements with respect to time and/or space, the comprehension of their meaning, and the projection of their status after some variable has changed, such as time, or some other variable, such as a predetermined event. SA is acquired by compiling observations of sensor systems and other data sources like databases or information from the internet into a data store to provide an image or picture of the current situation; in the military terminology, this is also denoted as the Picture Compilation process and the data store (or a subsets thereof) is also referred to as the Recognised Picture, the Recognised Air Picture, the Recognised Maritime Picture or the Common Operational Picture. In this chapter, this data store is referred to as the External Picture (EP) and an analysis of the EP provides the required external SA. In the expanded framework, the EA is complemented with the perception of the state of the available resources: are they still functioning correctly, is there sufficient fuel and ammunition available and is the crew fed and rested well enough to execute the required actions? The state of the resources can be seen as Internal SA (ISA) and the ISA is stored in the Internal Picture (IP). Similar to unexpected developments in the ESA may lead to the reconstruction of the plans and eventually to the reconsideration of the mission goals, this is also the case with changes in the ISA due to e.g. the breakdown of performers or an unexpected shortage of a consumable. The constructed frame work is able to determine the consequences and can assist in suggesting alternative resources or adaptation of the goals (consequence management).

Both the ESA and the ISA are stored on a regular basis in order to be able to analyse their development in time and to enable the evaluate the mission planning and execution within the assessment stage.

The Assessment Stage

In this stage, the analysis of the mission document, the constructed planning and the execution of the mission are reviewed. The data stores that were described previously provide an excellent means to perform this analysis. From this analysis, lessons learned can be constructed that can assist within the analysis and planning stages of future missions.

6.3.3 A C2 Framework

In Fig. 6.6 the processes that are executed during all mission stages in combination with the derived data stores and a Generic set of resources is shown. Parts of this framework were prototyped in order to analyse the viability of the framework.

[7] Endsley et al. 1997.

6.4 Task Oriented Programming

Task Oriented Programming[8] (TOP) is a novel way to develop software systems that support collaboration of parties (resources like people, computers and systems) in a distributed setting. Central to TOP is the concept of a *task*. A TOP application coordinates the tasks that have to be performed by the users of the system. Users can be either humans or other machines. The TOP application tells its users which task to do at what moment and provides the right information needed to perform that task at the right time.

In TOP, a developer only specifies an information model and a high-level task model. The Information model describes the information that is used within the application. The Task model describes when and by who information is processed (generated, viewed, altered). A fully working multi-user web-based application is generated automatically from these models. This feature makes TOP an environment to rapidly create complex cooperative applications that support and coordinate work and information between a multitude of people and machines.

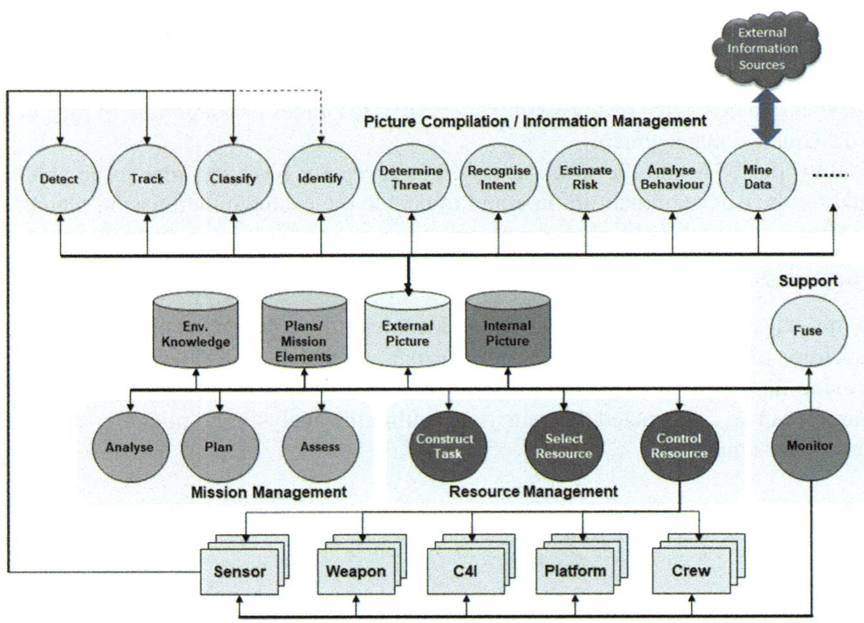

Fig. 6.6 C2 Model [*Source* F. Bolderheij, J.M. Jansen, A.A. Kool, J. Stutterheim]

[8] Geltink 2014; Plasmeijer et al. 2007, 2011, 2012; Lijnse et al. 2011, 2012; Jansen et al. 2010; Kool 2017.

6.4.1 Basic and Composite Tasks

Tasks are either basic tasks or composite tasks. Typical basic tasks are:

- enter, view or update information by a user in a user interface;
- provide information by a sensor;
- retrieve information from a data source;
- put information into a data source (the information may come from a user, sensor, a computer, etc.);
- do a calculation on previously obtained information.

All other tasks are sequential or parallel compositions of tasks. Sequential tasks are executed one after another. A subsequent task may depend on the result of a prior task. Tasks that are composed sequentially never have conflicting resource requirements. Parallel tasks can be executed independently at the same and may try to claim a resource that is used by another task.

6.4.2 Shared Stores: Information Sharing Between Tasks

Sequentially composed tasks pass the task result of one task directly to a subsequent task as input. Another way to pass information to another task is to use a shared store. Information in a shared store can be reached by any task at any time, independently of the way these tasks are composed.

Shared stores play a central role in TOP in general and C2 applications in particular. In C2 applications, they maintain shared Situational Awareness, by combining the internal and external picture as shown in Figs. 6.4 and 6.6. The shared stores Tasks can add, view or alter information in shared stores. The content of a shared store is described by an information model; the *type* of the store. The content of a shared store can, for example, be a list of contacts observed by the sensors in the C2 system, the current position of the ship itself, the status of the propulsion system, etc. All information that has to be shared between several tasks must be modelled using shared stores.

Shared stores can in turn also be composed to form virtual shared stores. For tasks, these virtual stores behave exactly in the same way as real shared stores. In this sense, virtual stores are comparable to views in relational databases. An example of a virtual store is a store of surface contacts that has been created by applying a filtering function to the store of all contacts.

Shared Stores as a Spreadsheet Metaphor

The use of (virtual) shared stores can be compared to spreadsheets. A normal store is the equivalent of a cell in which a user can enter (or view) information. A virtual store can be compared to a cell with a formula attached to it that combines the information of several other cells and that is automatically recalculated in case a value in one of these other cells is altered.

Watching Stores for Changes

It is also possible to attach a *watch task*, or *watch* to a shared store. A watch consist of a combination of a (virtual) shared store, a boolean function and a new task. The watch continuously monitors the content of the store. As soon as the boolean function returns true when applied to the content of the store, the new task is executed with the content of the store as input parameter.

There are many practical applications of these watch tasks. One such example is an automatic fire alarm that watches the temperature sensing task in a room. Another practical application is an automatic countermeasure against incoming missiles, which can be modelled as a watch task on the status of the outside world. In our case studies we will give some more examples of (virtual) stores and watches.

6.5 A Declarative Approach to C2: Formalizing the Command Aim

How does TOP applies for C2-systems? Command and Control from the TOP point of view consists of reaching the mission goals by performing the right activities (tasks) by the right entities or resources at the right moment using the right information.

The mission goals that have to be reached are described as the commanders intent: *the central goal and stand-alone reference that enables subordinates to gain the required flexibility in planning and executing. It is the standard reference point from which all present and future subordinates actions evolve. The design of commanders intent is not to restrain but to empower subordinates by giving them freedom of action to accomplish a mission.* The commander's intent is formalized in a Command Aim (CA, see also Fig. 6.4).

Because the Command Aim is the the driving force behind everything that is done, this command aim should be made an explicit part of the Situational Awareness (SA). This is the only way to make it possible to predict the operational consequences of resource failures etc.

6.5.1 Starting Point: Situational Awareness Maintained in Stores

Situational awareness during a mission is of paramount importance. SA not only comprises the operational picture (external SA) but also the state of all resources (internal SA) and also all restrictions one has to deal with during a mission (environmental conditions, rules of engagement, etc.). As motivated above, also the goals of the mission (the Command Aim) should be part of the shared SA, therefore is captured by the four stores from Fig. 6.6. The goal of building up shared situational awareness is to provide the right information at the right moment to the right entity

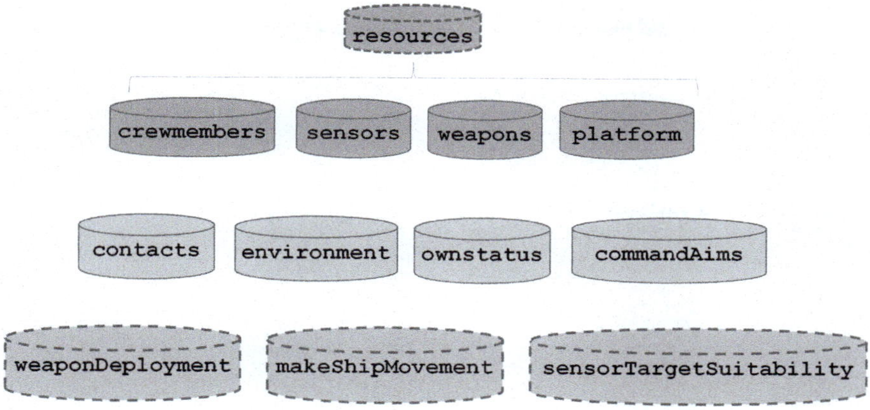

Fig. 6.7 Shared Stores for OPV [*Source* F. Bolderheij, J.M. Jansen, A.A. Kool, J. Stutterheim]

(person, machine or process). TOPs information stores offer exactly what is needed for this. Figure 6.7 shows the stores that are used for our case studies.

Currently, a large part of SA is only maintained in the people's mind. They know for example what the operational consequences are of the malfunction of a resource or what the goals of the mission are. To reach the higher levels of synchronicity this knowledge must be made explicit in the C2-system. This can be reached by explicitly modelling the relations between:

- the command aim;
- the operational activities needed to reach this goal;
- the resources that are needed to perform these activities;
- all internal and external factors that have influence on the resources that are needed (weather, sea state, health of crew, etc.).

In this way every change in one of these elements can be automatically translated to the consequences for the operation. For example, when the cooling system degrades it is automatically inferred that this has consequences for a radar system and that this now certain types of contact cannot be observed and that this has consequences for the current command aim. By modelling all these relations explicitly in the system the fact that the current command aim is in danger can now be automatically inferred. Figure 6.8 shows these relations for our case studies. These relations are described in more detail in Sect. 6.6.

6.5.2 Primitive Tasks

Starting point for every mission or operation is the command aim. Activities or tasks should be executed to reach this command aim. These activities can be decom-

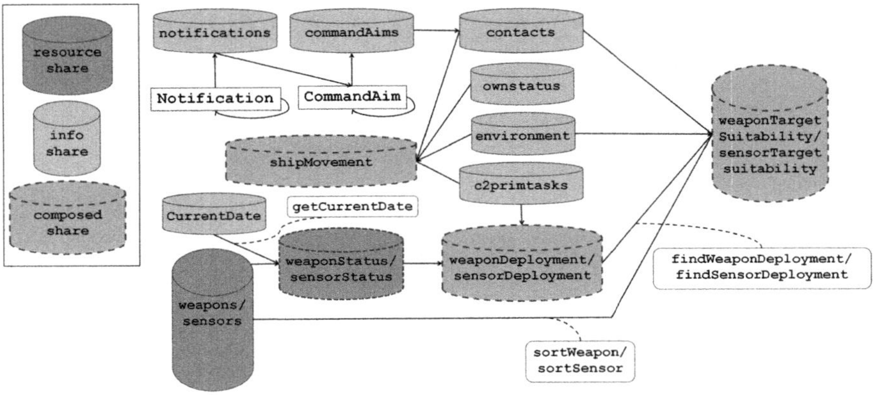

Fig. 6.8 Relations between Stores for OPV Case Study [*Source* F. Bolderheij, J.M. Jansen, A.A. Kool, J. Stutterheim]

posed into sub-activities until a point is reached that it makes no sense to further decompose the tasks. The lowest level tasks in this decomposition are the so-called primitive tasks. Primitive tasks are the basic activities that can be performed within an operation. A primitive task is always executed as a whole, it makes no sense to execute parts of a primitive task separately. Primitive tasks are the building blocks from which more complex operations can be built. They should be of the right grain size: there should be not too many of them because this complicates the execution of missions. But there should also be not too few of them: all real work that has to be done should be accomplished by a executing a primitive task. All other tasks on board are (sequential or parallel) compositions of primitive tasks. Finding the right primitive tasks of the right grain size for a military system is not a trivial exercise. This should be done in close co-operation with operational experts and its validation should be done by interactive simulations in an iterative way. Finding the primitive tasks for the OPV is therefore not the goal of this chapter. Examples of primitive tasks as they can be used in the maritime domain are:

- perform air surveillance;
- perform surface surveillance;
- illuminate a target;
- prepare the gun for shooting;
- calibrate the gun;
- fire the gun;
- cook a meal;
- disembark the ship;
- transit a ship at sea from one position to another;
- etc.

Note that primitive tasks are real actions that can be performed and that they are mostly described in an operational way. Nothing is said yet about the resources that are needed to do this. To achieve this we have to couple primitive tasks to resources that can execute them. We can do this directly: attach a list of resources to a primitive task. But it is better to have an indirect coupling. The reason to do this indirectly is that the choice for which resources should execute a task is not always fixed, but may depend on circumstances like: environmental conditions, rules of engagement, status of the resources, other actions currently performed, etc. Therefore, we model the needs for a primitive task by so-called roles that are needed. Resources are now entities that have the capability to execute certain roles. When a primitive task needs to be executed, all available resources are questioned for the roles needed for this task. In this questioning extra input parameters like weather, sea state, ROEs, etc. are also taken into account (see Fig. 6.8). In this way the most optimal choice of resources is found for executing the tasks at this moment in the current circumstances.

6.5.3 Utility Functions and the Generation of Possibilities

Primitive tasks are the building blocks for executing operations. Choosing the right resources to execute them is not a trivial task. The choice for a sensor for example may depend on the (maintenance) status of the sensors, environmental conditions, etc. In the current situation this type of information is mostly only available in the heads of the people involved. Again making this information explicit is of crucial importance. This is realized by the use of so-called utility functions. These functions calculate the performance of systems like weapons, sensors, platform systems given the circumstances in which they have to operate (weather, status of maintenance). The construction of the right utility functions is not a trivial task and will take considerable effort. One can imagine that these functions may have to be updated regularly and maybe machine learning strategies can be used to construct them.

Given a command aim the IMMS will generate suggestions for sensor and weapon systems to use. Using the above mentioned utility functions a ranking of these systems is made from which the user can choose. For every choice also the sensor and weapon plans needed to deploy these systems for action are displayed. In this way the user can evaluate the consequences of the choices made. The final plan can now be generated and consists of parallel and sequential compositions of primitive tasks (see for example Fig. 6.9). Examples will be given in the next sections.

6.6 Case Study 1: Potential Terrorist Threat on a Drilling Rig in the North Sea

In this case study (taken from Kool)[9] a patrol vessel from the Netherlands Navy has to taken action on a potential threat by terrorist on a drilling rig in the Dutch part of

[9] Kool 2017.

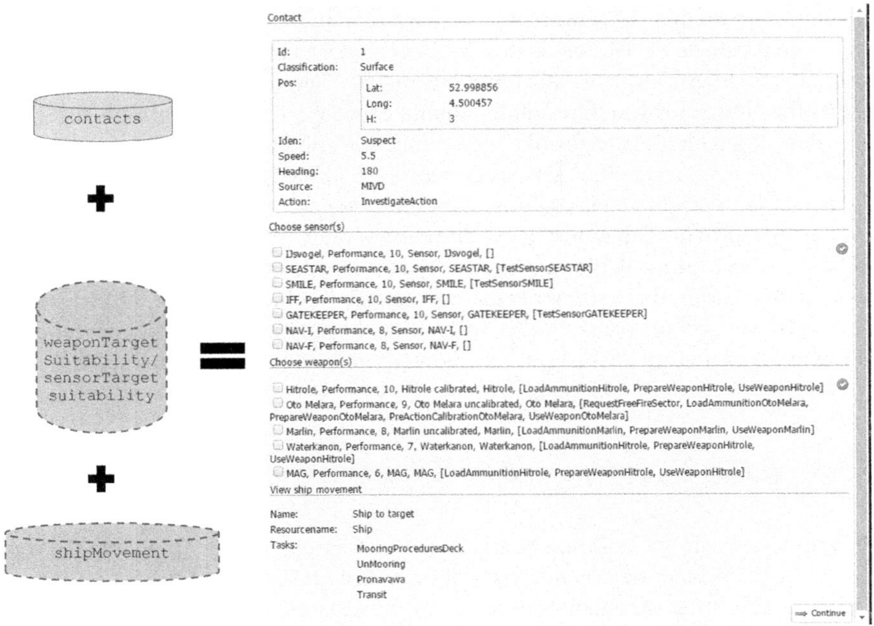

Fig. 6.9 Example Command Advice for a mission [*Source* F. Bolderheij, J.M. Jansen, A.A. Kool, J. Stutterheim]

the North Sea. Starting point for the mission is an Intel report from the Netherlands Military Security Service that states that there is a potential threat by terrorists against drilling rigs in the Dutch part of the North Sea. At the same time an unknown small sea vessel is reported in this part of the North Sea that does not respond to radio calls. The ship of the watch, a patrol vessel of the Holland class, has to take appropriate actions.

First, the commander of the vessel gets the information about the threat. The commander enters a command aim in the system, stating the goal of the mission (protect the oil rig against a possible threat). As part of the command aim also the possible position of the threat is entered as a virtual (assumed hostile) contact with the assignment to investigate this contact.

Because the C2-system is contact driven, the existence of a contact, its presumed location and its identification leads to the automatic creation of a plan based on constraints on the shared stores. In the first stage of planning it is determined which sensor and weapon systems are best suited for acting against this target. The sensor and weapon systems are ranked on suitability using the utility functions and the user can make a choice amongst the suitable sensors and weapons (see Fig. 6.9).

In the second part of the planning process: the chosen sensor and weapon systems, the current state of the ship (moored in the port of Den Helder), the position of the oil rig and the presumed position of the attacker, the type of vessel deployed by the terrorist and the environmental conditions are used to make three plans: a transition plan, a weapon deployment plan and a sensor deployment plan. The advice that is generated based on the information available in the different stores. The folllowing examples show how the plan depend on information in stores:

- if wind and sea state are worse the assistance of a tugboat will make part of the transition plan.
- if the status of a contact is switched from hostile to friendly the weapon plan for this contact will automatically disappear.
- if the calibration interval period for the gun is exceeded, a calibration task action make part of the weapon deployment task.
- in case of low visibility condition weapon systems like the 30 mm Oto Melara Marlin gun that depend on optical sensors will automatically get a low utility.

Once the user has chosen a plan, all task that make part of it are combined into one overall mission that consists of a paralel/sequential composition of primitive tasks. During the execution of these task resource allocation and relaxation is done automatically and possible conflicts are detected and the user is informed about them.

6.7 Case Study 2: Damage Control

In the first case the focus was on the external battle; the things taking place outside of the ship. In this second case study, the focus is on the internal battle and its relation to the external battle. This case study is concerned with a fire-fighting and damage control (FFDC) simulation. For example, if the external battle escalates and the ship takes damage, what are the consequences for the ship's systems? Conversely, how will damage to certain areas of the ship and the systems therein affect the ship's ability to influence the external battle?

To successfully reason about these things, the (internal) structure of a ship must be modelled in such a way that it both represents a sufficiently realistic ship on the one hand and that an algorithm can easily use the model on the other hand. With such a structure in place, the consequences of (fighting) calamities can be translated to the operational domain in a way that fits with the models represented by Figs. 6.8 and 6.9.

Again the concept of resources is applicable and the spaces in the ship can be modelled as such. Spaces can be seen as resources that provide space to other resources, like systems, items (including fire-extinguishers, etcetera), sensors (fire, water), connections (pipes and cables) or people. By modelling the spaces in the ship and the position of the systems, sensors, connections and people in these spaces, it is possible to predict/translate the consequences of fires, damage and leaks directly to the operational domain, reusing the already existing connection between the operational tasks and resources.

In the next two subsection these ideas are described in somewhat more detail.

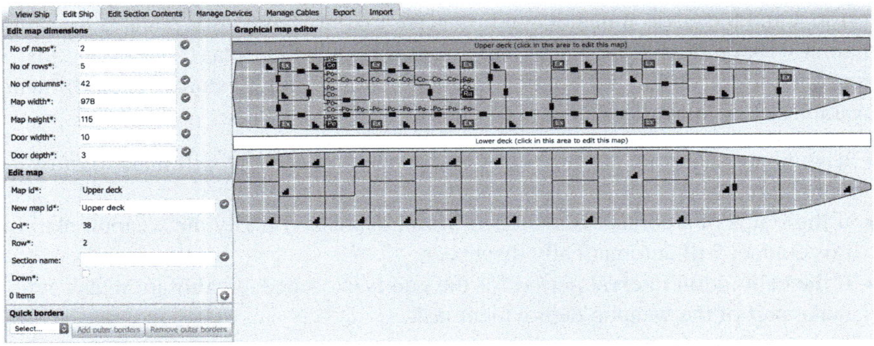

Fig. 6.10 Ship editor: modelling the ship's spaces [*Source* F. Bolderheij, J.M. Jansen, A.A. Kool, J. Stutterheim]

6.7.1 Ship Data Modelling

To reasoning about a ship, its resources and its internal- and external battle, a concrete model of a ship is needed. We present a ship modelling tool that facilitates the construction of a coarse-grained model of a ship. The screenshots in Figs. 6.10 and 6.11 show this tool in action.

In the bar on the left side of the screen a user can specify the number of decks and the ship's dimensions. Each deck is divided into a grid. Each grid cell wall can be absent, solid, or solid with a door. A user needs only click on a wall to cycle between those three states. Each grid cell is a section. A section can contain other resources (systems and people), connections and may have doors and stairs to other sections. Any change made in this editor view is immediately propagated to the rest of the application via the relevant shared stores, even if an FFDC simulation is already running.

All types of objects that have been mentioned before play a role in the FFDC simulation. Actors that have been tasked with extinguishing a fire will need to find a fire extinguisher first, pick it up, and then find a way to a fire before extinguishing it. Devices in the real world generally need power to operate. On a ship, many devices, such as radar or a power generator, also need an active cooling mechanism. Together, all of these dependencies form a network of devices with possibly cyclic dependencies. For example, the power generator requires cooling, while the cooling system requires power. Power or cooling water is transported via power cables and cooling pipes. The ship editor allows the user to make the systems and the connections between the systems explicit, creating a graph in which devices are nodes and cables and pipes edges. With this graph of devices, we can reason about the effects of devices or cables/pipes being disabled, for example when they are destroyed by a fire. In turn, we can reason about the effects this has on the ship's command aim.

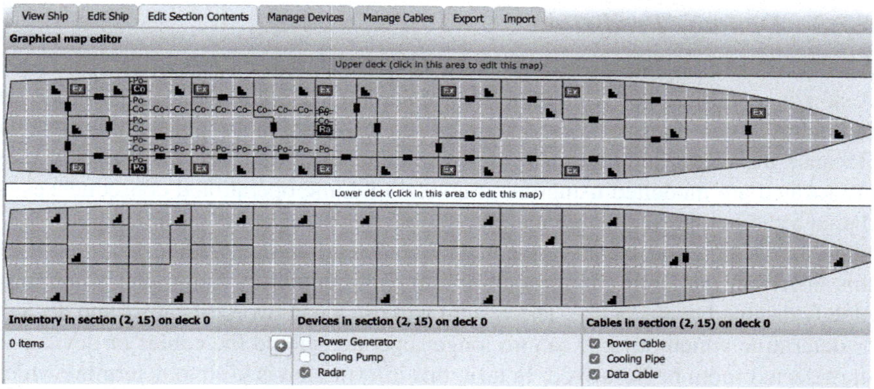

Fig. 6.11 Ship editor: laying out the systems, cables and items [*Source* F. Bolderheij, J.M. Jansen, A.A. Kool, J. Stutterheim]

6.7.2 FFDC Simulation

Now that we have a ship model, we want to be able to use it to simulate an FFDC scenario.

In our scenario, actors will walk around inside the ship until they are given a task by the Damage Control Officer (DOff). While walking around, actors may encounter items, such as fire extinguishers, which they may pick up. Items that have been picked up can be dropped at any time. Since users can walk around inside the ship, their location may change at any time. Such a change needs to be reflected in the rest of the application, so that the user interface may be updated accordingly. We use shared stores to model these changes. By relating this store with the store containing the ship model, the position of the user can be displayed on the map of the ship. In this way the DOff has a constant overview of the positions of the crew members.

In case one of the sensors in one of the sections notifies a fire or a leak the DOff is visually notified. The DOff is also immediately given a task to resolve the problem. The FFDC system will give an advice how to approach the problem. This advice takes into account the positions of the crew members, the position of the fire-extinguishers and the fire, and the routes a crew member has to walk picking up an extinguisher to a fire. Because these calculations are modelled as constraints on the relevant stores, every change in these stores (doors that are blocked, extinguisher that are removed) are immediately reflected into new advice.

6.7.3 Damage Prediction

A ship operates based on what its command aims are. The command aim is modelled by the tasks that need to be executed and the resources that are necessary for this. Because the relations between resources, connections and the spaces where they are located are modelled using the graphical tool, the operational consequences of damage can be inferred automatically.

In the DOff's user interface we have included a *damage prediction mode*. With this interface, the DOff can reason about the consequences of a room being completely disabled by e.g. a fire. The system will use the network of cables and devices to determine which devices can no longer operate, should the cables or devices in the selected room be destroyed. In turn, this information is used to determine which command aims are imperilled by the disabled devices. All of this information combined enables the DOff to determine which fires in which sections need to be put out first.

This feature can also be used in the design phase of a ship. By simulating fires, leaks and damage to the ship and relate the consequences of those calamities to the tasks a ship is expected to carry out, it is possible to spot bottleneck in the ship's design.

6.8 Conclusions and Future Work

This chapter describes some experiments we executed to use a declarative programming approach to deal with C2. Therefore a C2 framework was developed that uses operational guidelines to analyse the orders given to a military entity to execute a mission. From these order, the mission goals, operation area and opponent information are derived. This information can now be supplemented with environmental and climatological data and other information required to support the commander of the entity in determining what activities have to be executed to the achieve the formulated mission goals. The framework provides a class-model that describes the composition of the entity by means of the class attributes and the capability of its resources by means of the capability functions (class methods): this model thus enables the selection of the most appropriate resource to execute an activity. This method not only supports the planning of the deployment of the resources, but also provides an indication of capacity problems if resources are simultaneously assigned to more than one workflow. If this is the case, the method is capable of suggesting alternatives. All information needed to execute a mission, including the goals of the mission, are maintained in a shared information space on which constraint are defined that help to automatically find the best way to move forward given the current state of affairs. This declarative way of describing a C2 system leads to a more comprehensible and more compact description of systems, that are also easier to extend and better to maintain. Important advantages are: There is no need for explicit event handling. All actions that have to be taken can be modelled putting watches on (virtual) stores. Extensions can be made orthogonally by adding new stores, connecting them into (new) virtual stores and adding relevant watches on the contents of them.

6.8.1 Relation with NEC

Nowadays C2 and NEC are closely connected. NEC takes an information systems approach to deal with coherent integration of sensors, deciders, weapon systems and support systems to reach the desired goals of a mission. Sensors and weapon systems can be regarded as producers of information. This information based approach should lead to: Increased provision of timely information allowing quick response; better interoperability; increased speed of operations; more efficient C2 structures; shared situational awareness between alls actors leading to synchronized operations.

The integrated approach presented in this chapter, where mission goals, internal and external situational awareness are all available in a shared information space provides a coherent mode to reach this higher level of synchronicity.

6.8.2 Future Work

Not all aspects relevant to C2 mission where studied already. The aspect of time was not taken yet into account. A resource is mostly needed for a restricted period of time. Goals have to be achieved within a certain time frame. In the planning phase of a mission this should all be taken into account. This will be a subject of study for the next phase of our research.

Something similar should be done with respect to failure of resources. In the current system the status of resource is monitored and the consequences of a failure are presented to the user. The next step should be an automatic re-planning of activities to cope with the new situation and a graceful degradation of all other activities that were part of the task for which the resource failed. Also this will be subject for further study in the next phase of our research.

References

Bolderheij F, Absil F, van Genderen P (2005) Risk-based object-oriented sensor management. In: Proceedings of the 8th Int. Conf. on Information Fusion, Philadelphia

Bolderheij F, van Genderen P (2004) Mission driven sensor management. In: Proceedings of the 7th Int. Conf. on Information Fusion; 2004, Stockholm: pp 799–804

Boyd JR (1987–1992) A discourse on winning and losing, Unpublished briefing notes, various editions, http://dnipogo.org/john-r-boyd

Endsley MR, Kaber DB, Onall E (1997) The impact of intermediate levels of automation on situation awareness and performance in dynamic control systems. In: Proceedings IEEE 6th Conference on Human factors and power plants, Global Perspectives of Human Factors in Power Generation, Orlando

Geltink G (2014) C2 systems in iTasks. Bachelor thesis, Faculty of Military Sciences, Netherlands Defence Academy

Hornby AS, Wehmeier S (2000) Oxford Advanced Learner's Dictionary of Current English, 6th edn. Oxford University Press, Oxford

Jansen JM, Lijnse B, Plasmeijer R, Grant T (2010) Web based dynamic workflow systems for C2 of military operations. In: Selected Papers of the 15th International Command and Control Research and Technology Symposium, Santa Monica, CA, USA

Kool AA (2017) Integrated mission management for C2 support: An iTask prototype. Bachelor thesis, Faculty of Military Sciences, Netherlands Defence Academy

Lijnse B, Jansen JM, Nanne R, Plasmeijer R (2011) Capturing the Netherlands coast guard's SAR workflow with iTasks. In: Proceedings of the 8th Information System for Crisis Response and Management, ISCRAM Conference, Lisbon, Portugal

Lijnse B, Jansen JM, Plasmeijer R (2012) Incidone: A task-oriented incident coordination tool. In: Proceedings of the 9th Information System for Crisis Response and Management Conference, Vancouver, Canada

Ministry of Defence (Netherlands) (2014) Fundamentals of maritime operations, www.defensie.nl/downloads/publicaties/2014/02/13/grondslagen-van-het-maritieme-optreden-nederlandse-maritiemmilitaire-doctrine

Plasmeijer R, Achten P, Koopman P (2007) iTasks: executable specifications of interactive work flow systems for the web. In: Proceedings of the International Conference on Functional Programming, ICFP 2007, Freiburg, Germany, pp 141–152

Plasmeijer R, Achten P, Lijnse B, Michels S (2011) Defining multi-user web applications with iTasks. In: Proceedings of the Central European Summer School on Functional Programming, volume 7241 of LNCS, Eötvös Loránd University, Budapest, Hungary, pp 14–24

Plasmeijer R, Lijnse B, Michels S, Achten P, Koopman P (2012) Task-oriented programming in a pure functional language. In: Proceedings of the 10th International Conference on Principles and Practice of Declarative Programming, PPDP 2012, pp 195–206, Leuven, Belgium

The Horton Academy (2016) Combat estimate 7 questions booklet, http://www.mod.gov.sl/docs/doctrine%20-%207%20questions%20handbook.pdf

Chapter 7
Challenges for Cooperative Wireless Sensor Networks in Border Control Applications

H. Nikookar and H. Monsuur

Contents

Abstract A wireless sensor network (WSN) is a network of low-size and low-complexity devices that senses the environment and communicate the gathered data through wireless channels. The sensors sense the environment, and send data to a control unit for processing and decisions. The data is forwarded via multiple hops or is relayed to another network through a gateway. WSNs have a wide range of applications from monitoring the environment and surveillance, to precision agriculture, and from biomedical to structural and infrastructure health monitoring. One of the important application domains of wireless sensor networks is in the military. Technological advances in the past decades have resulted in small, inexpensive and powerful sensors

H. Nikookar (✉) · H. Monsuur
Faculty of Military Sciences, Breda, The Netherlands
e-mail: h.nikookar@mindef.nl

H. Monsuur
e-mail: h.monsuur@mindef.nl

H. Monsuur et al. (eds.), *NL ARMS Netherlands Annual Review of Military Studies 2018*, NL ARMS, https://doi.org/10.1007/978-94-6265-246-0_7

with embedded processing and radio networking capability. Distributed cooperative smart sensor devices networked through radio links and deployed in large numbers provide enormous opportunities. For border control applications, these sensors can be deployed on the ground and control and monitor borders. In this chapter, the challenges of the usage of WSNs for border control and monitoring are explained and cutting-edge technologies for these applications are discussed. Cooperation between nodes of a WSN will increase the performance in tasks like detecting, localisation or tracking intruders in border control. Game theory is used to describe how and why coalitions of nodes in a network form, using the trade-off between the advantage of cooperation (in terms of better performance) and the costs of cooperation (in terms of bandwidth, transmitting information). A general game-theoretic framework for WSN is presented, and illustrated by means of an example.

Keywords wireless sensor networks · cooperative game theory · border control · intruder detection · surveillance · heuristics · distributed networks

7.1 Introduction

A Wireless Sensor Network is a network of (micro)sensors which are low-size and low-complexity devices (nodes). These nodes sense the environment and communicate the information gathered from the monitored field through wireless links. The gathered data is forwarded, possibly via multiple hops relaying, to a sink that can use it locally, or is connected to other networks (e.g., the Internet) through a gateway. Wireless sensor networks improve the performance of detection and observation of the environment (such as border control and monitoring use cases) through the employment of geometric diversity. Development of sensor networks requires three technologies: Sensing, Communication and Computing.[1] One major example of early sensor networks is Air Traffic Control. However, the main driving force for the early application of (wireless) sensors was defence applications of military sensors. During World War II networks of acoustic sensors (hydrophones) were deployed in the oceans bottom to detect Soviet submarines. In the Cold War era networks of air defence radar were deployed including AWACS planes which was followed by distributed sensor networks research for DARPA (Defence Advanced Research Projects Agency) in 1980 using ARPANET (which was in fact the predecessor of Internet). Advances in MEMS (Micro-electro-mechanical system) technology, wireless networking, and inexpensive low-power processors are important factors for massive development of wireless sensor networks. Sensor networks in 21st century are ad hoc, especially for highly dynamic environments, and have network information processing capability. The WSN Technology trends perspective entails (i) Advances in wireless networks, (ii) Advances in chip capacity and processor production (causing energy/bit reduction for computing and computation), and (iii) Sensing, computing

[1] Nikookar 2015.

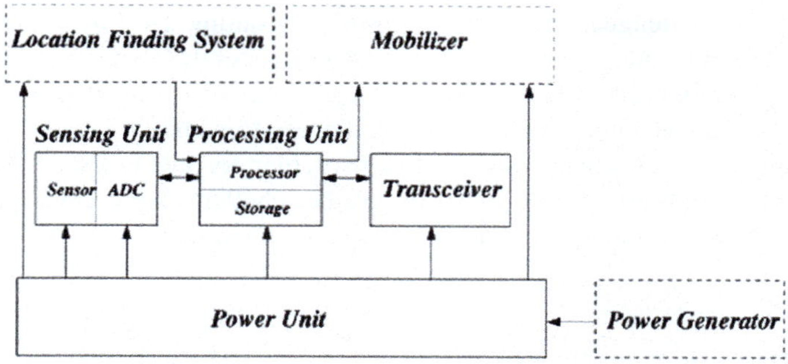

Fig. 7.1 Sensor Node Architecture (Gupta and Kumar 2013). [*Source* C.P. Gupta and A. Kumar 2013]

and communication integrated on a single chip resulting in cost reduction as well as deployment of sensors in large numbers.

A typical sensor node in a WSN for border control and monitoring applications has a small size (at the size of a button) which accommodates sensors, radio transceivers, a small processor, a memory and a power unit. See Fig. 7.1.

These sensors are deployed randomly in the region of interest for monitoring and surveillance. With the proliferation of wireless sensor networks in general, and with applications in border control, in particular, the requirements on prime resources like battery power and radio spectrum are put under severe pressure. In a wireless environment the system requirements, network capabilities and device capabilities have enormous variations giving rise to significant design challenges. There is therefore an emergent need for developing energy efficient, green technologies that optimize premium radio resources, such as power and spectrum, even while guaranteeing quality of service (for example the required security). Moreover, many wireless sensor networks in border monitoring and surveillance scenarios operate under dynamic conditions with frequent changes in the propagation environment and diversified requirements. All these trends point to flexible, reconfigurable structures that can adapt to the circumstances and the radio neighborhood and can also cooperate with other sensor networks. The nodes of future WSNs in border control scenarios will most likely be context aware, cooperative with energy harvesting capabilities.

7.2 Challenges in WSN

The challenges of WSN, in general, are manifold. Topology of sensor network can be seen as the first challenge. Each node needs to know the identity and location of neighbours in fixed or mobile scenarios. Therefore, a priori knowledge of planned networks is needed. Furthermore, for Ad hoc sensor networks the topology should be made in real time and updated, and failed nodes should be excluded, while new sensors be included in the network.

The second challenge is the network control and routing. Dealing with resources-energy, bandwidth and processing power, Protocols, Mobile IP (needing heavy overhead time, memory, energy), size and density of network, and trade-off between latency, reliability and energy are further challenges to name.

In addition to these challenges, and in particular for the WSN applications in border control and monitoring scenarios, further challenges are envisaged. In the following, these particular issues are discussed in more detail.

7.2.1 Propagation Channel

In wireless sensor networks, typically the nodes have low-height antennas. In these applications, the radio propagation channel characteristics and among others the path loss exponent is considerably different from the free-space channel. Therefore, routes with more hops and with shorter hop distances can be more power-efficient than those with fewer hops but longer hop distances. One of major research challenges in this regard is to investigate the impact of dynamic channels on the adaptive self-configuration topology mechanism of border monitoring sensor networks and see to which extent it can reduce energy consumption and increase network performance.

7.2.2 Cognitive WSNs

Current WSNs operate in the ISM (Industrial-Scientific-Medical) band. This band is shared by many other wireless technologies giving rise to degradation of performance of WSNs due to interference. WSNs can also interfere other services in this band. The proliferation of WSNs will result in scarcity of the spectrum dedicated to wireless sensor communications. Cognitive Radio (CR) technology for WSNs improves sensor nodes communications performance as well as spectral efficiency. It is foreseen that cognitive radio will emerge as an active research area for wireless networks in general and in particular in border control/monitoring scenarios in the coming years. Unlike conventional radios in which most of the components are implemented in hardware, cognitive radio uses software implementations (i.e., Software Defined Radio (SDR)[2] for some functionalities enabling flexible radio operation. The radio sensors are reconfigurable and therefore the need to modify existing hardware is reduced. In this context, the increasing number of sensing nodes equipped with wireless communication capability will require faster connectivity, and the adaptation to the new requirements (of bandwidth) of the wireless spectrum. Cognitive radio

[2] Software Defined Radio is a software-based, programmable and reconfigurable modulation and demodulation technique. With the flexibility that it provides, hybrid platforms can be deployed in the wireless sensor network. By integrating SDR technique in the WSN, with the same (programmable) hardware, more radio standards can be introduced to the network. Therefore, instead of designing hardware again, only the sensor nodes of the WSN need to be reprogrammed.

will prevent the need to implement hardware upgrades, in a large border monitoring area. It will allow the cognitive radio-enabled sensor nodes to search for the best frequency-based pre-determined parameters. Applying cognitive radio technology to WSNs for border surveillance is a challenge. It should be noted that CR-WSNs differ from conventional WSNs in several aspects. One of the important issues in this regard is interference to other wireless networks or Primary Users (PUs). Protecting the right of Primary users is the major concern of the CR-WSN. Therefore, miss detection probability of PUs should be minimized in order to minimize interference with the PUs. False alarm probability should also be minimized as large false alarm rates (which is not desirable in border control applications) will also cause the spectrum to be under-utilized. High false alarm and miss detection probability in CR-WSNs in border monitoring and control cases should be deeply studied as this can dramatically degrade the performance of wireless sensor networks for surveillance purposes.

7.2.3 *Joint Communication and Sensing in One Technology for WSNs*

Integrated sensing and radio communication systems have emerged in sake of system miniaturization and transceiver unification. With the current technological advancements, the radio frequency front-end architectures in sensing networks and radio communications become more similar. Orthogonal Frequency Division Multiplexing (OFDM) as a capable technology, already and successfully used in wireless communications (e.g., in IEEE802.11a,g,n,p standards), can be used in wireless sensor networks.

Among the state-of-the-art transmission schemes the seminal concept of joint ranging (location) and communication using OFDM technology[3] is important. In this context OFDM can find applications in future WSNs for border control where context-awareness (location information) is important and, in addition to sensing, data exchange among nodes or between nodes and the fusion center is essential.

By using OFDM technology, the bandwidth will be efficiently used. Furthermore, this technology provides reconfigurability and adaptation capabilities simultaneously. By using OFDM technology for border control applications (or Doppler effect), the movement of an intruder in border control applications can be detected in real time. This technology is also favourable in a UAV sensing network, monitoring large areas where the communication channel among sensing nodes is highly mobile.

[3] Van Genderen and Nikookar 2006.

7.2.4 Security of WSNs

Security is an extremely crucial issue in the application of WSNs. This is because the sensor nodes are prone to various kinds of malicious attacks. Therefore, security mechanisms will be required to safeguard transmission of sensed data. Security mechanisms of WSNs seem remarkably different from traditional secure communication systems. This is because sensor nodes of a WSN deployed in the region of interest interact with the environment and broadcast data. Major challenges for security of WSNs are the physical limitations of sensor nodes in terms of size, battery power and memory, which make the complete implementation of security mechanisms (encryption and decryption) a hard task. Furthermore, as mentioned above, in WSNs nodes broadcast the sensed data in a network. Therefore, there will be more chance for collision of data. Moreover, in a hostile environment the probability of trapping the sensed data is obviously higher. For the security of WSNs sensor nodes and base stations should authenticate the received data to verify whether they are sent from a trusted node. In the protocol layer of WSNs secure management mechanisms should be considered as encryption and routing information require a high level of security management. For full security at each sensor component of WSN a security mechanism must be implemented which with regard to limitations of sensor nodes constitutes a real challenge.

7.2.5 Cooperative Aspects of WSNs in Border Control

The cooperative scheme in WSNs for the border control and surveillance applications can effectively increase the probability of correct decisions on the detection of an intruder, reduce the probability of false alarms and can reduce the overall energy consumption as compared to non-cooperative methods. Many challenges in applying Game Theory to cooperative wireless sensor networks are envisioned. Among them theoretical methods to design cooperative WSNs, study of cooperation schemes, protocol design, and deployment of cooperative networking over existing infrastructure are just a few to name. In the next section, we focus on the game-theoretic aspect of cooperative WSNs, especially on dynamic node's coalition formation algorithms, and see how these can be applied to the border monitoring or the intruder detection case.

7.3 A Game-Theoretic Framework for WSN

As discussed above, the need for self-organizing, sometimes decentralized and autonomous networks, makes suitable game-theoretical tools of paramount interest. These tools can be used to analyse the behaviour and interaction of nodes in

WSN. As already mentioned, in a WSN a few nodes may cooperate to increase the performance of the system. In this chapter, we use game theory, to study the nodes' cooperation as a process of arriving at coalitions within WSN. Such a coalition of cooperating nodes is also called a cluster. These coalitions have to be flexible, have reconfigurable structures that can adapt to the circumstances, and also should be able to cooperate with other sensor networks. In studies on the process of coalition formation an important issue is how coalitions form, or by which rules they proceed before some kind of stability is reached. In the more classic approach of game theory, it is assumed that (for some reason) the grand coalition is formed, consisting of all players. Subsequently, the gain is divided between all players is such a way that players do not have an incentive to leave or defect from this grand coalition and form other coalitions instead.[4] In that approach, the issue of how coalitions form is not taken into consideration. But in forming coalitions for optimizing some task, like detecting or tracing an intruder using a WSN, generally this grand coalition is inefficient due to the costs of information exchange between the nodes. Instead some partitioning of nodes will emerge, where nodes work together in coalitions to perform tasks. In addition, when the intruder moves through the area of interest, the partitioning of the total set of nodes in a WSN may change over time for tracking purposes. Therefore, in applying game theory to WSN, one has to describe how coalitions form. In the literature, one may find models in which the formation of coalitions may be constrained by an underlying network, connecting the various nodes. It may even be the case that links are formed or deleted, like in social networks, where nodes try to obtain unique positions. In social networks analysis for example, the research question is what kind of networks do emerge, what is its topology.[5] In the discussion that follows here, we do not take these kinds of constraints into consideration, except for the case that some coalitions may need the presence of a node that transmits information to a ground station.

7.3.1 Aspect of Game Theory Relevant *for Cooperative WSN*

Coalition formation entails finding a coalitional structure which maximizes some technical welfare or utility. This technical welfare can be defined in various ways, depending on the application at hand.[6] Finding the structure that has the maximum welfare requires iterating over all partitions of nodes, each time determining its technical welfare. But, as for 10 nodes there already exist more than 115,000 partitions, this centralized approach is computationally complex and impractical. Therefore, some specific coalition formation algorithms are used, consisting of simple rules for forming or breaking coalitions. After several iterations of these rules, the stability

[4] Evers et al. 2013; Grant et al. 2014.

[5] Monsuur 2007; Jackson 2008.

[6] Bejar et al. 2010.

of the obtained partition of the set of all nodes is assessed. In our presentation, we closely follow the approach of[7] [6], [7] and [12].

7.3.2 Technical Welfare

Let N be the set of nodes in a WSN, and let $|N|$ be its size. A coalition (a cluster of nodes) is a non-empty subset of N. We assume that some value can be assigned to such a coalition. For a coalition S, this value is noted by $\upsilon(S)$. This value models the trade-off between the advantage of cooperation (in terms of better performance) and the costs of cooperation (in terms of bandwidth, transmitting power, or exchanging information). The value may depend on the topology within such a coalition (for example the presence of an information fusion centre), node's location within the area of interest, and on characteristics of the individual nodes.

A collection of the (grand) coalition N is any family $S=\{S_1, S_2, \ldots, S_t\}$ of mutually disjoint coalitions of N; its size is t. If, in addition, the union of these disjoint coalitions is N, it is called a partition of N. In forming flexible structures that can adapt to the circumstances, the set of nodes is partitioned into mutually disjoint coalitions. These mutually disjoint coalitions may be interpreted as alternatives structures that can perform some task that the WSN is constructed for. In the process of finding an optimal coalitional structure, a particular partition of nodes is compared to alternative partitions by means of a technical welfare function. Given a partition $\{S_1, S_2, \ldots, S_t\}$, this technical welfare is denoted by $tw(S_1, S_2, \ldots, S_t)$, which is a function of the values $(\upsilon(S_1), \upsilon(S_2), \ldots, \upsilon(S_t))$. By abuse of notation, it may also be written as $tw(\upsilon(S_1), \upsilon(S_2), \ldots, \upsilon(S_t))$. Technical welfare of two partitions can be compared in various ways. We give a few examples. Let $S=\{S_1, S_2, \ldots, S_t\}$, and $T=\{T_1, T_2, \ldots, T_k\}$ be two partitions of the set of nodes.

- *Utilitarian comparison*
  S is preferred to T if $\sum_{i=1}^{t} \upsilon(S_i) \sum > \sum_{j=1}^{k} \upsilon\left(T_j\right)$, so $tw(x_1, \ldots, x_t)=\sum x_i$
- *Nash comparison*
  S is preferred to T if $\prod_{i=1}^{t} \upsilon(S_i) > \prod_{j=1}^{k} \upsilon\left(T_j\right)$, so $tw(x_1, \ldots, x_t)=\prod x_i$
- *Maximum comparison*
  S is preferred to T if $\max_i \upsilon(S_i) > \max_j \upsilon\left(T_j\right)$, so $tw(x_1, \ldots, x_t)=\max_i x_i$

Which comparison function is used depends on the application in mind. Technical welfare combines coalitional values with the value generated by the WSN as a whole. (As an aside: if one also distributes the value $\upsilon(S)$ between the nodes of S, transforming the vector $\upsilon(S_1), \upsilon(S_2), \ldots, \upsilon(S_t)$ into a vector $(s_1, s_2, \ldots, s_{|N|})$ with $|N|$ entries, one may also use the *Pareto comparison*: S is preferred to Q if $(s_1, s_2, \ldots, s_{|N|})$ is preferred to $(q_1, q_2, \ldots, q_{|N|})$, meaning that $s_i \geq q_i$ and there exists an index j such that $s_j > q_j$.)

[7] Apt and Witzel 2006; Apt and Radzik 2006; Saad et al. 2009.

7.3.3 Transitions Between Partitions

Now we come to the issue of how coalitions form, or evolve over time. A transition from one partition to another one is feasible, or is likely to happen, if the technical welfare increases. To describe the possible alternative partitions, we need some simple yet rich enough rules by which one may proceed towards optimal partitions. Again, there are several choices for these rules that modify an existing partition. We give three examples of such rules that may be used to transition to a next partition.

- Merging coalitions
  $\{Z_1, Z_2, \ldots, Z_k\} \cup S$ becomes $\bigcup_{j=1}^{k} Z_j \cup S$ if $tw\left(\bigcup_{j=1}^{k} Z_j\right) > tw(Z_1, Z_2, \ldots, Z_k)$
- Splitting a coalition
  $\bigcup_{j=1}^{k} Z_j \cup S$ becomes $\{Z_1, Z_2, \ldots, Z_k\} \cup S$ if $tw(Z_1, Z_2, \ldots, Z_k) > tw\left(\bigcup_{j=1}^{k} Z_j\right)$
- Exchanging
  $\{Z_1, Z_2\} \cup S$ becomes $\{(Z_1 \backslash U_1) \cup U_2, (Z_2 \backslash U_2) \cup U_1\} \cup S$ where $U_1 \subset Z_1$ and $U_2 \subset Z_2$, if $tw(Z_1, Z_2) < tw((Z_1 \backslash U_1) \cup U_2, (Z_2 \backslash U_2) \cup U_1)$.

Clearly, these definitions assume that the technical welfare of a partition can be built from technical welfares of parts of the WSN. For example, if $tw\left(\bigcup_{j=1}^{k} Z_j\right) > tw(Z_1, Z_2, \ldots, Z_k)$, then $tw\left(\bigcup_{j=1}^{k} Z_j\right) > tw(Z_1, Z_2, \ldots, Z_k, S)$ for any S. See [5] for introducing the rules above and discussing this issue of monotonicity. The rules may, in some sense, be compared to defining neighbourhoods of a given point in a solution space if one uses heuristics for optimization, like simulated annealing.

To illustrate the use of the rules above, and investigate the sufficiency of these rules for reaching optimal partitions, we consider the following example.[8] Let $N = \{1, 2, 3, 4\}$, and let v be defined by:

$$v(S) = \begin{cases} 3 & if\, S = \{1, 2\} \\ |S| & otherwise \end{cases}$$

If we take the utilitarian comparison, the partitions with the highest *tw*-value are {{1,2}, {3,4}} and {{1,2}, {3}, {4}}, having a value of 5. Now start with any partition. Using the merging and splitting rule, we arrive at either of these two partitions, or at other partitions with two coalitions, where each coalition has two elements, like {{1,3}, {2,4}}. These partitions all have a value of 4. Note that if we only apply the merging and splitting rules, it is impossible to transit from {{1,3}, {2,4}} to the partition with value 5. For that to happen, we in addition need the exchange rule. Unfortunately, one may construct examples, where even the addition of this rule does not make it possible to reach the partition with the highest *tw*-value.

---

[8] Apt and Radzik 2006.

7.3.4 Testing Stability; D-Stable Partitions

In the classical game-theoretic approach, one assumes that the grand coalition will be formed. Then, a proposed solution for dividing the gains of cooperation has to be tested with respect to stability. A well-known concept then is the core of the game, consisting of payoffs for which no coalition of players can obtain a better payoff by leaving the grand coalition.

So far, we described transitions from one partition to another one by means of rules, like splitting and merging. To test the stability of a particular partition that may have emerged after iterations of the merging and splitting rules, we use the notion of defecting functions D. This defection function can be compared with testing whether or not the payoff structure within the grand coalition belongs to the core. Given any partition S of the nodes, the set $D(S)$ consists of partitions that serve as alternative to the existing partition. An example is the set D_{hp}. Here $D_{hp}(S)$ consists of partitions that can be reached from S in just one iteration of the merge or split rule. Repeated application of merge/split, starting at any partition, always terminates (due to the finite number of partitions) at what is then called a D_{hp}-stable partition. As illustrated in the example above, the outcome is not always unique, nor does splitting and merging guarantee maximal utility.

Another example is the set $D_c(S)$ consisting of all possible collections of coalitions, not necessarily a partition. Unfortunately, D_c-stable partitions may not exist. But, if a D_c stable partition exists, it is the unique outcome of applying merging and splitting to any partition. Given a partition S, we may also consider transitions due to a defecting collection T, where T is not necessarily a partition. Let $T = \{T_1, T_2, \ldots, T_k\}$, and let $\hat{T} = \bigcup T_i$. The collection may be evaluated in its defected form as $tw(T_1, T_2, \ldots, T_k)$. But in the frame of $S = \{S_1, S_2, \ldots, S_t\}$, the current partition, it may be evaluated as $tw(S_1 \cap \hat{T}, S_2 \cap \hat{T}, \ldots, S_t \cap \hat{T})$. Note that if $\hat{T} = N$, then these two evaluations are equal. A transition is possible if $tw(T_1, T_2, \ldots, T_k) > tw(S_1 \cap \hat{T}, S_2 \cap \hat{T}, \ldots, S_t \cap \hat{T})$. As generally speaking no partition S is immune for transitions including coalitions, we restrict ourselves to transitions between partitions.

7.3.5 An Illustrative Example (Intruder Detection)

Depending on the application in mind, there are several choices for assigning value to a coalition, as well as assigning the technical welfare to a collection or partition. Giving a task that the WSN has to perform, like detecting an intruder, the value v models the trade-off between the advantage of cooperation (in terms of better performance) and the costs of cooperation (in terms of bandwidth and power). The technical welfare function is tuned to resemble the quality of the partition in performing a task. To give an example, we consider the task of detecting an intruder, see Fig. 7.2.

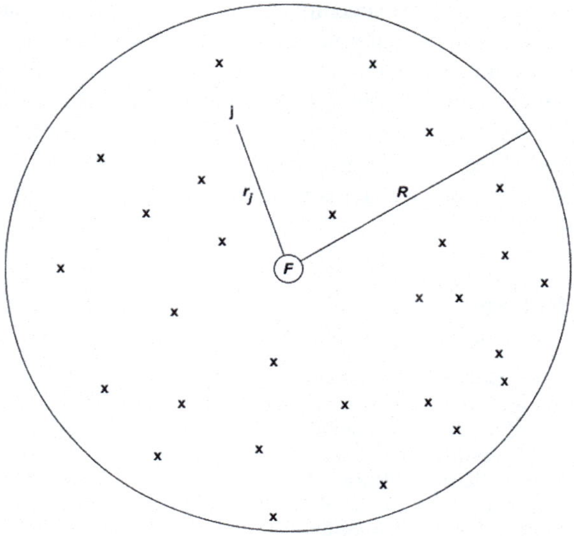

Fig. 7.2 WSN configuration for intruder detection. *R* is the coverage of the WSN; *F* is the fusion node; the *x's* are typical nodes of a WSN; r_j is the distance of node *j* to the fusion node. [*Source* H. Nikookar, H. Monsuur]

The gain or quality of cooperation *Q*(*M*) of a coalition *M* depends on how the coalition of nodes is able to distinguish signals from noise. In our (distributed) detection case, this gain is not a simple function. It depends on probabilities of false alarms, thresholds, and a particular decision scheme. Therefore, for this exposition, we only focus on the cost of cooperation *C*(*M*). For each node is given p_i, the power of the node. The parameter r_i is the distance of node i to the fusion center, while σ^2 is the noise variance. Then we define the cost of cooperation within the coalition *M* by $C(M) = \sum_{i=1}^{M} p_i \frac{r_i^2}{R^2} + \log_2\left(1 + \frac{\sum_{i=1}^{M} p_i \left(\frac{r_i}{R}\right)^2}{\sigma^2}\right)$. As a value for the coalition *M* we may take $\upsilon(M) = \alpha Q(M) - (1 - \alpha)C(M)$, where $0 < \alpha < 1$, thereby balancing costs and performance or quality. This approach may be used in simulations to investigate the flexible adaptation of coalitions to tasks and changing circumstances. This dynamic coalition formation process, with distributed nodes and a fusion center, is based on iterated application of the merging and splitting rules.

7.4 Summary

Game theory is used in studying cooperative wireless networks for two reasons.[9] The first is to understand incentives and strategies of nodes for cooperation. The second one is to devise distributed algorithms that can find optimal partitions of the set of

---

[9] MacKenzie and daSilva 2006.

nodes. Our distributed approach using merging and splitting can be suboptimal, but runs in polynomial time, contrary to a more centralized approach.

In future research, we will start simulations, using several intruder detection scenarios, with nodes having certain distinct characteristics. This will be used to validate the performance of the game-theoretic approach in these intruder detection scenarios. There we will also elaborate on the gain of cooperation, which will require more sophisticated probabilistic arguments.

References

Apt K, Radzik T (2006) Stable partitions in coalitional games. arXiv:cs/0605132v1 [cs.GT]

Apt K, Witzel A (2006) A generic approach to coalition formation. In: Endriss U, Lang J (eds) Proceedings of the International Workshop on Computational Social Choice (COMSOC). University of Amsterdam, pp 21–35

Bejar P, Belanovic P, Zazo S (2010) Cooperative localization in wireless sensor networks using coalitional game theory. Proceedings 18th European Signal Processing Conference, pp 1459–1463

Evers L, Barros AI, Monsuur H (2013) The Cooperative Ballistic Missile Defence Game. In: Das SK, Nita-Rotaru C, Kantarcioglu M (eds) GameSec 2013. LNCS. Vol. 8252:85–98

Grant TJ, Janssen RHP, Monsuur H (eds) (2014) Network Topology and Military C2 Systems: Design, Operation and Evolution. IGI Global Publishers

Gupta CP, Kumar A (2013) Wireless Sensor Networks: A Review, International Journal of Sensors. Wireless Communications and Control 3(1)1:25–36

Jackson MO (2008) Social and Economic Networks. Princeton University Press

MacKenzie AB, daSilva LA (2006) Game theory for wireless engineers. Synthesis Lectures on Communications 1(1):1–86

Monsuur H (2007) Stable and Emergent Network Topologies: A Structural Approach. European Journal of Operational Research 183(1):432–441

Nikookar H (2015) Wireless Radio Senor Networks: Looking Back, Moving Forward. Seminar on Human Bond Communications and Beyond 2050, Aalborg University, Denmark

Saad W, Han Z, Debbah M, Hjørungnes A, Basar T (2009) Coalitional Game Theory for Communication Networks: A Tutorial. IEEE Signal Processing Magazine 26(5):77–97

van Genderen P, Nikookar H (2006) Radar Network Communication, 6th International Conference on Communications, Bucharest, Romania, pp 313–316

Part III
Data Analysis and Deployment of Maritime Security Forces

Chapter 8
Optimizing Asset Deployment in Maritime Law Enforcement

E.R. van Veldhoven and H.J. Fitski

Contents

Abstract Maritime security operations, such as counter-piracy operations, often take place in vast areas of open sea. This requires operating in a coalition task force consisting of multiple task units, each composed of a number of naval assets such as frigates, helicopters, and unmanned aerial vehicles (UAVs). For the planning of these operations, we introduce a two-level approach. At the first level, the area of operations is divided into sectors and the available task units are assigned to these sectors. The second level consists of the tactical planning of the deployment of the individual assets of a task unit within the task unit's sector. In this paper, we propose algorithms to tackle both levels of planning. For maritime security operations in general, we introduce an allocation algorithm for dividing an area of operations,

E.R. van Veldhoven (✉) · H.J. Fitski
Military Operations Department, TNO, The Hague, The Netherlands
e-mail: edwin.vanveldhoven@tno.nl

H.J. Fitski
e-mail: hilvert.fitski@tno.nl

H. Monsuur et al. (eds.), *NL ARMS Netherlands Annual Review of Military Studies 2018*, NL ARMS, https://doi.org/10.1007/978-94-6265-246-0_8

based on the capabilities of the individual task units, in such a way that the expected effectiveness of the task force as a whole is optimal. For counter-piracy operations, where the focus is on the prevention of pirate attacks on merchant vessels, a search planning algorithm is introduced that allows generating effective search plans for the deployment of the task unit's assets within a sector of the area of operations.

Keywords Naval Forces · Maritime Law Enforcement · Maritime Security Operations · Counter-Piracy Operations · Allocation · Tactical Planning

8.1 Introduction

Naval platforms are increasingly being sent on international security missions to combat drug smuggling, piracy, illegal fishing, and human trafficking. These types of missions, called maritime security operations, differ from conventional warfare operations in the fact that they focus on law enforcement and should interfere with regular shipping as little as possible. The focus is on finding and eliminating specific targets.

In view of the vast area of operations that is usually involved, maritime security operations would require a large number of naval assets to be fully effective. However, long-term deployment of many assets can often not be accomplished due to other tasks and commitments, even if the operation is executed by a coalition task force.

The question then becomes: how can the limited number of available assets be optimally deployed in maritime security operations? We assume that the (coalition) task force consists of multiple task units. Each task unit consist of a number of naval assets (task elements)[1] such as frigates, helicopters, unmanned aerial vehicles (UAVs) and rigid hull inflatable boats (RHIBs).

For planning the deployment of these assets, we introduce a two-level approach. The first level of planning is the responsibility of the Officer in Tactical Command (OTC). This can be the Maritime Component Commander (MCC) or a task force commander appointed by the MCC.[2] At this level of planning, which we will call task unit allocation, the area of operations is divided into sectors and the available task units are assigned to these sectors.

The second level, for which the task unit commanders are responsible, is the daily tactical planning of the individual asset deployment of a task unit within the task unit's sector.

Figure 8.1 illustrates the command structure. In the example shown in this figure, there is one task force which consists of three task units. The mission is controlled by the OTC (which can be the MCC). The OTC can be stationed onboard one of the frigates, but can also be far away from the task force on land.

[1] For describing the organization structure, we use the terminology from Defensie 2014, Chapter 5, except for "task element", which we will simply call "asset".

[2] See Defensie 2014, pp. 114–115.

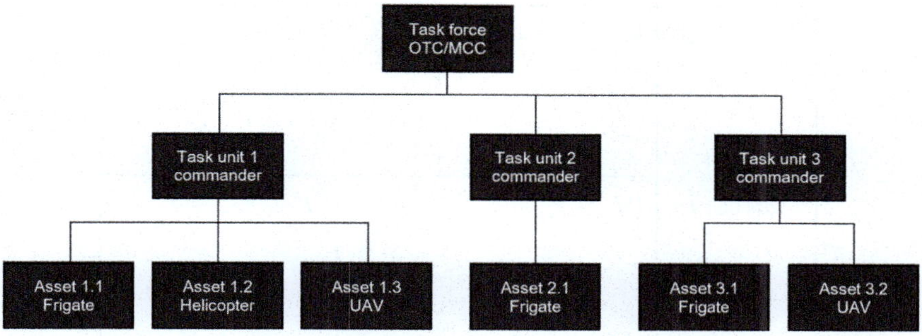

Fig. 8.1 An example of the command structure for the task force [*Source* E.R. van Veldhoven, H.J. Fitski]

The algorithms presented in this paper are results of the Dutch research programme "Maritime Situational Awareness", in which research has been performed on maritime security operations.[3] In this paper, all distances are in nautical miles (nmi), all times in 24-h time, and all speeds in knots (kts), unless otherwise stated.

8.2 Task Unit Allocation

The first step in planning an operation is deciding where the task units of the task force will be deployed. The task force commander must divide the entire area of operations into sectors, and assign all available task units to these sectors. The overall operational effectiveness of the task force as a whole must be optimized; therefore, the partition in sectors and the assignment of task units (at most one per sector) must be done in an optimal way.

The measure of effectiveness (MoE) that is used to quantify the operational effectiveness depends on the objective of the operation. The MoE may also depend on the phase of the operation: planning or execution. In the planning phase, a simulation tool can be used, in which full knowledge of the (simulated) world is available. For a mission to combat drug smuggling for example, the percentage of seized smugglers can then be used as MoE. In the execution phase, when only limited knowledge of the (real) world is available, e.g. the number of captured smugglers or the amount of seized contraband can be used as MoE. Because we are looking at the planning of maritime security operations, we use the percentage of seized (i.e. detected and boarded) targets as MoE.

We will assume that the area of operations is a rectangular area and that this area must be divided into rectangular sectors that do not overlap. Furthermore, we assume that the sizes of the area and the sectors are integer multiples of a certain unit of length (for example 1 nmi).

---

[3] See Smith and Van Dongen 2015.

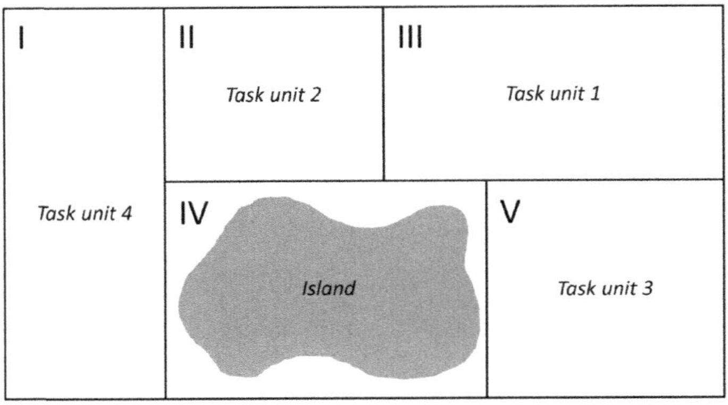

Fig. 8.2 Examples of an area of operations which is divided into five sectors, indicated by Roman numerals. Task units are assigned to four of these sectors; the sector containing an island is left "empty". [*Source* E.R. van Veldhoven, H.J. Fitski]

The composition of the available task units may differ, but we assume that the composition is fixed during the operation. For example, one task unit may consist of a frigate with a helicopter, another task unit may consist of a frigate with two UAVs, and yet another task unit may contain only a single frigate. The capabilities of the task units (for contributing to the overall operational effectiveness) may differ, due to differences in e.g. detection ranges, speed, and endurance of the individual assets of the task units.

Not every part of the entire area of operations may be interesting, for example because intelligence is available about the potential whereabouts of targets, or because certain conditions (e.g. the presence of islands, the lack of fish, or the lack of places to moor for smugglers) make it unlikely that targets will be operating in certain parts of the area. Therefore, there may be more sectors than task units. We will denote sectors without task units as "empty sectors" (see Fig. 8.2). We assume that the number of sectors is fixed and at least equal to the number of task units.

The problem of dividing the area of operations into sectors and assigning the available task units to these sectors is closely related to the Graph Partitioning Problem[4] and the Generalised Assignment Problem,[5] which are both NP-complete problems. Although the number of possible partitions of the area of operations and the number of possible assignments of the task units are finite,[6] the time required to find an optimal solution increases very quickly as the size of the problem grows. We decided to solve the problem using simulated annealing (SA) because this technique has been applied successfully to many partitioning and assignment problems.

---

[4] See Johnson et al. 1989.

[5] See Cattrysse and Van Wassenhove 1992.

[6] Note that, since we assume that the sizes of the area and the sectors are integer multiples of a certain unit of length, the number of possible partitions is finite.

Simulated annealing is a probabilistic technique for approximating the global optimum in a large search space.[7] In our case, the search space consists of all possible configurations of area partitions and task unit assignments. When searching for an optimum, the operational effectiveness is used as performance measure.

Simulated annealing is named so because of its analogy to the process of physical annealing in metallurgy, which is a technique involving heating and very slow cooling of a crystalline solid to reduce the number of crystal defects. The idea of slow cooling is implemented in the simulated annealing algorithm as a slow decrease in the probability of accepting worse solutions as the search space is explored.

Starting with an initial configuration (which will likely be far from optimal), the SA algorithm will search for configurations that approximate the global optimum using a "cooling schedule". In every step of the cooling schedule, a neighbour configuration is constructed, which is a slight modification of the current configuration. In our case, a neighbour configuration can contain a modified partition in sectors and/or a modification in the allocation of the available task units.

If the performance of the neighbour configuration is better than (or equal to) that of the current configuration, the neighbour configuration is accepted as the new current configuration. If the performance of the neighbour configuration is worse, the choice between accepting or rejecting it is based on an "acceptance probability". This probability depends on the temperature parameter T, which decreases as the cooling schedule progresses in time. As T decreases, the probability that a neighbour configuration with worse performance is accepted also decreases.

The cooling schedule ends when a certain stop criterion is reached. Provided that the decrease of T and the stop criterion have been chosen correctly, the end configuration will approximate the global optimum.

In pseudocode, our SA allocation algorithm reads as follows:

```
Initialize the temperature parameter T
Initialize the number of steps N
Construct an initial configuration S_0
S := S_0
Calculate the performance PERF_S of S
S_max := S
PERF_max := PERF_S
while stop criterion not reached do
    for i := 1 to N do
        Construct a neighbour configuration S* of S
        Calculate the performance PERF* of S*
        if PERF* ≥ PERF_S then
            S := S*
            PERF_S := PERF*
            if PERF_S > PERF_max then
                S_max := S
                PERF_max := PERF_S
            end if
```

[7] See Kirkpatrick et al. 1983, and Henderson et al. 2003.

```
        elsif e^((PERF* - PERF_S)/T) ≥ random(1) then
            S := S*
            PERF_S := PERF*
        end if
    end for
    Decrease the temperature parameter T
    Adapt the number of steps N
end while
```

As can be seen in the pseudocode, we also keep track of the configuration with the best performance (configuration S_{max} with performance $PERF_{max}$). This is done because it is possible that one of the constructed neighbour configurations has a better performance than the resulting end configuration. We use the configuration with the best performance as outcome for our algorithm.

Constructing the initial configuration can be done very easily, by simply dividing the overall area of operations into the desired number of equal horizontal or vertical sectors, and randomly assigning the task units in such a way that every sector contains at most one task unit.

In the remainder of this section, we first explain how neighbour configurations are constructed, then describe how we calculate the performance of a configuration, and finally show results of a case study that we did using our allocation algorithm.

8.2.1 Constructing a Neighbour Configuration

In our case, a configuration is the combination of the partition of the area of operations in sectors, and the allocation of the task units to these sectors. We define the neighbour configurations of a certain configuration as those configurations in which a single line segment (between two or more sectors) has been moved and/or in which the allocation of the available task units over the sectors has been changed.

We split the construction of a neighbour configuration into two separate steps: constructing a modified partition of the area of operations in sectors, and the allocation of the task units to the modified sectors.

Given a partition of the area, we construct a neighbour partition in the following way. First, we randomly select one of the sectors and randomly add a horizontal or vertical line in this sector. After this, we randomly select one of the lines that make up the sectors and remove this line. Finally, we extend any partial lines if necessary. This process is depicted in Fig. 8.3.

In this way, any starting partition can be transformed into any possible partition of the area (with an equal number of sectors as the starting partition) in a number of steps.

Once a neighbour partition has been constructed, the next step is the allocation of the task units to the sectors. For this step, we looked at three approaches. The first

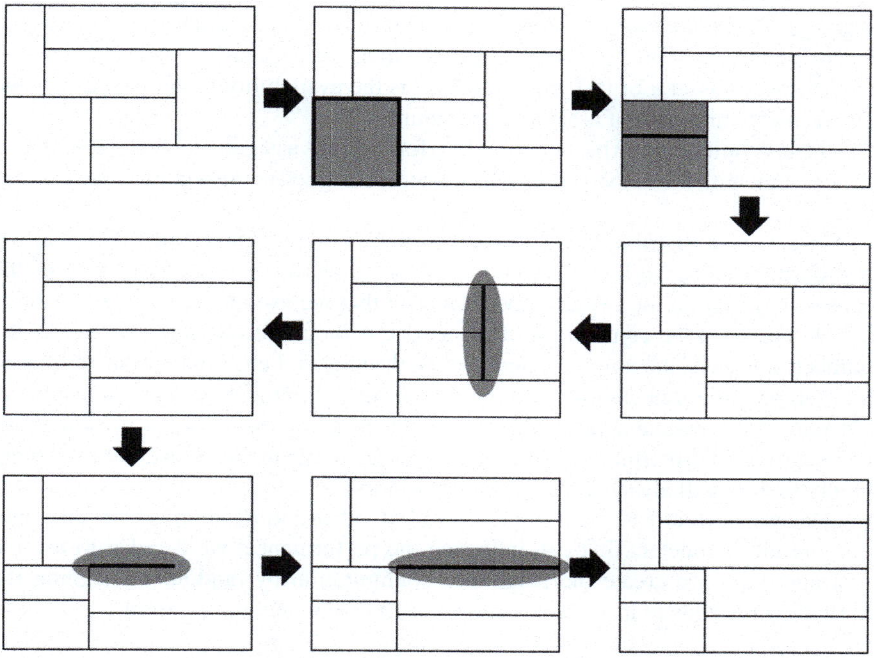

Fig. 8.3 Constructing a neighbour partition. Top row: randomly selecting one of the sectors and randomly adding a line in this sector. Middle row: randomly selecting one of the lines that make up the sectors and removing it. Bottom row: extending the partial line. [*Source* E.R. van Veldhoven, H.J. Fitski]

and simplest approach is randomly assigning the available task units to the sectors. If there are more sectors than task units, the remaining sectors stay empty.

The second approach is making a slight adjustment to the assignment of the task units, for example randomly exchanging two task units.[8] However, modifying the partition may already require reassigning task units. An example of this can be seen in Fig. 8.3: in which sector of the resulting partition should the task unit of the lower left sector of the original configuration be placed? Because this approach is algorithmically more difficult than the full random assignment of the first approach, we did not further investigate it.

In the third approach, the task units are assigned to the sectors based on their expected performance. The performance of a task unit i is calculated as the sum of the individual performances of the assets:

$$Perf(i) = \sum_{n=1}^{m_i} v_{n,i} \cdot r_{n,i} \cdot a_{n,i} \tag{8.1}$$

[8] If there are empty sectors, it is also possible to randomly move a task unit to an empty sector.

where m_i is the number of assets in task unit i, $v_{n,i}$ is the search speed of asset n of task unit i, $r_{n,i}$ is the detection range at which targets can be detected by one of the sensors of asset n of task unit i, and $a_{n,i}$ is the availability (expressed as a value between zero and one) of asset n of task unit i.

The task unit with the best expected performance is assigned to the largest sector, the task unit with the second best performance is assigned to the second largest sector, etc.

We expected that the third approach, which is more sophisticated than the first approach, would give better results. This was, however, not the case. One of the causes may be that the expected performance that we used to assign the task units is only based on the capabilities of the assets, without considering aspects like the number of targets, the targets' whereabouts, the targets' behaviour, or the number of other ships in the area. As a result, certain task unit assignments are never considered, whereas in the random approach, each possible task unit assignment has a chance of being chosen. Furthermore, if there are more sectors than task units, the remaining empty sectors will always be the smallest sectors.

Because it would be very complex to extend the third approach to take into account all parameters that can influence the performance, we decided to use the first approach: we create the neighbour configuration by randomly assigning the available task units to the sectors of the constructed neighbour partition.

8.2.2 Calculating the Performance of a Configuration

An essential part of our SA allocation algorithm is the performance calculation for the configuration of an area partition and task unit assignment. The inputs of the performance function are attributes of the area of operations, capabilities of the task units, intelligence about targets, sector partition, and the assignment of task units. Based on these inputs, the performance function should calculate the operational effectiveness of the task force as a whole.

We decided to use the SURPASS (SURface Picture ASSessment) simulation model to model the performance function (see Fig. 8.4). SURPASS is TNO's simulation model for maritime surface surveillance.[9] It provides an insight into the resources and tactics required for establishing and maintaining a recognized surface picture,[10] for example in an embargo or a counter-drug operation. The main assets considered in SURPASS are frigates, UAVs, helicopters, and maritime patrol aircraft. Sensors, such as radar, optical, infrared, ESM (Electronic Support Measures), and passive sonobuoys, are also included. SURPASS can be used as an analysis tool (e.g. for research into new platforms or new operational tactics) and as a training tool (e.g. for educational purposes).

---

[9] See Fitski et al. 2015.

[10] The recognized surface picture or RSP is a listing of the surface ships within a certain area, with additional information for each ship, such as position, speed, course, and ship type.

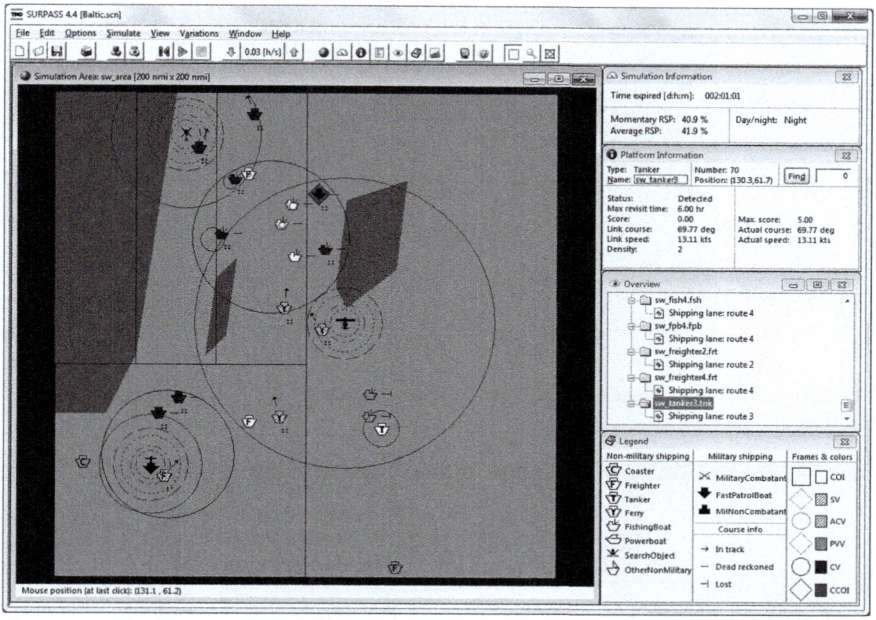

Fig. 8.4 Screenshot of SURPASS, showing a top view of a maritime operation [*Source* E.R. van Veldhoven, H.J. Fitski]

In this case, we used SURPASS as an analysis tool to calculate the operational effectiveness of an operation. In SURPASS, we can build a scenario containing the area of operations, the targets and their behaviour, and the assets of the task units. We can define identification criteria (IDCRITS)[11] such that boarded targets are identified as critical contacts of interest (CCOI), and all other ships as cleared vessels.

As the measure of effectiveness, we used the percentage of targets that are identified as CCOI. Note that the type of target, and hence the criteria for a contact to be identified as CCOI, depends on the type of operation. Targets can, for example, be illegal fishermen or smugglers.

When the performance of a configuration must be calculated in the SA algorithm, the partition and task unit assignment are sent to SURPASS, which inserts these in the scenario, gives all assets of the task units a basic search pattern (a ladder search pattern; see Fig. 8.5) and runs the scenario for a predefined number of simulation days. The resulting MoE value, which represents the performance of the configuration, is then returned to the SA algorithm.

[11] In SURPASS, it is possible to define IDCRITS using either the NATO Standard Identities (Unknown, Assumed Friend, Suspect, Friend, Neutral, Hostile) or the Maritime Interdiction Force (MIF) Identities (Contact Of Interest, Assessed Cleared Vessel, Suspicious Vessel, Potential Violator Vessel, Cleared Vessel, Critical Contact Of Interest).

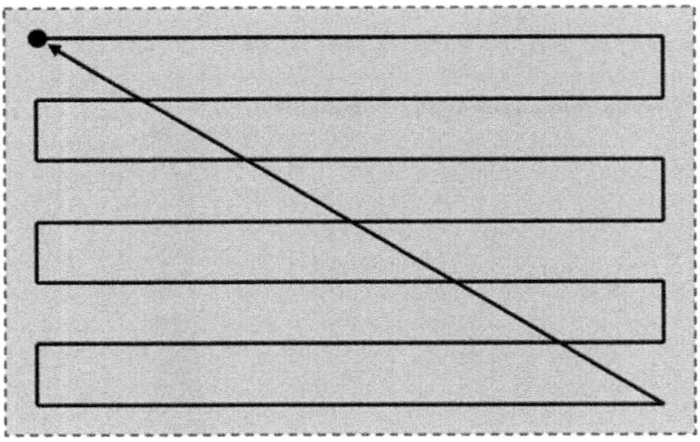

Fig. 8.5 An example of a ladder search in a rectangular search area [*Source* E.R. van Veldhoven, H.J. Fitski]

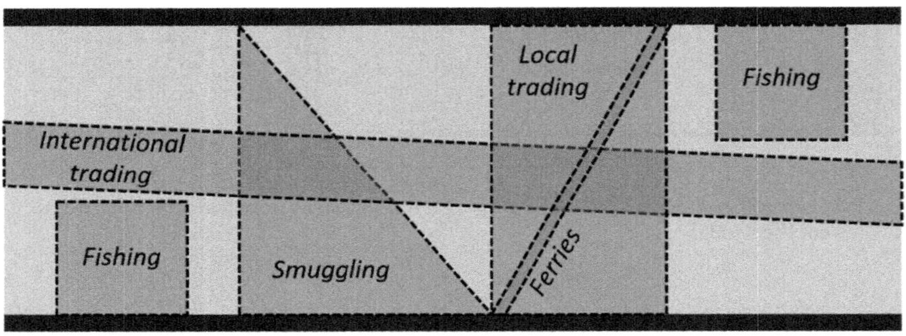

Fig. 8.6 Overall view of the shipping in the sea area of 150 nmi by 50 nmi [*Source* E.R. van Veldhoven, H.J. Fitski]

8.2.3 Case Study

To evaluate our allocation algorithm, we created the following scenario (see Fig. 8.6): in an area of 150 nmi by 50 nmi, bordered by northern and southern coastlines, tankers representing international trading passed through an east-west oriented sea lane, coasters representing local trading sailed through a north-south oriented sea lane, ferries sailed back and forth between the two coastlines, fishing took place in two fishing areas, and smugglers were active in a triangular area between the two coastlines. In addition, pleasure boats sailed throughout the area.

The task force consisted of a varying number of task units, each composed of one frigate and one organic helicopter. Both the frigates and the helicopters were equipped with radar and infrared sensors. Each helicopter could fly at most three sorties per day, had an endurance of six hours, and was unavailable (due to refuelling and maintenance) for two hours after each sortie.

The objective of the operation was to catch the smugglers. Note that in the above scenario, the best allocation for the task units is obvious: deploy them in and around the "smuggling" area. This scenario was intentionally simple: we wanted to see if the results of our allocation algorithm would match intuition.

We will show the results for the following combinations:

1. five task units, no empty sectors;
2. four task units, one empty sector;
3. three task units, two empty sectors;
4. two task units, three empty sectors.

The result of the allocation algorithm for the case with five task units is shown in Fig. 8.7. The area in which the smugglers were active is indicated by the grey triangle. The algorithm yielded a configuration with a very high MoE of 97.8%, where the highest concentration of task units is, as expected, in the smuggling area.

Figure 8.8 shows the resulting configuration for four task units and one empty sector, having an MoE of 95.2%. The SA algorithm placed three task units such that they have a large overlap with the smuggling area.

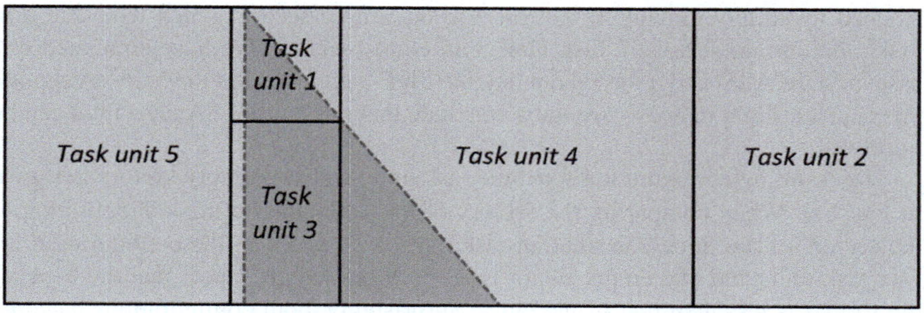

Fig. 8.7 Resulting configuration for five task units and no empty sectors [*Source* E.R. van Veldhoven, H.J. Fitski]

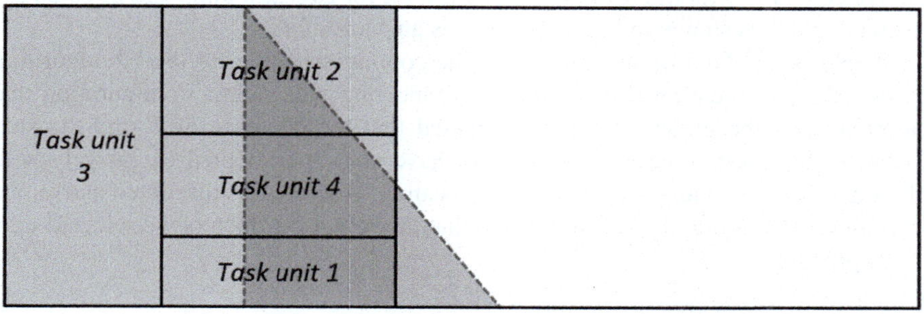

Fig. 8.8 Resulting configuration for four task units and one empty sector [*Source* E.R. van Veldhoven, H.J. Fitski]

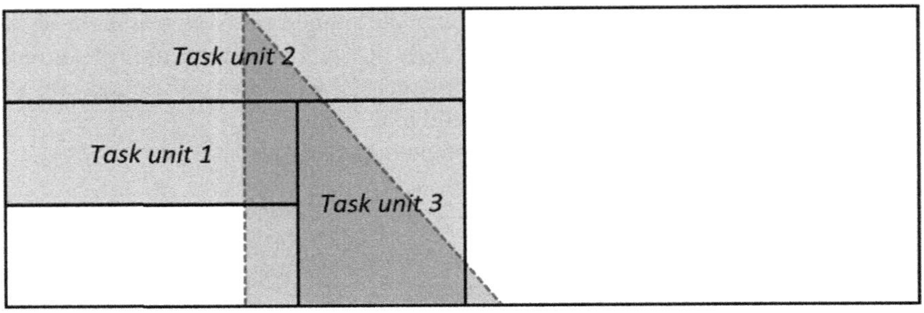

Fig. 8.9 Resulting configuration for three task units and two empty sectors [*Source* E.R. van Veldhoven, H.J. Fitski]

Interestingly, the right corner of the smuggling area is not covered[12] at all, while Task Unit 3 operates in an area where no smugglers are present in our scenario. Task Unit 3 contributes to the MoE because its assets can detect and identify other ships in the area, and hence the other task units have more time to investigate contacts that may be smugglers. Nevertheless, one would expect that a higher MoE could be reached by simply moving Task Unit 3 to the empty sector (which would in turn make the current sector of Task Unit 3 an empty sector). We have simulated this case in SURPASS, and it turned out that the MoE then increases to 95.5%. Although this is just a slight increase, we must conclude that our current SA algorithm can be improved.

The resulting configuration for three task units and two empty sectors is shown in Fig. 8.9. When comparing the sectors of the task units in this configuration to the sectors of the three contributing task units 1, 2, and 4 in the configuration for four task units and one empty sector (Fig. 8.8), one might expect that the MoE of the former is less than that of the latter. Surprisingly, both configurations have the same MoE of 95.2%. It is interesting to see that the allocation algorithm can produce configurations that are counterintuitive, but still have a good performance.

We conclude with the resulting configuration for two task units and three empty sectors, which is shown in Fig. 8.10 and has an MoE of 93.0%.

A final note about the parameters of the cooling schedule for the SA algorithm is in order. We mentioned that simulated annealing will yield a configuration that approximates the global optimum, provided that the decrease of T and the stop criterion have been chosen correctly. We have not experimented extensively with these parameters to tune the simulated annealing. However, as discussed above, the current results of our algorithm indicate that the initial parameters we selected may be improvable.

[12] It must be noted that the sectors do not fully correspond to "covered" area, since an asset that is near the border of its sector might perform detections outside its sector. In SURPASS, an asset is not allowed to move outside its sector, but it can already start intercepting a target that it detected outside its sector.

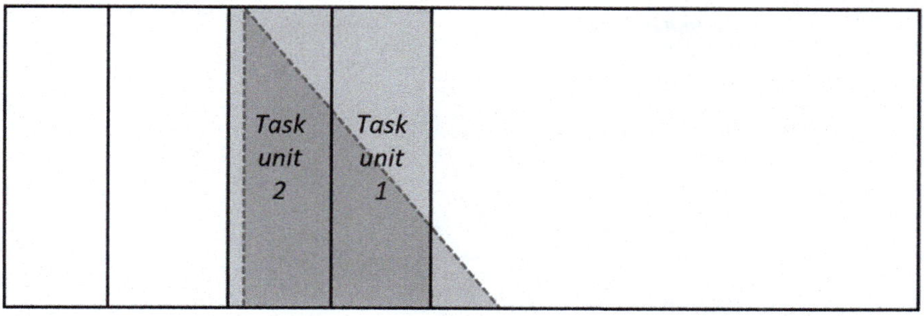

Fig. 8.10 Resulting configuration for two task units and three empty sectors [*Source* E.R. van Veldhoven, H.J. Fitski]

For our case study, we used a value of ten as the initial value for T and decreased T by halving it (an exponential decrease). For the number of steps N, we assigned a fixed value of five. For the stop criterion, we used $T < 0.001$. Another stop criterion could be the number of successive neighbour configurations that are rejected. For example, the SA could be stopped if none of the previous 100 configurations were accepted.

Furthermore, it would be interesting to investigate extensions of the current construction of neighbour configurations. For example, instead of completely changing the structure of the allocation, a neighbour partition could also be constructed by just moving one or more of the lines that define the sectors in the allocation. Another way of constructing a neighbour configuration could be the random exchange of two task units, without modifying the partition of the area of operations.

8.3 Tactical Planning

Once a task unit commander has been assigned a sector of the area of operations, he must plan the daily deployment of the individual assets based on the available daily Intelligence. Here, we look at the situation that every day at 06:00 h, the task unit receives threat information for the next 24 h, in the form of "threat maps" and "risk maps". The task unit commander must not only consider the intelligence when planning, but must also take into account that the deployment of assets like helicopters and UAVs may be limited due to endurance, refuelling, maintenance, and crew rest times.

The algorithm that we present in this section was developed primarily for counter-piracy operations. However, the general concept behind the algorithm can also be used for other missions, such as missions for countering illegal fishery or smuggling. We will indicate where the algorithm differs for these types of missions.

In Sect. 8.3.1, we explain the concepts of threat maps and risk maps. Sections 8.3.2 up to 8.3.5 present our search planning algorithm for tactical planning of the deploy-

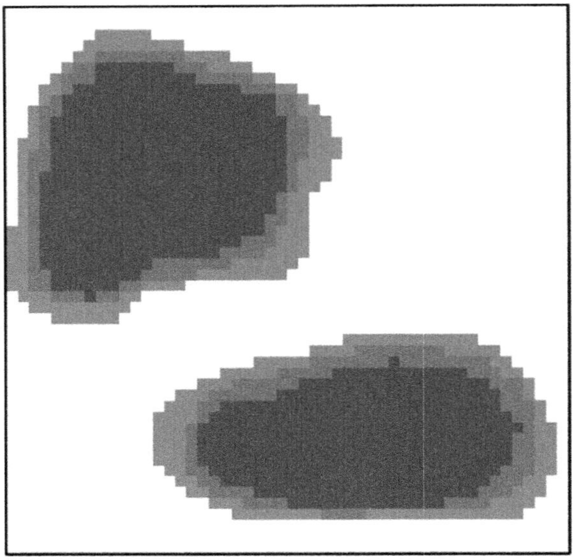

Fig. 8.11 An example of a daily threat map within the sector. The darkest coloured areas indicate the highest threat alert. The white area indicates there is no threat presence. [*Source* E.R. van Veldhoven, H.J. Fitski]

ment of assets. Finally, we discuss the results of a case study that we carried out using our algorithm in Sect. 8.3.6.

It must be noted that the problem of the tactical planning of the deployment of assets can also be solved using other techniques, such as game theory. In a game theoretic approach, the operation can be modelled as a game where an interceptor (for example an aircraft) needs to select a patrol route to detect intruders (for example illicit fishing boats or smugglers).[13]

8.3.1 *Threat Maps and Risk Maps*

For planning of the deployment of naval assets within a sector of the area of operations, information about the whereabouts of the targets is vital. We assume that this information is available in the form of a threat map. A threat map is a grid laid over the sector, where each cell indicates the probability of the occurrence of the threat within that cell.

We define the grid for the threat maps with $x = 1, \ldots, X$ and $y = 1, \ldots, Y$, where X and Y are constants defining the number of cells in horizontal and vertical direction, respectively. The probability of target presence in cell (x, y) is given by the threat map function $T(x, y)$, for $x = 1, \ldots, X$ and $y = 1, \ldots, Y$. An example of a threat map is shown in Fig. 8.11.

[13] See Atkinson et al. 2017, and Laan et al. 2017.

It is assumed that every day at 06:00 h, a new threat map for the next 24 h is received. It must be noted that, although we use one threat map per day in the algorithm that we present, it is possible to use more threat maps for a single day. During the course of a fishing inspection mission, for example, the locations of illegal fishing activities may vary during the day because the locations of schools of fish may change.

For most operations, the threat maps can be used for planning directly. In missions which combat drug smuggling and illegal fishing, the operational effectiveness can be measured in practice by counting the number of smugglers or illegal fishermen that are caught. In a simulation environment, the percentage of caught targets can be measured.

For counter-piracy operations, however, we use a different approach. The best way of measuring the effectiveness of these operations in practice is to look at the reduction in the number of hijacks. In a simulation environment, the ratio between the number of hijacks with and without the presence of the task force can be used as measure of effectiveness.[14]

As a result, the focus in missions to combat drug smuggling and illegal fishing should be on those locations where the threat map indicates a high probability of target presence. For counter-piracy missions, however, it is best to focus on the protection of merchant vessels instead of merely catching potential pirates. Searching for pirates should therefore be concentrated on locations where merchant vessels can be attacked by pirates. This is why we introduce the concept of risk maps.

A risk map is a representation of the actual risk for the merchant vessels, based on the threat map. Like the threat map, the risk map is a grid laid over the sector. Each cell of the risk map indicates the risk within that cell, which is at least zero, and the higher this value, the higher the risk.

We define the grid for the risk maps with $x = 1, \ldots, X$ and $y = 1, \ldots, Y$, where X and Y are the same as in the definition of the threat maps. The risk in cell (x, y) for hour i is given by the risk map function $R(x, y, i)$, for $x = 1, \ldots, X$, $y = 1, \ldots, Y$, and $i = 0, \ldots, 23$ (where the first hour starts at 06:00 h).

To produce the risk map, information about the location and routes of the vessels to be protected must be available. Note that this does not imply that we oblige all merchant vessels to provide this information. However, a vessel that does not share information regarding its location and route cannot and therefore will not be taken into account when planning the counter-piracy operation.

The calculation of the risk maps, which occurs once per hour, is performed as follows. For every merchant vessel, whether a pirate in a certain cell can detect *and* intercept the vessel within the time frame of one hour is checked. This depends on the expected detection capabilities and intercept speed of the pirates. If the pirate can both detect and intercept, the probability from the threat map cell multiplied by the vessel's vulnerability is included in the corresponding risk map cell.

The vulnerability of merchant vessels is incorporated in the risk maps because not every ship has the same vulnerability to pirate attack. The vulnerability depends

[14] See Fitski 2013.

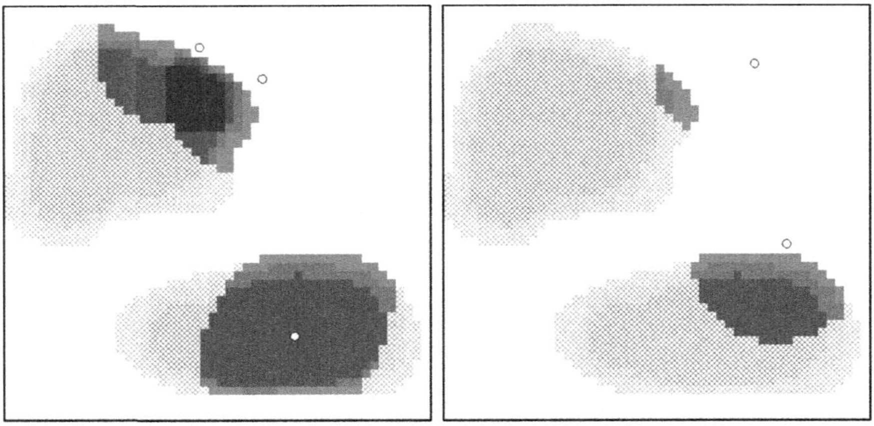

Fig. 8.12 Examples of two successive hourly risk maps based on the threat map from Fig. 8.11. The darkest coloured areas indicate the highest risk exposure for the merchant vessels for a particular hour. The shaded parts show the parts from original threat map where threats may be present, but which are not of interest within the current hour. The merchant vessels are depicted as white circles. [*Source* E.R. van Veldhoven, H.J. Fitski]

on aspects like the speed, size, freeboard, and cargo of the ship. We define the vulnerability as a value between zero and one.

We number the merchant vessels from one to M. The risk map for hour i is defined as follows:

$$R(x, y, i) = \sum_{m=1}^{M} T(x, y) \cdot V_m \cdot P(x, y, i, m) \tag{8.2}$$

where

$$P(x, y, i, m) = \begin{cases} 1 \text{ if a pirate in cell } (x, y) \text{ can detect and intercept} \\ \quad \text{vessel } m \text{ within hour } i \\ 0 \text{ otherwise} \end{cases} \tag{8.3}$$

and in which m denotes a merchant vessel and V_m is the vulnerability of m. Note that $R(x, y, i)$ can be greater than one.

Because the location of the moving merchant vessels heavily influences the risk maps, a new risk map will be calculated every hour. In Fig. 8.12, an example is shown of two successive risk maps, based on the threat map from Fig. 8.11.

Note that for missions other than counter-piracy operations, such as countering illegal fishing or smuggling, the risk maps can be considered equivalent to the threat maps.

8.3.2 The Search Planning Algorithm

We want to make a daily plan of action for the individual assets of the task unit, for every hour (which align with the hourly risk map updates). In the current version of our algorithm, which we will refer to as the search planning algorithm, we make the following assumptions:

1. the sector of the area of operations to which the task unit has been assigned is rectangular;
2. the one-hour search areas are squares;
3. all time-related parameters, such as the endurance, on-station time, and minimum time between successive sorties of an asset, are expressed in whole numbers of hours;
4. each search asset has a constant search speed and a constant transit speed;
5. the detection ranges of the search assets are omnidirectional, are equal during day and night, and are independent of the location in the sector;
6. the task unit's assets have a common operational picture, i.e. they are aware of the same information regarding detected targets;
7. a transit of an asset to another part of the sector will always occur at the start of an hour;
8. there are no restrictions on where a search asset may operate in the sector, such as a maximum distance from its home base.

The purpose of the search planning algorithm is to calculate the search plans for the assets of a task unit, within the task unit's sector. This includes scheduling the sorties (*when* should the assets be deployed) and determining the search areas within the sector (*where* should the assets be deployed).

The search plans are created by trying to cover as much risk as possible. We number the available search assets in the task unit from one to N. The goal is to find search areas $A_{n,i}$, for each asset $n = 1, \ldots, N$ and each hour $i = 0, \ldots, 23$, such that the following sum is maximized:

$$\sum_{i=0}^{23} \sum_{x=1}^{X} \sum_{y=1}^{Y} R(x, y, i) \cdot E(x, y, i) \tag{8.4}$$

where

$$E(x, y, i) = \begin{cases} 1 \text{ if there is an } A_{n,i},\ 1 \leq n \leq N, \text{ such that cell } (x, y) \text{ is in } A_{n,i} \\ 0 \text{ otherwise} \end{cases} \tag{8.5}$$

Notice that Eq. 8.4 reflects the total risk of those cells that have been covered by any sensor of any search asset. If a cell is covered by different assets during the same hour, the risk existing in that cell will be taken into account only once.

8.3.3 Risk Reduction

In Eq. 8.2, it is implicitly assumed that the risk maps are independent of the search efforts in the past. However, when compared with the risk maps, the real risk will be reduced at the places that were recently covered by a search asset. The influence of past search efforts decreases over time if no new searches are performed at the same locations.

To incorporate the concept of "risk reduction", we introduce "adaptive risk maps", in which the effects of past search efforts are taken into account. The adaptive risk maps are defined as follows:[15]

$$\tilde{R}(x, y, i) = \begin{cases} R(x, y, i) \cdot (1 - \alpha^{(p(x,y)-1)}) & \text{if there is an hour } h, 0 \leq h \leq i, \text{ in which} \\ & \text{cell } (x, y) \text{ has been covered} \\ R(x, y, i) & \text{otherwise} \end{cases} \tag{8.6}$$

where $0 \leq \alpha \leq 1$ and $p(x, y)$ is the number of hours since the last time that cell (x, y) has been covered by a search asset.

We assign α as the risk reduction factor. If α equals zero, the risk in the adaptive risk maps is zero in those cells where the assets have been searching in the previous hour, and the risk is equal to that in the original risk maps elsewhere. If α equals 1, the risk in the adaptive risk maps is zero in every cell that has once been covered by an asset.

It must be noted that we currently only adapt the risk maps based on the search efforts made during the period of 24 h. This could be changed such that the search efforts of the previous period are also taken into account.

8.3.4 Determining Sorties

The first part of the search planning algorithm focuses on the question of *when* the search assets should be deployed during the day. This is only relevant for assets with a limited endurance, such as helicopters or UAVs. We assume that the sorties of the search assets can be selected dynamically. If the task unit does not contain assets with limited endurance, or if the assets are supposed to use predefined sortie schedules, this part of the search planning algorithm can be skipped.

Regarding the planning of sorties, we make the following assumptions:

1. a search asset will always make the maximum number of sorties that it is allowed to make per day;
2. all sorties will last for the entire endurance period of the asset;
3. all sorties will be finished within the planning period of 24 h.

---

[15] In this equation, we define $0^0 = 1$.

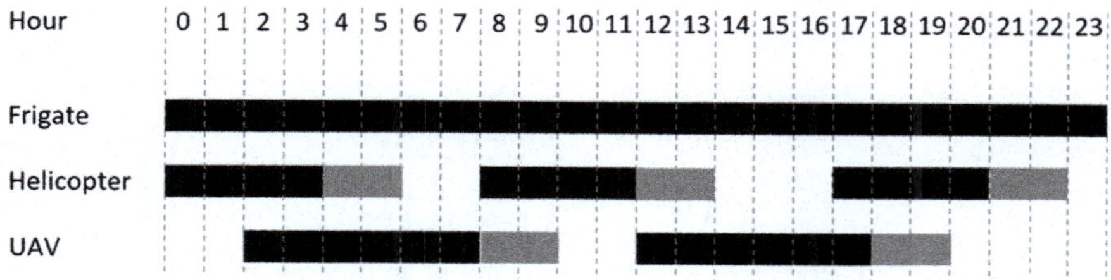

Fig. 8.13 An illustration of a sortie schedule. The black bars denote the on-station periods, the grey bars indicate the unavailable periods after sorties. [*Source* E.R. van Veldhoven, H.J. Fitski]

Figure 8.13 shows an example of a sortie schedule. In this example, we have a task unit consisting of a frigate, a helicopter, and a UAV. The frigate's endurance is considered unlimited, the helicopter has an endurance of four hours and the UAV's endurance is six hours (both indicated by black bars). Both search assets are unavailable for two hours after each sortie (indicated by grey bars). The number of sorties is three for the helicopter and two for the UAV.

The goal is to schedule the sorties during the day, in such a way that the covered risk can be maximized. Here, we make an approximation by looking at the maximum risk that could be covered during each hour by the search assets. The reason for this is that the actual amount of risk that can be covered depends on the course of the search, which depends on the actual presence and actions of the threat and cannot be foreseen.

We define the coverage rate of search asset n as follows:

$$C(n) = v_n \cdot 2 \cdot r_n \tag{8.7}$$

where v_n is the search speed of asset n and r_n is the detection/classification range at which targets can be detected by one of the sensors of asset n.

Since the one-hour search areas are supposed to be squares, we take as the maximum search area that can be covered in one hour a square with a length and width of a, where a is calculated as follows:

$$a = \left\lfloor f\left(\sqrt{1 \cdot C(n)}\right)\right\rfloor \tag{8.8}$$

where f is a function that maps the real distance to the distance in grid cells of the risk map.

We use the following procedure to determine the sortie schedules. We sort the search assets from the highest to the lowest coverage rate $C(n)$. Starting with the asset that has the highest coverage rate, we calculate the maximum risk coverage for the entire 24 h, for *every* possible sortie schedule of the unit, taking into account the unavailability after sorties (note that there may be remaining unavailable period from the previous day).

The maximum risk that can be covered by asset n during hour i is defined as follows:

$$R_{max}(n, i) = \max_{x=1..X-a+1}\left(\max_{y=1..Y-a+1}\left(\sum_{x^*=x}^{x+a-1}\sum_{y^*=y}^{y+a-1} R'(x^*, y^*, n, i)\right)\right) \tag{8.9}$$

$$R'(x, y, n, i) = \begin{cases} R(x, y, i) & \text{if cell } (x, y) \text{ is not in any search area already} \\ & \text{assigned for hour } i \text{ to an asset with a higher} \\ & \text{coverage rate than asset } n \\ 0 & \text{otherwise} \end{cases} \tag{8.10}$$

Note that in Eq. 8.10, we use the risk map function R. If risk reduction is to be taken into account, the adaptive risk map function $\tilde{R}$ should be used here.

The maximum risk that can be covered by asset n during the entire 24 h is:

$$R_{max}(n) = \sum_{i=0}^{23} R_{max}(n, i) \cdot S(n, i) \tag{8.11}$$

where

$$S(n, i) = \begin{cases} 0 & \text{if asset } n \text{ is not deployed during hour } i \\ 1 & \text{if asset } n \text{ is deployed during hour } i \end{cases} \tag{8.12}$$

For the sortie schedule, we determine the search areas that yield the highest risk coverage $R_{max}(n, i)$ for every hour that the asset is deployed in the sortie schedule, and (temporarily) assign them to asset n. This is necessary for Eq. 8.10. Note that this equation effectively assures that the risk map values $R(x, y, i)$ are taken as zero for the remainder of the calculation, for all cells (x, y) that are within the search area of asset n in hour i. This is done to prevent a situation where previously covered risk counted again as covered by any remaining assets to be scheduled.

Then we proceed to the next search asset and repeat this procedure until the sortie schedules for all assets have been determined.

8.3.5 Determining Search Areas

Once it has been decided *when* the search assets should be on-station during the day, it is possible to determine *where* they should be deployed in the sector. This is what the second part of the search planning algorithm focuses on.

This second part of the algorithm, the planning of the search areas within the sector, is done at the start of every new hour, based on the corresponding risk map. In this way, the current positions of the search assets can be taken into account. The

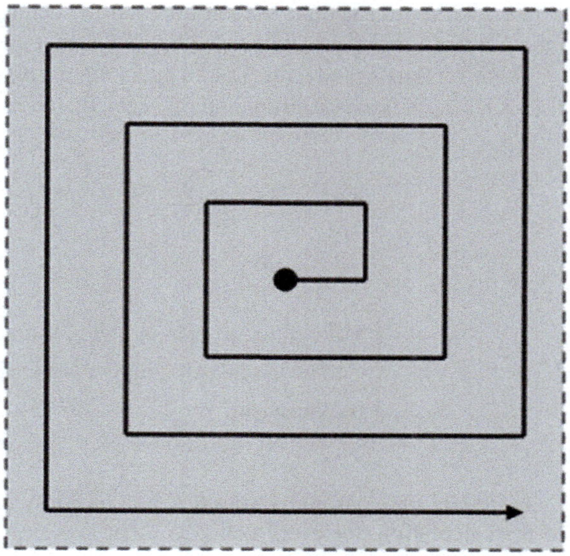

Fig. 8.14 An example of an expanding square in a square search area [*Source* E.R. van Veldhoven, H.J. Fitski]

positions of assets cannot be known exactly beforehand, since an asset may have to divert from the planned search route to investigate detected contacts during the search.

We assume that transits are performed at a higher speed or altitude than used for searching, and hence no detections occur during transit. The longer the transit, the less time is left for searching and the smaller the search area will be. The estimated total area $A(n, s)$ that asset n can cover in search time s is calculated as follows:

$$A(n, s) = C(n) \cdot s = v_n \cdot 2 \cdot r_n \cdot s \tag{8.13}$$

Note that, because the search time is at most one hour, the remaining search time is zero if the transit takes one hour (or more). We will only consider transits that are less than one hour. We decided to use an expanding square as search pattern (see Fig. 8.14), and hence we calculate the transit time from the current position of an asset to the centre of the possible search area.

If more than one search asset is involved, the algorithm first sorts the search assets in order of their coverage rate, from high to low. Starting with the search asset that has the highest coverage rate, all assets are considered one by one. For every possible search area that is reachable from the asset's current position within the maximum transit time of one hour, the total covered risk is calculated. Note that we assume that a search area is square and consists of whole risk map cells. The length and width a of the search area are calculated as follows:

$$a = \left\lfloor f\left(\sqrt{(1-t) \cdot C(n)}\right) \right\rfloor \tag{8.14}$$

where t is the transit time needed to reach the centre of the search area and f is a function that maps the real distance to the distance in grid cells of the risk map.

The asset is assigned to the search area with the highest covered risk. The covered risk of a search area A (during hour i) is calculated as follows:

$$R(A,i) = \sum_{x=1}^{X}\sum_{y=1}^{Y} R(x,y,i) \cdot H(A,x,y,i) \tag{8.15}$$

where

$$H(A,x,y,i) = \begin{cases} 1 \text{ if cell } (x, y) \text{ is in } A \text{ and not in any search area already assigned} \\ \quad \text{to an asset with a higher coverage rate than asset } i \\ 0 \text{ otherwise} \end{cases} \tag{8.16}$$

Effectively, the risk map values $R(x, y, i)$ are considered to be zero for the remainder of the calculation, for every cell (x, y) that is within the search area in the current hour i. Like in the calculation of the sortie schedule, this is done to prevent a situation where previously covered risk is again counted as covered by any remaining assets for which search areas are determined.

8.3.6 *Case Study*

In a case study, we have performed a limited analysis on several aspects of the search planning algorithm.[16] For this purpose, we used a simulation model in which the algorithm was applied to a fictitious counter-piracy scenario. The simulation allowed us to compare the operational effectiveness of our algorithm with the operational effectiveness in the situation without any form of security intervention. In this section, we highlight some of the results.

In the counter-piracy scenario, the task unit consisted of a frigate with two embarked assets, a helicopter and a UAV. The task unit's sector was an area of 50 by 50 nmi. The frigate was given a fixed search area in the centre of the sector and followed a square search pattern. Both flying assets made two sorties per day and used an expanding square search. After detection of a contact, an asset had to approach the contact for classification. The endurance was four hours for the helicopter and six hours for the UAV; both flying assets were unavailable for two hours after each sortie.

For the threat map, we assumed a uniform risk of 100%. The cell size of the threat maps and risk maps was 1 by 1 nmi. The shipping that passed through the area

---

[16] See Vermeulen and Van Veldhoven 2014.

Table 8.1 Shipping density variants (average number of ships in the sector) [*Source* E.R. van Veldhoven, H.J. Fitski]

	Variant I	Variant II	Variant III	Variant IV
Merchant vessels	4	4	4	2
Pirate ships	0.4	0.4	0.08	0.5
Neutral ships	3	8	3	1.5

consisted of merchant vessels, pirate ships, and neutral ships. We examined various notional shipping densities which are listed in Table 8.1.

In the simulation, the behaviour of the pirate ships was modelled as follows: a pirate ship sails straight on, until it detects a merchant vessel within its detection range. After detection, the pirate tries to intercept and hijack the merchant vessel. An attack on a merchant vessel was counted as successful if the pirate ship could intercept the merchant vessel without being classified by one of the surveying assets.

To analyse our planning algorithm, we compared the situation in which our planning algorithm was used with the situation without any form of military intervention. We defined the following measure of safety (MoS):

$$MoS = \frac{s}{m} = \frac{m-h}{m} = 1 - \frac{h}{m} \tag{8.17}$$

where h denotes the number of merchant vessels that sail through the sector and that are hijacked, s denotes the number of merchant vessels that sail safely through the sector, and m denotes the total number of merchant vessels that sail through the sector.

During the simulation, the MoS was calculated for both the situation without military intervention ($MoS_{no\ mil\ act}$) and the situation with military intervention, using our search planning algorithm ($MoS_{mil\ act}$). To evaluate the effectiveness of our algorithm, we used the following measure of effectiveness:

$$MoE_{counter-piracy} = \frac{MoS_{mil\ act} - MoS_{no\ mil\ act}}{(1 - MoS_{no\ mil\ act})} \tag{8.18}$$

Equation 8.18 can be rewritten as:

$$MoE_{counter-piracy} = 1 - \frac{h_{mil\ act}}{h_{no\ mil\ act}} \tag{8.19}$$

where $h_{mil\ act}$ denotes the number of merchant vessels that sail through the sector and that are hijacked in the situation with military intervention, and $h_{no\ mil\ act}$ denotes the number of merchant vessels that sail through the sector and that are hijacked in the situation without military intervention.

We highlight two aspects of our algorithm that we have analysed: using scheduled sorties versus fixed sorties, and whether adaptive risk is used.

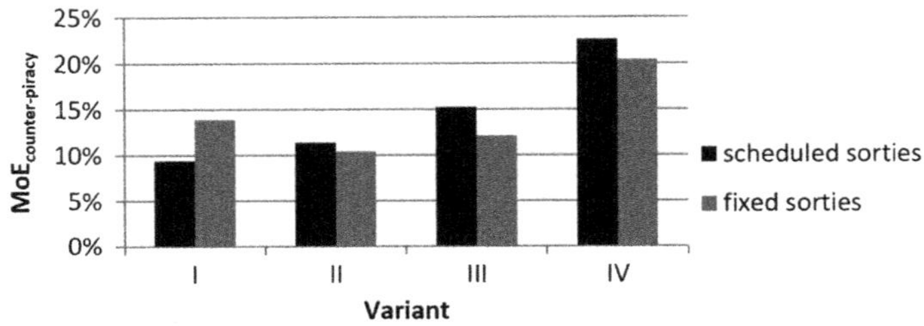

Fig. 8.15 Results for using scheduled sorties versus fixed sorties [*Source* E.R. van Veldhoven, H.J. Fitski]

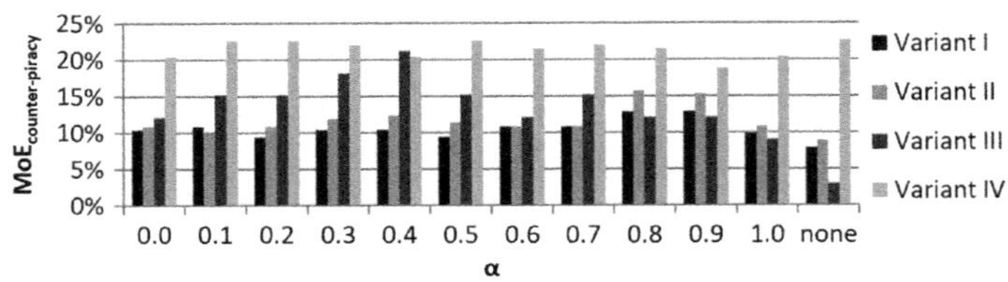

Fig. 8.16 Results for using adaptive risk (with various values for α) or using initial risk maps (indicated by "none") [*Source* E.R. van Veldhoven, H.J. Fitski]

8.3.6.1 Scheduled Sorties Versus Fixed Sorties

First, the use of sorties scheduled by the search planning algorithm is compared with the use of fixed sorties. For the fixed sorties, we examined one schedule, in which each of the flying assets started at 06:00 h and 14:00 h. The results are shown in Fig. 8.15.

There is only a marginal difference between the use of scheduled and fixed sorties. The explanation for this outcome is that, given the assumed shipping densities, there is usually much more risk than can be covered by the task unit. Only when there are few merchant vessels (e.g. Variant IV), and hence fewer high-risk areas, or if there are very few pirates (e.g. Variant III), the fixed schedule performs worse.

Two notes must be made here. The first is that in practice, the flexibility of the sorties is limited by the crew's watch schedule. The influence of this limitation has not been investigated. The second note is that we investigated only one fixed schedule. Other types of schedules may produce other results.

8.3.6.2 Using Adaptive Risk

We looked at different values for the α parameter (see Sect. 8.3.3) versus the use of the initial risk maps, to examine the effects of using adaptive risk. The results are shown in Fig. 8.16.

From the results, we conclude that using adaptive risk maps is useful: for most evaluated values of α, the operational effectiveness is either higher than when using no adaptive risk, or almost equal. This is logical since the probability that there are undetected pirates left in a search area after a one-hour search is, obviously, very low.

It is remarkable that, except for variant III, the actual value of α has hardly any influence on the operational effectiveness, especially for values lower than 0.7. We have no explanation for this yet.

8.4 Conclusions

In this paper, we introduced a two-level approach for the planning of maritime security operations. The first level of planning is task unit allocation, which is dividing of the area of operations into sectors and assigning the available task units to these sectors. The second level is the tactical planning of the deployment of the individual assets of a task unit within the task unit's sector. For both types of planning, we presented algorithms and the results of case studies that we executed to evaluate our algorithms.

The allocation algorithm shows promising results. Some of these results indicate, however, that the parameters that we chose for the cooling schedule of our simulated annealing algorithm can be improved. Furthermore, it is interesting to investigate extensions of the current construction of neighbour configurations. For example, instead of completely changing the structure of the allocation, a neighbour configuration could also be constructed by just moving one or more of the lines that define the sectors in the allocation.

The search planning algorithm calculates when and where search assets should operate within an assigned sector, provided that threat maps and the routes of the vessels to be protected are available. The algorithm can be improved in several ways, for example by allowing search areas to be rectangular instead of square, by allowing other search patterns than the expanding square search, and by taking into account the influence of day and night on the detection ranges.

References

Atkinson MP, Kress M, Szechtman R (2017) To Catch an Intruder: Part A - Uncluttered Scenario. Wiley Online Library https://doi.org/10.1002/nav.21730

Cattrysse DG, Van Wassenhove LN (1992) A survey of algorithms for the generalized assignment problem. European Journal of Operational Research 60:260–272

Defensie (2014) Grondslagen van het Maritieme Optreden, Nederlandse maritiem-militaire doctrine. Ministerie van Defensie, The Hague

Fitski HJ (2013) Effectiviteitsmaten voor counter piracy, counter smuggling en counter illegal fishing. TNO, The Hague

Fitski HJ, Van Veldhoven ER, Nienhuis B (2015) Simulatie van maritieme oppervlaktebeeldopbouw met SURPASS. Militaire Spectator 184:14–24

Henderson D, Jacobson SH, Johnson AW (2003) The Theory and Practice of Simulated Annealing. In: Glover F, Kochenberger GA (eds) Handbook of Metaheuristics. Springer, Boston MA

Johnson DS, Aragon CR, McGeoch LA, Schevon C (1989) Optimization by Simulated Annealing: An Experimental Evaluation; Part I, Graph Partitioning, Operations Research 37:865–892

Kirkpatrick S, Gelatt Jr CD, Vecchi MP (1983) Optimization by Simulated Annealing. Science 220:671–680

Laan CM, Barros AI, Boucherie RJ, Monsuur H (2017) Security Games with Probabilistic Constraints on the Agent's Strategy. In: Rass S, An B, Kiekintveld C, Fang F, Schauer S (eds) Decision and Game Theory for Security. Springer, Cham, pp 481–493

Smith AJE, Van Dongen MPFM (2015) Programme V1114 MSA - Final Report. TNO, The Hague

Vermeulen JFJ, Van Veldhoven ER (2014) Sector Search Algorithm for Maritime Situational Awareness. TNO, The Hague

Chapter 9
Security Games with Restricted Strategies: An Approximate Dynamic Programming Approach

C.M. Laan, A.I. Barros, R.J. Boucherie and H. Monsuur

Contents

Abstract In this chapter we consider a security game between an agent and an intruder to find optimal strategies for patrolling against illegal fishery. When patrolling large areas that consist of multiple cells, several aspects have to be taken into account. First, the current risk of the cells has to be considered such that cells with high risk are visited more often. Moreover, it is important to be unpredictable in order to increase the patrolling effectiveness countering illegal fishery. Finally,

C.M. Laan (✉) · H. Monsuur
Netherlands Defence Academy, Den Helder, The Netherlands
e-mail: c.m.laan@utwente.nl

H. Monsuur
e-mail: h.monsuur@mindef.nl

C.M. Laan · A.I. Barros
TNO, The Hague, The Netherlands
e-mail: ana.barros@tno.nl

C.M. Laan · R.J. Boucherie
University of Twente, Enschede, The Netherlands
e-mail: r.j.boucherie@utwente.nl

H. Monsuur et al. (eds.), *NL ARMS Netherlands Annual Review of Military Studies 2018*, NL ARMS, https://doi.org/10.1007/978-94-6265-246-0_9

patrolling strategies have to be chosen in such a manner that they satisfy given operational requirements. For example, the agent might be required to patrol some cells more often than others imposing extra restrictions on the agent strategies. In this chapter, we develop a dynamic variant of the security game with restrictions on the agent's strategy so that all these requirements are taken into account. We model this game as a stochastic game with a final penalty to ensure that the operational requirements are met. In this way, strategies are formed that both consider past actions and expected future risk levels. Due to the curse of dimensionality, these stochastic games cannot be solved for large scale instances. We develop an approximate dynamic programming algorithm to find approximate solutions.

Keywords Stochastic games · Security · Patrolling · Restricted strategies · Approximate dynamic programming · Aggregation

9.1 Introduction

The coast guard is responsible for patrolling the coastal waters. Patrolling strategies should be unpredictable, cover the entire region, and must satisfy operational requirements on e.g. the frequency of visits to certain vulnerable parts of the region (cells). We develop a special security game dealing with the protection of a large area in which the agent's strategy set is restricted. This area consists of multiple cells that have to be protected during a fixed time period. The agent has to decide on a patrolling strategy, which is constrained by governmental requirements that establish a minimum number of visits for each cell. Some cells have to be visited more often than others because these regions are more vulnerable. For example, cells close to a port have to be visited more often. A static version of this model is discussed in Laan et al.,[1] where a strategy for the complete time period is identified before the game starts. The requirements are modeled in such a way that they are met with high probability. However, this model does not allow patrolling strategies adjusted to the current situation. In this chapter, we consider a dynamic approach to the security game with restricted strategies in which the agent decides on his strategy for each day taking into account expected future rewards. This allows finding a more flexible strategy for the agent, where current payoffs and number of visits to each cell can be taken into account.

An example application of this model lies in countering illegal or unreported and unregulated fishing. These illicit activities endanger the economy of the fishery sector, fish stocks and the marine environment and require the monitoring of large areas with scarce resources subject to national regulations. To support the development of patrols against illegal fishing, in Haskell[2] a decision support system is developed. This system models the interaction between different types of illegal fishers and the

[1] Laan et al. 2017.

[2] Haskell et al. 2014.

patrolling forces as a repeated game. Moreover, in order to cope with the uncertainty on the adversary's strategy a robust optimization approach is used. More recently, Fang et al.[3] introduced a new game theoretical approach, the green security games, wherein a generalization of Stackelberg games is used to derive sequential agent strategies that learn from adversary behavior. However, in these papers restrictions to the patroller's strategy are not considered.

We model the dynamic variant of the security game with restricted strategies as a finite-time stochastic game in which the state depends on both the current payoff matrix and the remaining minimum number of visits left to each cell. The direct reward is given by the intruder's payoff and at the end of the time period a penalty is given if the operational requirements are not met. Solving stochastic games can be done by iterating over all states and time periods. However, the state space grows exponentially in the number of cells and we are unable to solve realistic sized games. Therefore, we develop an approximate dynamic programming (ADP) approach to find approximate solutions.

Due to the curse of dimensionality, many stochastic optimization models cannot be solved by iterating over all possible states. ADP is a technique that can be used to solve large scale Markov decision processes (MDPs). We develop an ADP framework to find approximate solutions for our stochastic game. A brief introduction in ADP can be found in Powell[4] and various examples are given in Mes and Rivera.[5] In the ADP framework, the optimal solutions are not found using standard backward dynamic programming, but by using a forward dynamic programming approach over only a fixed number of iterations. In this forward approach, different value function approximations can be used. In this chapter, we use multiple aggregation levels of the state space to approximate the value functions as discussed in George et al.[6] In the basic ADP algorithm, only a very limited number of states will be updated during each iteration. In our method using aggregation of the state space, multiple value function approximations are updated at the same time, possibly with different weight for different aggregation states. In this way, the value functions are updated more often and will converge faster.

Although most of the research in ADP focuses on solving MDPs, some models focus on solving games. In Perolat et al.,[7] the authors consider the error propagation for different approximation schemes of zero-sum stochastic games. However, this chapter does not provide a clear procedure that can be used to solve stochastic games using ADP. A solution technique that is very similar to ADP is reinforcement learning (RL), see for example Bucsoniu.[8] The main difference between ADP and RL is that RL is considered to be model-free, which means that information about transition probabilities is not necessarily required. In the field of RL, there is also limited

[3] Fang et al. 2015.

[4] Powell 2010.

[5] Mes and Rivera 2017.

[6] George et al. 2008.

[7] Perolat et al. 2015.

[8] Buşoniu et al. 2010.

research about applications to stochastic games. In Lin et al.,[9] the authors use RL to approximate unknown rewards and use an iterative algorithm to find a policy for both players, while we are interested in calculating this policy using approximation algorithms.

The main contribution of this chapter is twofold. First, we develop a model to solve security games with restrictions on the agent's strategy. Formulating this model as a stochastic game enables the agent to adjust the strategy to the current situation and actions that already have been chosen in the past. Second, we approximate optimal solutions of this stochastic game via an ADP approach. We adjust the standard ADP model that is often used to solve large scale MDPs to analyze stochastic games. Experimental results show that this method gives better payoffs for the agent's than using a static approach where strategies are fixed for the complete planning period.

The remainder of this chapter is organized as follows. In Sect. 9.2, we introduce the model and give the elements of the stochastic game. In Sect. 9.3, we first give a brief introduction in ADP and then describe our formulation for stochastic games. In Sect. 9.4, we give computational results and compare the static and dynamic approach. Finally in Sect. 9.5, we summarize the main findings and provide directions for future research.

9.2 Model Description

In this section, we give the formulation of the security game with restrictions on the agent's strategy. We first describe the basic model in Sect. 9.2.1. In Sect. 9.2.2, we briefly explain the solution method that is used to solve the game with a static strategy for the complete time period as studied in Laan et al.[10] In Sect. 9.2.3, we describe a new stochastic game approach which is used to enable strategies over the entire planning period.

9.2.1 *Basic Model*

The game is played between an agent and an intruder over a time period of N_D days. The area is given by a finite set of cells $C = \{1, \dots, N_C\}$. Each day, an intruder selects one cell to attack while the agent chooses a route from a finite set of routes $R = \{1, \dots, N_R\}$. The agent and intruder choose their action simultaneously. Routes consist of multiple cells where the agent is allowed to move between adjacent cells. The matrix A indicates which cells are visited by each route, such that a_{ij} equals 1 if route i visits cell j and 0 otherwise.

---

[9] Lin et al. 2017.

[10] Laan et al. 2017.

The risk of a cell is displayed in the payoff matrices. Cells with a high risk have higher payoffs than low risk cells. This payoff is interpreted as the intruders gain: the higher the gain for the intruder, the higher the probability that the intruder will attack there. The payoff matrix can change over time due to, e.g., weather conditions or seasonal fluctuations resulting in multiple payoff matrices. We assume that we have some information about how these payoff matrices change. Let $M^{(k)}$ be the k-th payoff matrix of size $N_R \times N_C$ out of a finite set of payoff matrices, $k = 1, \ldots, N_M$. The element $m_{ij}^{(k)}$ is the expected payoff if the agent uses route i and the intruder attacks cell j, $i = 1, \ldots, N_R$, $j = 1, \ldots, N_C$. We consider the payoff given by the intruder's expected gain:

$$m_{ij}^{(k)} = \left((1 - d_j)a_{ij} + (1 - a_{ij})\right) g_j^{(k)}, \quad i = 1, \ldots, N_R, \; j = 1, \ldots, N_C, k = 1, \ldots, N_M,$$

where d_j is the detection probability for cell j and $g_j^{(k)}$ is the intruder's gain if the intruder successfully attacks cell j. If the agent successfully intercepts the intruder, the payoff is 0.

There are operational requirements on the number of visits to the cells: the agent's strategy is restricted by the requirements that impose a minimum number of visits v_j for each cell j, $j = 1, \ldots, N_C$. During the time period, the agent has to decide on his actions such that cell j is visited at least j times.

Note that the model described in this chapter only describes a basic security game with one intruder. The methods developed in this chapter may be applied to extensions to matrix games obtained by changing the payoff matrices, such as including more (cooperating) intruders or detection probabilities depending on the cell or chosen action.

9.2.2 *Static Approach*

When using a static approach, the strategies are the same for each time period, but might be different for each payoff matrix $M^{(k)}$. The strategy of the agent is $p^T = (p^{(1)}, \ldots, p^{(N_M)})$, where $p_i^{(k)}$ is the probability that route i is chosen when the payoff matrix is $M^{(k)}$. The strategy of the intruder is $q^T = (q^{(1)}, \ldots, q^{(N_M)})$, where $q_j^{(k)}$ is the probability that cell j is attacked when the payoff matrix is $M^{(k)}$. The probability that the payoff matrix is $M^{(k)}$ equals $\mu^{(k)}$.

The restrictions to the agent's strategy are modeled by the constraint $f(p) \geq 1 - \epsilon$. The function $f(p)$ gives the probability that all the agent's restrictions on the minimum of visits for the cells are met, given the agent's strategy p. Randomized strategies are used to guarantee the unpredictability of the patrolling. Therefore, it is not possible to demand that the requirements are always met. By requiring $f(p) \geq 1 - \epsilon$, we guarantee that the requirements are met with high probability. For the experiments in this chapter, we use $\epsilon = 0.05$.

The value of the game is the expected payoff per day and can be found by solving the following optimization problem:

$$
\begin{aligned}
V = \min_{p} \max_{q} \quad & \sum_{k=1}^{N_M} \mu^{(k)} (p^{(k)})^T M^{(k)} q^{(k)} \\
\text{s.t.} \quad & f(p) \geq 1 - \epsilon, \\
& \sum_{i=1}^{N_R} p_i^{(k)} = 1, \quad k = 1, \ldots, N_M, \\
& \sum_{i=1}^{N_C} q_i^{(k)} = 1, \quad k = 1, \ldots, N_M, \\
& p, q \geq 0.
\end{aligned} \tag{9.1}
$$

Taking the dual of the inner linear program, $\max_q \{\sum_{k=1}^{N_M} \mu^{(k)} (p^{(k)})^T M^{(k)} q^{(k)} \mid \sum_{j=1}^{N_C} q_j^{(k)} = 1, k = 1, \ldots, n_M, q \geq 0\}$, the minmax formulation from (9.1) can be rewritten as a minimization problem to obtain the game value and optimal strategies for the agent.

We use approximations to determine $f(p)$. We explain the basic idea of these approximations and refer to Laan et al.[11] for a more detailed description. Consider the game with only one payoff matrix, so we omit the index k. Let $Y = (Y_1, \ldots, Y_{N_R})$ be the number of times that each route is chosen by the agent. The random variable Y is multinomially distributed with parameters p and N_D, where p is the probability distribution over the routes and N_D is the length of the planning period. For large N_D, Y can be approximated by a multivariate distribution with mean $N_D p_i$ and variance $N_D p_i (1 - p_i)$ and covariance $-N_D p_i p_{i'}$, $i, i' = 1, \ldots, N_R$. Let $X = (X_1, \ldots, X_{N_C})$ be the number of times that each cell is visited:

$$X_j = \sum_{i=1}^{N_R} a_{ij} Y_i.$$

Using the approximation of Y, X can be approximated by a multivariate normal distribution with mean $N_D a_j p$, variance $N_D a_j p(1 - a_j p)$ and covariance $\sum_{i=1}^{N_R} \sum_{i'=1}^{N_R} a_{ij} a_{i'j'} Cov(\tilde{Y}_i, \tilde{Y}_{i'})$, $j, j' = 1, \ldots, N_C$ (see Ross).[12] Now, the probability that the requirements are met can be calculated using the cumulative distribution for the multivariate normal distribution, but this function is difficult to implement. A lower bound for the probability that all requirements are met is:

[11] Laan et al. 2017.

[12] Ross 1996, Chapters 1.4 and 1.8.

$$f(p) \geq 1 - \sum_{j=1}^{N_C} \Phi\left(\frac{v_j - N_D a_j p}{\sqrt{N_D a_j p(1 - a_j p)}}\right),$$

where $\Phi(x)$ is the cumulative distribution of the standard normal distribution. Implementing this function in (9.1) gives an upper bound for the game value. Experimental results show that the error that is made by this lower bound is small ($\leq 2\%$).[13] A similar expression for $f(p)$ can be derived for the case with multiple payoff matrices.

9.2.3 Dynamic Approach

When considering a dynamic approach, strategies can change during the time window depending on the current payoff matrix and the number of times each cell already has been visited. We model this as a finite-time zero-sum stochastic game. We now describe the elements of this game.

The state space S of the game is given by the current payoff matrix and the number of visits that are still required for each cell:

$$S = \{s | s = (k, \bar{v}_1, \ldots, \bar{v}_{N_C}),\ k = 1, \ldots, N_M,\ 0 \leq \bar{v}_j \leq v_j,\ j \in C\}.$$

The action space of the agent and intruder are given by A_A and A_I. The intruder attempts to maximize the payoff by choosing which cell to attack, so the action set of the intruder is given by C. The agent tries to catch the intruder by selecting a route, so the action set of the agent is given by R:

$$A_A = R,\ \ A_I = C.$$

The matrix T gives the transitions between the payoff matrices. These transitions do not depend on the actions of the agent and the intruder. If the current payoff matrix is $M^{(k)}$, then with probability t_{kl} the next payoff matrix is $M^{(l)}$. The transition matrix of the game P depends on both T and the action i of the agent:

$$P(s'|s, i) = \begin{cases} t_{kl}, & \text{if } \bar{v}'_j = \max\{\bar{v}_j - a_{ij}, 0\},\ \text{for all } j \in C, \\ 0, & \text{otherwise.} \end{cases}$$

where $s = (k, \bar{v}_1, \ldots, \bar{v}_{N_C})$ and $s' = (l, \bar{v}'_1, \ldots, \bar{v}'_{N_C})$ and i is the agents action.

The direct reward is given by R and depends on the agent's strategy i, the intruder's strategy j and the current payoff matrix $M^{(k)}$:

$$R(s, (i, j)) = m_{ij}^{(k)}.$$

---

[13] Laan et al. 2017.

To ensure that the requirements are met, we introduce a final reward which is a penalty for the requirements that are not met. This can either be a penalty for each requirement that is not met or one penalty if the requirements are not met. For the results considered in this chapter we consider the last option:

$$R_f(s) = \begin{cases} B, & \text{if } \sum_{j \in C} \bar{v}_j > 0, \\ 0, & \text{otherwise,} \end{cases}$$

where B is chosen large enough such that it is never beneficial to violate one of the requirements.

Optimal strategies can be found by solving the game iterative (see Owen).[14] Let $V_t(s)$ be the game value at time period t, when the game is in state s.

$$V_{N_D}(s) = \text{Val}\left(M^{(k)} + \sum_{s' \in S} P(s'|s, \cdot) R_f(s') \right), \tag{9.2}$$

$$V_t(s) = \text{Val}\left(M^{(k)} + \sum_{s' \in S} P(s'|s, \cdot) V_{t+1}(s') \right), \quad t < N_D. \tag{9.3}$$

where $s = (k, \bar{v}_1, \ldots, \bar{v}_{N_C})$, so $M^{(k)}$ depends on the first element of state s, and $P(s'|s, \cdot)$ is the matrix consisting of the values $P(s'|s, i)$ for all agent's actions. The expression between brackets defines a matrix game. Val gives the value of this matrix game, so this is the game value when both players choose a strategy corresponding to a Nash equilibrium.

Solving Eqs. (9.2) and (9.3) will give an optimal value of the game. However, the size of the state space is exponentially increasing in the number of cells and conditions and we are unable to solve these equations analytically. In the next section, we present a model to deal with this large state space.

9.3 Solution Approach: Approximate Dynamic Programming

In this section, we present a method that can be used to overcome the large state space of the stochastic game formulation in Sect. 9.2. Approximate dynamic programming (ADP) is a technique that is often used to solve large scale MDPs. In Sect. 9.3.1, we give a short introduction in ADP for solving MDPs based on Powell.[15] In Sect. 9.3.2, we develop ADP to solve our stochastic game.

---

[14] Owen 1995, Chapter V.3.

[15] Powell 2010.

9.3.1 Introduction to ADP

Consider an MDP over time horizon T, with states s_t, actions a_t, transition matrix P, and cost functions C_t. The value of an MDP can be found by solving the Bellman equations:

$$V_t(s_t) = \min_{x_t} \left(C_t(s_t, x_t) + \sum_{s_{t+1}} P(s_{t+1}|s_t, x_t) V_{t+1}(s_{t+1}) \right).$$

When the state space is large, solving the Bellman equations is too time consuming. The main idea of ADP is not to solve the model by enumerating over all possible solutions but only over a limited number of states using a forward dynamic programming approach over a fixed number of iterations N. For each iteration, the random information is sampled using Monte Carlo experiments.

The random information that is revealed after action a_t is chosen is given by w_{t+1}. Both the action and the random information define the next state. For ADP, the post-decision state s_t^a is introduced. A post-decision state is the state after an action a_t is chosen, but before the new random information w_{t+1} is revealed:

$$V_t(s_t) = \min_{a_t} \left(C_t(s_t, a_t) + V_t^a(s_t^a) \right),$$

$$V_t^a(s_t^a) = \sum_{w_{t+1}} P(w_{t+1}) V_{t+1}(s_{t+1}|s_t^a, w_{t+1}).$$

By the use of the post-decision state, we only have to evaluate the possible outcomes over w_{t+1} for each action and not over all possible states s_{t+1}. This decreases the number of possible outcomes that have to be evaluated during each iteration significantly.

The output of the algorithm is an approximation $\bar{V}_t^n(s_t^a)$ of the value of the post-decision states. During each step, the approximation $\bar{V}$ is updating using the following update rule:

$$\bar{V}_t^n(s_t) = \begin{cases} (1-\alpha)\bar{V}_t^{n-1}(s_t^n) + \alpha \hat{v}_t^n, & \text{if } s_t = s_t^n, \\ \bar{V}_t^{n-1}(s_t), & \text{otherwise.} \end{cases} \tag{9.4}$$

where α is a step size between 0 and 1. In the next section, we discuss the value of α.

The basic structure of an ADP is given by the following algorithm.

Algorithm 1 ADP algorithm

1: Initialize:

- Choose an initial approximation $\bar{V}_t^0(s_t^a)$ for each t.
- Set $n = 1$ and choose an initial state s_0^1.

2: Choose a sample path $w^n = (w_1^n, \ldots, w_T^n)$.

3: For $t = 0, \ldots, T$

- Solve

$$\hat{v}_t^n = \min_{a_t} \left(C_t(s_t^n, a_t) + \mathbb{E}^w \left(\bar{V}_{t+1}^{n-1}(s_t | s_t^{a_t}, w) \right) \right),$$

and let a_t^n be the action that solves this minimization.
- Update $\bar{V}_t^n(s_t)$ using (9.4).
- Compute the next state to visit from the action a_t^n.

4: Set $n = n + 1$ and go to Step 2.

This algorithm is a basic outline and will in general not always give good approximation results. There are some methods for improving the algorithm, mainly in the step of choosing the next state (random or not), the choice of α and in the steps of the value function approximation. We discuss these methods in the next section.

9.3.2 ADP for a Stochastic Game

The ADP approach described in the previous section is used to solve large scale MDPs. In this section, we describe the adjustments we make to the ADP to solve the stochastic game in Sect. 9.2.3. The difference is that we deal with multiple players. Therefore, the Bellman equations are replaced by:

$$V_t(s) = \text{Val}\left(M^{(k)} + \sum_{s' \in S} P(s'|s, \cdot) V_{t+1}(s') \right).$$

As a consequence, we have to optimize over both the intruder's and the agent's actions. However, in our case, the next state does not depend on the intruder's action. Therefore, we can use an ADP algorithm similar to the ADP algorithm which is used to solve MDPs.

Due to the introduction of multiple players we are not dealing with discrete actions. Both agent and intruder choose as an action a probability distribution over the action spaces at each time step. Therefore, we are not able to calculate a value for each combination of actions and states. We modify the formulation and use of the post-decision state, which in our case only depends on the agents actions. Let s_t^i be the post-decision state at time t and state s when the agent chooses pure strategy $i \in R$:

$$\bar{V}_t(s_t^i) = \sum_{l=1}^{N_M} t_{kl} \bar{V}_{t+1}\left((l, (s_t(2) - a_{i1})^+, \ldots, (s_t(N_C+1) - a_{iN_C})^+)\right),$$

where $s = (k, \bar{v}_1, \ldots, \bar{v}_{N_C})$.

We now describe the basic ADP algorithm adjusted for our game:

Algorithm 2 ADP algorithm for stochastic game

1: Initialize:

- Choose an initial approximation $\bar{V}_t^0(s_t)$ for each t, s_t.
- Set $n = 1$ and choose an initial state s_0^1.

2: Choose a sample path w^n which describe the payoff matrices.

3: For $t = 0, \ldots, N_D - 1$

- Construct M, such that:

$$m_{ij} = m_{ij}^{(k)} + \bar{V}_{t+1}^{n-1}(s_t^i), \quad t < N_D,$$
$$m_{ij} = m_{ij}^{(k)} + R_f(s_t^i), \quad t = N_D.$$

- Solve

$$\hat{v}_t^n = \mathrm{Val}\,(M)\,,$$

and let π_t^n be the agent's strategy that solves this minimization.
- Update $\bar{V}_t^n(s_t)$ using (9.4).
- Compute the next state to visit: w.p. β decide on the next state using π_t^n and with probability $1 - \beta$ choose a random action.

4: Set $n = n + 1$ and go to Step 2.

We now discuss the choice of α and β and introduce aggregation, which can be used to speed up the convergence of the algorithm.

Choice of α The value of the step step size α can be chosen in different ways. A review of different step sizes that are used in literature is given in George and Powell.[16] Two popular step sizes that are often used are the harmonic and the polynomial step size.[17] We use a harmonic step size where α depends on the iteration n:

$$\alpha_n = \max\left\{\frac{a}{a+n-1}, \alpha_0\right\},$$

where the value of α_n decreases in the number of iterations. In Sect. 9.4, we conduct experiments to decide on the value of a and α_0.

[16] George and Powell 2006.

[17] Powell 2010.

Choice of β In Step 3 of the ADP algorithm, the next state is chosen. If the next state only depends on the strategy π_t^n, it is possible that some states will never be visited and the algorithm does not converge to the best possible value. To avoid this, a random action is chosen with probability $1 - \beta$. In Sect. 9.4, we show the results of experiments with the value of β.

Aggregation To have a good approximation of the value function of a state, this specific state has to be visited often enough. During one iteration, the value function of only one state is updated and when the number of states is large, a lot of iterations are necessary to ensure a good approximation. There are different methods that can be used to speed up the convergence by updating multiple states per iteration. Two methods that are commonly used are aggregation and the use of basic functions.[18] We use aggregation with multiple aggregation levels which is proven to work well for large scale MDPs.[19] An example of an aggregation level is to only consider the requirements and not the payoff matrix.

Let G be the number of aggregation levels and $S^{(g)}$, $g = 0, \ldots, G$, be the state space corresponding to the g-th aggregation level ($S^{(0)} = S$). The state $s^{(g)}$ is the state corresponding to s in the g-th aggregation level and $\bar{V}^{(g)}(s^{(g)})$ is the value function approximation for this state. The value function approximation of each state s is given by a weighted combination of the value functions of all the corresponding states for the different aggregation levels:

$$\bar{V}^n(s) = \sum_{g=0}^{G} w^{(g,n)}(s)\bar{V}^{(g,n)}(s^{(g)}),$$

where $w^{(g,n)}(s)$ is the weight of the g-th aggregation level for state s. We choose the weight by inverse mean squared errors as described in George et al.[20] using the bias and variance of each estimator:

$$w^{(g,n)}(s) \sim \frac{1}{\frac{(\tilde{\sigma}^{(g)}(s))^2}{N_s^{(g)}} + (\tilde{\mu}_s^{(g)})^2},$$

where $\tilde{\sigma}^{(g)}(s))^2$ is the sample variance of all the observations corresponding to the estimate $\bar{V}^{(g)}(s^{(g)})$, $N_s^{(g)}$ is the number of all these observations and $\tilde{\mu}_s^{(g)}$ is the bias from the true value $\bar{V}^{(0)}(s)$. A detailed description of these computations can be found in George et al.[21] Experiments with different aggregation levels can be found in Sect. 9.4.

---

[18] Powell 2010.

[19] George et al. 2008.

[20] George et al. 2008.

[21] George et al. 2008.

In this section, we have described a framework to enable us to deal with large scale dynamic games. In the next section, we show computational results to illustrate the performance of the ADP framework.

9.4 Experiments

We have developed a model and solution approach to solve a dynamic variant of security games with restrictions on the agent's strategy. In this section, we perform experiments to see how our model performs. First, we compare the static and dynamic approach in Sect. 9.4.1. In Sect. 9.4.2, we experiment with different input variables of the ADP approach and give computational results. Finally, in Sect. 9.4.3, we explore the model for an instance of realistic size.

9.4.1 Benefits of the Dynamic Approach

To show the benefits of the dynamic approach studied in this chapter, we compare it with the static approach as described in Sect. 9.2.2.

Consider a game with 9 cells and 8 routes as described in Fig. 9.1. In this example, the routes are chosen in such a way that the agent moves right, left or diagonal. The numbers are the cell numbers and the color of the cells correspond to the intruder's gain. The darker the color, the higher the intruder's gain: white cells have a payoff of 1, light gray cells have a payoff of 2 and dark gray cells have a payoff of 3. The transition probabilities for the payoff matrices are:

$$T = \begin{bmatrix} 0.7 & 0.3 \\ 0.3 & 0.7 \end{bmatrix}.$$

This means that on average both $M^{(1)}$ and $M^{(2)}$ occur with equal probability, so $\mu^{(1)} = \mu^{(2)} = 0.5$. The time period, N_D, equals 80.

In Table 9.1, the second and third columns show the game value for both the static and dynamic approach for different requirements on the agent's strategy. The value that is given is the expected value per day. The last column gives the running time for the stochastic game. The static game always runs within a second. All experiments in this section are implemented in Matlab version R2016b[22] on an Intel(R) Core(TM) i7 CPU, 2.4 GHz, 8 GB of RAM.

Both the static and the dynamic game are played over a time period of N_D days. Note that the strategies from the static game, can always be recreated using the dynamic approach. When there are no restrictions, the dynamic game gives almost the same strategies as in the static game because previous actions do not influence

[22] MATLAB 2016.

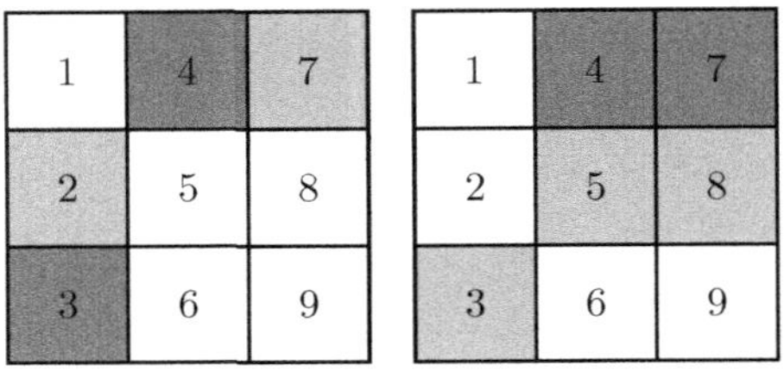

Routes	Cells visited by route
1	1, 5, 9
2	2, 3, 6
3	6, 8, 7
4	1, 4, 7
5	1, 2, 3
6	2, 6, 8
7	3, 5, 6
8	4, 5, 9

Fig. 9.1 Payoff matrices and routes [*Source* C.M. Laan, A.I. Barros, R.J. Boucherie, H. Monsuur]

Table 9.1 Expected payoff per day for different requirements [*Source* C.M. Laan, A.I. Barros, R.J. Boucherie, H. Monsuur]

Requirements	Static	Dynamic	
	Game value	Game value	Running time (s)
None	1.45	1.45	1.01
$v = (0, 0, 40, 0, 0, 0, 0, 0, 0)$	1.64	1.55	10.38
$v = (0, 30, 0, 0, 0, 0, 20, 0, 0)$	1.88	1.52	143.81
$v = (0, 30, 40, 0, 0, 0, 20, 0, 0)$	2.31	1.58	6513.91
$v = (0, 0, 40, 0, 0, 0, 30, 0, 0)$	–	1.85	275.19

the outcome and, when N_D is large enough, the number of times each payoff matrix appears is approximately the expected value μ as used in the static game. As can be seen in Table 9.1, the dynamic game approach gives better results for the agent when there are restrictions. This is because he has more flexibility in planning his strategy. The agent does not have to plan his complete strategy in advance anymore and can adjust his strategy depending on which routes were chosen before. Moreover, using the stochastic game approach, it is guaranteed that the requirements are met. Another advantage is that we do not have to require that each payoff matrix occur often enough because we do not need to apply the law of large numbers. Also, some requirements give an infeasible solution for the static approach, while they can be met for the dynamic case. This follows from the fact that for the static approach we use randomized strategies that are the same for each time period. To meet the requirements with high probability, the cells have to be visited more often on average than the requirements require. This is not necessary for the dynamic approach, since the strategies can be adjusted to the number of visits in the past. The disadvantage of the stochastic game approach is that the running time increases exponentially in the number of visits.

9.4.2 Computational Results of ADP

In this section, we explore the performance of the ADP approach for the dynamic game. Also, we test different inputs parameters and multiple aggregation levels. Consider the game as described in Sect. 9.4.1 with the requirements $v = (0, 30, 40, 0, 0, 0, 20, 0, 0)$. This example will be used to illustrate our experiments.

The running times of the experiments in this section depend on the level of aggregations: the more levels of aggregations, the higher the running time. For the case without aggregation, the running time of the experiments is approximately 1000 s and the running time for the case with for levels of aggregation, the running time was approximately 1500 s. For all the experiments, we used 3000 as the number of iterations.

First, we test the model without aggregation for different input parameters: the step size parameters, a and α_0, and the probability that a random action is chosen $1 - \beta$. The value function approximation of the initial state is displayed in Fig. 9.2 for a selection of different combinations of these parameters without aggregation. The ADP algorithm gives value function approximations for each possible state. Also, for each possible state, a strategy is calculated in Step 3 of the algorithm. We test this strategy by simulating the game after different numbers of iterations. The game is simulated 100 times, where the value approximations and strategies obtained by the ADP algorithm are used.

Tables 9.2, 9.3, 9.4 and 9.5 show the results for the model with and without aggregation. Tables 9.2 and 9.4 show the percentage that the requirements are met. In general, it holds that the better the value function approximations are, the higher the probability that the requirements are met. For the dynamic game, it is guaranteed that the conditions are met if this is feasible and the penalty is high enough. However, when using the value function approximations to decide on the strategies, this is not always guaranteed if the approximations are still too far from the optimal values.

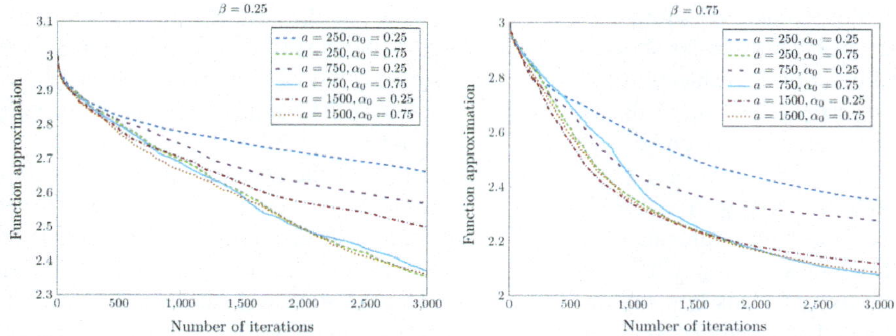

Fig. 9.2 Convergence of ADP for different values of α_0 and a and β, no aggregation [*Source* C.M. Laan, A.I. Barros, R.J. Boucherie, H. Monsuur]

Table 9.2 Percentage requirements satisfied, no aggregation [*Source* C.M. Laan, A.I. Barros, R.J. Boucherie, H. Monsuur]

β	a	250			750			1500		
	Iterations/α_0	0.25	0.5	0.75	0.25	0.5	0.75	0.25	0.5	0.75
0.25	1000	1%	0%	1%	1%	2%	0%	2%	2%	4%
	2000	4%	8%	5%	9%	5%	15%	16%	6%	6%
	3000	13%	8%	7%	17%	7%	5%	30%	14%	4%
0.5	1000	0%	9%	3%	3%	1%	1%	4%	1%	4%
	2000	2%	11%	9%	13%	20%	7%	29%	20%	3%
	3000	6%	20%	26%	18%	11%	68%	47%	18%	4%
0.75	1000	0%	25%	80%	9%	8%	43%	94%	34%	44%
	2000	77%	89%	63%	40%	91%	100%	99%	58%	98%
	3000	88%	100%	96%	99%	100%	99%	100%	99%	100%

Table 9.3 Average game value, no aggregation [*Source* C.M. Laan, A.I. Barros, R.J. Boucherie, H. Monsuur]

β	a	250			750			1500		
	Iterations/α_0	0.25	0.5	0.75	0.25	0.5	0.75	0.25	0.5	0.75
0.25	1000	1.73	–	1.76	1.87	2.04	–	1.92	1.84	2.11
	2000	1.84	1.87	1.98	1.97	1.99	1.93	1.97	1.93	1.82
	3000	1.93	1.91	1.92	1.99	1.90	1.86	1.94	1.92	1.85
0.5	1000	–	2.04	2.01	2.09	2.01	1.89	2.05	2.02	2.05
	2000	1.94	1.97	1.93	2.00	1.99	1.98	1.99	2.04	1.95
	3000	1.97	1.98	1.93	2.00	1.99	1.98	1.94	1.97	1.97
0.75	1000	–	2.20	2.17	2.17	2.07	2.22	2.16	2.22	2.16
	2000	2.23	2.13	2.06	2.13	2.14	2.07	2.07	2.15	2.06
	3000	2.16	2.12	2.00	2.13	2.09	2.00	2.00	2.10	2.00

Tables 9.3 and 9.5 show the average game value for the case that the requirements are met. These tables show that $\beta = 0.75$ gives the best results for all different step values. For the value of the step size, the results are less conclusive. However, higher step sizes gives better value function approximation. The choice of α_0 is hereby more important than the choice of a. This can also be seen in Fig. 9.2.

In Fig. 9.3 the value function approximation for the starting state is shown for both the ADP with and without aggregation ($a = 750$, $\alpha_0 = 0.75$, $\beta = 0.75$). For the case with aggregation, we use 4 aggregation levels. The first level considers the state without payoff matrix, the second level considers the state with only even number of visits left, the third level considers the state with the number of visits divided and rounded to the nearest integer above and the fourth level only considers the total number of visits. We use the first level for the case with one level, the first two for the case with two levels, etc.

Table 9.4 Percentage requirements satisfied, with 3 aggregation levels [*Source* C.M. Laan, A.I. Barros, R.J. Boucherie, H. Monsuur]

β	a	250			750			1500		
	Iterations/α_0	0.25	0.5	0.75	0.25	0.5	0.75	0.25	0.5	0.75
0.25	1000	0%	0%	2%	2%	0%	3%	2%	2%	2%
	2000	3%	9%	3%	7%	1%	9%	2%	5%	11%
	3000	18%	11%	9%	20%	9%	20%	10%	20%	21%
0.5	1000	3%	4%	8%	4%	1%	1%	4%	2%	3%
	2000	24%	29%	57%	14%	9%	6%	33%	27%	49%
	3000	48%	60%	88%	23%	27%	12%	62%	31%	72%
0.75	1000	83%	35%	84%	76%	85%	86%	32%	99%	80%
	2000	98%	94%	100%	41%	100%	100%	95%	100%	99%
	3000	100%	99%	99%	100%	100%	100%	100%	100%	100%

Table 9.5 Average game value, with 3 aggregation levels [*Source* C.M. Laan, A.I. Barros, R.J. Boucherie, H. Monsuur]

β	a	250			750			1500		
	Iterations/α_0	0.25	0.5	0.75	0.25	0.5	0.75	0.25	0.5	0.75
0.25	1000	–	–	2.06	2.04	–	1.97	1.89	2.06	1.93
	2000	1.85	1.88	1.86	1.98	1.91	1.97	1.93	1.91	1.98
	3000	1.91	1.97	1.90	2.01	1.92	2.01	1.96	1.99	1.92
0.5	1000	2.03	2.19	2.01	2.01	2.13	2.10	2.04	2.12	2.04
	2000	2.03	1.98	2.00	1.99	2.07	1.87	1.97	2.02	1.95
	3000	2.02	1.99	1.93	2.00	1.97	1.91	1.98	2.01	1.93
0.75	1000	2.26	2.21	2.11	2.16	2.18	2.13	2.19	2.12	2.17
	2000	2.16	2.09	1.98	2.06	2.08	1.98	2.09	2.01	2.03
	3000	2.11	2.00	1.92	2.03	2.01	1.92	2.07	1.94	1.99

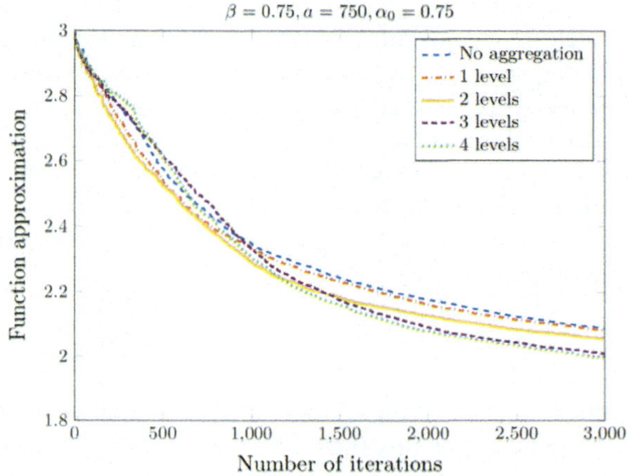

Fig. 9.3 Convergence of ADP for different aggregation levels [*Source* C.M. Laan, A.I. Barros, R.J. Boucherie, H. Monsuur]

Figure 9.3 shows that more aggregation levels give faster convergence. However in this example, the differences between the different aggregation levels are small. This can be explained by the fact that this is a relative small problem and the convergence for the case without aggregation is already fast. In the next section, we discuss a larger instance where it can be seen that the algorithm with aggregation converges significantly faster than without.

Recall the results in Sect. 9.4.1 as shown in Table 9.1. For the game with requirements $v = (0,\ 30,\ 40,\ 0,\ 0,\ 0,\ 20,\ 0,\ 0)$, the game value for the static approach is 2.31 and for the dynamic approach 1.58. In this section, we approximated the dynamic approach solution by using ADP, where we were able to obtain game values of 1.92 (see Table 9.5). These results show that the expected reward of when using the ADP approach is a higher than the optimal value of the stochastic game. However, it still outperforms the static approach. Moreover, this method can be used for larger instances where the stochastic game approach is too computationally expensive.

We tested the ADP approach for different instances, which gave similar results. The ADP approach usually outperforms the static approach, but not always in the cases where the game value of the static and dynamic case are close. This can explained by the fact that in these cases, the requirements do not have a large impact on the optimal strategy, so the static game already gives a solution close to the solution of the dynamic game. Since some approximation error is made in the ADP approach, it might occur that the static game gives a better value. Also, the optimal choice of input parameters vary a bit for different instances, so these have to be chosen carefully depending on the instance. From our computational results, we can say that a high value of β always gives good results and that the value of a needs to be chosen higher for larger instances.

9.4.3 Numerical Results for a Realistic Sized Instance

In this section, we give numerical results of a larger instance of the security game for which we cannot solve the stochastic game to optimality. The size of this instance is comparable to real world sized problems. However, we still consider a limited number of payoff matrices such that we can compare the game values with the game value of the static game as described in Sect. 9.2.2.

Consider the game as described in Fig. 9.4 with two payoff matrices and with requirements on Cells 1–5: $v = (10,\ 30,\ 30,\ 30,\ 10,\ 0,\ 0,\ 0,\ 0,\ 0,\ 0,\ 0,\ 0,\ 0,\ 0,\ 0,\ 0,\ 0,\ 0,\ 0)$. The time period, N_D, is 100. The transition probabilities for the payoff matrices are:

$$T = \begin{bmatrix} 0.3 & 0.7 \\ 0.4 & 0.6 \end{bmatrix},$$

which means that on average, the payoff matrix is $M^{(1)}$ with probability 0.36 and $M^{(2)}$ with probability 0.64. Solving the static game gives a game value of 2.57.

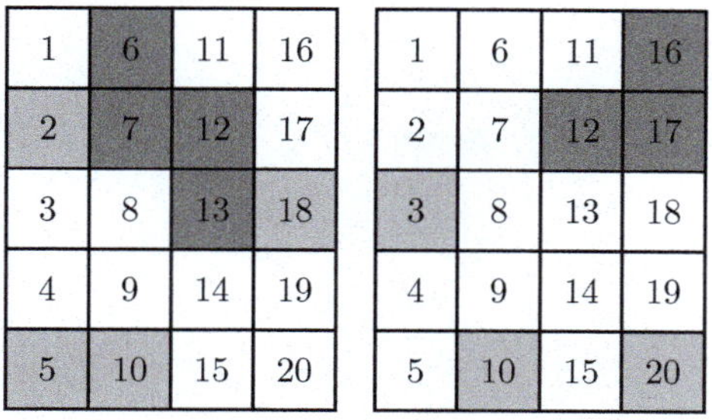

Routes	Cells visited by route
1	1, 2, 3, 8, 13, 18
2	5, 10, 14, 15, 19
3	4, 5, 6, 7, 8, 11
4	4, 9, 12, 13, 14, 17
5	16, 17, 18, 19, 20
6	1, 2, 6, 7, 11, 12
7	3, 8, 11, 12, 13
8	4, 5, 10, 15, 20
9	1, 2, 6, 11, 16
10	3, 8, 14, 19, 20
11	6, 7, 12, 16, 17

Fig. 9.4 Payoff matrices and routes for realistic sized scenario [*Source* C.M. Laan, A.I. Barros, R.J. Boucherie, H. Monsuur]

We ran the ADP algorithm with 4000 iteration with multiple aggregation levels in different configurations. We used the same aggregation levels as described in Sect. 9.4.2 with one additional aggregation level. The fifth aggregation level only considers the maximum number of visits over all cells.

The results for a selection of aggregation level configurations are shown in Fig. 9.5. This figure shows that aggregation ensures convergence a lot faster in this game. For this instance, the best convergence is obtained with levels 1, 2 and 4 combined. With these levels combined, the problems converge faster than without aggregation levels. This can also be seen in Table 9.6. However, not for all aggregation configurations outperform the algorithm without aggregation. For example, only using levels 3, 4 and 5 decreases the convergence speed. This can be explained by the fact that an error is made when aggregation multiple states. Aggregating many states will speed up the convergence, but may also lead to approximations far from the optimal solution. The right choice of aggregation levels depends on the instance and has to be chosen carefully.

Table 9.6 Percentage and average realistic sized scenario ($\beta = 0.75$, $a = 150$, $\alpha_0 = 0.75$) [*Source* C.M. Laan, A.I. Barros, R.J. Boucherie, H. Monsuur]

Iterations	No aggregation		3 levels	
	Average	Percentage (%)	Average	Percentage (%)
1000	–	0	2.47	98
2000	–	0	2.33	100
3000	2.08	83	2.25	100
4000	2.03	82	2.17	100
5000	2.01	98	2.07	100

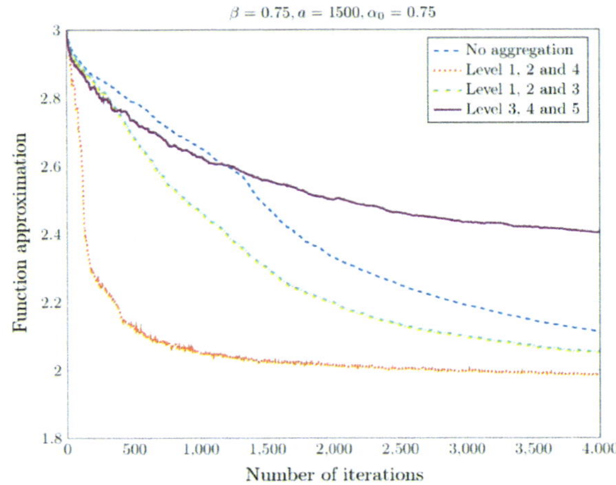

Fig. 9.5 Realistic sized scenario with and without aggregation [*Source* C.M. Laan, A.I. Barros, R.J. Boucherie, H. Monsuur]

9.5 Conclusion

In this chapter, we have developed a model for the dynamic decision making of an agent when his strategy is restricted by operational requirements. We have formulated the problem as a stochastic game and have shown that the use of a dynamic formulation outperforms the model in which strategies cannot be adjusted to the current situation: better game values for the agent can be obtained. Also, the stochastic game formulation can yield a feasible solution when more operational requirements are considered.

The disadvantage of the stochastic game formulation is that the solving time grows exponentially in the number of cells with requirements. This means that we cannot solve the game to optimality for real world instances. For that reason, we have developed an ADP approach to find approximate solutions. ADP is often used to solve large scale MDPs. With a limited number of adjustments, we have been able to develop a similar approach for our stochastic game.

Experimental results show that the game value which is found by the ADP algorithm is about 25% worse than the optimal solutions. However, using this algorithm we can solve much larger instances than for the full stochastic game. We also compared the ADP approach with a static approach and this showed that the ADP approach outperforms the static approach in our computational experiments.

For large instances, the convergence of the value function approximation can be slow, because states have to be visited multiple times before a good approximation can be given. We have used state space aggregation to speed up this convergence. For small instances, we do not gain a lot from this aggregation, because the algorithm without aggregation is already fast. However, for large instances, the speed of convergence is increased considerably with this aggregation.

The convergence of the ADP algorithm also depends on different input parameters which define the step size and the level of randomness. The optimal value of these parameters can vary for each instance and may also depend on the aggregation level. From our computational experiments, we can say that a large step size and a small number of randomness performs the best for our instances.

In this chapter, we have assumed that the evolution of the payoff matrices is defined by a given transition matrix and that at the beginning of each day, the payoff for that day is known. For future research, it would be interesting to investigate the case where not all payoff matrices are knows and only predictions for each day are given.

References

Buşoniu L, de Schutter B, Babuška R (2010) Approximate dynamic programming and reinforcement learning. Interactive collaborative information systems, pp 3–44

Fang F, Stone P, Tambe M (2015) When security games go green: Designing defender strategies to prevent poaching and illegal fishing. IJCAI, pp 2589–2595

George AP, Powell WB (2006) Adaptive stepsizes for recursive estimation with applications in approximate dynamic programming. Machine Learning, 65(1):167–198.

George AP, Powell WB, Kulkarni SR (2008) Value function approximation using multiple aggregation for multiattribute resource management. Journal of Machine Learning Research, 9(Oct):2079–2111

Haskell W, Kar D, Fang F, Tambe M, Cheung S, Denicola E (2014) Robust protection of fisheries with compass. Twenty-Sixth IAAI Conference

Laan CM, Barros AI, Boucherie RJ, Monsuur H (2017) Security games with probabilistic constraints on the agents strategy. International Conference on Decision and Game Theory for Security, pp 481–493

Lin X, Beling PA, Cogill R (2017) Multi-agent inverse reinforcement learning for zero-sum games. IEEE Transactions on Computational Intelligence and AI in Games (published online)

MATLAB (2016) version 9.1 (R2016b). The MathWorks Inc., Natick MA

Mes MRK, Rivera AP (2017) Approximate dynamic programming by practical examples. In: Boucherie RJ, van Dijk NM (eds) Markov Decision Processes in Practice, Springer, pp 63–101.

Owen G (1995) Game theory, 3rd edn. Academic Press

Perolat J, Scherrer B, Piot B, Pietquin O (2015) Approximate dynamic programming for two-player zero-sum Markov games, Proceedings of the 32nd International Conference on Machine Learning (ICML-15), pp 1321–1329

Powell WB (2010) Approximate dynamic programming: Algorithms. Wiley Encyclopedia of Operations Research and Management Science

Ross S (1996) Stochastic processes, 2nd edn. John Wiley & Sons, Inc

Chapter 10
Data Analysis Within the Netherlands Coastguard: Risk Mapping, Social Network Analysis and Anomaly Detection

J.P.H. Kalden

Contents

Abstract With trade concentrated in a few ports in today's global economy, even a single maritime terrorist incident has the potential to significantly disrupt our economic and financial processes. A (renewed) maritime focus for policy makers is not only of paramount interest for our economic wealth and progress, but also for our national security. This chapter highlights the role of the Netherlands Coast Guard (NCG) in controlling our borders and protecting our harbours. To improve its planning process for surveillance of the national maritime borders by air and by sea, the NCG has started a research program for maritime situational awareness. This program uses mathematical and computer science methods in data analysis, risk mapping, social network analysis and anomaly detection. These methods are described, and for the planning of optimal patrols and (future) capacity planning is discussed.

Keywords Coast Guard · Risk mapping · Social network · Anomaly detection · Maritime intelligence · Data analysis

---

J.P.H. Kalden (✉)
Netherlands Coast Guard, Den Helder, The Netherlands
e-mail: jph.kalden@mindef.nl

H. Monsuur et al. (eds.), *NL ARMS Netherlands Annual Review of Military Studies 2018*, NL ARMS, https://doi.org/10.1007/978-94-6265-246-0_10

10.1 Introduction

National security is one of the prime concerns of many European countries. As almost all terrorist attacks are directed at land-based people and objects,[1] the focus of policy makers is primarily directed towards providing security on the continent. However, in doing so, policy makers risk to ignore the maritime aspect of security. This maritime focus of national and homeland security should not be missed as harbours are clear and present chokepoints of life. To illustrate, Rose George, in her book Ninety Percent of Everything,[2] explains that 90 percent of everything we can observe around us is shipped overseas, where the North Sea is one of the busiest shipping routes in the world.[3] The shipping/maritime industry and the huge amounts of goods represent a value of trillions of dollars, and offers thousands of people a living. The majority of non-bulk cargo is carried in over 15,000,000 containers, making over 200,000,000 port visits annually.[4] Besides the goods being transported overseas, the fishing industries deliver 18% of the daily animal protein[5] needed to feed the ever-increasing populations of Europe.[6] Although transforming rapidly into a 'green energy' producing sector, the present offshore industry still presents a very large amount of the energy needed to keep the mainland of Europe going.[7]

With trade concentrated in a few ports in today's global economy, even a single maritime terrorist incident has the potential to significantly disrupt our economic and financial processes. A renewed maritime focus for policy makers is not only of paramount interest for our economic wealth and progress, but also for our national security. Maritime terrorism includes attacks against vessels (warships, cruise liners, tankers and other carriers, tugboats and barges), harbour/anchorage attacks, fixed land based targets near ports (oil refineries, oil storage depots, other port infrastructure, energy pipelines and undersea cables), hijacking commercial/passenger ships on high seas, and putting obstructions such as sinking a large ship in harbour entrances.[8]

[1] In 2003, the Aegis Research and Intelligence Database estimated between 1999 and 2003 that maritime targets represented less than one percent of all terrorist attacks. A similar analysis of the RAND terrorism database supports these figures; of the 40,126 terrorist incidents recorded between 1968 and 2007, only 136 (0.34%) were against the maritime domain. https://www.fairobserver.com/region/north_america/maritime-terrorism-how-real-threat/. Accessed 1 January 2018.

[2] George 2013.

[3] On a yearly average 260.000 ships pass through the Dutch Economic Exclusion Zone. More than 20% of these ships enter a Dutch port (Dutch Ministry of Infrastructure and Water management, https://www.rijkswaterstaat.nl/English).

[4] http://www.marsecreview.com/wp-content/uploads/2012/09/MSR-Viewpoint-02-Maritime-Terrorism-How-Real-is-the-Threat.pdf.

[5] https://nl.wikipedia.org/wiki/Visserij#Nederlandse_en_Belgische_visserij (not available in English, accessed 29 December 2017).

[6] In 2016 the Dutch export value of fish increased by 12 percent to 3,4 billion euro.

[7] In 2017 the revenue was 5.9 billion euro, whilst 44.000 people depend for their work on the offshore industry. http://www.maritiemnederland.com/dossiers/offshore/item55, accessed 29 December 2017.

[8] https://www.trackingterrorism.org/article/maritime-terrorism, accessed 1 January 2018.

To counter these threats from the sea, and to control our borders and protect ourselves against overseas transportation of terrorists, explosives, weapons, plans, and subversive knowledge, we have to achieve 'sea power'.[9] In modern terms, this means that we have to make use of mathematical and computer science expertise, and data and (social) network analysis. This will strengthen our maritime security and intelligence in terms of accuracy, reliability and redundancy. Maritime intelligence aides' decision-making and capacity planning: what (future) maritime risks need to be mitigated by what means, how many casualties and how much damage do we accept, against what (political) costs?

In this chapter, we will illustrate the role of the Netherlands Coastguard (NCG) in providing border security. Next, we will highlight the efforts undertaken to improve accuracy and reliability of maritime intelligence using modern Operations Research methods.

10.2 Netherlands Coastguard

The Netherlands Coastguard (NCG) is responsible for organising and monitoring all maritime traffic and activities in the Netherlands Economic Exclusion Zone (EEZ), keeping it safe, sound and secure.[10] The Coastguard is rescuing life and is trying to keep the Dutch part of the North Sea and the various waterways clean, by encountering oil and various other spillage. Altogether, this is a highly complex task of balancing the various needs of people. As mentioned before 90% of everything arrives over sea. Therefore, one could easily claim that at least 90 % of all illegal weapons and explosives pass through European harbours. This assertion is strengthened by the fact that the continental focus of terrorist groups is changing to the sea. Air transportation of weapons and explosives have become a non-issue, as security measures at European airfields are very strict and almost infallible. Also land borders are put under surveillance more closely. Terrorists seek and will find different routes and targets to create havoc, possibly by using the sea. It will therefore be no surprise that the number of trained people, modern ships, aircraft and equipment necessary to execute the task of providing maritime security is large.[11] The Netherlands EEZ covers approximately 2,5 times the land surface, and its maritime borders exceed the length of the land borders. Having sufficient maritime (safety and security) capacity (ships, aircraft, helicopters and trained personnel) at its disposal to mitigate and neutralise possible risks and damage to the Netherlands, is one of the biggest challenges of the NCG. By default, the latest reinforcements are too little and too late, as

[9] Alfred Thayer: Mahan https://en.wikipedia.org/wiki/The_Influence_of_Sea_Power_upon_History, accessed 27 December 2017.

[10] https://www.kustwacht.nl/en/aboutus.html, accessed 29 December 2017.

[11] https://zoek.officielebekendmakingen.nl/kst-30490-26.html (not available in English, accessed 30 December 2017).

terrorists' cadre are in a survival mode and will always think in alternatives, research and innovation.

Due to the enormous territory that needs to be kept under 24/7 surveillance and the scarce NCG capacity, the planning process of surveillance of national maritime borders by air and/or by maritime patrolling must be supported by accurate and reliable maritime intelligence. How to improve this maritime situational awareness is the subject of the following section.

10.3 Maritime Intelligence and Maritime Situational Awareness

The vast amount of structured (for example wave height, wind speed and direction, imagery data, AIS data)[12] and unstructured data (reporting of incidents) is growing exponentially. Therefore, the products of data analysis to extract forecasting information will help the structuring and manning of Maritime Intelligence (MI). MI will strengthen maritime situational awareness 'by foreseeing the future' and therefore assisting the NCG's effort to execute its capacity planning process more effectively and more efficiently. For planning purposes, the NCG needs to expand the forecasting horizon (with respect to what risks ships pose to the Netherlands) up to a distance of five days' sailing from the Netherlands.

To be able to assign the right assets at the right time and the right location we also have to be able to forecast the probability that these risks (effects) indeed will occur.

To create this forecasting power the research projects within the NCG are concentrating on three issues: (1) risk mapping based on temporal geospatial analysis, (2) social network analysis, and (3) anomaly detection (a fourth, text mining, is coming soon). All these approaches can be integrated, so the NCG will have several applications at its disposal. In the following subsections, these applications will be explained in more detail.

10.3.1 (Maritime) Risk Mapping

The essence of maritime risk mapping is to know in advance what the probability is that certain events will take place at a certain time (in the foreseeable future) and location (position Lat/Long). The approach the NCG uses is quite straightforward: the basic rule is that maritime grids (rectangular shapes with a standard length and in nautical miles) on a sea map can be given a colour. The colours represent the risk values calculated for that particular grid. These values depend on the geospatial correlation between various (logical) attributes with historical data of past events in the same area. For example, the number of SAR incidents or piracy attacks (Fig. 10.1)

[12] https://www.vesselfinder.com/historical-ais-data. Accessed 30 December 2017.

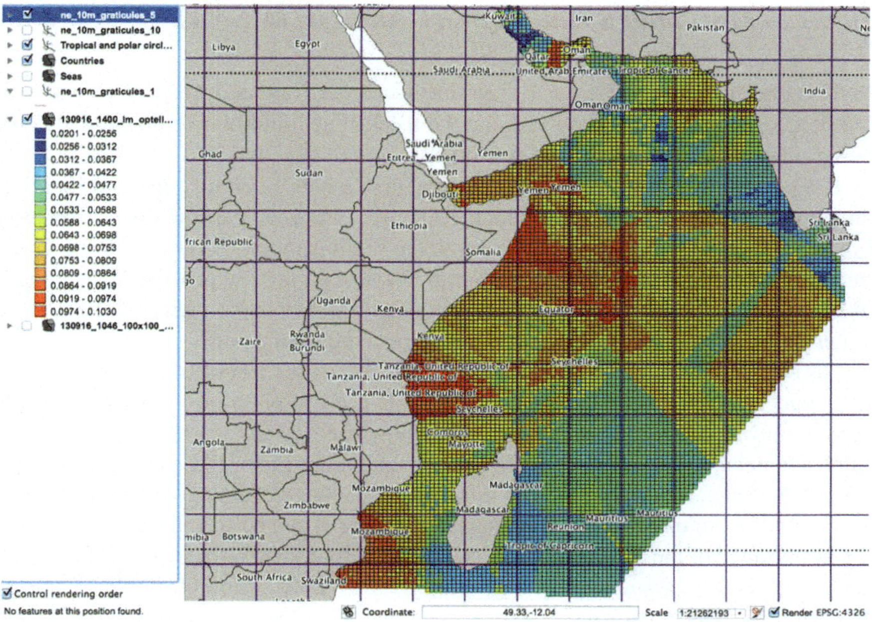

Fig. 10.1 Piracy Risk map and risk calculator (Big data analytics en Defensie: visie en aanpak, Prof. Dr. P.C. van Fenema, Dr. ir. S.J.H. Rietjens, J.P.H. Kalden, Drs. W. van der Sluis (RTD), R. Schimmel, Militaire Spectator, September 2015. http://www.militairespectator.nl/thema/bedrijfsvoering/artikel/big-data-analytics-en-defensie-visie-en-aanpak (accessed 30 December 2017).The calculator in Fig. 7.1 calculates the risk of a piracy attack with a given route, speed per track and the type of ship (Decision Support Tool)). [*Source* van Fenema, Rietjens, Kalden, van der Sluis (RTD), Schimmel, September 2015]

will correlate highly with the wind and the height of waves. The geospatial correlation between an attribute and an event at certain time and location will decline exponentially when the distance increases.[13]

This decision support tool, based on intel created by assets on board or provided by friendly ships and aircraft, can assist in improving the NCG's route planning process. When a ship sails a planned course (thick line in Fig. 10.1), its mere presence will neutralise the risk values in each grid it enters (with a certain radius from the centre of the ship). Future research could be focussed on time series analysis of the historic risk values at time t-n up to t to create future risk maps n time steps ahead. Maritime risk mapping based on data analysis is an innovative way to support maritime intelligence and may boost effectiveness by improving future capacity planning.

[13] Geospatial Analysis - 5th Edition, 2015 - de Smith, Goodchild, Longley. http://www.spatialanalysisonline.com/HTML/index.html?distance_decay_models.htm. Accessed 30 December 2017.

10.3.2 (Maritime) Social Network Analysis (MSNA)

In this paragraph, we will discuss maritime social network analysis (SNA). It reveals the people, organisations (entities) and the roles, that could lead to the risks that are being visualized in the maritime risk map.

If a certain activity is planned in an organisation at a certain time and location, an increase in the exchange of social media traffic between participants is expected. For example, participants in less professional organisations will always try to communicate. They may use Twitter whilst their location is switched on, or use words in the content of their messages that will reveal their location. This can be used to generate a mapping of the network of the terrorist organisation.

Network analysis (or social network analysis) makes use of mathematical tools and concepts that belong to graph theory. It is used in psychology, sociology, ethnology and anthropology.[14] Graphs show how the various actors (the nodes) are (inter)connected, also indicating the strength and direction of these connections (the edges). A connection is basically an information package/exchange that is directed or undirected (from one node to the other). These edges can be weighted, as a result of the importance of the connected nodes or as a result of the content itself. Information exchanges can be associated with operations, financials, training, public relations, etc. An information package could be anything that transports information. Examples are: e-mail messages, letters, notes, phone calls, faxes, messages by voice, social media.

Such a package (for example a letter) can be sent directly from the source to the receiving end, with no interference. It may also be sent from the source via various runners or ways of transportation to the receiving end. The process of sending and or receiving these weighted and or un-weighted information packages, the corresponding volumes and the fractions will give a good indication of the specific roles of each node, sub networks and cliques in a network at some point in time. The roles of nodes can be approximated by interpreting the outcome of the calculations of the various centrality measures (CM). Well known centrality measures are in and out-degree,[15] betweenness,[16] closeness[17] and eigenvector centrality.[18] Explanations and mathematical analysis of these measures may be found in the scientific literature.[19]

---

[14] https://en.wikipedia.org/wiki/Graph_(discrete_mathematics)#cite_note-10. Accessed 5 January 2018.

[15] In degree: number of incoming edges, indicating an information hungry node (analyst), out degree: number of outgoing edges indicating an information distribution role like a postman.

[16] Betweenness: how many shortest paths pas through a node, the glue or a bridge between edges and or communities.

[17] Closeness: Based on the length of all the shortest paths from a node to all other nodes in the network. A high score of a node indicates its connectiveness. Therefore, a node with a high closeness score could act as an 'alarm bell, trip wire' or security (advanced) guard.

[18] A node with a high score on Eigen vector centrality is connected to many influential nodes. When the network is approached randomly what is the change that a nod visited, the node with the highest Eigen vector centrality.

[19] Monsuur and Storcken 2004; Husslage et al. 2014.

Combined with expert knowledge, the CMs that are calculated at regular intervals can be used to estimate the present and (possible) future roles of nodes. It will also indicate future objectives of the (clandestine) network. By observing changes in centrality measures for some nodes, we might be able to foresee a change in phasing of a (clandestine) operation.

Using SNA and available information on edges, the individual hijackers of the 9/11 attack have been ranked and analysed.[20] Looking at the mission of the Netherlands Coastguard it is obvious that (Maritime) SNA improves our maritime intelligence and maritime situational awareness. Coastguard operations can proactive plan their scarce maritime assets.

10.3.3 (Maritime) Anomaly Detection (AD)

The third data analysis approach the NCG is testing is the so-called anomaly detection (AD).[21] In this paragraph, we will elaborate on the use of AD in the maritime world.

In general, a captain of any type of ship will minimize the changes in course and speed. Too many and too harsh alterations will cost the shipping company money as the ship will consume more bunker fuel. Therefore, the captain will keep a 'straight line' as long as possible. If for no reason, the captain is changing the course and/or the speed, we have identified an anomaly. We may use the IMO classification of ships[22] to standardize the average sailing pattern[23] per region and per class. Then, for each ship under observations, its AIS and or radar data may be used to calculate the standard deviation. Combined with expert knowledge, one may then decide per class of ship and per region on the anomaly thresholds. To model the expert knowledge, we can fine-tune[24] the thresholds (so the system can automatically identity an anomaly) using training data. Also vessels that stay longer in waiting areas for no particular reason (for example in case of the absence of mandatory assignments of harbour authorities) could indicate that they are waiting to meet up with other ships. This may also be classified as an anomaly detection.

The integration of maritime Intel (coming from data analysis, social network analysis, and anomaly detection) with expert knowledge, is input for the determination of risk values in maritime risk mapping.

---

[20] https://www.defensie.nl/organisatie/defensieondersteuningscommando/eenheden/nlda/wetenschappelijke-medewerkers/krijgswetenschappen/cyber-operations/inlichtingen-en-veiligheid-1/dr.-ir.-r.h.a.-roy-lindelauf. Dr. Ir. Roy Lindelauf is assisting the Netherlands Coastguard data scientists in setting up and exploring SNA as one of the maritime intelligence products and services. Ranking terrorists in networks, R. Lindelauf, Tilburg University, 2014.

[21] https://www.datascience.com/blog/python-anomaly-detection. Accessed 7 January 2018.

[22] http://www.imo.org/en/OurWork/Safety/Regulations/Pages/Default.aspx. Accessed 7 January 2018.

[23] These average sailing patterns are indicated as ships density maps.

[24] Fine-tuning reflects to minimizing the error rate (residuals) by automatically changing the weighing factors for the attributes in the algorithm.

10.4 NCG Data Analysis Put in Effect

Starting with anomaly detection (AD) and social network analysis (SNA), enhanced with expert knowledge, followed by risk mapping (RM), creates the most complete and integrated future Intel picture for the NCG necessary for decision support. By introducing the modular (data analysis and expert knowledge) approach the NCG is able to improve its effectiveness and efficiency.

The NCG, in close cooperation with TNO[25] was able to introduce an advanced data analysis proposal for the EU project MARISA (Maritime Integrated Surveillance Awareness).[26] As a result of its input it will organise a trial on the North Sea in September 2018 where the modules will be put to practise in a trial. With the help of the Royal Netherlands Navy[27] the NCG has organised a data science team located in the Navy harbour in Den Helder.

In close cooperation with the TNO, NLDA[28] and other partners, data analysis will help the NCG to balance its maritime (safety and security) capacity at the right time and place, to mitigate and neutralise possible risks and damage to the Netherlands.

References

George R (2013) Ninety percent of everything. Metropolitan Books

Husslage BGM, Borm PEM, Burg T, Hamers HJM, Lindelauf R (2014) Ranking Terrorists in Networks: A Sensitivity Analysis of Al Qaeda's 9/11 Attack. CentER Discussion Paper, Vol. 2014-028, Operations Research, Tilburg

Monsuur H, Storcken T (2004) Centers in Connected Undirected Graphs: An Axiomatic Approach. Operations Research, 52 (1):54–64

[25] https://www.tno.nl/en/about-tno/organisation/.

[26] http://www.marisaproject.eu/.

[27] https://english.defensie.nl/organisation/navy.

[28] Netherlands Defence Academy, Den Helder.

Chapter 11
Maximal Covering Location Games: An Application for the Coast Guard

L. Schlicher

Contents

Abstract It is well-known that maximal covering location games may have empty cores. In Schlicher et al. (2017) several sufficient conditions for core non-emptiness are derived for these games. In this chapter, we present another sufficient condition for core non-emptiness, which also has a practical interpretation when dealing with a real-life application of the studied game, namely the pooling of coast guard boats.

Keywords Cooperative game theory · Military operations research · Maritime application · Maximal covering location problem · Core non-emptiness · Totally unimodular matrices

11.1 Introduction

Various countries protect their coast lines with the help of governmental coast guard organizations (see, e.g., NACGF).[1] Typically, these organizations own a large fleet of resources (consisting of, e.g., cutters, boats, or aircraft), which are used to protect

L. Schlicher (✉)
Netherlands Defence Academy, Breda, The Netherlands
e-mail: lpj.schlicher@mindef.nl

[1] NACGF 2018.

H. Monsuur et al. (eds.), *NL ARMS Netherlands Annual Review of Military Studies 2018*, NL ARMS, https://doi.org/10.1007/978-94-6265-246-0_11

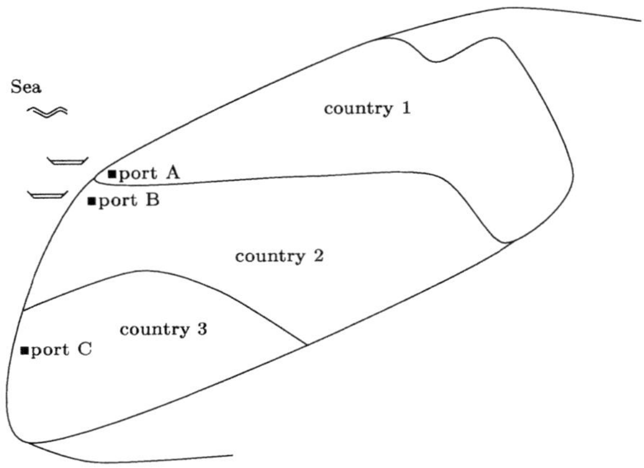

Fig. 11.1 An example with three countries and coast guard boats. [*Source* L. Schlicher]

their *own* coast only. Looking from a central perspective, one can (sometimes) use these resources more efficiently. Figure 11.1 illustrates this clearly. In this figure country 1 and country 2 both position their coast guard boat close to the border (to protect their important ports). But, looking from a central perspective, it may suffice to position one coast guard boat between port A and port B (to cover both ports) and one at port C. So, by pooling the coast guard boats, a larger part of the entire coast can be covered with less irregularities (e.g., accidents or attacks) as a consequence.

Although such a form of pooling may reduce the total number of irregularities, it is not straightforward how the costs (associated to inevitable irregularities) or cost savings (associated to prevented irregularities) should be allocated. The theory of cooperative games can be helpful here. This theory deals with the modelling and analysis of situations in which groups of players (i.e., coalitions) can benefit from coordinating their actions. In this chapter, we will use this theory, and in particular we will focus on cooperative games in which binding agreements are made between players and side payments are allowed. For such cooperative games, one lists for each possible coalition a single number, representing the associated costs (e.g., the costs associated to inevitable irregularities) or cost savings (e.g., the cost savings associated to prevented irregularities) for this group of players when they coordinate their actions. In the theory of cooperative games, an important question is then how to allocate the associated amount when all players decide to cooperate. A well-known solution concept that helps to answer this question is the core. The core is the set of all allocations that are efficient (i.e., for which the total amount is divided completely), and stable (i.e., for which it is not profitable (with respect to the allocation) for any coalition to leave the group and to work on its own). Indeed, under such an efficient and stable allocation, no individual player, nor any subgroup of players wants to split off from the collaboration.

In this chapter, we study an already existing cooperative game, which turns out to have an interesting relationship with the coast guard pooling situation. In these games, which are called maximal covering location games, there are several players that each may or may not own a single resource. Players can cooperate by pooling these resources. It is assumed that a resource *covers* all players (that are) located within a certain radius from the resource. Coverage of a player by (at least) one resource results into a player-specific profit (e.g., a cost saving). The aim of the players is to position the resources in such a way that the joint profit (i.e., the sum of the profits of the covered players) is maximized. Schlicher et al.[2] studied various properties of these games: they showed that these games are superadditive (i.e., that the value of the union of any two disjoint coalitions is at least the sum of the values of these disjoint coalitions) and monotonic (i.e., that the value of every coalition is at least the value of any of its subcoalitions), but can have empty cores. Moreover, they presented several sufficient conditions for core non-emptiness (e.g., in terms of the number of players, the type of graph, the number of resources, and an underlying integer linear programming problem). In this chapter, we introduce another sufficient condition for core non-emptiness, which has a practical interpretation when dealing with our real-life application, namely the pooling of coast guard boats.

The outline of this chapter is as follows. In Sect. 11.2, we introduce maximal covering location situations, the associated maximal covering location games, and present an already known sufficient condition for core non-emptiness (of these games). Then, in Sect. 11.3, we formulate a new sufficient condition for core non-emptiness (of these games) and in Sect. 11.4, we show its practical application when dealing with a real-life application of our studied game. In Appendix 1, we provide some basic elements of cooperative game theory and in Appendix B, we present the proof of our main theorem.

11.2 A Short Recap

In this section, we shortly introduce maximal covering location situations and the associated maximal covering location games, by closely following the formulation as presented in Schlicher et al.[3] Moreover, we present an already known sufficient condition for core non-emptiness of maximal covering location games.

11.2.1 Maximal Covering Location Situation

We consider an environment with a finite set $N = \{1, 2, \ldots, n\}$ of players and a finite set $L = \{n + 1, n + 2, \ldots, n + l\}$ of possible resource locations. The distance between player $i \in N$ and resource location $j \in L$ is denoted by $d_{ij} \in \mathbb{R}_+$. For any player $i \in N$, we introduce $r_i \in \{0, 1\}$, where $r_i = 1$ indicates that player $i \in N$ owns a resource and $r_i = 0$ indicates that player $i \in N$ does *not* own a resource. Every player $i \in N$ with $r_i = 1$ positions its resource at any resource location $j \in$

[2] Schlicher et al. 2017.

[3] Schlicher et al. 2017.

L and if $d_{ij} \leq \mathscr{D} \in \mathbb{R}_+$ (i.e., if the player is covered by the resource) a profit of $p_i \in \mathbb{R}_+$ is obtained. To analyse this setting, we define a *maximal covering location (MCL) situation* as a tuple $(N, L, p, r, d, \mathscr{D})$ with N, L, $p = (p_i)_{i \in N}$, $r = (r_i)_{i \in N}$, $d = (d_{ij})_{i \in N, j \in L}$, and $\mathscr{D}$ as described above. For short, we will use θ to refer to such an MCL situation $\theta = (N, L, p, r, d, \mathscr{D})$ and Θ for the set of MCL situations. In addition, for all $\theta \in \Theta$, we define $N_j = \{i \in N | d_{ij} \leq \mathscr{D}\}$ for all $j \in L$, $L_i = \{j \in L | d_{ij} \leq \mathscr{D}\}$ for all $i \in N$, and construct a corresponding (bipartite) graph $\mathscr{G} = (N, L, E)$ with N and L the sets of nodes and $E = \{\{i, j\}_{i \in N, j \in L_i}\}$ the set of edges. Note that an edge between player $i \in N$ and resource location $j \in L$ indicates that the distance between these nodes is no more than $\mathscr{D}$, implying that player i is covered when a resource is positioned at this location j.

11.2.2 Maximal Covering Location Game

Players can cooperate by pooling their resources. Then, for any group of players (i.e., coalition) $S \subseteq N$, we assume that coverage of any player $i \in S$ by one (or possibly multiple) resource(s) results into a profit of p_i. So, any $S \subseteq N$ faces the joint problem of where to position the resources such that the sum of the individual profits (of coalition S) is maximized. For every MCL situation $\theta \in \Theta$ and all $S \subseteq N$ this corresponding *maximal covering location problem* can be formulated as

$$
\begin{aligned}
MCL^{\theta}(S) : \max \quad & \sum_{i \in S} p_i \cdot y_i \\
\text{s.t.} \quad & y_i - \sum_{j \in L_i} x_j \leq 0 && \forall i \in S \\
& \sum_{j \in L} x_j \leq \sum_{i \in S} r_i \\
& x_j \in \{0, 1\} && \forall j \in L \\
& y_i \in \{0, 1\} && \forall i \in S.
\end{aligned}
$$

The first constraint ensures that the profit of player $i \in S$ is obtained only if at least one resource of coalition S is positioned within distance $\mathscr{D}$. The second constraint ensures that the total number of resources used does not exceed the number of available resources of coalition S. The third and fourth constraint enforce integrality of the variables. Note that a solution of the MCL problem indicates at which resource locations a resource is positioned and which players obtain a profit. In particular, if a resource is positioned at resource location $j \in L$, then $x_j = 1$ and otherwise $x_j = 0$. Similarly, if player $i \in S$ obtains profit p_i, then $y_i = 1$, otherwise $y_i = 0$.

In the remainder of this chapter, we denote for every MCL situation $\theta \in \Theta$ and all $S \subseteq N$ the optimal value of $MCL^{\theta}(S)$ by $\mathbf{opt}(MCL^{\theta}(S))$.

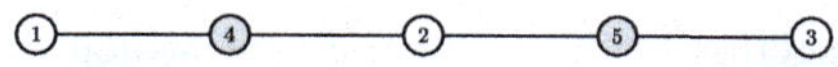

Fig. 11.2 Graph corresponding to MCL situation. [*Source* L. Schlicher]

Example 11.1 Let $\theta \in \Theta$ be an MCL situation with $N = \{1, 2, 3\}$, $L = \{4, 5\}$, $p = (3, 7, 6)$, $r = (1, 0, 0)$, $d_{14} = d_{24} = d_{25} = d_{35} = 1$, $d_{15} = d_{34} = 3$, and $\mathscr{D} = 1$. Observe that $L_1 = \{4\}$, $L_2 = \{4, 5\}$, and $L_3 = \{5\}$. The corresponding graph $\mathscr{G} = (N, L, E)$ with $E = \{(1, 4), (2, 4), (2, 5), (3, 5)\}$ is represented in Fig. 11.2.

For coalition $S = \{1, 3\}$, the maximization problem boils down to a trade off between a profit of 3, when the resource is positioned at location 4 and a profit of 6 when the resource is positioned at location 5. Hence, $\mathbf{opt}(MCL^{\theta}(\{1, 3\})) = 6$. ◇

We proceed with associating an MCL game to any MCL situation.

Definition 11.2 For every MCL situation $\theta \in \Theta$, we call the game (N, v^{θ}) with

$$v^{\theta}(S) = \begin{cases} 0 & \text{if} \quad S = \emptyset \\ \mathbf{opt}(MCL^{\theta}(S)) & \text{if} \quad S \subseteq N, S \neq \emptyset, \end{cases}$$

the associated MCL game.

Now, we present an example of an MCL game.

Example 11.3 Consider the situation of Example 11.1. The associated MCL game is presented in Table 11.1. ◇

Table 11.1 Corresponding profit per coalition of MCL game. [*Source* L. Schlicher]

S	$\emptyset$	$\{1\}$	$\{2\}$	$\{3\}$	$\{1, 2\}$	$\{1, 3\}$	$\{2, 3\}$	$\{1, 2, 3\}$
$v^{\theta}(S)$	0	3	0	0	10	6	0	13

Finally, we present one sufficient condition for core non-emptiness of MCL games formulated by Schlicher et al.[4] In doing so, we need to introduce a definition. For every MCL situation $\theta \in \Theta$ and all $S \subseteq N$ we define $RMCL^{\theta}(S)$ as a relaxation of $MCL^{\theta}(S)$ where $x_j \geq 0$ for all $j \in L$ and $0 \leq y_i \leq 1$ for all $i \in S$. Note that $x_j \in \{0, 1\}$ for all $j \in L$, $y_i \in \{0, 1\}$ for all $i \in S$, and $x_j \leq 1$ for all $j \in L$ are not taken into consideration. Based on this relaxation, Schlicher et al.[5] formulated the following sufficient condition for core non-emptiness of MCL games.

Theorem 11.4 *For every MCL situation $\theta \in \Theta$ with $\mathbf{opt}(RMCL^{\theta}(N)) = \mathbf{opt}(MCL^{\theta}(N))$, it holds that the core of the associated MCL game (N, v^{θ}) is non-empty.*

[4] Schlicher et al. 2017.

[5] Schlicher et al. 2017.

We conclude this section with an example for which this sufficient condition holds.

Example 11.5 Consider the situation of Example 11.3. For the relaxation of the MCL problem in standard LP-form, i.e., in matrix form $Ax \leq b$ with $x \geq 0$, we have the following A and b.

$$A = \begin{bmatrix} 1 & 0 & 0 & -1 & 0 \\ 0 & 1 & 0 & -1 & -1 \\ 0 & 0 & 1 & 0 & -1 \\ 0 & 0 & 0 & 1 & 1 \\ 1 & 0 & 0 & 0 & 0 \\ 0 & 1 & 0 & 0 & 0 \\ 0 & 0 & 1 & 0 & 0 \end{bmatrix}, \qquad b = \begin{bmatrix} 0 \\ 0 \\ 0 \\ 1 \\ 1 \\ 1 \\ 1 \end{bmatrix}.$$

Note that vector x stands for $(y_1, y_2, y_3, x_4, x_5)$ where x_4 and x_5 represent successively resource locations 4 and 5. Solving the relaxation of the MCL problem to optimality gives $\mathbf{opt}(RMCL^\theta(N)) = 13$, which equals the optimal value of the original MCL problem. Using Theorem 11.4, we conclude that the core of MCL game (N, v^θ) is non-empty. ◇

11.3 A New Sufficient Condition for Core Non-emptiness

In this section, we present a new sufficient condition for core non-emptiness of MCL games. In order to present this new sufficient condition, we introduce three definitions and three helpful theorems. Let $C = (c_{ij})_{i\in N, j\in M}$ be a matrix with $N, M \subseteq \mathbb{N}$. A *square submatrix* of matrix C is a matrix $C' = (c'_{ij})_{i\in W_1, j\in W_2}$ with $W_1 \subseteq N$, $W_2 \subseteq M$ and $|W_1| = |W_2|$. Moreover, matrix C is *totally unimodular* if every square submatrix of matrix C has determinant equal to $+1$, -1 or 0. Totally unimodular matrices have several interesting properties and two of them are presented below.

Theorem 11.6 *Let $A = (a_{ij})_{i\in N, j\in M}$ with $N, M \subseteq \mathbb{N}$ be a totally unimodular matrix and let $b \in \mathbb{Z}^N$ and $c \in \mathbb{R}^M$. Then the linear programming problem $\max\{cx \mid x \geq 0, Ax \leq b\}$ has integer optimal solutions, whenever it has a finite optimum.*

Proof See, e.g., Wolsey.[6]

Theorem 11.7 *Total unimodularity of a matrix is preserved under:*

(i) multiplying a row or column by -1;
(ii) adding a row or column with one non-zero, being $+1$ or -1.

[6] Wolsey 1998, p. 40.

Proof See, e.g., Schrijver.[7]

A matrix $A = (a_{ij})_{i \in N, j \in M}$ with $N, M \subseteq \mathbb{N}$ has the *consecutive ones property* if for each (row) $i \in N$ there exist a $k \in M$ and $l \in M$ with $k \leq l$ such that $a_{ij} = 1$ for all $j \in M$ for which $k \leq j \leq l$ and $a_{ij} = 0$ otherwise. It turns out that matrices with the consecutive ones property are totally unimodular.

Theorem 11.8 *A matrix with the consecutive ones property is totally unimodular.*

Proof See, e.g., Schrijver.[8]

We proceed by illustrating the introduced definitions and theorems in an example.

Example 11.9 Consider the situation of Example 11.5. Matrix A, as presented in Example 11.5, does not have the consecutive ones property, as some entries are not equal to zero or one. However, it can be shown easily (via our introduced theorems) that matrix A is totally unimodular. First, observe that matrix B, as presented below

$$B = \begin{bmatrix} 1 & 0 \\ 1 & 1 \\ 0 & 1 \\ 1 & 1 \end{bmatrix}, \overline{B} = \begin{bmatrix} -1 & 0 \\ -1 & -1 \\ 0 & -1 \\ 1 & 1 \end{bmatrix}, \widehat{B} = \begin{bmatrix} 1 & 0 & 0 & -1 & 0 \\ 0 & 1 & 0 & -1 & -1 \\ 0 & 0 & 1 & 0 & -1 \\ 0 & 0 & 0 & 1 & 1 \end{bmatrix}, \widetilde{B} = \begin{bmatrix} 1 & 0 & 0 & -1 & 0 \\ 0 & 1 & 0 & -1 & -1 \\ 0 & 0 & 1 & 0 & -1 \\ 0 & 0 & 0 & 1 & 1 \\ 1 & 0 & 0 & 0 & 0 \\ 0 & 1 & 0 & 0 & 0 \\ 0 & 0 & 1 & 0 & 0 \end{bmatrix},$$

has the consecutive ones property, and so, based on Theorem 11.8, is totally unimodular. Based on Theorem 11.7 (i), matrix $\overline{B}$ is totally unimodular as well as it results from matrix B by multiplying the first, second, and third row by -1. Based on Theorem 11.7 (ii), matrix $\widehat{B}$ is totally unimodular as it results from matrix $\overline{B}$ by adding three columns, each of them consisting of zeros only, except for one entry with value 1, which varies from the first entry in the first column to the third entry in the third column. Similarly, matrix $\widetilde{B}$ is totally unimodular as it results from matrix $\widehat{B}$ by adding three rows, each of them consisting of zeros only, except for one entry with value 1, which varies from the first entry in the first row to the third entry in the third row. Note, matrix $\widetilde{B}$ coincides with matrix A of Example 11.5 and so A is totally unimodular as well. ◇

Now, we are ready to formulate our new sufficient condition (in terms of the underlying MCL situation) for core non-emptiness.

Theorem 11.10 *For every MCL situation $\theta \in \Theta$ for which there exist for each $i \in N$ a $k \in L$ and $m \in L$ with $k \leq m$ such that $d_{ij} \leq \mathcal{D}$ for all $j \in L$ with $k \leq j \leq m$ and $d_{ij} > \mathcal{D}$ otherwise, it holds that the core of the associated MCL game (N, v^{θ}) is non-empty.*

[7] Schrijver 1998, p. 280.

[8] Schrijver 1998, p. 279.

The proof of Theorem 11.10 is relegated to appendix B. We provide a sketch of proof here. First, we show, in a similar way as we do in Example 11.9, that matrix A of the relaxation of the MCL situation in standard form (i.e., in matrix form $Ax \leq b$) is totally unimodular. Then, we conclude, based on Theorem 11.6, that the relaxation of the MCL problem has an integer optimal solution as the optimum is finite, vector b has all integer entries, and $p_i \in \mathbb{R}_+$ for all $i \in N$. Subsequently, we show that this optimal solution is a binary optimal solution. It then follows that the optimal value of the MCL problem coincides with the optimal value of the relaxation of the MCL problem and so, based on Theorem 11.4, we conclude that the core of the associated MCL game is non-empty.

We now illustrate how the new sufficient condition is applied in an example.

Example 11.11 Consider the situation of Example 11.5. For player 1, set $k = l = 4$ and observe that $d_{14} \leq \mathscr{D}$ and $d_{15} > \mathscr{D}$. For player 2, set $k = 4$ and $l = 5$ and observe that $d_{24} = d_{25} \leq \mathscr{D}$. For player 3, set $k = l = 5$ and observe that $d_{34} > \mathscr{D}$ and $d_{35} \leq \mathscr{D}$. So, based on Theorem 11.10, we (again) conclude that the core of MCL game (N, v^θ) is non-empty. ◇

11.4 An Application for the New Sufficient Condition

In this last section, we show that the new sufficient condition for core non-emptiness has a practical interpretation when dealing with a real-life application of the studied game, namely pooling of coast guard boats.

11.4.1 Model

Our starting point is the coast guard pooling situation of Fig. 11.1. In order to analyze this coast guard boat pooling situation, we use the following modelling approach.

- We model the coast of the three countries by a *line*, which is divided into several (small) districts of equal length (e.g., 2 km).
- We assign to each district a certain value, identifying its importance (e.g., the cost savings that can be realized by covering this district).
- In each district, a coast guard boat can be positioned and, in addition to the covering of this district, the coast guard boat covers a fixed number of neighbouring districts to the left and the right completely.
- A country is represented by a set of concatenated districts and a (possibly empty) set of coast guard boats.

Note that for this modelling approach, it holds that the smaller we set the length of a district, the more realistic the model represents reality.

In Fig. 11.3, we give a graphical representation of how the situation of Fig. 11.1 can be modelled. As an example, we divide the coast into 16 districts and we set the value of each district with a port at 4 and the value of each district without a port at 1. We assume that a guard coast boat can cover three districts: its own district and its two direct neighbouring districts. We assume that the first four concatenated districts (from the left) represent country 3, the subsequent four concatenated districts represent country 2, and the remaining concatenated districts represent country 1. Finally, we assume that country 1 and country 2 both own one guard coast boat and that country 3 does not own a coast guard boat.

11.4.2 Relation to Maximal Covering Location Games

For the model represented in Fig. 11.3, we can formulate an associated 3-person game. For this game, which we denote by (T, w), with $T = \{1, 2, 3\}$, where 1, 2, and 3 represent country 1, country 2, and country 3, respectively, we assume that each coalition positions its coast guard boats such that the sum of the values of the covered districts (of this coalition) is maximized. For instance, the value of coalition $\{1, 2, 3\}$ is obtained by positioning one coast guard boat at the third district (with a total value of 6) and one coast guard boat at the eighth or ninth district (with a total value of 9). In Table 11.2, all coalitional values are represented.

It is not difficult to see that the core of game (T, w) is non-empty. For instance, allocation $x = (6, 6, 3)$ is a core element. We can also show core non-emptiness via another way, namely via relating game (T, w) to an MCL game. In particular, for game (T, w) we can construct the following MCL game (N, v^{θ}) with $N = \{1, 2, \ldots, 16\}$, $L = \{17, 18 \ldots, 32\}$, $p_3 = p_8 = p_9 = 4$, $p_i = 1$ for all $i \in N\backslash\{3, 8, 9\}$, $r_8 = r_9 = 1$, $r_i = 0$ for all $i \in N\backslash\{8, 9\}$, $d_{ij} = |j - (i + 16)|$ for all $i \in N$ and all $j \in L$, and $\mathscr{D} = 1$. In Fig. 11.4, we present the corresponding graph of MCL game (N, v^{θ}).

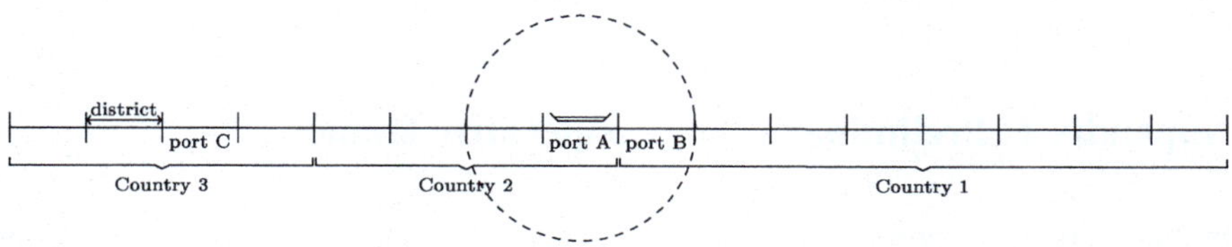

Fig. 11.3 Graphical representation of the situation of Fig. 11.1. [*Source* L. Schlicher]

Table 11.2 Coalitional values of game (T, w). [*Source* L. Schlicher]

S	$\emptyset$	$\{1\}$	$\{2\}$	$\{3\}$	$\{1, 2\}$	$\{1, 3\}$	$\{2, 3\}$	$\{1, 2, 3\}$
$w(S)$	0	6	6	0	12	6	6	15

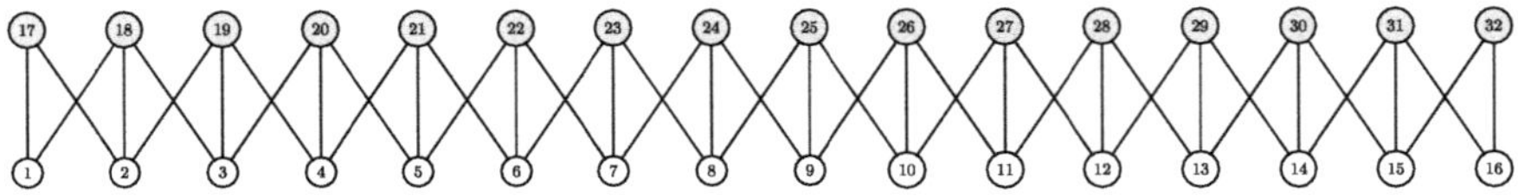

Fig. 11.4 Graph corresponding to MCL situation. [*Source* L. Schlicher]

For MCL game (N, v^θ) it is not difficult to find a $k \in L$ and $m \in L$ with $k \leq m$ for each $i \in N$ such that $d_{ij} \leq \mathscr{D}$ for all $j \in L$ with $k \leq j \leq m$ and $d_{ij} > \mathscr{D}$ otherwise. Namely, for player 1, we can set $k = 17$ and $l = 18$, for player 16, we can set $k = 31$ and $l = 32$ and for each player $i \in N\backslash\{1, 16\}$, we can set $k = i + 15$ and $l = i + 17$. So, based on Theorem 11.10, we can conclude that the core of MCL game (N, v^θ) is non-empty. With this result, we can also show that the core of game (T, w) is non-empty. Let $G_1 = \{1, 2, 3, 4\}$, $G_2 = \{5, 6, 7, 8\}$, and $G_3 = \{9, 10, \ldots, 16\}$. Now, observe that $w(S) = v^\theta\left(\bigcup_{i\in S} G_i\right)$ for all $S \subseteq T$. Let x be a core allocation of game (N, v^θ) and $y_i = \sum_{j\in G_i} x_j$ for all $i \in T$. We will show that allocation y is a core element (i.e., that $\sum_{i\in T} y_i = w(T)$ and $\sum_{i\in S} y_i \geq w(S)$ for all $S \subseteq T$). First, recall that $\sum_{i\in N} x_i = v^\theta(N)$ and $\sum_{i\in S} x_i \geq v^\theta(S)$ for all $S \subseteq N$ as allocation x is a core element of game (N, v^θ). Now, observe that $\sum_{i\in T} y_i = \sum_{i\in T}\sum_{j\in G_i} x_j = \sum_{i\in N} x_i = v^\theta(N) = w(T)$, which implies that allocation y is efficient. Let $S \subseteq T$. Now, observe that $\sum_{i\in S} y_i = \sum_{i\in S}\sum_{j\in G_i} x_j \geq v^\theta\left(\bigcup_{i\in S} G_i\right) = w(S)$, which implies that allocation y is stable as well. Hence, allocation y is a core element of game (T, w) and thus the core of game (T, w) is non-empty.[9]

It is not difficult to see that this result can be generalized to any game arising from a coast guard pooling situation that is modelled in the spirit of Sect. 11.4.2: for these coast guard pooling situations, one can construct a corresponding MCL game in which the resource locations are positioned such that the condition of Theorem 11.10 is satisfied. This result may stimulate coast guard organizations to consider coast guard boat pooling.

Acknowledgements A word of thanks to Marco Slikker and Erwin van Wingerden for the fruitful discussion on the modelling aspect of coast guard boat pooling situations.

Appendix 1: Preliminaries on Cooperative Games

In this section, we provide some basic elements of cooperative game theory. Consider a finite set $N = \{1, 2, \ldots, n\}$ of *players* and a function $v : 2^N \to \mathbb{R}$ called the *characteristic function*, with $v(\emptyset) = 0$. The pair (N, v) is a *cooperative game with transferable utility*, shortly *game*. A subset $S \subseteq N$ is a *coalition* and $v(S)$ is the worth

[9] We want to emphasize that this result can also be obtained via other MCL games. For instance, for the MCL game we introduced above, it does not matter if we reposition the ownership of the first resource to one of the other three districts of country 2 or reposition the ownership of the second resource to one of the other seven districts of country 1.

that coalition S can obtain by itself. The worth can be transferred freely among the players. The set N is the *grand coalition*. A game (N, v) is *superadditive* if the value of the union of any two disjoint coalitions is larger than or equal to the sum of the values of these disjoint coalitions, i.e., $v(S) + v(T) \leq v(S \cup T)$ for all $S, T \subseteq N$ with $S \cap T = \emptyset$ and *monotonic* if the value of every coalition is at least the value of any of its subcoalitions, i.e., $v(S) \leq v(T)$ for all $S, T \subseteq N$ with $S \subseteq T$. An allocation for a game (N, v) is an n-dimensional vector $x \in \mathbb{R}^N$ where player $i \in N$ receives x_i. An allocation is *efficient* if $\sum_{i \in N} x_i = v(N)$. This implies that all worth is divided among the players of the grand coalition N. An allocation is *stable* if no group of players has an incentive to leave the grand coalition N, i.e., $\sum_{i \in S} x_i \geq v(S)$ for all $S \subseteq N$. The set of efficient and stable allocations of (N, v) is the *core* of (N, v) and denoted by $\mathscr{C}(N, v)$.

Appendix 2: Proof of Theorem 11.10

Let $\theta = (N, L, p, r, d, \mathscr{D}) \in \Theta$ be an MCL situation for which there exist for each $i \in N$ a $k \in L$ and $m \in L$ with $k \leq m$ such that $d_{ij} \leq \mathscr{D}$ for all $j \in L$ with $k \leq j \leq m$ and $d_{ij} > \mathscr{D}$ otherwise. Let $N^* = N \cup \{n + 1\}$. Now, consider matrix $B = (b_{ij})_{i \in N^*, j \in L}$ with $b_{ij} = 1$ for all $i \in N$ and all $j \in L$ with $d_{ij} \leq \mathscr{D}$ and $b_{ij} = 0$ for all $i \in N$ and all $j \in L$ for which $d_{ij} > \mathscr{D}$ and with $b_{n+1,j} = 1$ for all $j \in L$. So, for each $i \in N^*$, there exist a $k \in L$ and $m \in L$ with $k \leq m$ such that $b_{ij} = 1$ for all $j \in L$ for which $k \leq j \leq m$ and $b_{ij} = 0$ otherwise. Hence, matrix B has the consecutive ones property, and based on Theorem 11.8, is also totally unimodular. Let $\overline{B} = (\overline{b}_{ij})_{i \in N^*, j \in L}$ be given by $\overline{b}_{ij} = -b_{ij}$ for all $i \in N$ and all $j \in L$ and $\overline{b}_{n+1,j} = b_{n+1,j}$ for all $j \in L$. Based on Theorem 11.7 (i), matrix $\overline{B}$ is totally unimodular (as well) as it results from matrix B by multiplying the first n rows by -1. Now, let $\widehat{B} = (\widehat{b}_{ij})_{i \in N^*, j \in N \cup L}$ be given by $\widehat{b}_{ij} = \overline{b}_{ij}$ for all $i \in N^*$ and all $j \in L$, $\widehat{b}_{ij} = 1$ for all $i \in N^*$ and all $j \in N$ for which $i = j$, and $\widehat{b}_{ij} = 0$ for all $i \in N^*$ and $j \in N$ for which $i \neq j$. Based on Theorem 11.7 (ii), matrix $\widehat{B}$ is also totally unimodular as it results from matrix $\overline{B}$ by adding n columns, each of them consisting of zeros only, except for one entry with value 1, which varies from the first position (in the first column) to the n-th position (in the n-th column). Now, let $N^{**} = \{n + 2, n + 3, \ldots, 2n + 1\}$ and matrix $\widetilde{B} = ((\widetilde{b}_{ij})_{i \in N^* \cup N^{**}, j \in N \cup L}$ be given by $\widetilde{b}_{ij} = \widehat{b}_{ij}$ for all $i \in N^*$ and all $j \in N \cup L$ and $\widetilde{b}_{ij} = 1$ for all $i \in N^{**}$ and all $j \in N \cup L$ for which $i = j + n + 1$ and $\widetilde{b}_{ij} = 0$ for all $i \in N^{**}$ and all $j \in N \cup L$ for which $i \neq j + n + 1$. Based on Theorem 11.7 (ii), matrix $\widetilde{B}$ is totally unimodular as it results from matrix $\widehat{B}$ by adding n rows, each of them consisting of zeros only, except for one entry with value 1, which varies from the first position (in the first row) to the n-th position (in the n-th row). Now, observe that $\widetilde{B} = A$, where A represents the matrix of the linear programming formulation $RMCL^{\theta}(N)$ in standard form (i.e., in the form $Ax \leq b$). As the optimum of the linear programming formulation $RMCL^{\theta}(N)$ is finite, vector b has all integer entries, and $p_i \in \mathbb{R}_+$ for all $i \in N$, it follows, based on

Theorem 11.6, that $RMCL^{\theta}(N)$ has integer optimal solutions. As $0 \leq y_i \leq 1$ for all $i \in N$, it follows that there always exist optimal solutions of $RMCL^{\theta}(N)$ for which $0 \leq x_j \leq 1$ for all $j \in L$. So, $RMCL^{\theta}(N)$ has an integer optimal solution with not only $y_i \in \{0, 1\}$ for all $i \in N$, but also $x_j \in \{0, 1\}$ for all $j \in L$. This implies that $\mathbf{opt}(RMCL^{\theta}(N)) = \mathbf{opt}(MCL^{\theta}(N))$ and so, based on Theorem 11.4, the core of (N, v^{θ}) is non-empty, which concludes this proof. □

References

North Atlantic Coast Guard Forum NACGF (2018) Governmental coast guard companies, http://www.kustwacht.nl/en/nautical.html, accessed 5 January 2018

Schlicher L, Slikker M, van Houtum G (2017) A note on maximal covering location games. Operations Research Letters, 45: 98–103

Schrijver L (1998) Theory of linear and integer programming. Wiley-Interscience Series in Discrete Mathematics & Optimization, John Wiley & Sons

Wolsey L (1998) Integer Programming. Wiley-Interscience Series in Discrete Mathematics & Optimization, John Wiley & Sons

Part IV
Natural-Scientific Aspects of Border and Port Protection

Chapter 12
Vulnerability of Harbours and Near-Shore Infrastructure to Underwater Explosions

L. Koene and A.J.M. Schmets

Contents

Abstract Underwater explosive devices, such as improvised explosive devices (IED), offer a high-risk threat within the maritime domain. An attack on ships in harbours, coastal infrastructure, such as locks and quays, by underwater explosives could have a detrimental effect on infrastructure functionality and national economy. Here, the physical effects of underwater explosives are reviewed and compared to surface firings. Next, a few examples in the maritime domain are treated in more detail: ships, divers and swimmers, tourist beaches, dikes, infrastructural assets and near-shore sea-bed communication. Moreover, possible detection methods and counter-strategies are discussed. A methodology for risk analysis of underwater explosion threats is outlined. Finally, conclusions and challenges for the future, focused on scientific research and preventive approaches are given.

L. Koene (✉) · A.J.M. Schmets
Faculty of Military Sciences, Den Helder, The Netherlands
e-mail: l.koene@mindef.nl

A.J.M. Schmets
e-mail: ajm.schmets@mindef.nl

H. Monsuur et al. (eds.), *NL ARMS Netherlands Annual Review of Military Studies 2018*, NL ARMS, https://doi.org/10.1007/978-94-6265-246-0_12

Keywords Underwater explosions · shock wave effects · risk assessment · protection · underwater unmanned vehicle (UUV) · unmanned surface vehicle (USV) · drones · harbours · near-shore · ships · infrastructure

12.1 Introduction

The Netherlands, as well as its overseas Caribbean territories, owes many of its socio-economic achievements to the close presence of the sea and a system of rivers that connects its coastal areas to a densely populated hinterland. From a national security point of view, the close presence of the sea requires the Dutch authorities to seriously consider the risk and impact of security threats originating near-shore and off-shore, and to define strategies and countermeasures to mitigate these threats. Obviously, this emphasizes the importance of the level of training and expertise of the Royal Navy and coastal guard.

One class of security disrupting maritime incidents are underwater and near-surface explosions. Such explosions may have physically and psychologically damaging impact on humans and sea life, infrastructures and the environment. Explosions may originate from accidents or intentional, for example, by state or terrorist aggressors.[1] Preparedness and rapid response of governments relating to the threats imposed by marine explosion requires a good level of knowledge on physical and damage-related aspects of these phenomena. However, the body of knowledge related to underwater explosions does still rely heavily on scientific work and battle-field experience from World War II, for instance the 1948-monography of Cole.[2] In-depth scientific analyses are often lacking. For example, recent scientific work[3] has revealed that the safety distance guidelines as commonly used by authorities are completely inconsistent (i.e. ten times smaller) with data derived from an extensive study that related human injury data to underwater blast. In this contribution, first we summarize the phenomenology and physics of underwater and near-surface explosions. Then, this approach is complemented with an outline of the associated risks for harbours and near-shore infrastructure. These risks are both actual and very real. A recent report by the British MP Rishi Sunak[4] emphasises both the importance and the potential vulnerability of the submarine cable infrastructure, especially in the context of hybrid warfare.

The first reported use of explosives to damage vessels at or below the waterline was in the Eighty Years' War by the *Dutch*[5] during the siege of Antwerp by the Spanish in 1585. The Spanish barricade of the river Scheldt was a bridge formed by ships,

---

[1] Eski 2011; Chalk 2008.

[2] Cole 1965.

[3] Lance et al. 2015.

[4] Sunak 2017.

[5] In the 16th Century, Belgium did not exist as a nation yet. For the (Catholic) Southern Netherlands their participation in the Eighty Years' War ended with the Fall of Antwerp in 1585.

effectively closing off the city from the sea. The *Dutch* insurgents tried to destroy the bridge using two ships transformed into floating mines and several smaller fire ships. The explosion is estimated to have caused between 800 and 1000 deaths among the curious Spanish onlookers, and a breach was made in the barricade.[6] Despite this result, the Dutch insurgents were not successful in liberating Antwerp and its harbour. Davies[7] suggested that the ship *Hoop* remains the Improvised Explosive Device (IED) that has killed most victims in history.[8] Moreover, the experience of exploding ships was not easily forgotten, with the expression 'hellburners of Antwerp' entering the vocabulary.[9] More recent examples of similar occurrences are the raid on the USS Cole by a small boat laden with explosives in 2000, or the attack on the French tanker 'Limburg' off the coast of Yemen in 2002. These attacks, together with 9/11, have inspired 'new anti-terrorism policies and tighter surveillance of the maritime realms'.[10] It has also led to additional regulations and standards issued by the United Nations maritime branch, the International Maritime Organisation (IMO): the *International Ship and Port Facility Security* (ISPS) amendment to the *International Convention for the Safety of Life at Sea* (IMO 2003).

The field of underwater explosions is complex as well as fascinating. An underwater explosion is defined as an explosion where the point of detonation is below the water surface. A plume due to an underwater explosion is shown in Fig. 12.1. The detonation of a high explosive underwater produces initially two pulses: a shock wave followed by a bubble pulse, associated with the gas produced by the explosive reaction. Shock waves in water can be analysed in a similar way to shock waves due to explosions in air. But, of course the bubble pulse, to be discussed in more detail in the theory section below, does not occur in air.

Thus, the main objective of this contribution is to provide an overview of relevant aspects related to the vulnerability of harbours and near-shore infrastructure to maritime explosion. The chapter provides an overview of the current body of knowledge related to underwater detonation of conventional high explosives and their interaction with structures and humans. Next to the interaction with the shock wave, the additional effects of the bubble pulse and cavitation are discussed.

The structure of this chapter is as follows. First, the phenomenology and physics of underwater explosions and their effects are reviewed. Next, both threats in this domain are discussed, followed by possible measures to mitigate these threats. Then a method of risk assessment and quantification is proposed. Then, this model is applied to two scenarios: explosion risk on dikes and dams, i.e. hard infrastructural targets, and on a tourist beach, obviously a soft target. Finally, a number of general conclusions are drawn, together with practical recommendations to counter threats and directions for future research.

---

[6] Bulson 1997; Groen 2013; Revill 2016.

[7] Davies 2018.

[8] Of course, the method of using an unmanned surface vehicle (USV) to deliver an explosive can still be applied.

[9] Revill 2016.

[10] Eski 2011.

Fig. 12.1 Baltic Sea (May 16, 2014). A Canadian explosive ordnance disposal (EOD) team detonates a World War II German naval mine after safely removing it from the wreck of a German minelayer worked by them and U.S. Navy Explosive Ordnance Disposal Mobile Unit (EODMU) 8. [*Source* U.S. Navy photo by Mass Communication 1st Class David R. Krigbaum/Released]

12.2 Theory

12.2.1 Explosions in Air

In air detonation of a high explosive produces a blast wave. A conventional chemical explosion occurs when an explosive compound undergoes a decomposition reaction at rates much faster than the speed of sound in the explosive material. Such a rapid decomposition process is named a detonation, which can be understood reasonably well by the one-dimensional ZND-model developed by Zel'dovich, Von Neumann and Döring.[11] The result of the detonation process is the almost instantaneous and localised creation of pressurised gases (one gram of TNT decomposes into about one litre—equivalent ambient pressure—gases) at elevated temperatures (order of 3000–4000 K). These gases forcibly expand like a spherical piston, pushing the surrounding atmosphere back, initiating an outward moving, large amplitude pressure wave in the surrounding medium. In the (high) pressure range, which is typically measured near an explosion centre, the local outward pressure-wave velocity is pro-

[11] Zel'dovich and Raizer 2002; Ficket and Davis 1979.

portional to the magnitude of the pressure, leading to steepening of the pressure wave (high pressure fronts of the wave outrun the corresponding pressure troughs), ultimately forming a shock wave, which is also named blast wave when the surrounding medium is air.

These shock waves propagate away from the explosion centre at high velocity, i.e. at Mach numbers of the order of 10, as measured at 1 m distance from the spherical detonation of 12 kg TNT in air at ambient conditions.[12] At larger distances from the volume of detonation the shock velocity decays monotonically with distance R, until it approaches asymptotically the ambient sound velocity in the medium. This experimental observation can be understood in terms of the problem of an idealised, strong point explosion in a homogeneous atmosphere. The problem was originally formulated by Taylor,[13] and it was completely solved by Sedov.[14] In a simplified treatment, the shock front is characterised by the variable C. For short times, that is until the shock velocity has decayed to the ambient velocity of sound, the motion of the wave front $R(t)$ is governed by the similarity relationship

$$R = C\left(\frac{E}{\rho_0}\right)^{\frac{1}{5}} t^{\frac{2}{5}} \tag{12.1}$$

with E the energy released by the explosion, ρ_0 the ambient mass density, t the time after detonation, and $R = R(t)$ the distance from the centre of the explosion.

The shock wave can be described either by the variation of shock wave parameters as a function of distance from the explosion source, or by the complete time history of the shock wave parameters at a specific distance. The latter representation of a blast wave can be characterised by the so-called Friedlander waveform, which is given by the relation between overpressure P and time ($t > t_0$):

$$P(t) = P_{\max}\left(1 - \frac{t - t_0}{t^+}\right)e^{-b\frac{t-t_0}{t^+}} \tag{12.2}$$

with $P_{\max}$ the peak overpressure, b the decay coefficient of the waveform, and the positive phase duration $t^+ = (t_p - t_0)$. The positive phase duration is defined as the difference between the time of arrival (at the detector location R), t_0, and the time t_p where the pressure has reached the ambient value again. The coefficient b controls the division of momentum between the shock waves' positive and negative phases. For $b = 1$ the positive and negative impulses are equal. These four parameters completely characterise a shock wave at a given distance from the detonation centre, see Fig. 12.2.

In the left part of Fig. 12.2 the key features of an air shock wave passing a pressure detector at given distance is presented using the waveform of Eq. (12.2). Typical features are the steep rise of pressure at arrival of the blast wave, its subsequent

---

[12] Swisdak 1975.

[13] Taylor 1946.

[14] Zel'dovich and Raizer 2002; Landau and Lifshitz 1987

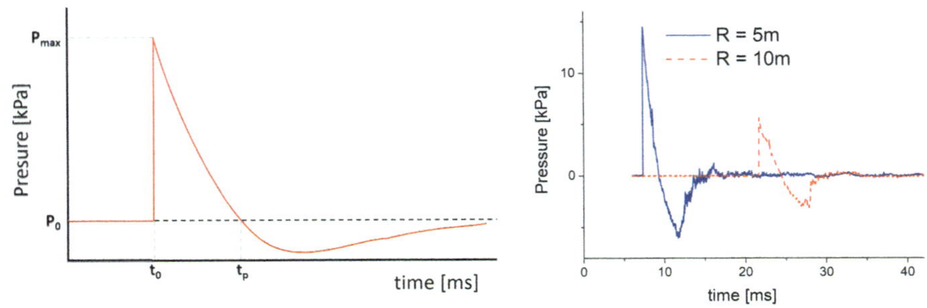

Fig. 12.2 The Friedlander waveform (left) typical for shock waves in air, and an example of a measured pressure-time dataset for 167 g of aluminium-cased C4 explosive (right), measured by the authors at the test site Elsenborn, Belgium, February 2017. Note that the time-axis in the right figure is at atmospheric pressure. [*Source* The authors]

exponential decay, towards pressures below the ambient pressure. The positive phase of the shock wave carries an impulse per unit area (product of force per unit area and time)

$$i = \int_{t_0}^{t_p} P(t)dt. \tag{12.3}$$

Damage and injury criteria are usually formulated in terms of the maximum pressure and impulse carried along by the shock wave.[15] However, most damage inflicted by shock waves is due to drag loading of the structure: the pressure gradient generates a so-called blast wind which loads the structure. The blast wind is characterised by the particle velocity of infinitesimal air volume. Fortunately, these velocities follow a similar pattern as the pressure in Fig. 12.2. Moreover, through the thermodynamic Rankine-Hugoniot relations the particle velocities, thus the drag load, can be expressed as a function of the maximum pressure at given distance.[16]

The right part of Fig. 12.2 shows pressure-time data for a 127 g C4 explosion at distances of 5 and 10 m from the explosive centre. The main features of a blast wave as described earlier are present. From the difference in arrival times one finds the average shock velocity between the two detectors to be in the order of the ambient sound velocity, hence the shock wave velocity at 5 m is well above Mach = 1. From data in literature[17] one finds for 12 kg spherical TNT charges in air, shock velocities larger than Mach = 10 at 1 m and at 10 m attenuated to Mach numbers slightly larger than 1. Obviously, the peak pressure decreases with the distance, as can be expected from properties that 'dilute' through spherical expansion. The relation between shock wave parameters, such as maximum pressure, and distance relies

[15] Baker et al. 1983.

[16] Kinney and Graham 2013.

[17] Swisdak 1975.

Fig. 12.3 Example of a simulated shallow-underwater explosion in air, with (left) the moment of detonation, and (right) snapshot of the violent gas expansion phase. The 'upright object' in the right figure is a pressure detector, connected to one of the multiple channels of the measurement setup. [*Source* Images recorded by the authors, Reek, November 2017]

on empirical formulae derived from simulations.[18] Fortunately for all known explosives the shock parameters scale with respect to charge mass over several orders of magnitude. Therefore, shock wave parameters are often expressed or tabulated as a function of scaled distance $Z = \frac{R}{\sqrt[3]{w}}$, with R the distance and w the mass of the charge, the so-called Hopkinson-Cranz scaling.

12.2.2 Underwater Explosions

The detonation process of an energetic material detonated under water, is analogous to the same process taking place in air. Once the detonation wave in the explosive material is complete, i.e. it has reached the charge's wet surface, the highly-compressed gas in the small bubble propels the surrounding liquid radially outward.

Figure 12.3 shows the effects of a simulation of an underwater explosion. A plastic bucket was filled with 20 L of water, then 0.25 kg spherically-shaped C4-explosive was mounted in the middle. The system was attached to a metal support 2 m above ground. The explosive was set off electrically, and the moment of detonation, characterised by an immediate rise of temperature to several thousand degrees, was visible by a flash of light in the bucket (left part of Fig. 12.3). Then, the rapid outward expansion of the decomposition gases pushed away the surrounding water. The gas-expansion front is preceded by a spherical shock wave in air (hardly visible), initially moving out at supersonic velocities relative to air.

[18] Brode 1955.

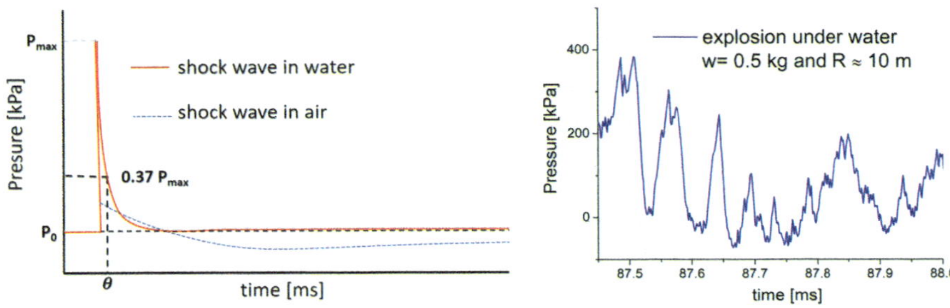

Fig. 12.4 The proposed waveform (left) for typical underwater shock waves, and example of a measured pressure-time dataset for the detonation of 0.5 kg C4 explosive (right) at a depth of 6 m below the water surface (and close to the bottom of the test site lake). The data were measured in the water 1 m below the water-air interface by the authors at the Mineursberg, Reek, February 2017

It is obvious that the underwater explosion model-experiment shown in Fig. 12.3 mimics the initial processes that accompany an underwater detonation: the almost instantaneous conversion of solid material into hot explosion gas induce a shock wave transmitted to the surrounding water and propagate spherically away from the source.[19] The initial temperature of the gas is of the order 3000 °C and the initial pressure is about 5000 MPa.[20] The underwater explosion pressure-time history is also described by a decay equation,[21] though here the decay follows a simpler form than the Friedlander form of Eq. (12.2), given by

$$P(t) = P_{\max} e^{-\frac{t}{\theta}}, \tag{12.4}$$

where θ is the decay constant, e.g. Fig. 12.4.

From extensive testing programmes in the 1950s and 1960s, it was found that most shock wave parameters follow power law dependence with inverse scaled distance $\left(\frac{w^{1/3}}{R}\right)$ for distances larger than a couple of charge radii from the explosive.[22] This power law behaviour suggests scale invariance or similitude, and indeed these scale relations are commonly used in the field of shock wave physical phenomena.[23]

[19] Cole 1965.

[20] Rajendran and Narasimhan 2006.

[21] Cole 1965.

[22] Costanzo 2011.

[23] Smith and Hetherington 1994; Zel'dovich and Raizer 2002.

Table 12.1 Shock wave constants for various explosives, adopted from Hsu (2015)

	HBX-1	TNT	PETN	Nuclear
k_1	53.51	52.12	56.21	1.06×10^4
α_1	1.144	1.18	1.194	1.13
k_2	0.092	0.0895	0.086	3.627
α_2	−0.247	−0.185	−0.257	−0.22

The maximum pressure as a function of spatial separation from the explosion centre is found to follow a two-parameter scale relation:

$$P_{\max} = k_1 \left(\frac{w^{1/3}}{R} \right)^{\alpha_1}, \tag{12.5}$$

and the decay constant θ scales, with an extra $w^{\frac{1}{3}}$, as

$$\frac{\theta}{W^{\frac{1}{3}}} = k_2 \left(\frac{w^{1/3}}{R} \right)^{\alpha_2}. \tag{12.6}$$

In Eqs. (12.4)–(12.6) w signifies the mass of the explosive (the power $\frac{1}{3}$ makes it proportional to a length), and P is the pressure. The constants k_1, k_2, α_1 and α_2 dependent on the type of explosive charge and can be obtained from experiments, see for example Swisdak.[24] In Table 12.1 values adopted from Hsu[25] are given for three different high explosives and for the shock wave originating from a nuclear explosion. Obviously, the constants for the nuclear case are very distinct from the others.

From Eq. (12.4) it is clear that in the case of an underwater explosion the shock wave does not possess a negative phase, hence the definition for the impulse per unit area i from Eq. (12.3) has to be adjusted for the underwater case[26] as

$$i = \int_{t_0}^{t_0+5\theta} P(t)dt \tag{12.7}$$

where $P(t)$ is either measured or calculated from Eqs. (12.4)–(12.6). Similar to Eqs. (12.5) and (12.6), also the impulse per unit area i follows a scaling relation

[24] Swisdak 1978.

[25] Hsu et al. 2015.

[26] Smith and Hetherington 1994; Cole 1965.

$$\frac{i}{W^{1/3}} = k_3 \left(\frac{W^{1/3}}{R} \right)^{\alpha_3}, \tag{12.8}$$

with parameters k_3 and α_3 to be determined experimentally for various explosive materials and geometries. Finally, from the relations formulated above, the energy flux density associated with the underwater shock wave can be formulated as

$$E' = \frac{1}{\rho_0 c_0} \int_{t_0}^{t_0+5\theta} [P(t)]^2 dt, \tag{12.9}$$

with $\rho_{0,} c_0$ the density and speed of sound in water respectively ($c_0 \cong 1400$ m/s). It should be noted that from thermodynamic considerations the sound velocity in a medium can be related to the square root of the ratio of elastic to inertial material properties. For fluids, this means that the velocity of sound reads $c_0 \sim \sqrt{P/\rho}$. The pressure in this expression is the hydrostatic pressure, which changes with depth. The density is a function of water salinity, which is also a function of depth. This may lead to anisotropic energy dissipation channels, originating from the layered nature of the sea water properties. Thus, great care should be taken when utilizing the expressions presented in this section, Eqs. (12.4)–(12.9).

In Fig. 12.4 an idealised pressure-time dependence for underwater shocks is presented, together with the same plot for shocks in air (cf. Fig. 12.2): the peak pressure of underwater explosions is 1–2 orders of magnitude larger than in air and decays much faster, less than 0.5 ms compared to several ms in air. The right part of Fig. 12.4 shows (measured) pressure-time data of 0.5 kg explosive charge at 6 m depth.

The data were recorded by a pressure detector at 1 m below the water-air interface and at 10 m distance from the detonation centre. Comparison with Fig. 12.2 shows that the peak pressures—although less explosive is used—are typically an order of magnitude higher, and the decay time is also much smaller: 1–5 ms in air shown in Fig. 12.2 and 0.1 ms under water. The many oscillations in Fig. 12.4 originate from reflections from the bottom and the cylindrical sidewall of the experimental pool. One also observes that pressures below the reference pressure (0) are detected. Here, the reference level signifies the hydrostatic pressure at the location of the pressure gauge (1 m deep), thus about 10 kPa. Although rarefaction waves at the location of the pressure probe might have caused the drop of pressure below hydrostatic levels, it seems more likely that interaction of the detector with the explosion-generated bubble pulse has caused the observed anomaly.

Based on the yield and the water depth, underwater explosions can be classified in terms of the depth parameter:[27]

$$D = \frac{d}{w^{1/3}} \tag{12.10}$$

[27] Le Méhauté and Wang 1996.

in which d is the water depth and w is the mass of the explosive. Depth d is expressed in meters and w in kilograms TNT equivalent explosive. This leads to the following empirical criteria for shallow, intermediate and deep underwater explosions:[28]

$$\text{Deep-water explosions:} \quad D > 5.6 \tag{12.11a}$$

$$\text{Intermediate-water explosions:} \quad 0.4 < D < 5.6 \tag{12.11b}$$

$$\text{Shallow-water explosions:} \quad D < 0.4 \tag{12.11c}$$

From this it follows that the explosion whose pressure-time data have been presented in Fig. 12.4 can be considered deep-water events ($D \sim 7.5$), whereas the explosion of Fig. 12.3 simulates a shallow-water explosion ($D \sim 0.2$).

Altogether, there are (obviously) many similarities between the physics of detonation and shock propagation in air and water. For example, the decomposition gases after detonation rapidly expand, where the means of energy (overpressure) transport is through a supersonic shock wave front. However, there are two circumstances that severely complicate the situation for an explosion under water compared to an explosion in air:

1. The presence of water as the surrounding medium leads to a two-phase problem: initially hot gases expanding in a liquid;
2. The presence of two interfaces: the gas-to-water interface, and the water-to-atmosphere interface.

The consequence of the first complication above gives rise to multiple energy dissipation channels of underwater explosions: next to shock waves in the surrounding medium, i.e. pressure waves in water, bubbles of exhaustion gases—dirty bubbles—are created. This also leads to additional modes of interaction of the explosion energy dissipation channels with structures and living species in the water. Fortunately, the time scales involved with the shock wave (milliseconds) and bubble pulses (seconds) are sufficiently different to allow for an uncoupled treatment.[29]

The second complication mentioned above, gives rise to scattering at the water-air interface, leading to downward rarefaction waves into the water bulk and transmission of mechanical (acoustical) energy through the water-air interface into the atmosphere. Finally, rising gas bubbles will cause plumes and surface waves. The various energy dissipation channels of underwater explosions are schematically depicted in Fig. 12.5. In the next section, additional detail will be provided on the dynamics of the gas bubbles formed after detonation.

12.2.2.1 Shock Pulse and Bubble Pulse Dynamics

As discussed, the underwater detonation of a high explosive generates two pressure pulses: a shock wave followed by a bubble pulse associated with the expansion of

---

[28] Le Méhauté and Wang 1996.

[29] Cole 1965; Geers and Hunter 2002.

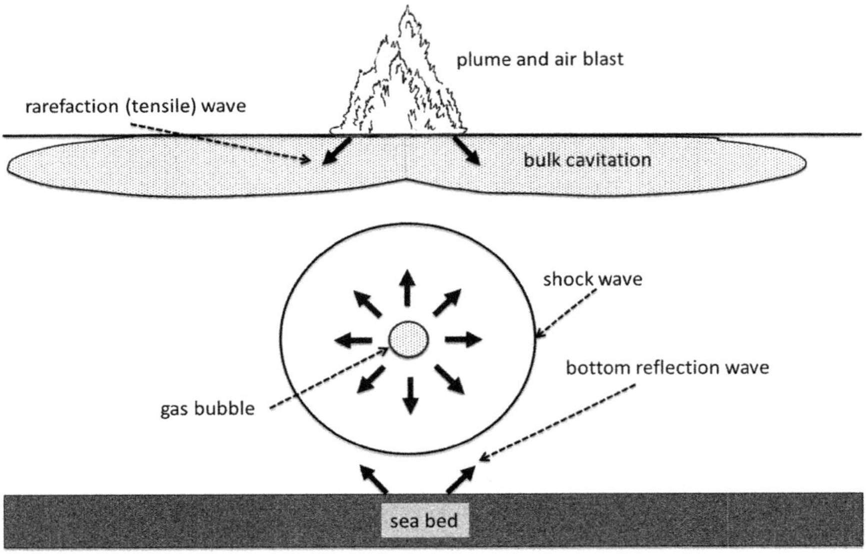

Fig. 12.5 Physical processes involved with the underwater detonation of explosives; multiple energy dissipation mechanisms are presented, each of them may give rise to interactions that cause damage or injury. The two complications of the underwater setting are apparent: bubble dynamics and surface effects like plumes

the products of detonation. The sequence of events is illustrated in Fig. 12.6. It qualitatively shows both the shock wave pulse and the evolution of the bubble size with time and depth. Thus, the explosive products form a high-pressure gas bubble which expands because of its high pressure and temperature (expansion phase). Inertia causes the bubble to overexpand, leading to pressures inside the bubble lower than the hydrostatic pressure in the surrounding water. This marks the start of the contraction phase, which continues until the bubble cannot contract any further due to the compressibility and pressure of the gases inside the bubble. Then the contraction of the bubble is reversed, which causes the first bubble pressure pulse, Fig. 12.6. This process of gas bubble expansion and contraction repeats until the bubble reaches the surface or the energy stored in the bubble system has become zero.

Next to the force due to pressure imbalances and fluid momentum, other relevant forces that affect the motion of the gas bubble are the forces of gravity and buoyancy. As the bubble expands its gas density decreases with increasing diameter. As a consequence, the buoyancy force rapidly increases (less dense gas at larger bubble diameters). Simultaneously, as the bubble tries to move upwards, fluid drag forces resist its upward migration. For each of the subsequent expansions and contractions the maximum bubble diameters are becoming progressively smaller while the minimum bubble diameters are becoming progressively larger. The expansion phase is accompanied with a corresponding negative pressure in the gas bubble. The pressures

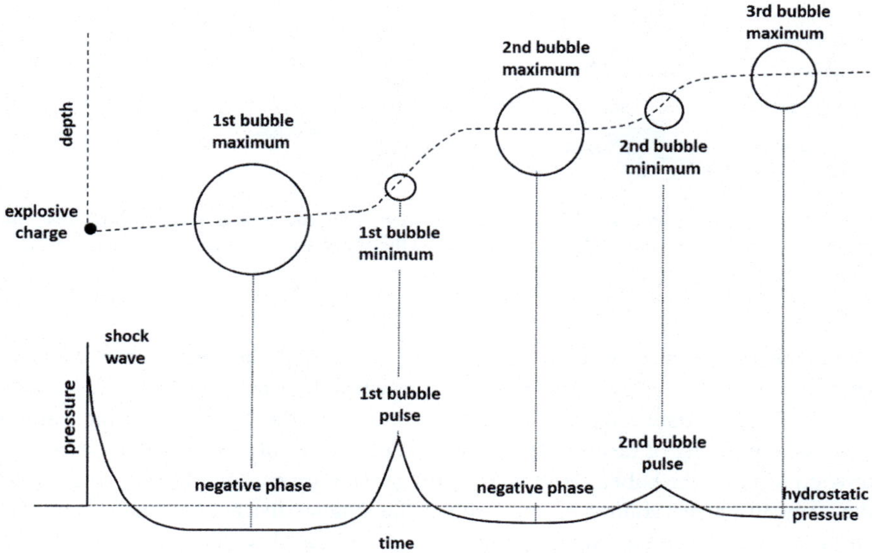

Fig. 12.6 The—idealised—pressure-time signature for an underwater explosion, adapted from Harris (Harris 1988). The snapshots of the bubble are continuously offset to the right for clarity. The bubble diameter and depth are not to the same scale

corresponding to minimum and maximum bubble sizes diminish in amplitude after each oscillation.

After the initial contraction of the bubble, a second outward-propagating wave is generated, which carries nearly as much impulse as the shock wave. The pressure profile of this wave is called the first bubble pulse. Following rebound, the bubble expands again to a second maximum and then contracts until it collapses and rebounds again. Altogether, the sequence of events following an underwater detonation resembles a series of (ever weaker) detonations. As mentioned before, bubble radius pulsation is accompanied by bubble translation, in which the bubble migrates in the direction of the water-air interface under the force of buoyancy. The surface of the gas bubble remains basically spherical when the bubble is large, but it approaches a mushroom cap profile as it collapses. At very large deformation the bubble may become toroidal, with a water jet shooting through the hole. In Fig. 12.7 the jetting process is sketched schematically: the main mechanism is that a vapour bubble of very low internal pressure deforms through anisotropic hydrostatic surface forces. When this deformation is 'fast', the shape may get unstable and become donut-shaped. The central opening of the donut will act as a pressurized nozzle that forms strong vortices and a high velocity—up to 1000 m/s has been observed—water jet, which may damage nearby structures. Eventually, the bubble reaches the surface, and surface waves together with plumes are formed. These are the signature surface

Fig. 12.7 The jetting process (left), which may occur when the bubble pulse or cavitation bubbles rapidly deform near a solid object, and (right) the spray dome (surface effect) caused by the rarefaction wave

manifestations of underwater detonation, Fig. 12.1: parabolic spray domes when the shock wave scatters at the surface, and plumes when the bubble arrives at the surface.

It has been found[30] that the upward movement of the bubble is an intermittent process, consisting of fast upward jumps and periods of almost constant depth. The upward force on the bubble originates from buoyant forces, countered by drag forces that depend on the volume of the bubble: the smaller the bubble, the lesser drag, so faster rise. Thus, the bubble jumps in more or less discrete steps upward, with decreasing jump lengths.

The bubble dynamics characteristics have been measured extensively and are theoretically well understood.[31] The maximum bubble diameter is found proportional to the size of the explosive ($w^{1/3}$) and the depth of detonation ($h^{-1/3}$), while the period time of pulsation also scales with the size of the explosive ($w^{1/3}$) and depth ($h^{-5/6}$).

A last effect associated with underwater explosion is cavitation, see e.g. Fig. 12.5. After detonation, a shock (compressive) wave spherically expands, until the shock front reaches the water-air interface. At the interface, the shock wave reflects downward, meanwhile changing its mode from a compression wave to a rarefaction (tensile) wave. The downward rarefaction wave creates an inhomogeneous zone of low-pressure vapour bubbles and liquid water, the bulk cavitation layer. Implosion of these cavitation bubbles can create a new shock wave (depending on the boundary conditions). It is weaker than the primary detonation, but significant.[32] It is also an important damage cause for rotor blades moving in water.

12.2.3 Explosions in Air and Underwater Compared

Two main characteristics of underwater and air explosions are compared in Fig. 12.8.

At very small distances and times, the peak pressure is completely determined by details of the detonation process, hence no large differences between underwater and

[30] Cole 1965.

[31] Cole 1965; Henrych 1979.

[32] Costanzo 2011.

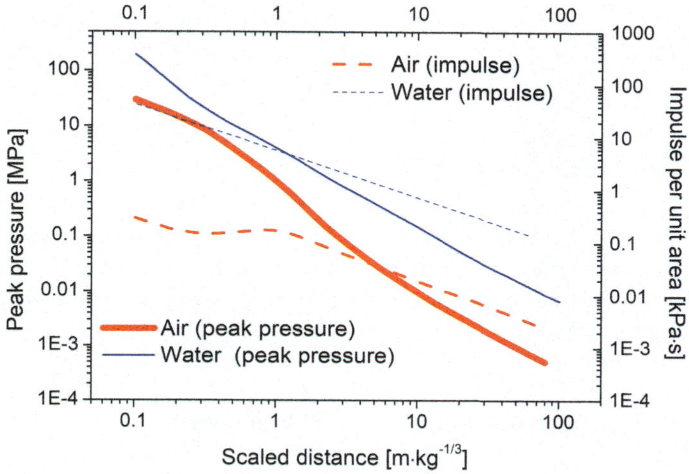

Fig. 12.8 Measured peak pressures and impulses per unit area compared for explosions in air and water (Kingery and Bulmash 1984; Swisdak 1975; Swisdak 1978)

air explosions are to be expected. Here, the pressure is determined by the detonation or C-J (Chapman-Jouget) pressure.[33]

Though, obviously shock waves in water and air have similarities, the following differences are apparent:[34]

- The primary peak pressure is much higher in water than the primary peak pressure in air (at the same scaled distance the peak pressure in water is 10–20 times higher than the same in air);
- The duration of the pulse of the primary shock wave in water is much shorter than the primary shock wave in air;
- The negative phase of the shock wave—as is described by the Friedlander waveform—is absent in water, because water is incompressible;
- The impulses in water are at least 40 times higher than in air;
- The blast wave in air has only one positive pressure phase, while under water the primary wave is followed by one or more consecutive shock waves, resulting from the bubble dynamics;
- Due to one extra interface in water (air shock waves scatter at a ground-air interface, whereas water-borne shockwaves have a ground-water and a water-air interface), there are three instead of two shock loads on structures to be expected in water;
- In air, material fragments originating from blast loaded structures can cause impact damage. Due to the drag in water, the ranges of secondary fragments are very short. Thus, their damaging potential can be safely neglected.

[33] Ficket and Davis 1979.

[34] Cole 1965; Henrych 1979; Bulson 1997.

Altogether, the mechanisms leading to damage are more complex in the case of underwater detonations. This will be outlined further in the next few paragraphs.

12.2.4 Damage Mechanisms

In this section the interaction of the underwater explosion phenomena with structures is briefly discussed. The main distinction to be made here is between contact explosions, where the distance between the explosive and the explosively loaded structure is essentially zero and non-contact explosions.

12.2.4.1 Underwater Damage by Contact Explosions

When controlled demolition of hydraulic structures like obsolete oil production platforms, shipwrecks or bridges, is required, the method of choice is to attach contact charges at the weakest parts of the construction. By common sense, one knows that this is the most effective way of demolition: here effectiveness is defined as the amount (kg) of explosive charge required to achieve demolition. When in close contact to an object, explosives have a very high shattering potential or 'brisance'. At present, a generally accepted definition of brisance does not exist. At very close separation distances peak pressures and impulses are very high, Fig. 12.8. But distance alone does not explain brisance. The formulation of a convincing and experimentally accessible definition of brisance has been a topic of fundamental research since Cranz.[35] An example of the underwater demolition of a massive steel bar of 5 cm diameter at 6 m below the water surface, using 0.5 kg of explosive is presented in Fig. 12.9.[36]

Finally, it should be noted here that, as for demolitions in air, the most effective way to breach a structure is by applying hollow charges to the structure. Details of these are beyond the scope of this work.

12.2.4.2 Underwater Damage by Non-Contact Explosions

As mentioned before, the explosive effects under water differ on a few fundamental aspects from the same in air. Whereas the loading of structures by side-on (peak)pressure and impulse is in principle similar as in air, the values of these characteristics are much higher under water; underwater blasts propagate further and decay less with distance than equivalent air blasts. The combination of peak pressure and impulse determines the amount of damage inflicted on a structural member. A useful tool is the pressure-impulse (PI) diagram, where iso-damage curves separate differ-

[35] Cranz 1926.

[36] de Both 2017.

Fig. 12.9 Metal rod (left) with attached explosive (0.5 kg) prior to sinking down into the underwater test facility. Once at depth in the water, divers of the Dutch Corps of Engineers attach a detonator. The right figure shows the damage (completely cracked rod) after the detonation (de Both 2017)

ent stages of failure. Another important method in the study of structural response to explosive loading is finite-element modelling. A structural benefit for objects loaded explosively under water, is the strong damping that is caused by the water that surrounds the submarine object. Resonant response of a structure to shock wave loading is less likely to happen under water than in air, as overdamped structural response will now dominate. Besides these considerations, the formation of bubbles and their interaction with structures constitute yet another major distinction with explosive loading of structures in air.

Shock Wave

The energy that accompanies an underwater explosion is partitioned among a range of modes or dissipation channels: the kinetic and potential energy of the water, kinetic and potential energy of the gas bubble, gravitational potential energy due to buoyancy, potential energy due to surface tension, acoustic radiation into the liquid, molecular relaxation in the product gas, heat and mass transfer at the bubble surface. Experimentally, the fractional division of energy over the various channels has been established. Figure 12.10 shows the division of energy from an underwater explosion. For TNT, the shock wave energy has been measured at 2345 kJ/kg and the bubble energy at 2000 kJ/kg. Consequently, the total energy is 4345 kJ/kg which is very close to the heat caused by a detonation of TNT, which is approximately 4520 kJ/kg.[37]

Similar to shock waves in air, shock waves in water impose dynamic loads on objects they encounter. As said, this dynamic load is characterised by a rapidly reached peak value which then decreases as the shock wave decays. The net effect of the load depends both on the nature of the shock wave and on the geometry and construction of the object (e.g. a ship). Experimentally it was found that damage to structures due to the shock alone, is proportional to a shock factor $w^{1/2}/R$.[38] A value of this shock factor of 0.8–1.0 was found to destructively damage smaller,

[37] Kaye 1983.

[38] Swisdak 1978.

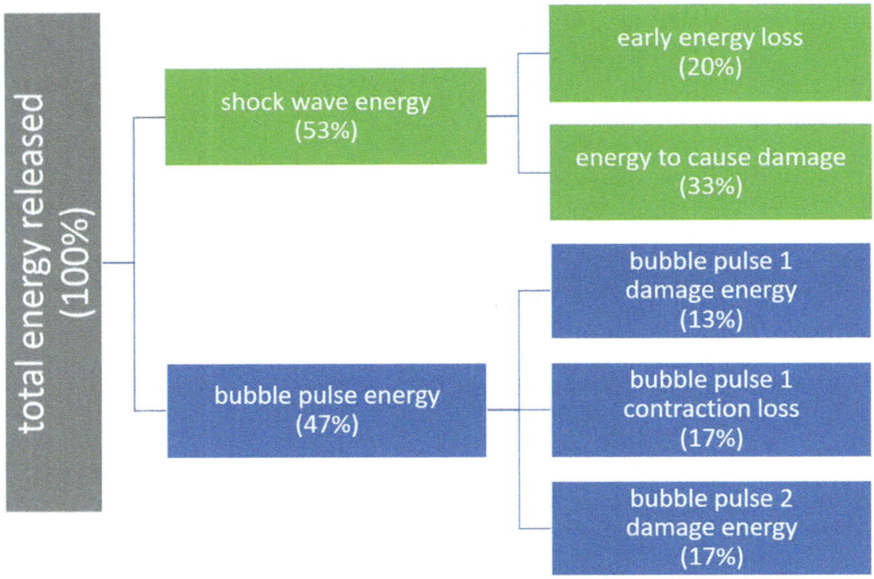

Fig. 12.10 The partition of energy from a TNT underwater explosion (Smith and Hetherington 1994; Swisdak 1978)

wooden vessels, whereas values in the range 2.0–2.2 would lead to fatal damage to double-walled battleships.

When the shock wave arrives at the surface of the water (i.e. the water/air interface) rarefaction of the shock wave occurs and the original shock wave profile is modified. Consequently, the impulse loading on a near-surface target will be less than that experienced by a submerged target. This means that submarines and underwater drones (UUV) are likely to be more severely loaded than surface vessels.

Similar to a charge detonated on the surface of the earth in air, a charge detonated on the sea bottom will produce a crater. The dimensions of the crater are a function of the mass of the charge, the nature of the explosive material, the depth of the water and the geomechanical properties of the bottom. Moreover, surface reflection will lead to a second branch of the same shock wave that may hit the structure. Very close detonation to the sea bottom will lead to a more intense (almost double) hemispherical shock wave; the same holds for surface bursts in air. Thus, for shallow underwater explosions ($D < 0.4$, see above), the effective pressure field is complicated by reflections from both the surface and the bottom. Consequently, the pressures observed will be a superposition of direct and reflected shock waves. In general, shock waves of deep-water explosions ($D > 5.6$) are simpler to describe.

Explosion Bubble Pulse Effects

The interaction of the bubble pulse with structures is not simple, also because it constitutes a three-phase system: water, gas and the material of the structure. The dynamic load on an object due to the bubble dynamics is caused by the rapid movement of the water phase. When the period of the bubble expansion-contraction process is similar to the eigenfrequency of a structural member, resonance effects ('whipping') may lead to even more damage.

In a shallow-water explosion ($D < 0.4$), a small fireball accompanies the detonation and a bubble of intensely hot gases and steam is formed which will burst through the surface after detonation. As a result, a hollow column of water is shot upward and there is a small partial transmission of the shock wave to the air, forming an air blast. Conversely, in a deep-water explosion ($D > 5.6$), there is little evidence of a fireball.

Bubble Jetting

A final effect of underwater explosions that can cause damage to structures is bubble jetting, see Fig. 12.7. A bubble consisting of gases from the explosive reaction near rigid objects can form a jet, thus generating a highly localised pressure on its wall. The interaction between these underwater explosion bubbles and ships is important. It should be noted that bubbles are attracted by solid surfaces. Using computer code, it has been shown that bubble jetting can result in significant late-time loading (i.e. compared to the shock loading) for vertical structures.[39] The bubble jet loading can potentially impart as much impulse as the initial shock loading, while its force is restricted to a smaller surface area. Unfortunately, relatively few studies on this topic exist.[40] Moreover, the few studies that deal with the jetting phenomenon are almost exclusively numeric in nature, experimental evidence and verification is hardly provided. Obviously, this phenomenon deserves further scientific study. The dynamic interaction process between the bubble pulse and a surface structural member is sketched in Fig. 12.11, inspired by Zhang.[41]

12.2.5 Determination of Safety Zones for Humans and Ships

To determine so-called safety zones for humans, sea mammals, fish, and ships knowledge of the vulnerability to underwater blast is required. For air blasts damage criteria are based on the structural loading of objects by both the peak pressure and the impulse carried by the shock wave. This leads to the concept of pressure-impulse representation of damage criteria, with iso-damage curves separating areas of different stages of failure.[42] Similar criteria have also been derived for human injury due to air blast.[43]

---

[39] McKeown et al. 2004.

[40] Zhang et al. 2008; Klaseboer et al. 2005; Li et al. 2015.

[41] Zhang et al. 2008.

[42] Jarrett 1968.

[43] Smith and Hetherington 1994.

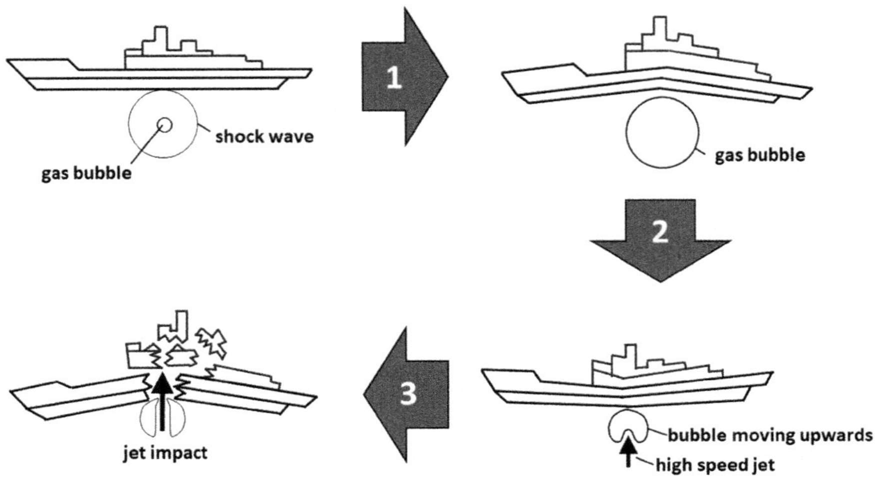

Fig. 12.11 Interaction of a bubble pulse and a ship

12.2.5.1 Humans

For humans, Lance and collaborators[44] have used open literature data to compile a human injury dataset. Based on these extensive human data they found that the 50% risk fatality from underwater blast occurs at an impulse per unit area of 302 ± 16 kPa-ms. A conservative calculation shows a 20% risk of pulmonary injury at a kilometre distance from a 20 kg TNT equivalent charge. Lance and team used $k_3 = 6698$ and $a_3 = 0.94$ (see Eq. (12.8)) in their study, which values they adopted from Arons.[45]

Actually, the findings of Lance are rather dramatic. They found for instance that the current US Navy Guideline for 'safe distance' was found to offer quite often lethal combinations of peak pressure and impulse ('The current US Navy guideline for "probable injury" is at a peak pressure value higher than most of the fatalities in this study'). The safety distances according to existing guidelines are about 90% off, in the dangerous direction. Moreover, they found that previous assumptions that impulse is the best predictor of human injury are false: peak pressure and impulse correlate strongly, so both are good predictors of human injury. Finally, the quality of Lance's study is exemplified by the finding that injury levels of organs that are close to the water surface (10 cm), e.g. the lungs, are significantly lower than abdominal injuries (30 cm below surface for swimmers). The effect of the rarefaction wave at the surface leads to a layer of lower peak pressures. The advice to swimmers and divers is to have blast sensitive organs (pulmonary and abdominal organs) in the upper 10 cm of the water, i.e. a horizontal position as close as possible to the water surface is advised.

[44] Lance et al. 2015.

[45] Arons 1954.

12.2.5.2 Ships

The safety zones for ships can be determined in a similar way as those for human beings. Recently, this has been done by Szturomski.[46] As long as the peak pressure of the shock wave of the explosion is below 4 MPa every floating vessel should retain manoeuvring and combat capabilities. Using empirical formulas, such as the ones proposed by Cole[47] shown above, describing the detonation wave, the safe distance of the ship from the epicentre of the explosion can be calculated for a specific mass of the charge and determine quantity-distance (mass and distance) perimeters for characteristic pressure values. Assuming the charge mass as 150 kg for small mines, 300 kg for medium mines and torpedoes, 500 and 800 kg for large ones and 1200 kg for the largest, one can estimate the damage they will cause as a function of distance of the hull from the epicentre, following the equations proposed by Cole. Thus, it was found that explosions of sea mines containing even 800–1300 kg of TNT at a distance over 80 m do not pose any major threat to warships. For small mines containing up to 150 kg of TNT the safe distance is 50 m.[48]

Damage to vessels and structures originating from gas bubble dynamics is twofold: dynamic loading by the secondary (tertiary etc.) shock pulses, and collision with the gas bubble. For the latter to happen, the maximum bubble radius should vertically project on the vessel or structure. Thus, structures within a vertical cylinder with diameter of the maximum bubble radius would be prone to bubble related damage modes (including jets). In Fig. 12.11 the interaction between a gas bubble and a ship is shown. Finally, the earlier mentioned surface effects of bulk cavitation and surface waves may cause serious damage to surface vessels. It should however be noted that the most dramatic surface wave effects are obtained by explosions in air, close to the water-atmosphere interface.

12.3 Threats

The threat to vessels and static structures to underwater explosion damage depends on the means of delivery of the explosive charge and its distance to the target. Delivery of the charge close to the structure may be realised through movement of the charge to the target, e.g. torpedoes or by manned or unmanned vehicles (USV, UUV). Movement of the charge towards the target puts an upper limit on the amount of explosive: it depends on the means of transport. Actually, this method is the most prominent threat for static structures, i.e. for most coastal and near-shore infrastructure. Another threat is due to static charges (sea mines, seabed munition dumps, etc.) that detonate at contact or when triggered by proximity to the target. For static charges the limits

[46] Szturomski 2015.

[47] Cole 1965.

[48] Szturomski 2015.

of explosive mass are less restricted. The charges mentioned here might consist of conventional munitions, or improvised munitions.

Above the waterline, ships are particularly vulnerable to shells, bombs, improvised explosive devices (IED), and guided missiles. Although flying drones, unmanned aerial vehicles (UAV), in combination with IED are certainly a relevant and possible present-day threat, these threats are not the topic of the present work. However, they may become relevant in the context considered here in case the drone can dive and manoeuvre underwater. The explosive effects of these explosive carrying drones are assumed to be identical with explosive carrying conventional submarine drones. A surface or underwater drone (i.e. USV or UUV) can carry the explosive until physical contact with the target object is achieved, and the explosive is detonated. In this work, it is generally assumed that the explosive is below the waterline before impact. The explosive charge can also be moved using an unmanned surface vehicle (USV).

Below the waterline, one of the most common threats near harbours and in coastal areas are mine warheads. There are two main types of sea mines in use: bottom and moored. Bottom mines rest on the sea floor. Mines use underwater blast effects to cause damage to the target ship, submarine or submarine infrastructural assets. As outlined before, the energy of the explosion is divided between the initial shock wave and the expanding gas bubble. In case the detonation depth increases, particularly deeper than 55 m, the probability to cause damage dramatically decreases. Consequently, bottom mines are rarely used in waters deeper than 55–60 m (Payne 2006). So, only moored mines are a relevant threat near harbours and in coastal areas. In addition, these mines are not very expensive and thus accessible to non-state actors.

12.3.1 Typical Charge Mass of Explosive Threats

To get an impression of the size of possible threats, the typical charge masses of some well-known threats were collected, see Table 12.2. The minimum mass of the explosive charge of an anti-personnel mine is estimated to be about 0.05 kg.[49] The minimum mass of the charge of a modern sea mine is about 40 kg.[50] One should note that the mass ranges given do not imply that higher or lower charge masses are not possible or do not exist. The masses presented also show boundaries for means of delivery to the target structure. Though, if merely the psychological effect of fear is intended, it is rather the unpredictability of when and where the explosive is being detonated, that makes an underwater attack successful for perpetrators, rather than the amount of explosive employed.

[49] Snyman and Dyk 2010.

[50] Szturomski 2015.

Table 12.2 Typical explosive mass range for selected types of threats

Threat	Typical explosive mass range (kg)	References
Land mines	0.05–14	Care 2010; Snyman and Dyk 2010
Modern torpedo warheads	40–350	Wikipedia 2018
Sea mines	40–9000	NRC 2000; Szturomski 2015
IEDs	0.5–5000	Various Authors 2015

12.3.2 Mitigating Threats

12.3.2.1 Limit Use of Drones by Civilians

It is well-known that air drones (UAV) flown by amateurs can be dangerous to air planes. In an article in *The Jerusalem Post*,[51] Neri Yarkoni, former director-general of the Civil Aviation Authority in Israel and an aviation attorney and pilot, stated that drones are becoming a menace to flights across the globe. "The drones are very, very dangerous and can damage an airplane very seriously, depending on the weight of the drone and speed of the aircraft," he said. In addition, the prices of such drones are getting lower and lower and they are getting increasingly easy to use. To remedy the problem of proliferation of civilian drones Yarkoni proposed to register the drones with identifiable serial numbers that are monitored via radar by a computerized central database coordinated with airports. In the meantime, although there are aviation laws in Israel forbidding drones from flying into commercial airspace, the laws are nearly impossible to enforce without adequate traceability of drones.[52] Following these thoughts on air drones, one may think of limiting the use of unmanned underwater vehicles underwater (UUV) and unmanned surface vehicles (USV) in a similar way.

In the same line, but from a scientific point of view, is the recent proposal of La Cour-Harbo (2017). He combines a series of established models and methods to provide a foundation for an explosive payload (mass) threshold. He assumes a 10^{-7} fatality rate per flight hour to be acceptable, which is within the generally accepted range for unmanned aviation. His probabilistic approach is based on the following formula:

$$P_{\text{fatality}} = P_{\text{crashing}} \times P_{\text{impact}} \times P_{\text{fatal injury}} \quad (12.12)$$

where P_{crashing} is the probability of the drone crashing at (near) top speed, P_{impact} the conditional probability of hitting a person in the crash, and $P_{\text{fatal injury}}$ the conditional probability for the impact resulting in fatal injury. Based on his risk analysis La Cour-Harbo proposed a mass threshold of 250 g for drones, below which it is thought

[51] Eisenbud 2017.

[52] Eisenbud 2017.

reasonable to classify drones as harmless. Also, for unmanned underwater vehicles underwater (UUV) and unmanned surface vehicles (USV) one may propose mass thresholds following a similar analysis to prevent abuse or harm.

12.3.2.2 Detection

Wang[53] described a method to detect TNT using a carbon-fibre electrochemical sensor with a voltammetry analyser integrated onto an unmanned underwater vehicle (UUV). This integration was part of a program to demonstrate the effectiveness of advanced sensor technology for detecting explosives (leaking out of mines) in coastal regions of the ocean. The (electro)chemical detection of explosives within a marine environment is a very challenging problem, because the seawater easily dilutes the trace amount of explosive below the detection level. Thus, one needs highly sensitive sensors to detect plumes containing trace amounts of explosives that leak into the seawater. This detection can be used to identify and mark sea mines, but also other static explosive charges. The electrochemical sensor was tested in a UUV to track TNT plumes in several field missions lasting between 2 and 3 h.[54]

The carbon-fibre-based voltammetric sensor technology was also integrated into a diver-held unit. This integration relied on the incorporation of a commercial compact hand-held voltammetric analyser (PalmSens) within a pressure vessel, with the electrode assembly sticking out of the vessel surface. Preliminary underwater testing has been very promising.[55]

12.3.2.3 Interception Methods

Seizing Control of a Drone

One of the well-known methods to seize control of a drone is by hacking. This possibility was demonstrated in October 2016 by the Federal Trade Commission (FTC) with three different commercial off-the-shelf drones, all costing less than USD 200. The three drones tested were the AR Drone Elite Quadcopter from Parrot, the Hawkeye II 2nd FPV Motion Sensing Quadcopter from DBPower and the oneCase CX-10w made by Cheerson. Obviously, the FTC did not specify which hacks worked on which drones.[56]

Unfortunately, an unmanned underwater vehicle (UUV) cannot be hacked using the same method, because radio waves do not propagate well in good electrical conductors like sea water. However, one could try to control a UUV by misleading or disturbing its sensors.

---

[53] Wang 2007.

[54] Wang 2007.

[55] Wang 2007.

[56] Glaser 2017; Sneiderman 2016.

Example: The SAAB Sea Wasp Underwater Vehicle

To fight the growing terrorist threat of underwater IEDs, SAAB has developed a Waterborne Anti-IED Security Platform (Wasp). This Remotely Operated Vehicle (ROV) is designed for the successful location, identification and neutralization of IEDs specifically in the confined areas and challenging environmental conditions of ports and harbours.

The Sea Wasp is equipped with a number of sensors, including wideband sonar, LED lights and video cameras. All of these provide means for the Sea Wasp and its operators to collect the data necessary to defuse bombs. The sensor suite also enables them to work effectively in areas underwater where there is limited visibility. The Sea Wasp is equipped with a five-function manipulator arm. The arm has a camera attached to it that helps with examining and processing the IED, very similar to the Bushmaster IED interrogation arm (Thales) for similar land operations. The arm also carries tools to neutralize and remove the bomb. The operator can use the manipulator arm to place a disruptor next to the explosive device. When its job is done, the Sea Wasp is brought back to the surface, where it is recovered by the team. The disruptor is then fired from the surface. It detonates and the threat is destroyed.[57] An important limitation of the Sea Wasp is that it is not wireless; thus, the operational staff have to operate it from relatively near distances.

12.3.2.4 Physical Methods

The most obvious method to prevent damage from underwater explosives is to guarantee a large stand-off distance (see Sect. 12.2), which can be achieved by thorough hardening and surveillance of the coast and its vital structures. This is especially a formidable challenge when it comes down to protect tourist beach areas.[58]

Controlled Deflagration

A possible destructive method to mitigate the threat of explosives is controlled (forced) deflagration of the explosive. Unfortunately, scientific studies in which this tentative idea was investigated were not found. Perhaps, further possibilities can be investigated in the future.

Application of Blast Mitigating Technologies

In a combined experimental and numerical study, the effects of different blast mitigating technologies on the deformation induced on a steel plate under near-field

---

[57] Barrie 2016.

[58] Lance et al. 2015.

blast loading have been investigated recently by Bornstein[59] in air. Six different fill materials (mitigants) were considered for attributing the targets with the desired near-field blast mitigation effect. The mitigants investigated were bulk water, aerated water, sand, expanded polystyrene (EPS), a combination of EPS and water, and shear thickening fluids. The performance of the mitigants depended on their mass. Sand provided the best protection and EPS the worst for a given volume. Inspired by these experiments conducted in air, the effects of blast mitigants in water should be investigated. For example, recently the effect of corn starch liquid armour for underwater blast mitigation has been investigated.[60] Moreover, in the design process of marine structures the typical frequencies of gas bubble pulses should be adopted as a design parameter: eigenfrequencies of waterborne structures should be designed out of the range of possible bubble pulse frequencies (prevention of whipping).

Bubble Screens for Underwater Shock Attenuation

Protection of submerged structures from the shock wave can be achieved using so-called bubble screens or bubble curtains. For example, one can consider an offshore gas or oil production platform. Sometimes it is necessary to repair or modify submerged parts of the structure by using explosive cutting charges. Evidently, explosive loading should be confined to the component being cut and any dynamic loading on adjacent structural elements should be minimized. Localisation of the shock wave effect can be achieved by shrouding the work area in a screen of gas bubbles. This can be achieved by gas from a diver's bottle.[61] However, protection against the bubble pulse is more difficult to achieve. In this case, the loading is provided by the movement of a dense fluid. This motion will not be suppressed by a bubble screen. So, to protect against the bubble pulse a physical barrier such as a sacrificial metal shield may be required.[62]

12.4 Towards Risk Assessment

Hitherto, the phenomenon of underwater blast and the threat of underwater explosion from non-state actors has been discussed. Of course, the threat could also have included actions along the aforementioned line by actors that can bring about more destructive resources at a time. For example, in August 2017 a newspaper reported that a vessel from a non-NATO Navy stayed for several days at the same location in the North Sea, close to a submarine hub of transatlantic data cables.[63] These cables form

59 Bornstein et al. 2018.

60 Hawass et al. 2015.

61 Costanzo 2011.

62 Barnes et al. 1988.

63 Klopper 2017; Sunak 2017.

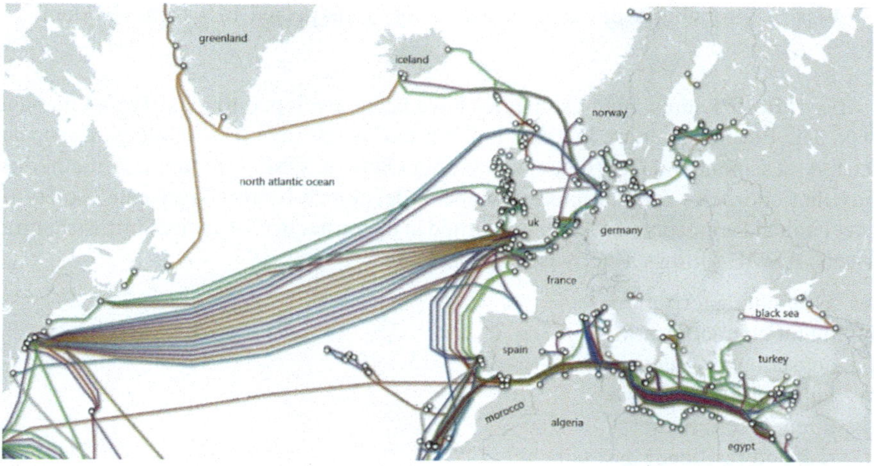

Fig. 12.12 Deep-sea cables in the North Sea (www.submarinecablemap.com. Accessed 15 Feb 2018)

a crucial infrastructure, see Fig. 12.12. Damaging these has serious consequences for economy and communication. Depending on the depth and construction of an infrastructural asset, it may be prone to both terrorist and state actor inflicted damage. However, deep-sea cables or pipelines would be difficult targets for terrorist attacks. On the other hand, for state actors it could be a relatively easy way to inflict serious damage to an opponent. In the remainder of this chapter, an outline of risk assessment of the threat of underwater detonations for harbour and near-shore infrastructure will be presented.

First, the concept of infrastructure asset should be explained. An infrastructure is a framework of tangible systems that are essential for the smooth functioning of a society, e.g. economic activity or providing for safe and healthy living conditions. Examples of infrastructural assets are harbours or systems of embankments and dikes for water safety, but also offshore platforms and wind farms, tourist beaches, etc. A threat to an infrastructural asset is the possibility of inflicting functional loss or damage. These threats may have a natural cause such as accidents, natural forces, technological failures, or the threat can be man-made, e.g. in the case of terrorism.[64] Terrorism is a persistent topic of concern. It can be defined as the premeditated use or threat to use violence by individuals or subnational groups to obtain a political or social objective through the intimidation of a large audience beyond that of the immediate non-combatant victims.[65]

To estimate the risk of underwater explosion threats for harbours and near-shore structures, one has to adopt a workable definition of risk:

---

[64] DCSI 2006.

[65] Sandler 2015.

$$\text{Risk} = (\text{probability of accident occurring}) \times (\text{expected loss from accident}) \quad (12.13)$$

For infrastructures, many strategies have been developed to identify and manage risk. The European Union has developed a risk assessment methodology, European Risk Assessment and Contingency planning (EURACOM). Another risk methodology that addresses infrastructures has been developed by the American Society of Mechanical Engineers (ASME). It is aimed at the protection of critical infrastructural assets. ASME follows a stepwise approach:

a. asset characterisation;
b. threat characterisation;
c. consequence analysis;
d. vulnerability analysis;
e. threat assessment;
f. risk and resilience assessment;
g. risk and resilience management.

Advantages of the ASME-approach are the avoidance of unnecessary detail in the analyses, the built-in cross-sectoral risk comparison, and the central role of resilience. Here, resilience of an asset is considered as its rapid return to full function after disruptive events. From a holistic point of view, risk analysis requires answering the following questions:[66]

1. What can happen?
2. How likely is it to happen?
3. Given that it occurs, what are the consequences?

Ad 1 (what can happen): This question has been explored, from a physical point of view, in Sect. 12.2. Given the mechanical loading from the underwater explosion of an asset, one can quantify its structural damage in relation to its desired function. Most harbour and near-shore constructions are made from either (reinforced) concrete or steel. Damage criteria for various structural elements made of these materials are provided in Table 12.3. The level of damage depends on the parameters that govern the destructive properties of an underwater explosion, such as pressure and impulse.

Ad 2 (How likely is it to happen?) It is difficult to exactly determine the probability of terrorist incidents in harbours and near-shore areas. This would require a thorough probabilistic study. However, the probability of falling victim to a terrorist incident is relatively small, roughly equivalent to that of drowning in one's bathtub.[67] The following attributes for ranking levels of probability of damage due to underwater explosions are suggested (P1–P4):

P1 Dynamics: dynamic structures versus static structures (e.g. buoy versus ship);
P2 Size: small versus large structures (e.g. large is easier to hit);

[66] Bedford and Cooke 2001.

[67] Mueller 2006.

Table 12.3 Damage criteria for various structural elements of infrastructural assets (Mays and Smith 1995)

Element type	Material	Failure type	Criteria	Damage		
				Light (%)	Medium (%)	Severe (%)
Beam	Concrete	Bending	Ratio centreline bending to span (δ/L)	4	8	12
	Steel	Bending	(δ/L)	5	12	25
Slab	Reinforced concrete	Bending	(δ/L)	4	8	15
		Shear	Average shear strain across section	1	2	3
Column	Reinforced concrete	Compression	Shortening/height	1	2	4
	Steel	Compression	Shortening/height	2	4	8

P3 Accessibility: difficult-to-access versus easy-to-access (e.g. data cables at great depth in the oceans are difficult-to-access, i.e. effectively no threat);

P4 Protection level: high versus low level of reinforcement/protection (e.g. public access quays versus force protected military coast assets).

The probability for each attribute can be quantified on the scale 0–100 (zero probability to certainty). Obviously, the probability depends on the vulnerability of the target.

Ad 3 (What are the consequences?) Probability has been treated above. Here we consider the consequences when a threat results in a loss for the specific case of harbours and near-shore structures. Therefore, a—non-exhaustive—set of attributes of consequences is proposed. These attributes can be quantified per asset (e.g. small versus large, cheap versus expensive), leading to a systemized overview of consequences for structures confronted with underwater explosions (C1–C8):

C1 Community: individual, group or society;
C2 Human lives: minor injuries versus fatalities;
C3 Economy: small versus significant impact (also logistics, transport, energy);
C4 Psychology: random, soft target versus symbolic target;
C5 Interdependence: singular object or chain-reaction towards crisis;
C6 Time: Temporary versus permanent;
C7 Communication: minimal versus large disruption of available digital data;
C8 Criticality: non-critical versus critical, strategic asset.

An overview of possible consequences of (terrorist) attacks by underwater explosives is presented in Table 12.4 for both static and dynamic targets in harbours and

Table 12.4 Probability and consequences for both static and dynamic threats of near-shore infrastructure for a preliminary risk analysis, with two example cases: dikes and tourist beaches

	Infrastructure asset	Probability	Consequence	Description
Static civil infrastructure and water management	**Dikes and dams**	**P1: 100** **P2: 100** **P3: 70** **P4: 50**	**C1: 100** **C2: 40** **C3: 70** **C4: 80** **C5: 90** **C6: 70** **C7: 20** **C8: 90**	**– Traffic hindered** **– Evacuations** **– Loss of houses (temporary)** **– Economic effects (shut down of industries)** **– Especially harmful in delta areas** **– Food production struck** **– Health: outbreak of diseases** **– Cascade of effects might lead to ecological disaster (eco-terrorism)** **– Energy production and distribution possibly at stake**
	Embankment			
	Quays			
	Tunnel (Benelux)			
	Terminal			
	Military assets			
Transport and signage	Cables (data, electricity, telecom)			
	Pipelines (gas/oil)			
	Beacons			
	Radar installations			
Energy and industry	Offshore windfarms			
	Offshore production platforms			
	Shore-based industry or storage (Botlek, The Netherlands etc.)			
Dynamic objects	***Beach and near shore tourism and recreation***	*P1: 10* *P2: 10* *P3: 100* *P4: 10*	*C1: 50* *C2: 100* *C3: 20* *C4: 100* *C5: 10* *C6: 10* *C7: 10* *C8: 10*	***– Psychological effects (fear society, loss of trust)*** ***– Limited number of casualties, but media blow up the scale*** ***– Limited impact on any important societal asset, though long term psychological fear may influence all sectors of society very negatively***
	Civil ships: – Cruise ships – Transport ships – With pollutant payload – With explosive payloads			
	Military vessels: – Subsea vessels – Transport vessels – Battle vessels			

near-shore areas. For each threat, the probabilities and consequences can be quantified. Two examples of this method applied to near shore infrastructure are shown in the table: dikes and tourist beaches. Certainly, the choice of attributes, their relative importance, and the corresponding quantification for a specific asset is open for further research. An example of thorough failure analysis of a dam structure is given by Wang.[68]

Next, the probabilities and consequences are collected into a single risk parameter that can serve as a decision tool:

[68] Wang and Zhang 2014.

$$\text{Risk} = \prod p_i P_i \times \prod c_j C_j. \tag{12.14}$$

Here P_i and C_j are the probabilities and consequences respectively, and p_i and c_j are weight factors.

A proposed quantification of probabilities and consequences can guide prioritisation and efforts of protective measures against threats. As defensive or protective counterterror action one can, apart from technological barriers, increase the costs for attempted terrorist attacks. One may increase the costs and scarcity of materials needed for their operation(s) by: (i) decreasing the availability of suitable underwater drones, (ii) increasing costs for these underwater drones, (iii) decreasing the availability of payloads and electronics, and (iv) increasing costs for payloads and electronics.

Other protective measures include target hardening, such as defensive perimeters around harbours, critical near-shore infrastructure and energy facilities. Defensive measures can also take the form of issuing terrorism alerts in harbours and for ships within a certain range and enhancing first-responder capabilities. Of course, this list of possible defensive actions is not exhaustive. Proactive counterterror measures may destroy terrorists' resources, hamper their finances, eliminate their safe havens, and kill or capture the members of their group. The latter may also imply a loss of prestige of the terrorists.

12.5 Conclusions

For centuries, the Netherlands has been a maritime nation, strongly dependent on the sea for commerce and transport. For this reason, it is very important to protect its harbours and near-shore infrastructure. This work has focused on the vulnerability of harbours and infrastructure to underwater explosions.

The first successful use of an improvised floating mine was in the Netherlands (now Belgium) by insurgents during the siege of Antwerp by the Spanish in 1585. The mine was capable of breaching a bridge, estimated to be about 730-m-long, made of ships over the river Scheldt. However, the Dutch were not successful in liberating Antwerp and its harbour. Nevertheless, this early example of the use of a IED in a harbour clearly shows the vulnerabilities of harbours to such threats.

Here, the physics of underwater explosions and its effects have been examined in depth. The interaction and mechanical loading of assets, and possible damage mechanisms were presented. The sources of actual threats, and the consequence of these threats for actual infrastructural assets has been outlined. As an example, the risk methodology has been outlined in detail for two types of assets: dikes and tourist beaches.

Also, possible countermeasures to decrease or compensate for vulnerability to underwater explosion were presented, include the following:

- Prohibition and/or limitation of non-professional use of underwater drones;

- Limitation of the mass for underwater drones used by non-professionals (see also further research in this section);
- Early detection combined with conventional measures of destruction;
- Usage of waterborne anti-IED platforms, such as the Sea Wasp.

Areas for further research in the field of underwater explosions and damage control include the following:

- Application of underwater blast mitigants, e.g. of bubble screens;
- Resilient engineering of near-shore infrastructure;
- Bubble jetting: effects and protection;
- Determination of a mass threshold for underwater drones used by non-professionals, essentially applying the method proposed by La Cour-Harbo (2017) for air drones on underwater drones;
- Investigation of methods to mislead or impair the sensors of USV and UUV;
- Further research on the (mathematical) risk assessment, i.e. probabilities and consequences assessments.

Acknowledgements Mr. D. Krabbenborg has been instrumental in the design and construction of experimental test set-ups, as well as for fruitful discussions on the subject matter of experimentally accessing the nature of air and underwater explosions. S.T.P. Blankestijn, C.G. Leibbrandt and K.M. Elsing, all Aspirant Officers of the Dutch Corps of Engineers, are thanked for their practical work during their lab session for the course Pyrotechniek I: they enabled the (mayonnaise) bucket experiment, under abominable field conditions. Sergeant-major M.H.M.T. Franken was the Safety Supervisor of the Explosive Experiment (in Dutch, LDSO: Leider der Springoefening) during the experiments. Lieutenant J.G.M. Albers provided the air blast pressure-time data for bare explosives in air. The underwater demolition of steel study was initiated and performed by lieutenant S.W. de Both, assisted by the Engineer Divers of the 105th Engineer Company. Finally, KLTZ E.C.L. Jolink from the Royal Dutch Navy is acknowledged for fruitful discussions on the topic of underwater explosions at large.

References

Arons AB (1954) Underwater explosion shock wave parameters at large distances from the charge. The Journal of the Acoustical Society of America 26(3):343–346

Baker WE, Cox PA, Westine PS (1983) Explosion hazards and evaluation. Elseviers Scientific Publishing Company

Barnes RA, Hetherington JG, Smith PD (1988) Bubble screens for underwater shock attenuation. Explosives Engineering 2(3):6–9

Barrie A (2016) The “Sea Wasp” will be a potent threat to terrorists and their underwater bombs. bgr.com/2016/05/19/the-sea-wasp-will-be-a-potent-threat-to-terrorists-and-their-underwater-bombs/ Accessed on 15 December 2017

Bedford T, Cooke R (2001) Probabilistic Risk Analysis: Foundations and Methods. Cambridge University Press

Bornstein H, Ryan S, Mouritz AP (2018) Blast mitigation with fluid Containers: Effect of mitigant type. International Journal of Impact Engineering 113:106–117

Brode HL (1955) Numerical solutions of spherical blast waves. Journal of Applied Physics26(6):766–775

Bulson PS (1997) Explosive loading of engineering structures: A history of research and a review of recent developments. Taylor & Francis, London
Care (2010) Facts About Landmines
Chalk P (2008) The maritime dimension of international security: terrorism, piracy, and challenges for the United States. Rand Corporation
Cole RH (1965) Underwater explosions. Dover Publications, New York
Costanzo FA (2011) Underwater explosion phenomena and shock physics. Structural Dynamics. Volume 3, Springer, pp 917–938
Cranz C (1926) Lehrbuch der Ballistik (Band II). Julius Springer, Berlin
Davies R (2018) Hellburner Hoop. Standing Well Back : IED & EOD evolutions. www.standingwellback.com/home/2011/9/16/hellburner-hoop.html Accessed 6 February 2018
DCSI (2006) Critical Infrastructure Threats and Terrorism
de Both SW (2017) Een experimenteel onderzoek naar de uitwerking van explosieven op staal onder water. Faculteit Militair Technische Wetenschappen, Nederlandse Defensie Academie, Den Helder
Eisenbud DK (2017) Drones becoming greatest threat to planes, says expert. Jerusalem Post. Accessed 15 December 2017
Eski Y (2011) Port of call: Towards a criminology of port security. SAGE Publications https://doi.org/10.1177/1748895811414593
Fickett W, Davis WC (1979) Detonation: theory and experiment. Dover Publications, New York
Geers TL, Hunter KS (2002) An integrated wave-effects model for an underwater explosion bubble. The Journal of the Acoustical Society of America 111(4):1584–1601
Glaser A (2017) The U.S. government showed just how easy it is to hack drones made by Parrot, DBPower and Cheerson. www.recode.net/2017/1/4/14062654/drones-hacking-security-ftc-parrot-dbpower-cheerson, Accessed 18 December 2017
Groen P (ed) (2013) De tachtigjarige oorlog: Van opstand naar geregelde oorlog, 1568–1648. NIMH, Boom, Amsterdam
Harris GS (1988) Introduction to the Underwater Explosion Problem. Conventional weapons underwater explosions. Office of Naval Research Report, Atlanta, GA
Hawass A et al (2015) Cornstarch liquid armour for underwater shock wave mitigation. In: International Autumn Seminar on Propellants, Explosives and Pyrotechnics. Qingdao, Shandong Province, China, pp 711–720
Henrych J (1979) The dynamics of explosion and its use. Elsevier, Amsterdam
Hsu CY et al (2015) The Study on the Dynamic Response of Cylindrical Pressure Hull on the Different Shock Loading Empirical Formula. In: Mechanical and Electrical Technology VII. Applied Mechanics and Materials. Trans Tech Publications, pp 604–609
IMO (2003) International convention for the safety of life at sea. International Maritime Organization
Jarrett DE (1968) Derivation of the British explosives safety distances. Annals of the New York Academy of Sciences 152(1): 18–35
Kaye SM (1983) Encyclopedia of Explosives and Related Items. Volume 8, New Jersey, USA: US army research and development command: warheads, energetics and combat support center
Kingery CN, Bulmash G (1984) Airblast Parameters from TNT Spherical Air Burst and Hemispherical Surface Burst. US Army Armament Research and Development Center, Balistics Research Lab, Aberdeen Proving Ground, Maryland, ARBRL-TR-02555
Kinney GF, Graham KJ (2013) Explosive shocks in air. Springer Science & Business Media
Klaseboer E, Khoo BC, Hung KC (2005) Dynamics of an oscillating bubble near a floating structure. Journal of Fluids and Structures 21(4):395–412
Klopper R (2017) Provocaties op zee: Russen en Chinezen koersen vaker en dichter langs onze kust. De Telegraaf. Accessed 15 December 2017
la Cour-Harbo A (2017) Mass threshold for “harmless” drones. International Journal of Micro Air Vehicles 9(2):77–92
Lance RM et al. (2015) Human Injury Criteria for Underwater Blasts. PLOS ONE 10(11):1–18.
Landau LD, Lifshitz EM (1987) Fluid mechanics. Pergamon Press

Le Méhauté B, Wang S (1996) Water waves generated by underwater explosion. World Scientific.
Li S, Li Y, Zhang, A (2015) Numerical analysis of the bubble jet impact on a rigid wall. Applied Ocean Research 50:227–236
Mays G, Smith PD (1995) Blast effects on buildings: Design of buildings to optimize resistance to blast loading. Thomas Telford, London
McKeown HR, Dengel O, Harris G, Diekhoff HJ (2004) Development and Evaluation of DYSMAS Hydrocode for Predicting Underwater Explosion Effects. Indian Head Naval Surface Warfare Center, Maryland
Mueller JE (2006) Overblown: How politicians and the terrorism industry inflate national security threats, and why we believe them. Simon and Schuster, New York
NRC (National Research Council) (2000) Oceanography and Mine Warfare. Washington DC: The National Academies Press, www.nap.edu/catalog/9773/oceanography-and-mine-warfare Accessed 12 January 2018
Payne CM (2006) Principles of naval weapon systems, 2nd edn. Naval Institute Press, Annapolis, MD
Rajendran R, Narasimhan K (2006) Deformation and fracture behaviour of plate specimens subjected to underwater explosion—a review. International Journal of Impact Engineering 32(12): 1945–1963
Revill J (2016) From the Gunpowder Revolution to Dynamite Terrorism. In: Improvised Explosive Devices : The Paradigmatic Weapon of New Wars. Palgrave Macmillan, Cham, pp 1–18
Sandler T (2015) Terrorism and counterterrorism: an overview. Oxford Economic Papers 67(1):1–20
Smith PD, Hetherington JG (1994) Blast and ballistic loading of structures. Butterworth-Heinemann, Oxford
Sneiderman P (2016) Johns Hopkins scientists show how easy it is to hack a drone and crash it. hub.jhu.edu/2016/06/08/hacking-drones-security-flaws/ Accessed 23 January 2018
Snyman I, Dyk T van (2010) The imparted impulse of a PMN anti-personnel mine. In: Proceedings of the National Ballistics Symposium of South Africa
Sunak R (2017) Undersea Cables: Indispensable, insecure. Policy Exchange, policyexchange.org.uk Accessed 7 February 2018
Swisdak MM (1975) Explosion Effects and Properties. Part I. Explosion Effects in Air. Naval Surface Weapons Center White Oak Lab Silver Spring, Maryland
Swisdak MM (1978) Explosion effects and properties. Part II. Explosion Effects in Water, Naval Surface Weapons Center White Oak Lab Silver Spring, Maryland
Szturomski B (2015) The effect of an underwater explosion on a ship. Scientific Journal of the Polish Naval Academy 201(2):52–73
Taylor GI (1946) Dynamics of a mass of hot gas rising in air. Technical Information Division, Oak Ridge Operations
Various Authors (2015) Factsheet IED attack
Wang G, Zhang S (2014) Damage prediction of concrete gravity dams subjected to underwater explosion shock loading. Engineering Failure Analysis 39:72–91
Wang J (2007) Electrochemical Sensing of Explosives. In: Yinon J (ed) Counterterrorist detection techniques of explosives. Elsevier, Amsterdam, pp 91–107
Wikipedia (2018) List of torpedoes by name
Zel'dovich YB, Raizer YP (2002) Physics of shock waves and high-temperature hydrodynamic phenomena. Dover Publications, New York
Zhang AM, Yao XL, Li J (2008) The interaction of an underwater explosion bubble and an elastic–plastic structure. Applied Ocean Research 30(3):159–171

Chapter 13
Coastal Border Control Using Magnetic Field Signatures

A.F. Vermeulen

Contents

Abstract The present chapter is about coastal border control for threats entering the coastal waters under the water surface. This threat consists mainly of covertly operating submarines. Acoustic sensors are commonly used for the detection of these submarines, as illustrated by the recent (renewed) deployment of networks of acoustic sensors by several Asian nations. However, acoustic conditions in shallow (littoral) water are relatively poor and this increases the importance of other sensors to detect the entering submarine. We review technology for detecting submarines by exploiting their magnetic field signature. Detection of submarines by their magnetic field signature is not new. For example during World War I the first inductive loops were installed on the seafloor in front of English harbours to detect German submarines. A line of mines laid near or in these loops could be triggered after detection of an enemy submarine. In World War II induction loops were used by the Allies to protect about 50 of their harbours worldwide, but all loops were dismantled after the

A.F. Vermeulen (✉)
Netherlands Defence Academy, Den Helder, The Netherlands
e-mail: af.vermeulen.02@mindef.nl

H. Monsuur et al. (eds.), *NL ARMS Netherlands Annual Review of Military Studies 2018*, NL ARMS, https://doi.org/10.1007/978-94-6265-246-0_13

war. Magnetic Anomaly Detection (MAD) from maritime patrol aircraft was introduced in World War II, it was commonly used during the Cold War, and remains an important sensor in modern anti-submarine warfare. Nowadays portable underwater magnetic barriers and swarms of long-endurance UAVs equipped with MAD are a realistic scenario. Is it not time to reconsider induction loops in the control of the underwater coast line, and in particular the entrance to harbours? What is the order of magnitude for the detection thresholds of these systems? Does an optimal geometry exist for the induction loop for harbour control? Which sources on board the submarine are related to the magnetic signature, and which level of variation of the recorded signature can be expected? These questions will be addressed in the present chapter by using open sources and some basic calculations.

Keywords Magnetic field signature · Harbour protection · Induction loop · Submarine detection · Surveillance system

13.1 Introduction

Underwater surveillance systems for detecting an underwater threat, in particular submarines, have been important since World War I. Recently the development of such surveillance systems in several Asian countries such as Japan,[1] India[2] and China[3] has come to light. The systems are mainly passive sonar systems using an array of hydrophones in order to 'listen' to the surrounding area and detect noise emitted by the submarine, for example by its propeller or engine. The most famous example of a surveillance system is the long-range Sound Surveillance System (SOSUS) developed by the United States in the Cold War.[4] The system was primarily developed for detection and tracking (Russian) submarines in the deep ocean ('blue water') and it has been installed on the sea floor at key locations on the East and West Coast of the United States, near Hawaii and also at the Greenland-Iceland-United Kingdom (GIUK) gap for example.[5] In the 80s the SOSUS became part of the Integrated Undersea Surveillance System (IUSS) with SOSUS as a static array, and the mobile capabilities of the Surveillance Towed Array Sensor System (SURTASS) employed by several vessels to give worldwide coverage. However, after the Cold War the

[1] Ball and Tanter 2015.

[2] Singh, A. (2016) India's "undersea wall" in the eastern Indian ocean (http://amti.csis.org/indias-undersea-wall-eastern-indian-ocean/, last visited 7-6-2017).

[3] Trevithick, J. (2017) South China Sea Underwater "Environmental" Sensor Net Could Track U.S. Subs (http://www.thedrive.com/the-war-zone/10906/south-china-sea-underwater-environmental-sensor-net-could-track-u-s-subs, last visited 7-6-2017).

[4] Whitman, E. (2005) SOSUS: The 'Secret Weapon' of Undersea Surveillance Undersea Warfare, *Undersea Warfare* (http://www.public.navy.mil/subfor/underseawarfaremagazine/Issues/Archives/issue_25/sosus.htm, last visited 20-12-2017).

[5] Integrated Undersea Surveillance System (IUSS) History 1950–2010 (http://www.iusscaa.org/history.htm, last visited 20-12-2017).

system was quickly downsized, in 1994 there were only five sites and eight vessels.[6] As pointed out by Makell, the IUSS was also capable of assisting in law enforcement tasks such as counter-drug operations and locating illegal fisheries. These latter tasks were probably done by the SURTASS component of IUSS because SURTASS could also operate, and be deployed, in shallow water.

Detection of submerged vessels—submarines but also Autonomous Underwater Vehicles (AUVs)—for coastal border control can also be done by using remote sensing techniques. These techniques are discussed briefly in Kopp,[7] and reviewed in May.[8] The classical method is to detect changes of the local magnetic field induced by the submarine, called Magnetic Anomaly Detection (MAD), from maritime patrol aircraft such as the P-3C Orion. This aircraft was in service by the Netherlands Navy until 2006, and is still in service in the United States, Germany and Portugal for example. Non-magnetic methods to detect submarines from the air are (i) by Synthetic-Aperture Radar (SAR) because submerged submarines will cause some physical surface characteristic, such as microwave scattering from induced wake,[9] that may be detectable by SAR.[10] Detection of the wake by (ii) infrared and (iii) optical systems might also be possible if the submarine triggers a change in the bioluminescence of the sea.[11] Although remote sensing techniques are interesting, in particular if done by Unmanned Autonomous Vehicles (AUVs), the present chapter focuses on stationary surveillance systems in coastal (or littoral) waters which are relatively shallow, in particular around the Netherlands.

As outlined by Holmes,[12] the acoustic conditions in shallow coastal water, also called 'brown water' are relatively poor. This renders the use of non-acoustic sensors a relevant research topic. The present chapter is about the induction loop, also called indicator loops, which is a sensor to detect changes of the magnetic field as induced by a submarine. These changes are called the submarine's magnetic signature or, more generally, the ship's magnetic field signature. Three classical works on these signatures are written by Holmes; concerning modeling of these signatures,[13] about the exploitation of the signatures by (magnetic) mines or by a surveillance system,[14] and about reducing the signatures by periodically 'demagnetizing' the ship,[15] also called deperming, or adding a certain number of coils to the ship ('degaussing system') which can actively induce a magnetic field to counteract the ship's magnetic field. However, such a degaussing system will never work perfectly and an indication of the magnetic field changes (flux density) of a submarine as a function of distance

[6] Maskell 2001.

[7] Kopp 2010.

[8] May and Wren 1997.

[9] Zhang and Wang 2017.

[10] Chen et al. 2005.

[11] Moline et al. 2013.

[12] Holmes 2008.

[13] Holmes 2007.

[14] Holmes 2006.

[15] Holmes 2008.

are given in Chen;[16] for example 13.33 nT at 0.5 km, 0.21 nT at 2 km and 0.01 nT at 5 km.

The history of induction loops is reviewed by Walding.[17] Firstly, Walding points out that the loop, invented by William H. Bragg during World War I, was used in combination with a row of mines which could be detonated from the shore in order to make a 'loop controlled mine field' for harbour protection against submarines. Next, Walding summarizes the further development of the loops and discusses the worldwide use of about 50 of these loops for harbour protection during World War II; for example by the United States,[18] the United Kingdom and Australia. Finally, Walding explains that after World War II, sonar and MAD became the techniques of interest, but that this might well be because the antisubmarine warfare (ASW) had moved mainly towards hunting submarines in the deep oceans ('blue water') which surfaces are far too large for surveillance by induction loops, and these oceans have favourable properties for the propagation of sound. However, with the shift to shallow coastal water in the case of border control, we address in the present chapter the question: is it not time for a revival of the induction loop for coastal border surveillance, and in particular for harbour surveillance?

Figure 13.1 shows an example of a possible layout of a harbour control system for surveillance of harbour access with induction loops. The induction loops will detect changes in the magnetic field when a ship or a submarine crosses the loops. For this reason another sensor (for example a radar, a camera or simply a watchman during Word War II) is needed to distinguish between a ship and a (submerged) vessel—the submarine. The dimensions of the loop are not specified in Fig. 13.1 because we also want to investigate in the present chapter what the relation is between the recorded signature and the dimensions of the loop; such an analysis has not been found in the literature.

The outline of the present chapter is as follows: before looking into the induction loop, we explain in Sect. 13.2 why a submarine has a magnetic signature. Section 13.3 presents the models to calculate the magnetic flux density caused by the submarine, and the potentials induced in the induction loops according to Faraday's law. The magnetic signature as recorded by the induction loop is shown in Sect. 13.4, and the relationship between the dimensions (geometry) of the induction loop and the recorded signature is also discussed. Other techniques to detect changes in the magnetic field caused by submarines are briefly reviewed in Sect. 13.5. Finally, we address the research question about the need for revival of the induction loop for harbour defence in Sect. 13.6.

---

[16] Chen and Yuan 2015.

[17] Walding 2006.

[18] Walding R. (2017) Anti-submarine indicator loop defence in the United States (http://indicatorloop.com, last visited 10-12-2017).

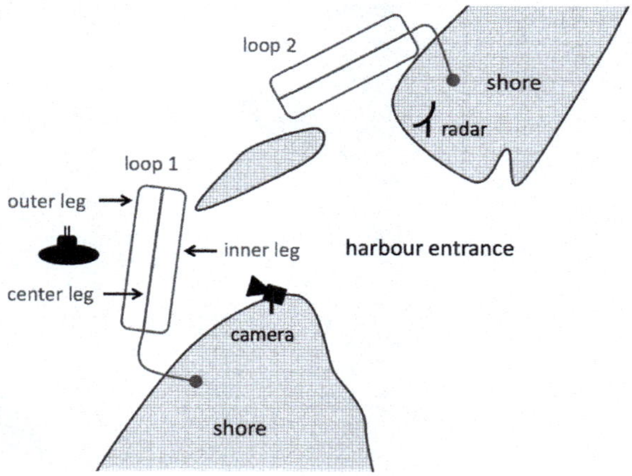

Fig. 13.1 Possible layout to control harbour access with two induction loops. A submarine sailing over the loop will induce a potential in the loop. The camera or radar can be used to decide if a ship or a submerged vessel (submarine) is entering the harbour. [*Source* A.F. Vermeulen]

13.2 Why Does a Ship or Submarine Have a Magnetic Signature?

Typically four sources are assumed to produce a magnetic field around a ship.[19] The combination of these fields produces a unique result for each ship due to certain characteristic elements (in particular in the frequency domain, or the distribution along a certain axis). The term 'signature', just like for a vessel's underwater sound pressure field, has been given to describe the pattern of the ship's magnetic field. The relative importance of each of the four sources depends on the design, and selection of materials, of the ship. The four sources are:

1. The most important source of the magnetic signature is ferromagnetism. The steel ship (or steel parts of the ship) will become magnetized when placed in a magnetic field such as the earth's magnetic field, and for 'hard' steels (e.g. cobalt and tungsten steel) this magnetization will remain if the field is removed ('permanent magnetism'). The ship will then act as a magnet producing its own magnetic field.
   Vibrations during the construction process, vibrations caused by heavy seas or explosions, magnetic storms or lightning, or if the ship has the same heading for a long period, can also (permanently) magnetize a ship. An interesting consequence of the difference in the earth's magnetic field orientation at different positions (latitude) on the world is that the initial direction of the (permanent) magnetization of a ship is related to the place of construction; the magnetization direction of a ship built in the Northern hemisphere is the opposite of one built in the Southern hemisphere, see the orientation of the field lines in Fig. 13.2, and it is possible to talk about North-down and South-down ships.[20]

[19] Holmes 2006.

[20] Walding 2006.

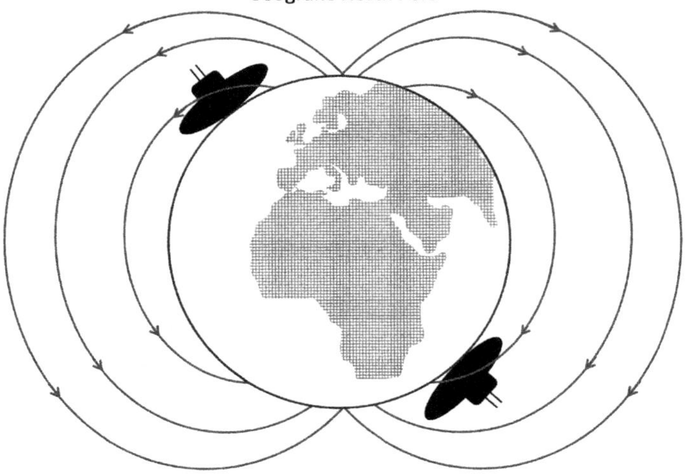

Fig. 13.2 A ship or submarine in the Earth's magnetic field. Notice the difference of the orientation of the field at different positions around the world. [*Source* A.F. Vermeulen]

Next to permanent ferromagnetism, another form of ferromagnetism exists: temporary or induced (ferro)magnetism. This form of magnetism is strongly related to magnetic permeability (μ) which is a measure to express the degree of magnetization that a material obtains in response to an applied magnetic field. Seawater, but also copper, has a permeability roughly the same as vacuum ($\mu = \mu_0 = 4\pi \cdot 10^{-7}$ H/m). However the permeability of High-Strength Steel (HSS) is about 180 times higher[21] and, consequently, the presence of steel will deform the earth's magnetic field locally. This deformation depends strongly on the orientation of the ship and can be predicted relatively easily with knowledge of the location and orientation of the ship, the earth's magnetic field at that location and a model that includes the magnetic permeability of the material of the structure of the ship.

The ferromagnetic properties of steel can be changed by alloying elements. For example, steel made of iron alloyed with nickel and chromium is non-magnetic (low magnetic permeability). In particular the choice of the material for the ship's hull will have important consequences on the amount of (permanent or induced) ferromagnetism of the hull. The magnetic signature caused by the hull would be greatly reduced by using aluminum, composites and non-magnetic steels for their construction, as done for mine counter vessels. However, other materials might have other disadvantages for example the construction might be more expensive due to the price of the material, and it could impact the construction process because of the need for special welding techniques.

[21] Holmes 2008.

Two other measures to reduce the magnetic signature of Naval vessels due to ferromagnetism are commonly used. Firstly a *deperm* takes place periodically (in particular before deployment). In a deperm the permanent magnetism of the ship is removed by measuring the ship's magnetic signature in a special range, and subsequently placing the ship in coils and applying a current to these coils to counter the permanent magnetism. After a deperm the ship should (in theory) be free of permanent (ferro)magnetism. The second measure is *degaussing* in which on board coils are used to oppose the (remaining) permanent magnetic and the induced magnetic field. The first field has to be measured in a special range, but the second can be predicted as mentioned above.

2. Eddy currents induced in conducting material on board as it rotates in the earth's magnetic field, also produce a magnetic field. The relevant rotations are the movement of the ship in all directions (roll, pitch, or change in heading). It is important to notice that Eddy currents are induced in all *conducting* material if the ship rotates. In particular, the roll induced currents are important because the amplitude is proportional to the angular rotation rate, and the rotation rate is usually largest in this direction. The rate, and consequently the induced magnetic field, depends strongly on the sea-state and will be small for a submerged vessel. Until recently, no active compensation (degaussing) was used to counter the induced magnetic field by Eddy currents, however, a new area of research[22] is to develop (finite element) models to predict Eddy currents, as these are usually the second most important source for the magnetic signature; they are in particular important for a ship with a non-magnetic hull.
3. Corrosion currents also produce a magnetic field. Corrosion is the deterioration of a material (usually a metal) because of an (electro)chemical reaction with its environment. A good example is galvanic corrosion which occurs because metals (or alloys) have different electrode potentials, and when they come into contact in an electrolyte, one metal acts as an anode and the other as a cathode. For a ship the two metals are generally the ship's hull (anode) and the bronze propeller (cathode). The seawater acts as the electrolyte. Electrons travel from the hull towards the propeller, where they are consumed, and an ion flow excists through the electrolyte in the opposite direction. This induces corrosion but also a magnetic field. Most (larger) naval vessels have an impressed current cathodic protection (ICCP), which actively impresses a current through contacts mounted on the ship's hull in the seawater, turning the hull into a cathode and preventing the hull from corroding. These currents must constantly be monitored and adjusted and they result in a so-called Corrosion Related Magnetic (CRM) signature. Although this signature is normally smaller than the magnetic fields caused by the first two sources, it is interesting to note that its magnitude decreases more slowly with distance and that it might be the prime source of the magnetic signature for ships with a properly tuned degaussing system.[23]

[22] Birsan and Tan 2016.

[23] Holmes 2006.

4. Electrical systems on board might produce a magnetic (stray) field. Current flowing in electrical systems, such as electric motors, generators and distribution cables, will generate a magnetic field. The basic example mentioned in an elementary physics course is that of current flowing through a wire which generates a magnetic field that circulates the wire according to the right-hand rule.[24] The same mechanism exists for current in the electrical systems on board, and the magnetic field might be significant for the large currents occurring in the power distribution system, for example. The resulting magnetic fields are not uniformly distributed along the ship's (longitudinal) axis and they will have an important frequency component. The functioning of electrical power systems on board, such as the electric motor or a generator, relies on magnetic fields, and some stray fields might well be present. The proper design of the electrical installation on board (including shielding) is essential to reduce most of these (stray) fields as measured outside the vessel, in particular if the hull is constructed from non-conducting material (i.e. no Faraday cage exists).

13.3 Modeling of a Submarine's Magnetic Signature and an Induction Loop

13.3.1 Modeling a Submarine's Magnetic Signature

Different models exist to predict the magnetic signature produced by a submarine, see Holmes.[25] These models vary in complexity from a spherical dipole model, also called point dipole, to detailed finite-element models which include the ship's structure (for example the model developed by TNO)[26] and the location of the electrical systems. The latter models are important in the design of a ship's degaussing system but they are too complex in the context of the present work. On the other hand, the spherical or point model is too simple because the distances at which the magnetic flux density has to be calculated, are similar to the length of the submarine. For these short distances the submarine might be represented by a triaxial spheroidal dipole with length l (longitudinal direction in the x_{sub} direction) and width b (beam in the starboard-port or y_{sub} direction). This model takes into account mainly the ferromagnetism and assumes a uniform distribution. The z_{sub} direction is orthogonal (downwards) on these directions. The magnetic flux density $\vec{B}$ for this model is given in Holmes.[27] In the present work only the downward (z_{sub}) component B_z is important because we assume that the submarine remains at the same depth, that it stays parallel to the induction loop which is on a flat horizontal seafloor, and, consequently, only the

[24] Young and Freedman 2004.

[25] Holmes 2007.

[26] Birsan and Tan 2016.

[27] Holmes 2006.

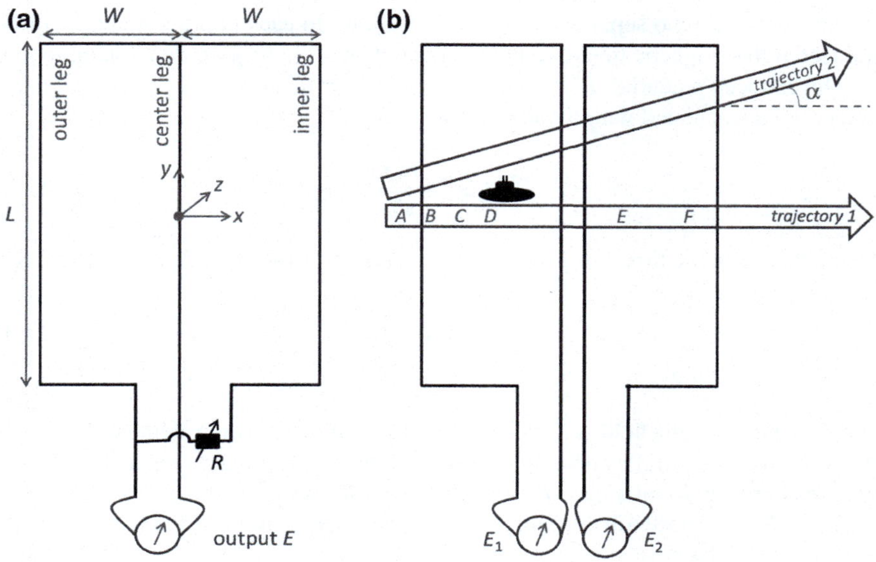

Fig. 13.3 Topview of the geometry of an induction loop (**a**). The geometry of the loop can be considered as two separate coils (**b**) for which the induced potentials are subtracted to get the output voltage of the induction loop. Two different headings (trajectory 1 and trajectory 2) of the submarine are shown in (**b**). The locations in (**b**) indicated by the letters ($A, B, \ldots, F$), are related to the recorded signature shown in Fig. 13.5. [*Source* A.F. Vermeulen]

vertical moment M_z is non-zero. Under these assumptions, the value of B_z is given by

$$B_z = \frac{3\mu_0 M_z}{4\pi c^3}\left(\frac{1}{4}\ln\left(\frac{r+1}{r-1}\right) - \frac{r}{2(r^2-1)} + \frac{z_{sub}^2 r}{R_1 R_2 (r^2-1)^2}\right), \tag{13.1}$$

with $c = \frac{1}{2}\sqrt{l^2 - b^2}$, $r = \frac{R_1+R_2}{2c}$ and

$$R_1 = \sqrt{(x_{sub}+c)^2 + y_{sub}^2 + z_{sub}^2},$$
$$R_2 = \sqrt{(x_{sub}-c)^2 + y_{sub}^2 + z_{sub}^2}.$$

13.3.2 *Modeling a Magnetic Induction Loop*

Figure 13.3a shows the geometry of a typical induction loop as used in World War II. The loop consists of two coils (here we assume with one turn) and the center leg of the induction loop belongs to both coils. For this reason the loop can also be considered as two separate coils, see Fig. 13.3b. In each coil a potential will be induced if the magnetic field through the coils changes in magnitude, or in direction.

This induced potential, E_i, for each coil ($i = 1$ for the outer coil or 2 for the inner coil) can be calculated with Faraday's law,[28]

$$E_i = -\frac{d\Phi}{dt}, \tag{13.2}$$

where the magnetic flux Φ is given by the integral over the area (S) enclosed by coil i,

$$\Phi = \int_S \vec{B} \cdot d\vec{A}, \tag{13.3}$$

and $\vec{B}$ is the magnetic field at the location of the infinitesimal area element $d\vec{A}$ within the coil. Equation (13.3) can be simplified under the assumptions given in Sect. 13.3.1 because in this particular case $\vec{B} \cdot d\vec{A}$ reduces to B_z as given by Eq. (13.1).

The voltage recorded at the output of the induction loop is the difference in induced potential of both coils;

$$E = E_2 - E_1. \tag{13.4}$$

In the original design of the induction loop (shown in Fig. 13.3a), a resistance R is included in order to balance both coils such that the voltage $E = 0$ V if no vessel is sailing over the induction loop.

13.4 Simulation Results: Magnetic Signature of a Submarine

13.4.1 Magnetic Flux Density for the Submarine's Model

The magnetic flux density $\vec{B}$ around the triaxial spheroidal dipole model of the submarine is shown in Fig. 13.4 for the three orthogonal components of the vector $\vec{B}$: B_x, B_y and B_z. The component B_z is calculated with Eq. (13.1) and the equations for the other components can be found in Holmes.[29]

Figure 13.4 shows that the magnetic signature varies with the location (x,y) and the component of interest (B_x, B_y or B_z-axis). These differences—already present with this simple model—are important to take into account when designing the ship's degaussing system, because the reduction of a ship's magnetic field signature[30] is essential for minimizing the threat of magnetic mines, and detection from maritime

---

[28] Young and Freedman 2004.

[29] Holmes 2006.

[30] Holmes 2008.

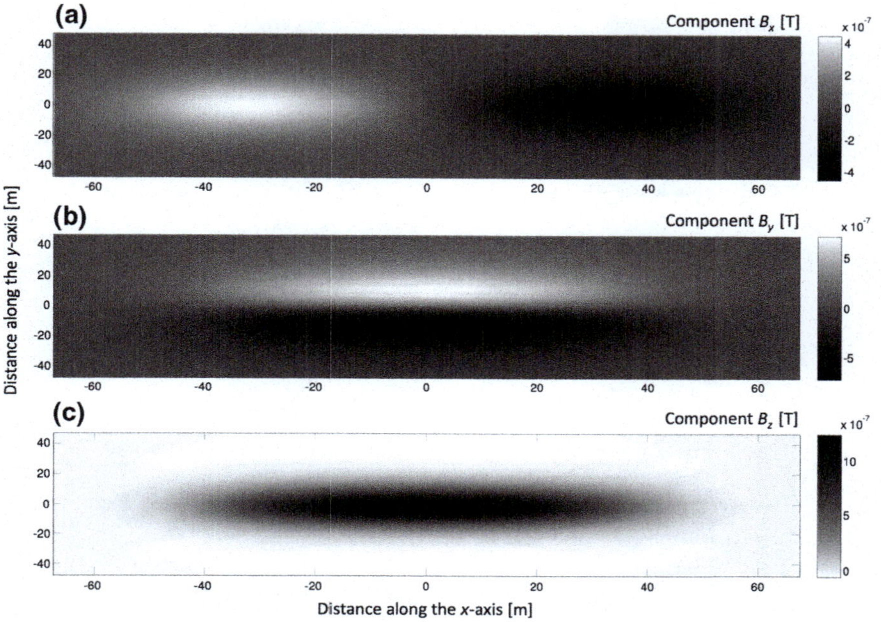

Fig. 13.4 Example of the magnetic flux density $\vec{B}$ around a submarine located at the origin (0, 0, 0) pointing towards the positive x-axis. The three components of $\vec{B}$, (**a**) B_x, (**b**) B_y and (**c**) B_z, are shown at the level of the seafloor which is assumed to be 20 m below the submarine. Parameters from Holmes (2006): $l = 90\,\text{m}$, $b = 7.5\,\text{m}$, $M_z = 150\,\text{kAm}^2$. [*Source* A.F. Vermeulen]

patrol aircraft with MAD capabilities. In the present study, only the flux density along the B_z-axis (at the level of the seafloor) has to be considered, and Fig. 13.4c shows that the spatial distribution of this component is relatively simple because it has a maximum value at (0, 0) and it decays in all directions.

13.4.2 Magnetic Signature as Recorded by the Induction Loop

The induction loops consists of two coils and the signal of interest is the difference in induced potential in both coils (Eq. (13.4)). This configuration is chosen in order to eliminate variations in the local magnetic field not induced by a ship, for example variations due to electric currents in the ionosphere (related to solar winds). Such variations will induce the same potential in both coils because the coils are next to each other, and consequently the influence of the variations theoretically vanish when taking the difference between both potentials; as argued by Holmes[31] this is

[31] Holmes 2006.

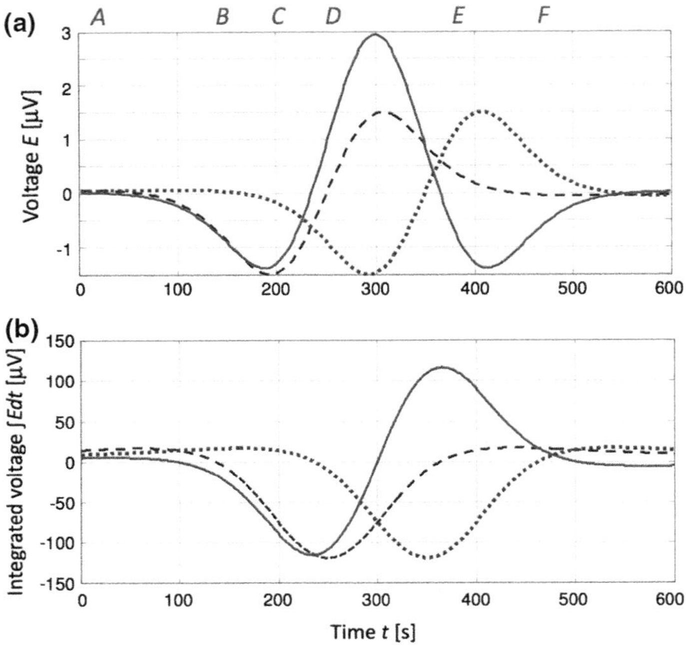

Fig. 13.5 Typical signature recorded by the induction loop for a heading along the x-axis (trajectory 1 in Fig. 13.3a) and relation with the location of the submarine (letters A–F in Fig. 13.3b). (**a**) The induced voltages in both coils (dashed and dotted lines) and the recorded voltage of the loop E (continuous line) which is the difference between both potentials. The typical 'W'-shape can be observed for the voltage E. (**b**) The integrated voltage $\int E dt$. Parameters: see Fig. 13.4, $\alpha = 0°$, $v = 2$ m/s, $z_0 = 200$ m, $L = 5$ km, $W = 200$ m. [*Source* A.F. Vermeulen]

only partly true because of nearby sub-bottom conducting anomalies in the coils such that the induced potentials will not be exactly opposed.

The voltage recording of the induction loop (E) is shown in Fig. 13.5a for a submarine with a heading along the x-axis (trajectory 1 in Fig. 13.3b) with a constant velocity v of 2 m/s at an altitude of $z_0 = 200$ m above the seafloor. The figure shows three lines: the induced potential of the first coil (outer coil) E_1 as a dashed line, the induced potential of the second coil (inner coil) E_2 as a dotted line, and the difference between both potentials E which is the output voltage of the induction loop, as a continuous line. The shape of the induced potential of the first coil (dashed line) is easy to understand because the flux density along the B_z-axis of the submarine has its maximum at $(x_{sub}, y_{sub}) = (0, 0)$ and, consequently, the induced potential is zero when the submarine is still largely outside the coil (point A in Figs. 13.3b and 13.5a). Near the coil the flux density increases and according to Eq. (13.2), this results in a decrease (negative value) of the induced potential. As long as the submarine passes the outer leg of the coil (point B), the potential is non-zero and it decreases until the entire submarine has passed the outer leg (point C) and the minimum value of the induced potential is reached. The induced potential returns to zero when the submarine is at the center of the coil (point D), and increases further when approaching the other leg of the coil; this is the center leg of the induction loop. The maximum value of the induced potential is reached (point E) when crossing the other leg, after which the potential decreases to zero again (point F).

When properly tuned, the potential induced in the second coil (dotted line) has the same shape as the potential in the first coil, but it is shifted in time because of its different location on the seafloor. The voltage recording of the induction loop (continuous line) is the difference between both potentials and consequently shows a typical 'W' pattern with its maximum value when sailing over the center leg. The magnitude of the maximum value is twice the magnitude of the minimum value. As pointed out by Walding,[32] the navy analysts called this the 'Inverted William' because *William* was the letter used in the military phonetic alphabet for the letter 'W' at the time of the World War II, and the negative axis was typically shown pointing up.

The theoretical voltage recording shown in Fig. 13.5a is nice and smooth, but it would deteriorate in the presence of sensor noise, or not-modeled local variations in the magnetic field of the submarine (for example because of electrical power systems on board). The common approach to reduce the (non-stationary) noise level is to filter the recorded signal E; an easy filter to use in the present study is an integrator, its output is shown in Fig. 13.5b. This figure shows that the submarine crosses the center leg of the induction loop when the output signal $\int E dt$ changes sign and the running average before and after the crossing is considerably different from zero, and of opposite sign. It would be wise from a practical viewpoint to present both output voltages to the analyst to facilitate the interpretation of the (noisy) signals and to reduce the false-alarm rate.

13.4.3 Influence of the Loop-Geometry on the Recorded Signature

The simple model of the submarine is defined by three variables: its length l, its beam b, and the magnetic moment M_z. The magnitude of all signatures scales linearly with M_z so its influence is straightforward to interpret. Furthermore, the ratios $\frac{b}{l}$ and $\frac{W}{L}$ will always be small and it is not the exact dimensions of the submarine which are important, but its relative size compared to the size of the coils. From this viewpoint, it is interesting to study the influence of *four parameters* on the recorded signature: (i) the height of the submarine above the seafloor (altitude: z_0), (ii) the width W of the coils of the loop (in relation to the length of the submarine) for (iii) different headings (trajectory 2 in Fig. 13.3b with different values for α), and (iv) for different velocities v_0 of the submarine.

---

[32] Walding 2006.

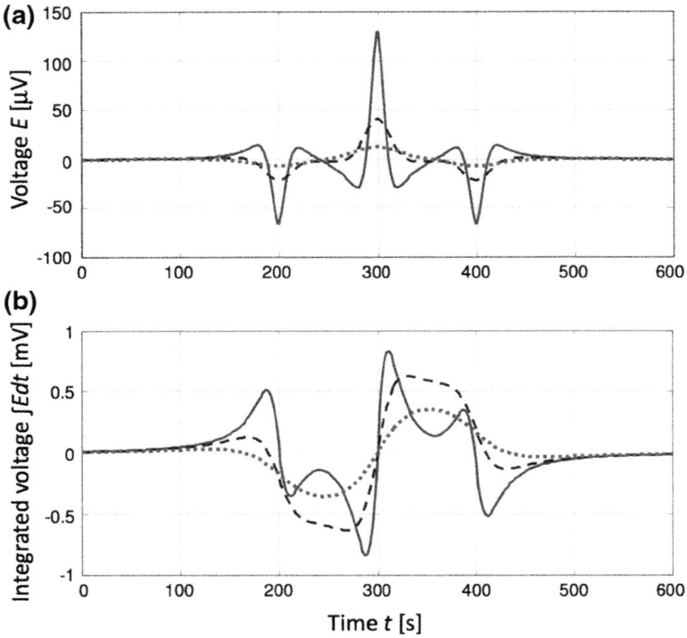

Fig. 13.6 Recorded voltage E (**a**) and integrated voltage $\int Edt$ (**b**) of the induction loop for different altitudes z_0 of the submarine above the loop: 20 m (continuous line), 50 m (dashed line) and 100 m (dotted line). For lower altitudes the typical 'W'-shape of the signature disappears and becomes three distinct peaks. Parameters: see Fig. 13.5. [*Source* A.F. Vermeulen]

The default voltage recording shown in Fig. 13.5a is calculated with the parameters from Holmes[33] and $v = 2$ m/s. The submarine is quite long (90 m; about 0.45 times the width of one coil) and it is sailing at an altitude of 200 m above the induction loop also used 100 m). The water in the North Sea is not so deep, and consequently, the altitude z_0 will be much smaller. Figure 13.6a shows the voltage recordings E for an altitude of 100, 50 and 20 m above the loop; the maximum value increases (and is roughly proportional to C/z_0 where C is a constant) but more importantly, the shape of the 'W' changes and the recording looks more like three distinct peaks (with the center response of opposite sign and twice the amplitude). The reason seems to be that the B_z distribution of the submarine is mainly pointing downwards (and spreads with the distance z_0; see Fig. 13.4c) such that for smaller values of z_0 the induced voltage in the coils reduces sharply if the distance between the submarine and a leg of the loop increases. Decreasing the coil's width W—the second parameter, see Fig. 13.7a, shows that the 'W'-shape can be brought back. The maximum value does not change much with the width W (from 133 to 150 μV in Fig. 13.7a), and might be detected with a level detector but the response for large W seems to be less

[33] Holmes 2006.

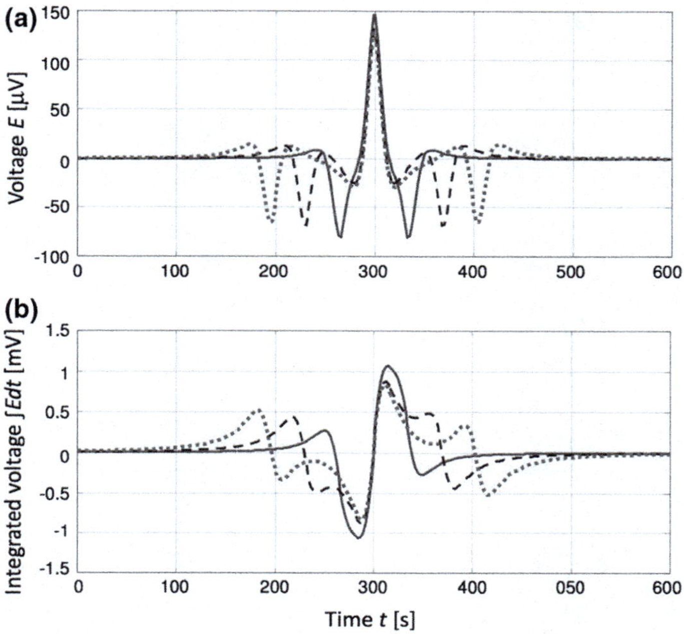

Fig. 13.7 Recorded voltage E (**a**) and integrated voltage $\int Edt$ (**b**) of the induction loop for different sizes of the loop. The width W of the loop changes from 70 m (continuous line), to 140 m (dashed line) to 210 m (dotted line). The typical 'W'-shape is apparent only for a low value of width W. This low value is similar to the length of the submarine. Parameters: see Fig. 13.5, $z_0 = 20$ m. [*Source* A.F. Vermeulen]

characteristic and more difficult to find in noise with a matched filter. The same can be observed for the integrated signals $\int Edt$, see Fig. 13.7b, or if the loop width W is kept constant and the size of the submarine (l) changes (not shown).

The third parameter to be considered is the heading of the submarine. Figure 13.8a shows the voltage recordings for four headings: $\alpha = 0°, 30°, 45°$ and $60°$ (see Fig. 13.3b for the definition of the angle α). In this figure the velocity of the submarine is always 2 m/s. It can be seen that the signature widens with the heading α. This is due to a lower component of the velocity along the x-axis (v_x) and, consequently, a longer time needed to cross the loop. Figure 13.8b shows the same results when the time is expressed as relative time ($t^\star = \frac{v_x}{W}t$) such that the time to cross the loop is identical. It can be noticed that the peak value of E decreases with the heading, roughly by the value cos(α). The integrated voltage recording $\int Edt$ is shown in Fig. 13.8c. Interestingly, this later voltage does not depend on the heading. The integrated voltage $\int Edt$ seems thus to be a good measure to detect the submarine without being affected by the heading of the submarine.

Does changing the last parameter—the velocity of the submarine v_0—bring back the typical 'W' shape for a wide loop? The answer seems to be negative because

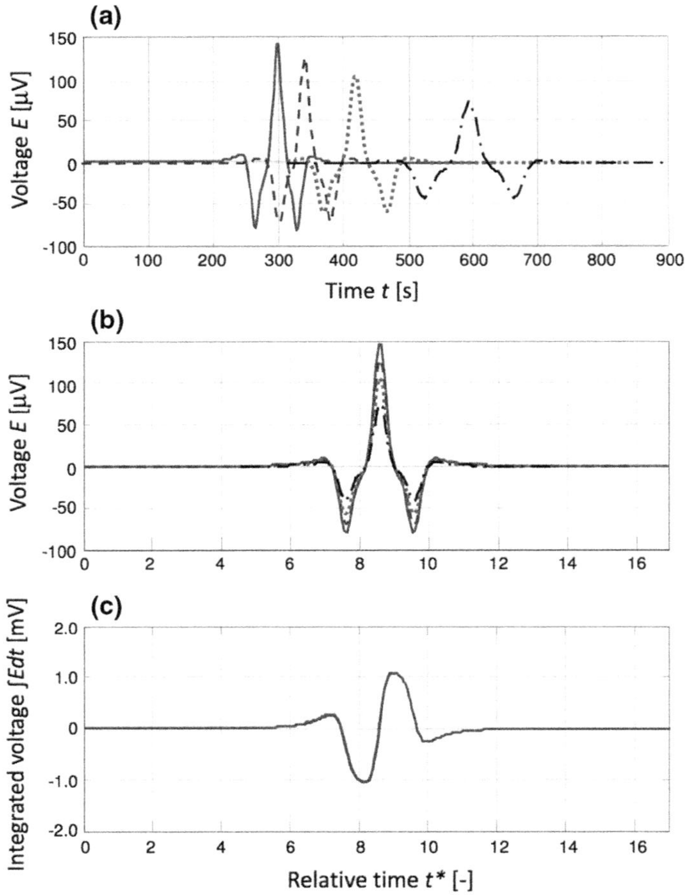

Fig. 13.8 Recorded voltage E (**a**, **b**) of the induction loop for different headings of the submarine: $\alpha = 0°$ (continuous line), 30° (dashed line), 45° (dotted line) and 60° (dash-dot line). **c** Integrated voltage $\int Edt$. In (**b**, **c**) the time is expressed as the relative time to cross the induction loop. The shape of E (**b**) does not change but its maximum value decreases slightly with α. The integrated voltage $\int Edt$ is entirely independent of the heading. Parameters: see Fig. 13.5, $W = 70$ m, $z_0 = 20$ m. [*Source* A.F. Vermeulen]

Fig. 13.8 suggests that only the velocity v_x is important, and an increase of this value does not change the overall shape of the potential. This can be further studied by considering the same velocity of the submarine along the x-axis, for example 2 m/s, and to change the heading (α), thereby increasing the velocity of the submarine from 2 m/s (for $\alpha = 0°$) up to 4 m/s (for $\alpha = 60°$). Interestingly, the voltages E and $\int Edt$ are now both independent of the heading (not shown) and only the velocity along the x-axis (v_x) is important. However, only the integrated voltage $\int Edt$ does not depend on either the heading or the velocity of the submarine.

The target size (length of the submarine l) seems to be closely related to the altitude z_0 and the width of the coil W. An intriguing question is whether an optimal width exists for each target size. However, changing the length of the submarine will also change the total magnetic flux created by the submarine and it is for this reason difficult to compare possible threshold levels for different lengths. In order to obtain the typical 'W' shape, a coil width similar to the size of the submarine seems most appropriate.

The recorded potentials were quite large in Figs. 13.7 and 13.8, such that a 40 dB reduction (factor 100) of the recorded potential—which means a similar change in magnitude of the magnetic signature of the submerged vessel—seems to be acceptable for the surveillance system to operate at a threshold in the order of one μV.

Different error sources exist for the voltages recorded with the induction loop. The geomagnetic noise mentioned in Sect. 13.4.2 is one error source (but it will largely be compensated by the design of the loop), two other potential sources, as argued by Holmes,[34] are motion noise because of the movement of the induction loops in the earth's magnetic field (but this can be largely eliminated by properly burying the loop in the seafloor) and thermal noise of the conductors (also called Johnsen noise). The latter noise level can be calculated but it is very small (below 10^{-3} μV). The last error source discussed by Holmes[35] seems to be the most important for induction loops, it is the magnetic field created by the ocean's waves. Small electric currents are induced in the electrically conducting seawater when the wind drives sea waves through the earth's magnetic field. The amplitude of this noise source is in the order of 3.8 μV at high sea state (6) if the seafloor is at 100 m depth. A threshold of several μV of the induction loop seems sufficient.

13.5 Other Technical Solutions for Magnetic Detection of Submarines

The classical method for detecting the magnetic signature of submarines is using long-endurance airplanes equipped with MAD capabilities, such as the P-3C Orion. However, the Netherlands does not have this capability anymore after selling these planes last decade.

Recent developments in China suggest an increase in their MAD capabilities because of the use of an array of high sensitive (low temperature) superconducting quantum interference devices (SQUIDs) as magnetometers.[36] Research into airborne MAD[37] is relevant for China in ASW, but it can also be considered to be one of their

---

34 Holmes 2006.

35 Holmes 2006.

36 Hambling, D. (2017) Chinas quantum submarine detector could seal South China Sea, *Daily News*, 22 August, https://www.newscientist.com/article/2144721-chinas-quantum-submarine-detector-could-seal-south-china-sea/, accessed 20 December 2017.

37 Zhang and Wang 2017.

(long-range) border surveillance systems because induction loops, as discussed in the present work, will not be practical for most of China's (deep water) border.

Employing drones, or more precisely UAVs, with a MAD system is also an area of research,[38] but endurance is relatively low at present. The development of these systems is also important for the United States because the Boeing P-8A Poseidon, which will replace the P-3C Orion, has no MAD capabilities.

An alternative method to measure magnetic field signatures is by using a field of buoys with magnetic sensors; such a swarm of sensors sounds modern, flexible and easy to deploy. However, two error sources related to variations in the local magnetic field, which were not important for the induction loop, might be a serious concern for a system based on buoys: the movement of the sensor in the earth's magnetic field and geomagnetic noise. Holmes[39] shows, with a numerical example, that a movement of the sensor with a fraction of a degree might render the magnetic sensor useless; consequently, a good and stable fixation of the sensor to the seafloor is a must. This makes the concept of buoys difficult and it seems more appropriate to think about a field of sensors attached to the seafloor. Several independent magnetic sensors might be necessary in order to counter the influence of geomagnetic noise, their location and orientation must be precisely known to be able to counter the effect of (geomagnetic) noise with a numerical algorithm. Furthermore, Holmes[40] shows that each sensor will mainly detect variations in the magnetic field which are in the same direction as the earth's magnetic field. The author has not researched these problems further, and can not judge how far these problems have been solved, and to which degree of accuracy.

Finally, Autonomous Underwater Vehicles (AUVs) have been described as a threat in the present chapter but can also be used for coastal surveillance,[41] and can be employed at places where no (stationary) surveillance system is present.

13.6 Discussion and Conclusion: Is It Time for a Revival of the Induction Loop?

As pointed out by Benedict,[42] surveillance and technical superiority have been major elements in antisubmarine warfare (ASW) for the US, and they will also remain important in the future.[43] SOSUS integrated in IUSS was an important component in ASW but it is not clear (to the author) what the status is nowadays of this surveillance

---

[38] Keller J (2015) BAE Systems to develop MAD ASW drone to help Navy P-8A find submarines from high altitudes, *Military & Aerospace* (http://www.militaryaerospace.com/articles/2015/01/bae-subhunting-drone.html, last visited 20-12-2017).

[39] Holmes 2006.

[40] Holmes 2006.

[41] Kemna et al. 2011.

[42] Benedict 2005.

[43] Christian 2007.

network. Surveillance also remains important in modern ASW and is a key element for every underwater threat, also in coastal or harbour defence.

Induction loops, which consist of a very simple reliable technique, have been used in World War II to control harbour access. These loops were dismantled after World War II, probably because the focus in ASW shifted entirely to the deep oceans. Whether other (non-NATO) nations use them nowadays remains unclear.[44] The present work has discussed the principles of the induction loop and has shown that the induction loop is a relatively easy surveillance system to implant for harbour control; it is reliable because it does not need underwater electronics, and the risk of damage to the system by recreational ships or fishing boats is small because the cables are buried in the seafloor. With modern signal processing tools it would be relatively easy to automate the interpretation of the recorded output voltages of the induction loops, and if a system is constantly operational it should be possible to build up a database with the magnetic signatures of all 'normal' ships such that it is relatively easy to detect suspicious activity, or an attempt to sail into harbour under cover of another ship (magnetic signatures can be expected to add up). The author thinks that it is time to think about a surveillance system for harbour control which can also detect an underwater threat. The induction loop is a good candidate and for this reason it might well be time for its revival. More in-depth research will be needed to judge if the induction loop is indeed the best system or if other systems such as buoys with magnetic sensors, probably in combination with sonar capabilities, are a better (or cheaper) option.

At present, induction loops might no longer be used but the reduction of the ship's magnetic signature remains an important topic for the mine threat, and recent research underlines this importance. For example, Baynes[45] presents a fast procedure for deperming, and research about a reconfiguration technique for the degaussing coils of a ship is given in Varma[46] and Choi.[47] The special case that some degaussing coils break down at sea such that a reconfiguration is necessary, is discussed in Kim,[48] and an indirect method for detecting a breakdown (or more generally a fault) is given in Jeung.[49] Degaussing has been a research topic at the Netherlands defence Academy, and in particular the potential use of superconductivity for degaussing.[50] In the Netherlands, TNO is currently working on degaussing systems. Their focus is on the optimization of the design of the ship's degaussing system with, for example, the so-called Least-Angle-Regression (LARS), see Bekers,[51] but they have also

---

[44] Daniel 2007.

[45] Baynes 2004.

[46] Raveendra Varma 2014.

[47] Choi et al. 2012a, b.

[48] Kim et al. 2016.

[49] Jeung et al. 2014.

[50] Ross et al. 2012, 2013; Somsen and Wagemakers 2015.

[51] Bekers and Lepelaars 2013.

developed a finite element method to predict the ship's magnitude signature due to (roll- and pitch-induced) Eddy currents.[52]

References

Ball D, Tanter R (2015) The Tools of Owatatsumi: Japanese Ocean Surveillance and Coastal Defence Capabilities. ANU Press http://www.jstor.org/stable/j.ctt13wwvvt

Baynes T (2004) Making Submarines Magnetically Silent. Magnetics Business & Technology Winter 2004, p 16

Bekers DJ, Lepelaars ESAM (2013) Degaussing System Design Optimization. Proceedings of the 8th International Marine Magnetics Conference (MARELEC)

Benedict JR (2005) The Unravelling and Revitalization of U.S. Navy Antisubmarine Warfare. Naval War College Review, 58(2), http://www.jhuapl.edu/ourwork/nsa/papers/art4-sp05.pdf

Birsan M, Tan R (2016) The Effect of Roll and Pitch Motion on Ship Magnetic Signature. Journal of Magnetics, 21(4): 503–508

Chen Y, Feng J, Minhui Z (2005) Detection methods of submerged mobile using SAR images. Proceedings of the Geoscience and Remote Sensing Symposium (IGARSS'05), Vol 3: 1717–1720

Chen Y, Yuan J (2015) Methods of Differential Submarine Detection Based on Magnetic Anomaly and Technology of Probes Arrangement. Proceedings of the 2nd International Workshop on Materials Engineering and Computer Sciences (IWMECS 2015): 446–449

Choi NS, Jeung G, Yang CS, Chung HJ, Kim DH (2012a) Optimization of degaussing coil currents for magnetic silencing of a ship taking the ferromagnetic hull effect into account. IEEE Transactions on Applied Superconductivity, 22(3): 419–422

Choi NS, Jeung G, Jung SS, Yang CS, Chung HJ, Kim DH (2012b) Efficient Methodology for Optimizing Degaussing Coil Currents in Ships Utilizing Magnetomotive Force Sensitivity Information. IEEE Transactions on Magnetics, 48(2): 419–422

Christian RJ (2007) Next-Generation Undersea Warfare and Undersea Distributed Networked Systems. Report No. NUWC-NPT-TR-11. Naval Undersea Warfare Center, Division Newport, USA

Daniel DCF (2007) ASW and superpower strategic stability - three years on. Report No. 8-89, Naval War College, Newport, USA

Holmes JJ (2006) Exploitation of a Ship's Magnetic Field Signatures. Synthesis Lectures on Computational Magnetics # 9, Morgan & Claypool Publishers, Denver (https://doi.org/10.2200/S00034ED1V01Y200605CEM009)

Holmes JJ (2007) Modeling a Ship's Ferromagnetic Signatures. Synthesis Lectures on Computational Magnetics # 16, Morgan & Claypool Publishers, Denver (https://doi.org/10.2200/S00092ED1V01Y200706CEM016)

Holmes JJ (2008) Reduction of a Ship's Magnetic Field Signatures, Synthesis Lectures on Computational magnetics # 23, Morgan & Claypool Publishers, Denver (https://doi.org/10.2200/S00150ED1V01Y200809CEM023)

Jeung G, Choi NS, Yang CS, Chung HJ, Kim DH (2014) Indirect Fault Detection Method for an Onboard Degaussing Coil System Exploiting Underwater Magnetic Signals. Journal of Magnetics, 19(1): 72–77

Kemna S, Hamilton MJ, Hughes DT, LePage KD (2011) Adaptive autonomous underwater vehicles for littoral surveillance. Intelligent Service Robotics, 4(4): 245–258

Kim DW, Lee SK, Kang B, Cho J, Lee W, Yang CS, Kim DH (2016) Efficient Re-degaussing Technique for a Naval Ship Undergoing a Breakdown in Degaussing Coils. Journal of Magnetics, 21(2): 197–203

[52] Birsan and Tan 2016.

Kopp C (2010) Evolving ASW Sensor Technology. Defence Today, 8(5): 26–29
Maskell DM (2001) The Navy's Best-Kept Secret: Is IUSS Becoming a Lost Art? MA thesis, USMC Command and Staff College, Quantico http://www.dtic.mil/get-tr-doc/pdf?AD=ADA401150
May D, Wren GG (1997) Detection of submerged vessels using remote sensing techniques. Australian Defence Force Journal, 127: 9–15
Moline MA, Oliver MJ, Orrico C, Zaneveld R, Shulman I, Watson J, Zielinski O (2013) Bioluminescence in the sea. In: Watson J, Zielinski O (eds) Subsea optics and imaging. Woodhead Publishing Series in Electronic and Optical Materials, pp 134–170 (https://doi.org/10.1533/9780857093523.2.134)
Raveendra Varma RA (2014) Design of Degaussing System and Demonstration of Signature. Reduction on Ship Model through Laboratory Experiments. Physics Procedia, 54: 174–179
Ross R, Bosklopper JJ, van der Meij KH. (2012) Operational merits of maritime superconductivity. Physics Procedia, 36: 985–988
Ross R, Meijer CG, Hunik R (2013) Maritime superconductivity perspectives. IEEE Transactions on Applied Superconductivity 23(3): 3601405–3601405
Somsen OJG, Wagemakers GPM (2015) Separating Permanent and Induced Magnetic Signature: A Simple Approach. Proceedings International Conference on Electronics, Information and Communication Engineering (ICEICE 2015): 1556–1559
Walding R (2006) Indicator loops and anti-submarine harbour defence in Australia in WWII. Journal of Australian Naval History 3(1)
Young HD, Freedman RA (2004) University Physics with Modern Physics, 11th edn. Addison Wesley, Boston
Zhang M, Wang J (2017) Microwave scattering from submerged object induced wake over rough sea surface. Proceedings of the 32nd URSI GASS meeting

The manufacturer's authorised representative in the EU is Springer Nature Customer Service Centre GmbH, Europaplatz 3, 69115 Heidelberg, Germany. If you have any concerns regarding our products, please contact ProductSafety@springernature.com

Printed and bound by CPI Group (UK) Ltd, Croydon, CR0 4YY
01/10/2026
02225871-0003